*Also by the same Author*

BLOODLINE OF THE HOLY GRAIL

REALM OF THE RING LORDS

Laurence Gardner, a Fellow of the Society of Antiquaries of Scotland, is an internationally known sovereign genealogist and historical lecturer. Distinguished as the Chevalier Labhràn de St. Germain, he is Presidential Attaché to the European Council of Princes, a constitutional advisory body established in 1946. He is also Prior of the Sacred Kindred of St. Columba, a Knight Templar of St. Anthony and Attaché to the Grand Protectorate of the Imperial Dragon Court, Hungary 1408. Formally attached to the Noble Order of the Guard of St. Germain, founded by King James VII of Scots in 1692 and ratified by King Louis XIV of France, he is the appointed Jacobite Historiographer Royal.

*Dedicated to the memory of Lawrence Percy,*
*father and fellow traveller of the Grail highway*

"A man may imagine things that are false, but he can only understand things that are true."
*Sir Isaac Newton*

# GENESIS OF THE GRAIL KINGS

THE EXPLOSIVE STORY OF GENETIC CLONING
AND THE ANCIENT BLOODLINE OF JESUS

**Laurence Gardner**

*le Chevalier Labhràn de St. Germain*

FAIR WINDS
PRESS

First edition published in Great Britain by Transworld
Publishers Ltd. in 1999
First USA edition published by Element Books Inc. in 2000

Paperback edition published in 2002 by
Fair Winds Press
33 Commercial Street
Gloucester, MA 01930

10 9 8 7 6 5

Printed in Canada

ISBN 1-55267-756-7



Library of Congress Cataloging-in-Publication data available

Typeset by Multi MediaQuest International Ltd., UK

Jacket design by Adrian Wagner and Stephen Knight
Cover illustration by Peter Robson

# CONTENTS

# CHARTS AND TABLES

# PLATES

# MAPS AND ILLUSTRATIONS

# ACKNOWLEDGEMENTS

For their invaluable assistance in the compilation of this work, I am indebted to the good offices of the Sacred Kindred of Saint Columba, the Royal House of Stewart, the European Council of Princes, the Order of Knights Templars of Saint Anthony, the Noble Order of the Guard of Saint Germain and the Imperial and Royal Dragon Court and Order. I would similarly like to thank all the archivists and librarians who have facilitated this project, notably those at the British Library; the Bibliothèque Nationale de France; the Bibliothèque de Bordeaux; the Louvre Museum, Paris; the Oriental Institute Museum, University of Chicago; the University of Pennsylvania Museum; the Natural History Museum, London; the Ashmolean Museum, Oxford; the Warburg Institute, London; the Royal Irish Academy, Dublin; the National Library of Scotland; the Somerset and Devon County Libraries; Birmingham Central Library, and the Departments of Western Asiatic Antiquities and Egyptian Antiquities at the British Museum.

My utmost gratitude is due to the directors and staff of MediaQuest International for working with me on this edition, along with HRH Prince Michael of Albany for affording me privileged access to Household and Chivalric papers. I am also thankful to my wife Angela, whose tireless effort has brought this work to fruition, and to my son James for his encouragement during my quest. Most grateful thanks, of course, to Greg Brandenburgh and all at Fair Winds Press who have seen the special transatlantic edition of this book through to its publication.

My recognition is due to all those whose own committed work has aided my research, especially Christian and Barbara Joy O'Brien. Also to the composer Sir Adrian Wagner who, in his family's tradition of such masterworks as *Lohengrin* and *Parsifal*, has endorsed this book with his companion music album, *Genesis of the Grail Kings* <www.mediaquest.co.uk/awggk.html>. Likewise to Sir Peter Robson for his valued artistic liaison and specially designed fine artwork <www.entropic-art.com>.

To those many friends who have smoothed the path of this venture in one way or another I offer my appreciation. In particular, I am grateful to Helen Wagner, Tracy Knight, Stephen Knight, Scarlett Nunn, Karen Lyster, Gretchen Schroeder, Laura

Wagner, Marge Jacob, Chev. David Roy Stewart, Herbert Kessler, Chev. Jack Robertson, Rev. David Cuthbert Stalker, Tony Skiens, Dr. Joe Dispenza, Jaz Coleman, Nigel Blair of the Wessex Research Group and Edmund Marriage of The Patrick Foundation.

For their generous support in aiding my work internationally, my special thanks to Eleanor Robson and Steve Robson of Peter Robson Studio; to Duncan Roads, Ruth Parnell, Marcus Allen, Jeffrey Williams and Tom Bosco of *Nexus;* to Adriano Forgione of *Hera;* to JZ Knight and all at Ramtha's School of Enlightenment. Also to Christina Zohs of *The Golden Thread,* Nancy and Mike Simms of Entropic Fine Art, Whitley and Ann Strieber, Laura Lee, Daniel S. Ward, Lucie Blanchard, Neil and Ursula Freer, Robert Ghost Wolf and Shoshanna of the Wolf Lodge Foundation, Terri and Bob Brown of the International UFO Congress, La Vern De Wilde and Robert L. Siblerud of The International Association for New Science and Charlie Bear Wiechert of The Society for Psi Research and Education.

Finally, I must convey my gratitude to all those readers who have supported and encouraged my work over the years—especially to those many who have written to me with such a variety of useful comments and contributions.

*Laurence Gardner, August 2001*

## PICTURE CREDITS

Thanks must go to those below in respect of the following photographic illustrations and copyright images:
1, Peter Robson Studio <www.entropic-art.com> and Entropic Fine Art Inc; 2, 6, 9, The Patrick Foundation; 3, The Iraq Museum, Baghdad; 4, University of Pennsylvania Museum; 5, 14, Réunion des Musées Nationaux and the Louvre Museum, Paris; 7, 13, 15, The Oriental Institute Museum, Chicago; 8, 19, The British Museum, London; 10, Princeton University Press; 11, Ernest Benn, London; 12, The Hebrew University, Jerusalem; 16, 20, The Metropolitan Museum of Art, New York; 17, Saint Catherine's Monastery, Sinai; 18, 22, 21, Cleminson Collection; 23, 25, 27, 28, John Murray, London; 24, Nancy Vann; 26, Michael Gerrish

While every effort has been made to secure permissions, if there are any errors or oversights regarding copyright material, we apologise and will make suitable acknowledgement in any future edition.

# PREFACE

*Genesis of the Grail Kings* is one of a related series of books, along with *Bloodline of the Holy Grail*, *Realm of the Ring Lords* and the forthcoming *Destiny of the House of Gold*. However, although mutually supportive, these books are each designed to stand alone and, despite their sequence of publication, it is not necessary that they be read in any particular order of preference.

The common thread is that the individual works are concerned with aspects of history from scriptural and cultural documents which were not included in the canonical Bible—those that were omitted for various reasons of vested interest. Also taken into account are numerous other archival resources which have, for one reason or another, been strategically ignored by authorized academic and clerical establishments through the centuries. In pursuing this line of comparative research, it becomes clear that first-hand writings from any given period often have little in common with the interpretations and spurious rewritings of subsequent ages—but it is from these later renderings and expositions that we are generally taught.

*Genesis of the Grail Kings* is chronologically structured to deal with the history of very ancient times—concentrating specifically on the first two books of the Bible's Old Testament: Genesis and Exodus. *Bloodline of the Holy Grail* looks at the New Testament era and the history of subsequent times, while *Realm of the Ring Lords* considers the relationship between history and mythology through the ages. Here, then, for those who are perhaps new to this series, is a brief summary of the main content of *Bloodline of the Holy Grail*—an overview that will illustrate the style and purpose of these correlative investigations:

Following the Jewish Revolt in Jerusalem in the 1st century AD, the Roman authorities were reputed to have burned all records (public and private) concerning the Davidic sovereign legacy of Jesus's family. However, the destruction was far from complete and relevant documents were retained by the royal inheritors, who progressed the heritage of the Messiah from the Holy Land into the West. These inheritors were called the *Desposyni* (Heirs of the Lord) and they were pursued by Roman dictate, to be put to the sword by Imperial command. Writing as long afterwards as AD 200, the historian Julius Africanus confirmed that the persecution was still formally operative, although the *Desposyni* remained politically active by way of a strict dynastic progression.

After the decline of the Western Empire, the torment was continued by the emergent Church of Rome, despite appeals from the family who promoted the opposing Nazarene Church of Jesus. They constantly denounced the Roman interpretations of the Virgin Birth and Resurrection, claiming that religion was to be found in the teachings of Jesus—not in the veneration of his person.

Through medieval times, support grew for the Messianic dynasts, but they were still harassed by the Popes, leading to the brutal Inquisitions of the Middle Ages. Only by suppressing the sovereignty of the *Desposyni* could the Church of Rome survive.

Now, in *Genesis of the Grail Kings*, we investigate the origins of the royal bloodline to establish when, why and how the dynastic family of Jesus was established, and by whom. In this we discover the historical identities of Adam and Eve, and how a powerful strategy of religious doctrine sought to break with all previous tradition by introducing the 'male only' concept of God.

*Laurence Gardner*

# 1

# The Cradle of Civilization

## Dawn of the Dragon

During the past two thousand years much has been written about the line of Messianic kingly descent from the family of Jesus — the dynastic bloodline which became known as the *Sangréal* (the Blood Royal). This was the line of King David of Judah, the family whose heirs, from the time of Jesus, were hounded by the Christian Church authorities for centuries — as recorded by such eminent historians as Hegesippus of Palestine, Julius Africanus of Edessa and Eusebius of Caesaria.[1] But what was it that made this sovereign line so special in the first place? What was the original legacy of their Messianic kingship — the legacy so feared by the orthodox establishment?

By studying pre-biblical texts concerning the Old Testament patriarchs of this family, the answers to these questions are stunningly revealed, but not necessarily in a form that we might expect. No longer are Adam, Noah, Abraham and the well-known characters of Genesis a humble band of territorial pioneers; instead they emerge as a formidable cast of players in one of history's most enlightening portrayals, for it was they who witnessed the astonishing dawn of the Grail Kings — the original House of the Dragon.

From the very earliest of recorded times, dragons have featured at the forefront of cultural lore, where they have been portrayed in various conflicting guises. The ancient Greeks believed that dragons were benevolent creatures with the ability to convey the wisdom and secrets of life, while in contrast the early Hebrews saw dragons as the meddlesome purveyors of sin. The mighty dragon was the emblem of the Chinese Empire, being a national symbol of good fortune, and outside the Hebrew tradition dragons were generally seen as the guardians of universal knowledge and the benign protectors of humankind.

To the Celtic races of Europe, the dragon was the ultimate symbol of sovereignty (hence, the Dark Age Pendragons: the Head Dragons or Kings of Kings), but in AD 494 Pope Gelasius I[2] challenged the Celtic Church by canonizing a certain Bishop George of Alexandria, who was said to have slain a dragon.[3] This violent and unpopular Turkish churchman was reputed to have insulted and persecuted dissenters, and was eventually killed by a Palestinian mob in AD 361. He emerged, however, as the famous martyr St. George, with surrounding legends that grew ever more exaggerated. At the Council of Oxford in 1222, it was proclaimed that St. George's feast day should be 23 April, and in the 14th century he became the Catholic patron saint of England by decree of King Edward III Plantagenet.

*The Chinese Dragon.*

From the 4th century, the Roman Church denounced and terrorized upholders of the Celtic Christian faith, and in this regard St. George the dragon-slayer personified the vengeful Catholic inquisition against the supporters of the Messianic bloodline. The dragons of Christian mythology were adopted from those of the Hebrew tradition and are often portrayed with wings and breathing fire, but historically dragons were the epitome of the royal crocodile or sea-serpent (the *Bistea Neptunis* of the Dark Age Fisher Kings and the medieval Merovingian kings of the Franks[4]).

By way of a manipulated tradition in western Christendom, the dragon has been portrayed rather differently from its original representation in the eastern cultures. It has also been diverted into the realms of legend and mythology, whereas it was with the fat of the historical *Messeh* or *Mûs-hûs* (the sacred dragon, or crocodile) that the Egyptian pharaohs and Mesopotamian kings were anointed upon installation.[5]

It is an apparent fact that what one culture defines as history, another will define as mythology; this is especially the case in religious affairs where opposing cultures are in spiritual conflict. Christians, for example, consider the deities of other beliefs to be mythical, but maintain that their own deity is not. The same might, of course, be said in reverse—so where in all of this lies the truth of that which is called 'history'?

The *Oxford English Dictionary* defines history as the 'continuous methodical record of important or public events'. Other reference books give similar definitions, and it is evident from these that the term 'history' does not constitute the events themselves, but relates to the documented records of the events. Sometimes these records are compiled first hand, and sometimes second or third hand, but whatever the case they are always subject to bias, opinion and vested interest. When history deals with matters of conflict (whether military, political, social or religious), it becomes a device for conveying sectarian or national leaning, and the details of individual events vary in accordance with the attitudes, commissions and objectives of the writers concerned.

Hence, the history of, say, a war will be differently perceived by each opposing side, as will the histories of political or religious disputes. The formal overall history that one learns is, therefore, that which has been approved by one's governing establishment. It is authorized, countenanced, sanctioned and academically warranted, but it is not necessarily the explicit truth—it is truth tempered by partisan interpretation and subjective opinion.

When documentary record is related to matters of science, then it is automatically constrained by ongoing research, and it can only communicate the facts as they are known at the time of writing. Only a few decades ago, it was (as far as anyone knew) quite impossible to converse with someone thousands of miles away. It was equally impossible to fly over the oceans, or to watch relayed coverage of live events from around the world. Now, such things are not only possible but commonplace, and the coming centuries will undoubtedly hold their own share of possibilities that were hitherto regarded as impossible.

By virtue of this, history cannot afford to be dogmatic; it can only record given points of view at given points in time because there are always areas of uncertainty and elements of the unknown which have to be conceded. When some huge, unfathomable bones were unearthed in China 2000 years ago they were recorded as being the bones of a dragon, for it was traditionally thought that a great dragon's tail had marked the river channels which drained the land in primeval times.[6] We now know these to be dinosaur bones, but the people of the era could not possibly have identified them as such because they had no knowledge that dinosaurs ever existed. In fact, everything that we know today about dinosaurs and their environment has been learned since the 1820s. (Their name comes from the Greek *deinos-saurus*, meaning 'terrible lizard'.)

Sometimes, for want of any comparative record, certain documented information is taken on board as history until a related and perhaps contradictory discovery sheds new light on the subject. In this regard, the Old Testament of the Jewish and Christian Bibles holds a primary position for, just like the Chinese dinosaur bones, no one had access to any more specific information through the same 2000 years. The Old Testament as we have come to know it was a largely retrospective work, first compiled between the 6th and 2nd centuries BC, but relating to the events of hundreds and even thousands of years before. There are references within the Old Testament to a number of material sources, but since these earlier works have not been available, the best that generations of people could do was to take the scripture as read, to treat it as being symbolic, or perhaps to ignore it altogether. The difference between the Bible and much other history lies, however, in the word 'scripture', for the Old Testament was not only a work of ancestral record, but became the basis for an evolving, widespread religious doctrine.

It was not until the 1850s that documentary evidence of pre-biblical history first came to light, and this was followed twenty years later by some published texts. Not until the late 1920s were the first in-depth translations released into the public domain—translations of scribal record considerably older than the original Old Testament. As the archaeologists progressed their excavations, these ancient clay tablets and engraved cylinders emerged in their tens of thousands from the very Bible lands of Adam, Noah and Abraham, and they were in large measure contemporary with the Old Testament's patriarchal and dynastic eras. More importantly, and perhaps surprisingly to some, many of their accounts were immediately familiar, and it soon became obvious that these were the models for stories written down in retrospect by the Israelite compilers of Genesis.

Throughout the best part of the common era, these informative texts had been hidden, unbeknown to anyone, beneath the Mesopotamian and Syrian deserts, and their discovery (like the discovery of dinosaurs) should have been greeted with enthusiasm by all—but it was not. The historical accounts were familiar, and the characters and places were recognizable as being the Old Testament prototypes, but the literal emphases were so different from the approved scripture that indoctrinated society and its governing authorities felt immediately threatened.

Quite suddenly, it was clear that the long-supposed authentic history of the Bible was not authentic at all: it had been contrived by adjusting original records to suit an emergent religious movement from 2500 years ago. This movement, at first a localized sectarian Hebrew cult, had subsequently expanded into mainstream Judaism and then branched off into Christianity, with the Old Testament becoming a common factor of teaching. But what had also transpired was that this series of books (originally compiled to underpin a cultural doctrine in troubled times) had become a repository of established dogma, which had itself become regarded as absolute history.

As previously stated, history cannot afford to be dogmatic, but it was too late; the die had been cast through religious application. Even now, the dogma of contrived scriptural history is still taught in our schoolrooms and churches, while the original documents from which the scripture was constructed are ignored. This is particularly unfortunate because the more ancient documents are far more explicit than the Old Testament in their detailing of the patriarchal era. In these texts the Bible stories are not only placed in a better chronological context, but their social and political relevance becomes far more understandable.

## The Fertile Crescent

In our quest for the Messianic heritage we shall be delving back to the ancient origins of the kingly tradition—back into the distant world of Genesis, to the time of Adam and beyond. In order to set the scene, however, it is first necessary to establish our geographical base since Old Testament history spans three distinct regions: Mesopotamia (the land encompassed by present-day Iraq), Canaan (Palestine) and Egypt. This overall territory, with the Mediterranean Sea bordering Egypt and Canaan, includes three great rivers: in the west is the north-flowing Nile, while in the east the Tigris and Euphrates run south into the Persian Gulf.

From about 10,000 BC, towards the end of the last Ice Age, this Near Eastern land mass was especially suited to irrigation, particularly in its river plateau and delta regions. In consequence, it was the earliest cradle of civilization and, for reasons of both culture and agriculture, it has been dubbed the Fertile Crescent.

In Mesopotamia, the temperate, moist conditions gave rise to large tracts of open woodland, and a variety of long grasses were developed to produce barley and wheat on a large scale. Harvesting of cereal crops can also be traced back to Canaan in about 10,000 BC, to northern Syria around 9000 BC and to the Jordan valley in 8000 BC. As the cereal and grain culture advanced by way of improved seeding, fertilization and ripening methods, so too were pulses and legumes (such as peas and lentils) cultivated. In this well-nurtured grazing environment certain animals were tamed and herded, with gazelles and goats being the primary meat providers, while the latter were also used for milking. Sheep farming was additionally popular in northern Mesopotamia from about 9000 BC, and from around 6000 BC pigs, dogs and cattle were also domesticated.

Throughout this period, the local farming communities were settled into villages and townships, with houses commonly built of mud brick. The settlements were often set upon hills, surrounded by trenches for protection against wild animals, and the domestic herds were further sheltered within wooden stockades. Because of the extensive grain crop, stone-grinding was an early introduction, as was the manufacture and use of pottery, and trade between communities was also encouraged. To expedite this trade, various natural resources were frequently used as means of exchange, particularly decorative items such as volcanic glass, shells and semi-precious stones.[7] It was during this period that Jericho was established as an urban residential centre in Jordan, and soon afterwards the plough and the wheel were in widespread use in the region.

The era from 8000 BC was that which we generally classify as the New Stone Age, but soon after 6500 BC the advanced culture of the Fertile Crescent had moved into the Bronze Age—the first age of metallurgy wherein copper was alloyed with tin to produce the highly durable bronze. The singularly impressive level of Near Eastern advancement becomes apparent when one realizes that, in contrast, the oldest pottery unearthed in Britain dates back only to about 2500 BC, and the earliest barley farming commenced about half a century later. Britain did not enter her Bronze Age until the Belgic tribes arrived in about 2000 BC.

By 6000 BC, the people of the Mesopotamian Near East were using ships on the open sea, while Britain was still 4000 years away from a simple weaving industry. It therefore comes as no surprise that the most prominent stories of earthly beginnings emerged from the Bible lands of the Fertile Crescent, for as far as the people of those lands were concerned the outside world was

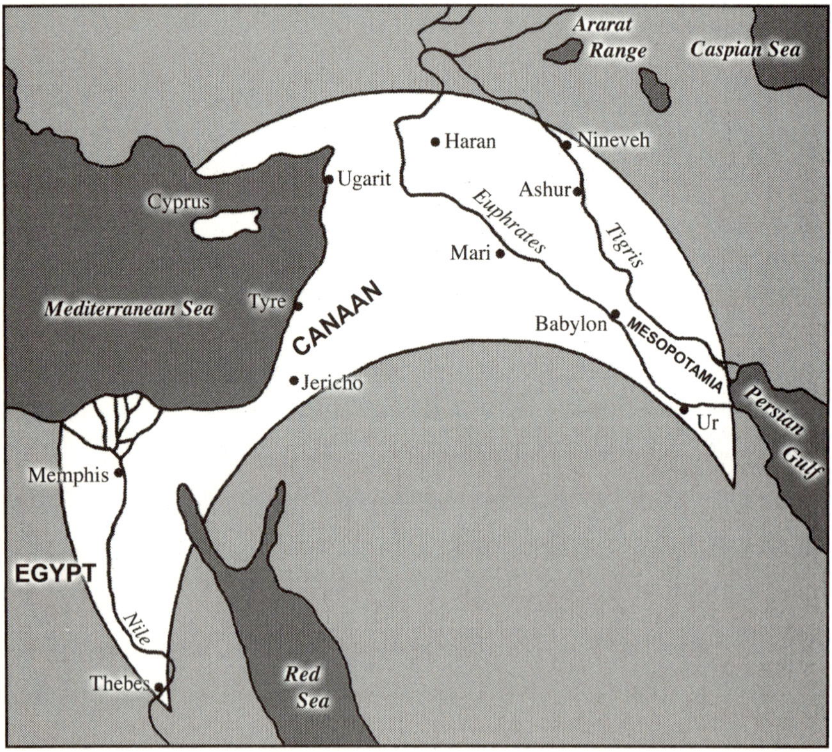


*The Fertile Crescent.*

still asleep in a forlorn and primitive environment. Indeed, it can be said with no reserve whatever that cultural history certainly began in those very countries described in the book of Genesis. (The title *Genesis* was introduced by Greek Bible translators in the 3rd century BC, and relates to 'origin' or 'beginning'. The Hebrew opening for the book was *Bereshit* (*B'rei-shêeth*): 'At the beginning'.[8]

It is not until we reach the 19th patriarchal generation of the Genesis account that Canaan and Egypt begin to feature in the narrative. This occurs after Abraham's emigration from his native Mesopotamia. And so, it is in Mesopotamia that our story must begin—in southern Mesopotamia to be precise, for in Genesis (11:31) we are told that Abraham (originally called Avram or Abram) came from Ur of the Chaldees. Earlier biblical references (back to the time of Adam) cement the family's tradition very firmly in the Tigris-Euphrates region above the Persian Gulf.

The name Mesopotamia means 'Land between the Rivers', and it was technically the country between the Tigris and Euphrates. But, geographically, the Mesopotamian boundaries enveloped these two rivers from the northern Taurus Mountains down to the Gulf. Northern Mesopotamia is perhaps better known as Assyria, while the central region was called Akkad (wherein sits present-day Baghdad, north of Babylon). Soon after 4000 BC, southern Mesopotamia was identified as Sumer (pronounced 'Shumer'),[9] and it was here that the early patriarchs prevailed.

One of the foremost cities of ancient Sumer was Uruk (modern-day Warka), from which derived the country's eventual name of Iraq. South-east of Uruk was the city of Ur in the Sumerian region of Chaldea (the Chaldees). These days, the Persian Gulf sweeps below Iraq to Iran (Persia) from northern Kuwait, but in those early times the Gulf extended a good deal further inland, so that Ur was practically on the coast.

The word 'city' is not used lightly in this context, for these important centres were undeniably cities from about 3800 BC, and Uruk, with its great temple, was the first true city on earth. Municipal society with community councils had actually evolved from about 5500 BC, when the farming Halafans of Tel Halaf introduced cobbled streets and drainage systems more than 3000 years before the primitive Stonehenge is reckoned to have been constructed in Britain—at which time Western Europeans had barely invented the crude wooden plough. In the Mesopotamian town of Arpachiya there were large beehive-shaped public buildings called *tholoi*, measuring on average about 32 feet (around 10 m) in diameter. One of the main Halafan communities (near subsequent Ur) was established as a delta settlement at Ubaid, a noted centre of metallurgy and pottery, and nearby emerged Sumer's most sacred city of Eridu. Other important cities of the area were Kish, Nippur, Erech, Lagesh and Larsa, and, just as today's cities are distinguished by their great cathedrals, so too did these highly cultural centres have their richly decorated skyward temples.

Although Mesopotamia was a world leader in numerous aspects from around 10,000 BC, there appears to have been a very marked further advancement from about 4000 BC when southern Mesopotamia became identified as Sumer and the truly municipal cities flourished. By that time they were formally recognized as city-states which operated as individual kingdoms, and it is the story of the amazing rise of Sumer which provides the very thrust of the patriarchal narrative in Genesis. This sudden cultural expansion was not simply a matter of general evolvement; it was a mighty technical and academic revolution which has long baffled scholars and historians worldwide.

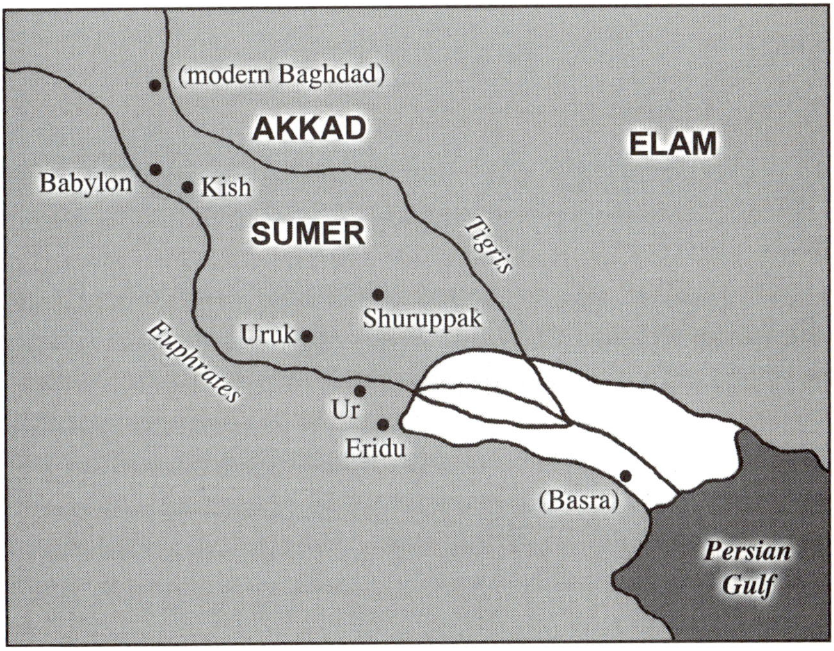


*Shoreline of the Gulf.*
*(White area identifies former extent of the Persian Gulf)*

# 2

# Like Migrating Birds

## The Adamite Chronicles

It is now time to consult our Bibles and to consider the Genesis text with ancient Sumer in mind. In so doing, we should think also about the natural evolutionary process of the wider world arena, and of how (from 4000-2000 BC) Sumerian society surged ahead of the natural process by thousands of years. We shall look at the individual details of this surge and its specific implications later on, but for the time being we should remember that, were it not for the extraordinary lead provided in old Mesopotamia, our present civilized culture would not exist in the form that we know it today.

In current times, in various parts of the world, there are still many tribes of bushmen and the like whose lives, although disciplined, are very primitive by our accepted standards. It is said that this has happened because they are sheltered from the world at large. But what is the world at large? These people have certainly not been sheltered from evolution because, according to scientists, evolution is a natural ongoing process. In fact, by virtue of their environment these people are the very epitome of natural evolution, but that evolution has sustained them in a protracted Stone Age culture.

In his *Earth Chronicles*, the eminent scholar Zecharia Sitchin makes the point that the real puzzle lies not in the backwardness of the bushmen, but in our own advancement. It took man over a million years to progress from using stones as he found them to the realization that they could be chipped and flaked to better purpose. It then took another 500,000 years before Neanderthal man mastered the concept of stone tools, and a further 50,000 years before crops were cultivated and metallurgy was discovered. Such was the long and arduous natural process which brought humankind to about 5000 BC. Hence, by all scales of evolutionary reckoning, we should still be far removed from any basic understanding of mathematics, engineering or science. We should naturally have evolved in line with the bushmen—but here we are, only 7000 years later, landing probes on Mars.

In real terms, the bushmen are the true inheritors of nature's own slow progression. It is we of the civilized races who have advanced far ahead of spontaneous evolution by way of our strategically applied wisdom. But this cannot have taken place by accident; we cannot invent wisdom, it has to be acquired and inherited. So, how did we inherit wisdom, and from whom? As we shall discover, the answer is to be found in the preserved texts of ancient Sumer—and in relating the story of Adam and Eve, the Bible calls the source of this advanced wisdom the Tree of Knowledge (Genesis 2:9).

Ever since Charles Darwin published his *Descent of Man* in 1871, a dispute has prevailed over whether humankind evolved by a gradual process through millions of years, or whether Adam and Eve were the first mortals, created by God, as told in the Old Testament book of Genesis.

If we discount the entire evolutionary process from the most primitive anthropoids of 30 million years ago, we still end up with positive proof that Neanderthal man existed before 70,000 BC. This race became extinct after some 40,000 years, and in the meantime Cro-Magnon man had appeared by 35,000 BC, thus beginning the era of *homo sapiens* ('thinking man'—from the Latin *sapienta,* meaning 'wisdom') with his art, clothing and community structure. So, if we presume that Adam was indeed the first man (or even symbolically representative of the first man), then with which date should we credit him: 35,000 BC, 70,000 BC or somewhere before that?

In 1996, Pope John Paul II claimed that the theory of evolution was 'more than a hypothesis'. He made this statement at a conference of the Papal Academy of Sciences, and it set the religious world thinking. How could the writings of Darwin and Genesis be compatible? As a result, Cardinal John O'Connor of New York announced at St. Patrick's Cathedral that perhaps Adam and Eve were not human after all, but some form of lower animal. Before long, numerous members of the High Christian establishment were questioning their traditional interpretation of the biblical text. But were they perhaps overreacting?

The fact is that Genesis positively describes Adam as a 'man' — a thinking man no less, and in terms of general earthly evolution, the text is seemingly quite accurate, even though chronologically ambiguous with its account of the 'six days' of Creation. In line with Darwin and others,[1] Genesis tells that prior to man (Adam) there were plants, fish, birds and animals (1:11-25), and these various life-forms are detailed in a scientifically logical progression, with humankind ultimately gaining dominion over the others (1:28). The story of Adam was not the prerogative of the early Hebrew writers, for his details were set down in writing long before Genesis was compiled. Nevertheless, the sequence of events portrayed in Genesis appears wholly in line with geological and archaeological discovery, except for the reality of a more general long-term evolutionary process.

In Genesis, the emergence of Adam is sudden, but that apart, he is emphatically described as a rather unique form of human who followed the early life-forms. This, of course, takes Adam and Eve out of the realms of Cardinal O'Connor's 'lower animal' speculation, but it still does not give them a date. We are left, therefore, with our original dilemma, and if we separate Adam from the unintelligent anthropoids such as *homo habilis* (of about 2-million BC) and *homo erectus* (about 1-million BC), the question remains: Was Adam a prehistoric Neanderthal or a later Cro-Magnon man?

The fact that Adam is credited with the knowledge of good and evil, having eaten from the tree that made him wise (Genesis 3:6), determines that he was of the strain called *homo sapiens*. In practice, he would actually have been of the further advanced modern strain called *homo sapiens-sapiens*. Adam's date, consequently, falls into a post-35,000 BC category. But the Neanderthalers and others preceded this era—so how could Adam be said to be the 'first' man? Of what particular strain was he the first?

In historical terms, Adam can be identified rather more precisely than in the Genesis account, and in making this identification his biblical heritage is not lost, for he was certainly the first of a kind. Before pursuing this, however, we should consider the Genesis chronology in greater depth so that Adam and Eve can be cemented into a more reliable time-frame.

In Christian Church theology, Adam is generally dated at 4004 BC, and this has been the case since AD 1650 when Ireland's Protestant Archbishop, James Ussher of Armagh, published his famous *Annales Veteris Testamenti*. His method of calculation was very straightforward, being based on the said ages of the early patriarchs when they fathered their respective sons in the Bible's key succession (*see* Chart: Biblical Ages of the Early Patriarchs). Genesis tells that Adam was aged 130 when his son Seth was born; Seth was 105 when he fathered Enos, who was 90 at the birth of his son Cainan, and so on. To that point (Adam to Cainan) 325 years had passed. Progressing then from Cainan to Noah adds another 731 years, and from Noah to Abraham another 890 years—a total of 1946 years from the emergence of Adam to the birth of Abraham. In such a calculation, the great final ages of the individual patriarchs (with Methuselah living for 969 years) are quite irrelevant: only their procreational ages of fatherhood are important.

Genesis gives us nineteen complete generations from Adam to Abraham, and 1946 years divided by 19 indicates an average generation standard of about 102 years, as against the 30-year average standard that is applied today. It is easy enough for a sceptical mind to dismiss the given longevity of the early patriarchs, but let us not be too hasty in this regard for intuitive scepticism is the best route to learning absolutely nothing. The main problem with Ussher's tabular method was that at some point the resultant age totals had to be counted back from the date of some historical event and the first such date given by Ussher is 2348 BC, said to be the year of the biblical Flood.[2]

If we go back to the birth of Noah, midway in the Adam-to-Abraham list, we see that 1056 years had passed from the advent of Adam. Genesis tells that Noah was aged 600 at the time of the great Flood. So, according to Genesis, the Flood was (1056 + 600) 1656 years after the emergence of Adam. According to Ussher, the biblical Flood was in 2348 BC; so if we go back 1656 years from then we get to 4004 BC, which is the standard date for Adam by the Christian reckoning. Indeed, only two centuries ago in 1779, the Church-approved *Universal History* went so far as to say that God's work of Creation actually began on 21 September 4004 BC![3]

In 1654, more than a century before the *Universal History* was published, the Vatican Council had decreed that anyone daring to contradict the 4004 BC date was a heretic—an attitude that was not relaxed until Pope Pius XII addressed the 1952 Papal Academy of Sciences in Rome. In this address, he announced that theologians must not ignore the discoveries of geological science, and that it was clear that the Earth had existed for thousands of millions of years. In making this statement, Pope Pius maintained that time was not really a factor in the Bible's Creation story because the six days of Creation were symbolic, and that, despite all discovery in this regard, God was still left in position as the paramount creator of all. This was really no different to Pope John Paul's announcement in 1996, but many churchmen had, for some reason, forgotten the papal address of forty-four years earlier, and were taken by surprise when their leader pronounced Genesis and natural science to be, to a point, compatible.

But what do the Jews make of Archbishop Ussher's date? The Old Testament is, after all, the essence of the Jewish Bible. Do they agree with 4004 BC? The answer is that they do not agree, but the Jewish reckoning for Adam is not far adrift at 3760 BC, the emergent year for the Jewish calendar. There are bound to be some differences in calculation because the Hebrews traditionally used a lunar calendar of 354 days per year, as against the early solar calendar of 364 days. The ancient book of Jubilees (6:29-36) makes the point that the lunar cycle is a corruption of ordained time, stating, 'Thus it is ordained in the tablets of heaven... and thou commanded the children of Israel that they should observe the years in this number, three-hundred and sixty-four days'.

The book of Jubilees is wholly related to time, and it begins, 'These are the words of the division of days according to the law and testimony'. On that account, the truly ascetic Jews (such as the 1st-century BC/AD Essenes of Qumrân) admonished the Pharisees and Sadducees of the Jerusalem Temple for erring against the Sabbath. They pointed out that their own solar year of 364 days was equally divisible into 52 weeks of 7 days, whereas the Hebrews' 354-day lunar year was not—and this was very likely one of the reasons why Jubilees was not included in the Hebrew-approved Old Testament.

In more precise terms, the solar year has approximately 365.25 days, as introduced by the Julian calendar of Julius Caesar from 45 BC, and this is the calendar that Archbishop Ussher would have used for his calculations in 1650. This calendar operated through a 365-day regular cycle, adding an extra day (the four quarter-days) every fourth year—a 'leap year'.[4]

And so Adam's mean date (between the Christian and Jewish reckonings) is 3882 BC—but this is substantially removed from the *homo sapiens* of 35,000 BC! In fact, it places Adam well forward of the Old, Middle and New Stone Ages, and sets him firmly into the Near Eastern Bronze Age, by which time the wheel, the metal plough and the sailing ship were all in widespread use. But Adam's date is not at all removed from some very dramatic events which occurred in his homeland of southern Mesopotamia from about 4000 BC—events which quite positively made the recorded Adam a unique first of his kind.

At this stage, it is perhaps worth considering the later patriarch Abraham who, some eighteen generations after Adam, left his native Ur in southern Mesopotamia and journeyed north to Haran. Then, after his father Terah had died, Abraham headed west into neighbouring Canaan with his wife Sarai and his nephew Lot (Genesis 12:4-5). This he supposedly did at God's bidding—but is there by chance any historical mention of something which might have prompted a migration at that time? There certainly is.

Abraham's home, Ur of the Chaldees, was a prominent city of the Sumerian Empire, and contemporary texts record that Ur was sacked by the king of nearby Elam soon after 2000 BC. Although the city was rebuilt, the centre of power then moved north to Haran in the kingdom of Mari. This was the very city to which Terah took Abraham and the others. But Haran was not just the name of a flourishing city: it was also the name of Abraham's brother (the father of Lot), who had died before the family left Ur of the Chaldees (Genesis 11:27-28). Other cities in northern Mesopotamia were also named in accordance with Abraham's forefathers, as discovered by archaeologists excavating the region from 1934. In studying the clay tablets of reports from governors and commissioners of the era, they found the names of Terah (Abraham's father), Nahor (Terah's father), Serug (Nahor's father) and Peleg (Serug's grandfather).[5]

Clearly, the patriarchs represented no ordinary family, but constituted a very powerful dynasty. But why would such a long-standing heritage of prominence and renown come to an abrupt end and force Abraham out of Mesopotamia into Canaan? A Sumerian text from 1960 BC (at about the time Terah moved his family from Ur to Haran) could well hold the initial key, for it states, 'The gods have abandoned us like migrating birds. Smoke lies on our cities like a shroud'.[6]

This is an interesting development: 'the gods'. What gods? To answer this we should now revert once more to the beginning of Genesis where, in connection with the creation of Adam, God says, 'Let *us* make man in our image, after *our* likeness' (1:26).

*The Ancient Near East.*

Then later, God says, in respect of the tree of the garden, 'In the day ye eat thereof, then your eyes shall be opened, and ye shall be as *gods*' (3:5). This is followed by: 'The Lord God said, Behold, the man is become as one of *us*' (3:22).

Old Testament entries such as these are quite indicative of historically recorded texts of the Sumerian era ('The gods have abandoned us', etc.), but they are surprisingly different from our traditional religious conditioning that there was but one God. Here is God himself, in no less a work than the Bible, talking about *us, our* and *gods* in the plural. To whom was God supposedly talking when he made the statement, 'Behold, the man is become as one of *us*'? Certainly not to the others of the Holy Trinity, as some straw-clutching bishops have suggested. (The Trinity concept of the Father, Son and Holy Ghost is strictly Christian and was not established as a doctrine until the Council of Nicaea in AD 325.)

## Ur of the Chaldees

Although the city name of Ur has been familiar for centuries because of its biblical mentions, it was not until the 20th century that anyone knew where it was located, and its discovery was made almost by chance.

In the early 1900s, the builders of the Baghdad railway placed a station about 120 miles (*c.*193 km) north of Basra because the landmarked site was a recognized travellers' rest. Here, an enormous solitary hill rose above the desert—a hill known to the Bedouins as Tell al Muqayyar (Mound of Pitch). But some thousands of years ago this desert waste was a lush, fertile valley with cornfields and date groves. As was soon to be discovered, within this great mound was the towering multi-levelled Temple of Ur, along with the rest of the ancient city.

In 1923, the archaeologist Sir Charles Leonard Woolley, with a joint team from the British Museum and the University of Pennsylvania, set out to excavate the mound because some years earlier a collection of very old texts, engraved on stone cylinders, had been unearthed near the summit.[7] One of these cylinder-seals (as they became known) had revealed the name of Ur-nammu, King of Ur in about 2010 BC, and so it was determined that this was probably the location of Abraham's home.

Within the structure of the great hill, Woolley detected numerous smaller table plateaux and it became apparent that these were the uppermost limits of successive habitable constructions, each built above the accumulated building rubble of a bygone age. Five of these constructions were discovered to be temples, built like fortresses with enormous walls. Each had an integral paved court with surrounding rooms, and fountains fed by bitumen-clad water troughs were found intact, as were a variety of ovens and large brick tables. On rekindling one of the ancient ovens, Woolley wrote in his diary, 'We were able to light the fire again, and put into commission once more the oldest kitchen in the world'.[8]

The main temple shrine within the massive Tell al Muqayyar actually crowned a four-storey mud-brick building with flat terraces surrounding the core constructions on each upper level. These rising platforms were consecutively reduced in size to form a staged pyramid with outside stairs leading from one level to the next, and the perimeter terraces were once planted with trees, shrubs and hanging gardens. Such buildings are now known to have been typical of the great Sumerian cities; they were called ziggurats, literally meaning 'towers rising to the sky'. More importantly, they were designated as 'sacred mountains' or 'hills of heaven'.

The best-known biblical ziggurat was the Tower of Babel (Genesis 11:1-9), built on the Babylonian plain of Shinar—an alternative name for Sumer.[9] This ziggurat fell into ruin long ago, but it was replaced by another, built by Nebuchadnezzar II (604-562 BC) who also constructed the famous Hanging Gardens of Babylon, one of the Seven Wonders of the World.[10] Although also now long gone, the ground-plan of the second Babylon ziggurat shows that it was actually a larger-scale replication of the ziggurat of Ur.[11]

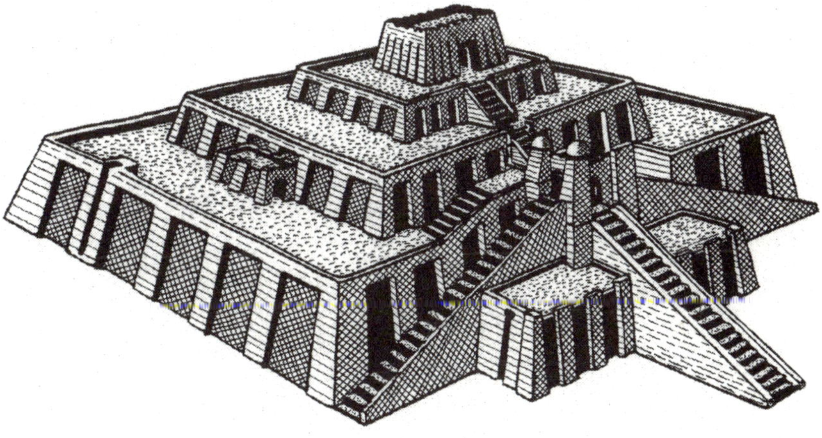

*The Ziggurat of Ur.*
*The base wall stands about 50 feet (around 16.5 m) and the whole tower about 70 feet (around 23 m) high. The lower two baked-brick sections were black, and the upper stage red, while the topmost shrine was faced with blue glazed tiles and crowned with a canopy of gold. These colours represented the dark Netherworld, the habitable Earth, the sky and the sun.*

Within the overall complex of the Ur Temple ziggurat and its associated lesser temples were found the preserved remains of offices, factories, warehouses, shops, hospitals, law courts and schools. Not only that, but a good deal of the old documentation was still extant: lawyers' records, taxation records, mill-owners' records, shopkeepers' records, educational records, medical records, even fashion-house records, all in a unique Sumerian style of wedge-shaped cuneiform writing. Additionally, mathematical calculators were found, including tables for extracting square and cube roots, and triangular formulae as manifest in the mathematics of Euclid who lived some 1700 years later.[12]

The Anglo-American excavations continued year upon year, and eventually, beneath the red slopes of Tell al Muqayyar, the whole city of Ur began to appear within great walls of baked brick 26 feet (*c*.8.5 m) high and 77 feet (*c*.25.5 m) thick at the base. There were rows of houses with streets between them – and what spacious houses they were. These were not the modest homes of primitive people; they were two-storeyed villas with up to fourteen rooms. The walls were plastered and whitewashed, and there were washbasins to remove sand from feet and hands in the entrance lobbies. The inner courts were neatly paved, with staircases rising to the upper floors, and all around, from the ground floor and gallery, were the family and guest rooms – even indoor lavatory provision and drainage systems.

These houses were built in the 2nd millennium BC, but by today's standards they were mansions of the utmost luxury. If Abraham came from the city of Ur, then he was doubtless a magnate of high esteem, for there were no humble dwellings here, and Sir Charles Leonard Woolley duly noted in his journal: 'We must radically alter our view of the Hebrew patriarch when we see that his earlier years were passed in such sophisticated surroundings. He was the citizen of a great city, and inherited the traditions of an old and highly organized civilization'. Indeed, as will be revealed, Abraham was actually descended from a daughter of the great king Ur-nammu who built the ziggurat Temple of Ur.

As if such monumental discoveries were not enough, there was more to follow. When the Woolley team investigated beneath the foundations of the 4000-year-old ziggurat and its confines, they found the remains of another great ziggurat and a buried city from even more ancient times,[13] with courtyard bricks dating back to the 4th millennium BC. Also, there were graves and artefacts from 3700 BC, around the time of Adam,[14] along with numerous archaeologically valuable items from a far more distant era. They even discovered a kingly burial ground, together with documentary records and cultural treasures unsurpassed in all Egypt. Here was positive proof of the world's oldest and greatest civilization—a highly advanced culture which had already existed for 2000 years before the ancient Egyptian civilization began, and which had emerged 4000 years before the earliest civilization in Greece.

# 3

# Crimson Robes and Silver Combs

## The Great Flood

Since we are looking at the unearthed history of ancient Sumerian Mesopotamia, a good test of the generally applied biblical chronology would be to compare some particular Genesis event with a modern archaeological discovery. What better in this regard than the great Flood as related in the story of Noah (Genesis 7:10-24). This was said to have taken place nine generations after Adam, and a further nine generations before Abraham. So, if we can find the historical Flood, then perhaps it would present a suitable peg upon which to hang a mean date in the early patriarchal succession.

As mentioned, the standard reckoning for the Flood is 2348 BC, as given by Archbishop Ussher. But the fact is that there was no possible way prior to the 1920s for Ussher or anyone else to have known the date of the Flood—nor even if there actually was a flood in the region. Not for nearly three centuries after Ussher's lifetime did any noteworthy archaeological excavations begin in Mesopotamia.

About 13,000 years ago (*c*.11,000 BC), a milder world climate ensued as the last Ice Age drew to a close. This abrupt change would have caused severe slippage in the ice sheets of the Arctic and Antarctic, displacing enormous quantities of water and leading to tidal waves of immense proportion in the great oceans. But was this the biblical Flood? It would seem not, although it was clearly the turning-point which heralded the Domestic Age of crop cultivation in the Fertile Crescent. What followed the biblical Flood, however, was not agricultural domestication which already existed, but the Age of Civilization and the rise of the Sumerian city-states.

In our search for the Flood of Genesis, we can once again join Sir Charles Leonard Woolley and his team in the 1920s, for it was they who first discovered the pre-Flood remains of old Mesopotamia. It has to be remembered, however, that in those distant times Mesopotamia was considered the hub of a somewhat limited geographical world. For a good many generations the kings of the region were designated 'Kings of the Four Quarters of the World',[1] so a major flood of the area would have been regarded as an event of worldwide consequence, just as it is presented in the Old Testament.

Six years after beginning their excavations at Ur, Woolley's archaeologists found an intriguing complex of ancient graves dating to about 3500 BC, including a stone-built tomb of unusual significance. It was significant because stone has never existed in this desert area; barely a pebble can be found within 30 miles (*c.*48 km) of Ur. Such an underground construction was clearly an extravagance, and the team knew they had found the grave of some very important person.

On entering the tomb, the men were truly amazed, for they were confronted by treasures such as they had never seen.[2] There were golden goblets, fine ornaments decorated with chips of red limestone and lapis lazuli (a deep blue mineral), bronze tableware, silver jewellery, mother-of-pearl mosaics, exquisite shell-decorated harps and lyres, a magnificent chariot with the golden heads of lions and bulls, vessels of silver, alabaster, copper and marble, tools and weapons made of gold—and all manner of wonderful artefacts outweighing the splendour of the Egyptian tomb of Tutankhamun from 1600 years later.

Round and about, soldiers were buried with helmets, spears and shields of copper, silver and gold. And there were the remains of ladies in crimson robes, with ornate headdresses, golden earrings and silver combs. These many attendants were the staff and guardians of the main tomb, which was found to be that of Queen Shub-ad, who reigned before the earliest dynasty of Egypt. Nearby was the grave of her husband A-bar-gi.

A-bar-gi's remains had been badly damaged in times long gone, but Shub-ad's were quite unmoved. She lay in state on a golden bier with a gold cup by her hand and two maid-servants kneeling at her side. Shub-ad's body was lavishly adorned with a beaded cloak of gold, silver, lapis lazuli, agate, carnelian and chalcedony (types of quartz). On her arms were gold and silver amulets representing fish and gazelles, and her headdress was an exquisite wreath of golden beech and willow leaves.

A further discovery was made close by when a second royal tomb was opened—a tomb bearing the inscription, 'Mes-kalam-dug, the King'. Another inscription, on a golden bowl within, identified King Mes-kalam-dug as the 'Hero of the Good Land'. Here was, presumably, a relative of Shub-ad and A-bar-gi, and amid the general fineries of his tomb was the most magnificent example of the ancient goldsmith's art ever found. On Mes-kalam-dug's head was a helmet of beaten gold, moulded to fit with cheek-pieces to protect the face. This helmet, now about 5000 years old,[3] is in the form of a wig, parted in the middle with locks of hair in wonderful relief, falling in wavy tresses and bound with a twisted fillet to form curls around the perfectly shaped ears. Even individual hairs are delicately engraved within the separated locks, and it is all made from one sheet of 15-carat electrum gold. A cylinder-seal inscription denotes that the wife of Mes-kalam-dug was Nîn-banda,[4] and we shall learn a good deal more about this influential couple in due course.

At this stage, the archaeologists had excavated down to more than 1700 years before the time of Abraham, and back more than 1000 years beyond the time of Noah, but so far they had come across no sign of any flood. Having found the royal burial ground, they continued to dig into the past, determined to discover what lay beyond. Shafts were sunk through dozens of feet of rubble, until suddenly they came upon wood-ash and numerous inscribed clay tablets. They struck down still further, pulling up pieces of pottery and household items until, at length, they appeared to have hit solid ground. They were at the very bottom—or so they thought.

Woolley then took himself into the depths of the pit, and there to his astonishment he found that he was not standing upon bedrock, but on solid clay—a type of clay that could only have been deposited by water.[5] His first thought was that, since Ur was closer to the coast in olden times, this must be the accumulated silt of the early Euphrates delta—but a ground study of the surrounding area led to a quite different conclusion. Such a concept was impossible for, even having dug down so deeply, they were still far above sea-level and certainly much higher than the river-bed of the Euphrates. So they kept on digging. Down they went through more than 8 feet (*c*.2.5 m) of clay, and then quite suddenly it ended as abruptly as it had begun.

What they came upon was pure virgin soil, the kind of soil that would have been the perfect ground for irrigation in the once Fertile Crescent. Then came further evidence of human habitation: pottery, jars, bowls and the like. Beneath the great thickness of the water-borne clay belt was yet another settlement, and when the clay was analysed it was found to contain the fossils of marine life from a time when the sea had flooded the whole area. The levels of strata were examined and, like all geological strata, they provided their own calender.[6] The bed of clay had been laid down over the old settlement in about 4000 BC—and Woolley duly sent a telegram to London: 'We have found the Flood.'

Subsequently, other archaeologists conducted surveys in various parts of the Tigris-Euphrates valley and, a good way north-west of Ur at Kish near Babylon, the clay was found to have reduced to a thickness of 18 inches (46 cm), but it was still a consistent layer. Overall, the flood was reckoned to have covered an area of 400 miles (644 km) north to south, and 100 miles (161 km) east to west. In its day, it would surely have been catastrophic and would undoubtedly have been perceived as being of worldwide proportion.

So, if Adam's date is correct according to a mean standard reckoning of around 3882 BC, and if Noah lived nine generations after Adam, then something is wrong, because the flood strata of Mesopotamia has been scientifically dated to about 4000 BC, which puts the Flood before the time of Adam. There is absolutely no trace of there being a flood at any time around 2348 BC, and therefore Archbishop Ussher's date is incorrect. So, if Noah was present at the time of the Flood as the Bible relates, then perhaps we have the wrong starting date for Adam. In this regard, the old Mesopotamian texts come into play and, in contrast to the Bible, they indicate that Adam prevailed 'after' the Flood.

Where, then, does this leave Noah? Well, in relation to the Flood it leaves him absolutely nowhere. Among some 20,000 preserved clay tablets, excavated from the world's most famous ancient library at Nineveh (old Ninua) in Mesopotamian Assyria, are twelve which tell the story of the Flood. According to these texts, the hero of the epic, who was commanded by the gods to 'build a ship', was King Uta-napishtim of Shuruppak, who reigned around 4000 BC. His story even states that when the waters had abated, 'All mankind had turned to clay; the ground was flat like a roof'.

Before looking at the Mesopotamian Flood saga in greater detail, we should first consider how it was that the original Hebrew compilers of Genesis, nearly 3500 years after the Flood, grafted Uta-napishtim's story into the lifetime of the much later Noah. Once we know the truth of this, we shall be in a far better position to identify the historical Adam.

## The Hebrew Tradition

It is generally agreed by scholars that there are two consecutive Creation stories in Genesis.[7] The first (Genesis 1:1-2:4) is considered to be the work of a priestly writer of the 6th century BC, and its purpose is the glorification of God by way of his bringing the Earth out of the darkness of Chaos.[8] It also establishes the principle of the seventh-day Sabbath as a customary day of rest. The second Creation account (Genesis 2:5-25) has a somewhat older tradition, and its author is often called the Jahvist because he introduced the godly name of Jehovah.

The name Jehovah (or *Yahweh*, from *YHWH*: 'I am that I am') was given as an alternative to the more original Canaanite term *Elohim*, which is commonly said to mean God.[9] But *Elohim* is actually a plural noun, the singular of which is *El* or *Eloh*, meaning 'Lofty One'. The *Elohim* were the early gods of Canaan, which explains the use of plural terminology in the Old Testament—e.g. 'Ye shall be as gods' (Genesis 3:5).

Clearly, when the Old Testament was being consolidated, the plural use of 'Elohim' in the original texts was applied to the single concept of Jehovah. Be that as it may, the early Canaanite writings determine that Jehovah's nominal predecessor was the great El Elyon,[10] whose powers included the bestowing of lordships in consultation with the Master Craftsmen, a definition which will be discussed later.

El Elyon's seat was said to be 'at the headwaters of the two rivers' (the Tigris and Euphrates), where he would receive ambassadors and settle disputes. His principal son was Baal (meaning Lord),[11] whose brothers included Yamm the Leviathan or sea-monster (Psalm 74:14), Mot (death),[12] Shahar (dawn), and Shalem (peace)—whence derives *Yuru-shalem* (Jerusalem): city of peace. Their sister was Anath, Queen of the Heavens. But if El Elyon's seat was located relative to the two great rivers, then his establishment must have been Mesopotamian before becoming Canaanite. Hence, it appears that El Elyon's tradition was originally brought from Mesopotamia into Canaan (the Land of

Purple),[13] probably by Noah's grandson Canaan, whose descendants were 'spread abroad' (Genesis 10:6-18). In fact, since *El* means no more than Lofty One, that same lofty one did indeed have a personal name in ancient Sumerian times.

Prior to the 20th century, little was known of the Canaanite religious tradition, but from 1929 a large number of ancient texts were found at Ras Shamra (the old city of Ugarit) in north-western Syria.[14] These writings, from around 1400 BC, detail that the female consort of El Elyon was called Asherah (or Ashtoreth),[15] and the Canaanite religion was firmly centred around fertility, both in the family and on the farm. Other goddesses of the era were Padriya, Talliya and Arsiya.[16] For the Israelites, the god-and-goddess concept came to an end when they dismissed Ashtoreth and pledged their allegiance to the one and only Jehovah, who was appropriated from El Elyon, being in essence the same character. But this pledge of singular allegiance was not made in the time of Abraham, nor even in the time of Moses—it occurred much later, in the time of Samuel the judge, when 'the children of Israel did put away Baal and Ashtoreth, and served the Lord only' (1-Samuel 7:4). This was in about 1060 BC.

Notwithstanding that the Old Testament's early Hebrew writers supplanted El Elyon with Jehovah, the plural concept of the Elohim gods was, for the most part, ignored and translated into the singular definition of 'God'. But Psalm 82 relates to the plural Elohim, and to an incident when Jehovah-El 'judgeth among the gods'. The early Christian historian, Julius Africanus of Edessa (AD 200-245),[17] observed that, as well as having godly status, the Elohim were defined in some non-canonical works as 'foreign rulers' and 'judges'.[18]

Just as the first Creation story in Genesis concludes with the institution of the Sabbath, so the second account concludes with the institution of marriage: 'Therefore shall a man leave his father and his mother, and shall cleave unto his wife, and they shall be one flesh' (Genesis 2:24). Both Creation stories, however, detail that humankind gained dominion over the animals (Genesis 1:28, 2:20).

In Genesis 1:27, it is related that God created Adam, and then, in Genesis 2:7, Adam is seen to be created again, thereby determining that the same story is being told by two different writers whose separate accounts have been grafted together.

It is apparent that, prior to the composition of the Jewish Old Testament, the Hebrew culture was largely founded upon Canaanite lore. But it is just as plain that Sumerian tradition was equally embodied. In this respect, it must be remembered that the nineteen inclusive generations from Adam to Abraham were natives of Mesopotamia; therefore when Abraham migrated to Canaan in about 1900 BC, he arrived neither as a Jew, nor as a Canaanite, but as a Sumerian. He was, nonetheless, the first of the succession to be formally classified as Hebrew and he is regarded as the ultimate patriarch of the Jewish race. This stems from his covenant with Jehovah (Genesis 17)—or more correctly with El Elyon (called El Shaddai in early Bibles). Henceforth, Abraham became the designated father of his people and male circumcision was adopted by his descendants (*see* Chapter 16).

The designation 'Hebrew' derives from the patriarch Eber (Heber/Abhâr), six generations before Abraham.[19] The term 'Israelite' comes from the renaming of Abraham's grandson Jacob, who became known as Israel (Genesis 35:10-12). By way of translation, *Is-ra-el* means 'soldier of El', while some say that *Ysra-el* means 'El rules', and others prefer 'El strives'. Whichever is correct, the name is plainly indicative of the Canaanite tradition of El Elyon or El Shaddai, rather than of the later tradition of Jehovah. Also, the place called Lûz, where Jacob received his new name, had itself been renamed *Beth-el* (Genesis 28:19), meaning 'House of El'.

As for the term 'Jew', this comes from the style 'Judaean'—that is the Israelites of Judaea in Canaan—and it has traditionally become an all-embracing style for the Hebrew nation. In the strict terms of the old Jewish *Halakhah* (traditional law), a Jew is an individual born to a Jewish mother,[20] but the modern view is rather more accommodating and affords Jewishness to adherents of the Jewish faith whatever the nature of their parentage.

Abrahamic descent is therefore not a factor in itself, neither was genetic descent from the Hebrew patriarchs ever a feature of Jewishness in many family lines, except in a symbolic and emotional sense.[21]

## The Old Testament

The truly fascinating thing about Jewishness is that it defines not simply a religion, but an age-old cultural tradition dating from the time of Abraham. The term 'Jew' is quite unlike the term 'Christian' because it has the unique quality of defining a national identity, rather like that of an extended family. For this reason, wherever in the world a Jew might be resident, he or she can always be distinguished by the Jewish cultural heritage. Christianity, in contrast, is neither cultural, racial, nor family orientated, being more of an international religious society to which one may or may not belong.

Judaism has evolved by way of firm attachment, or through an inherent birthright which, although seemingly having its roots in Canaan, has its patriarchal origin in ancient Mesopotamia. It is hardly surprising that the early Mesopotamian and Canaanite traditions have become entwined, and it is easy to see how truly ancient stories, such as that of the Flood and the Ark, were chronologically confused by writers collating the history so long after the event. So, when was the Old Testament written—and by whom?

As we have seen, the opening verses of Genesis were composed in the 6th century BC, roughly 1400 years after the time of Abraham, 2000 years after Noah and 3500 years after the Mesopotamian flood. But from where would such ancient genealogical records have been obtained? Who would have recorded and maintained the patriarchal lineage through so many centuries?

Today, when tracing back into an individual family tree, it might take very few ancestral generations before the task became quite difficult—maybe even impossible. In contrast, if that tree were of a noble family, then the task would be straightforward because registers of peerage house the archives of nobility through the ages. For the Old Testament compilers of the 6th century BC the same would have been the case since the patriarchal succession, through Noah and Abraham, was the equivalent of a noble lineage, with its offshoots to the royal houses of Egypt and Judah. The most intriguing factor is not that this influential line was recorded from early times, but that it was designated 'prestigious' in the first place some 6000 years ago, long before the Israelites wrote up the story. Why this should be the case we shall discover as we pursue our investigation of the sacred heritage that descended to Jesus and beyond.

The first five books of the Old Testament—Genesis, Exodus, Leviticus, Numbers and Deuteronomy—are referred to as the *Torah* (the Law), or as the *Pentateuch* (from the Greek, meaning a five-part work).[22] They are traditionally regarded as having been inspired by the teachings of Moses (from the 14th century BC), as indicated by Flavius Josephus (the one time military commander of Galilee, born AD 37) in the opening chapter of his *Antiquities of the Jews*. However, scholars generally agree that the modern *Pentateuch* is a composite work, structured from various writings dating from the 9th century BC, and first consolidated in the 6th century BC. This may well be so, inasmuch as these five books incorporate the Mosaic Law, but it is further evident that their ancient historical content was obtained from much older Mesopotamian records—and we know from the Bible that many Israelites were Babylonian hostages in the 6th century BC.

The Old Testament book of 2-Kings tells of how, from 606-586 BC, Nebuchadnezzar of Babylon (King Nebuchadnezzar II from 604 BC) laid siege to Jerusalem. He captured King Jechoniah of Judah and carried him off to Babylon along with 'all of Jerusalem, and the princes, and all the mighty men of valour, even ten thousand captives, and all the craftsmen and smiths; none remained save the poorest sort of people of the land' (2-Kings 24:14). This was ostensibly done at Jehovah's bidding, because

Jechoniah's great-grandfather, King Manasseh, had once set up a temple to Baal, the son of El Elyon (2-Kings 21:3). And since Jehovah and El Elyon were synonymous with God (by Hebrew and Canaanite definition, respectively), Manasseh had apparently defied the supreme deity by worshipping God's son. Nevertheless, whatever the interpretation at the time, Nebuchadnezzar ravaged Jerusalem and Judah, destroying the High Temple of Solomon 'at the commandment of the Lord... to remove them out of his sight for the sins of Manasseh, according to all that he did' (2-Kings 24:3).

From 586 BC, more than 10,000 Israelites were held captive in Babylon - kings, priests, prophets and all. Their descendent families remained there until the first group of 50,000 returned to Jerusalem in 536 BC. It was here, in this 6th-century BC Mesopotamian environment that many of the books of the Old Testament were compiled, with the scribes aided both by the Babylonian records of old Mesopotamia and by an old Hebrew Book of the Law (the crux of the book of Deuteronomy).[23] This had been found by High Priest Hilkiah in the Jerusalem Temple shortly before Nebuchadnezzar's invasion (2-Kings 22:8).

Although the main compilation of the Old Testament was undertaken during this period of Israelite exile, certain additional works, such as the book of Daniel, were written some while after the event in the 2nd century BC. Even by the 1st century AD, at the time of Jesus, there was no single composite text available to the Jews at large. The various books existed only as individual texts, as indicated by the thirty-eight scrolls of nineteen Old Testament books found at Qumrân, Judaea, between 1947 and 1951. These included a 23-foot (*c*.7 m) Hebrew scroll of the book of Isaiah,[24] the longest of all the Dead Sea Scrolls. Having been dated to about 100 BC, it is the oldest biblical text in existence.[25]

The first set of amalgamated books to be generally approved as the Hebrew Bible appeared after the fall of Jerusalem to the Roman general Titus in AD 70, and it was compiled in an endeavour to restore faith in Judaism at a time of social turmoil.

(The word 'Bible' comes from the Greek plural noun *biblia*, meaning 'a collection of books'.)

In its composite 1st-century form, the Old Testament was written in a Hebrew style consisting only of consonants. In parallel with this, a Greek translation emerged for the benefit of the growing number of Greek-speaking Hellenist Jews. This has since become known as the *Septuagint* (from the Latin *septuaginta*: seventy) because seventy-two scholars were employed in the translation. Later, in the 4th century AD, St. Jerome made a Latin translation from the Hebrew for subsequent Christian usage: this was called the *Vulgate* because of its 'vulgar' (general) application.

In about 900 AD, the old Hebrew text emerged in a new form, produced by Jewish scholars known as the Massoretes because they appended the *Massorah* (a body of traditional notes) to the text. The oldest existing copy of this comes from little more than 1000 years ago, in AD 916.[26]

These days, we may work from the Massoretic text, from the Latin *Vulgate*, or from English and various other language translations. But, whatever the case, the fact remains that these books are all from our present era, and have each been subjected to some translatory and interpretational amendment. The Greek *Septuagint* is somewhat older, being compiled between the 3rd century BC and the 1st century AD. How fortunate it is that, through the work of latter-day archaeologists such as Sir Charles Leonard Woolley, we can now consult the wealth of inscribed clay tablets and cylinder-seals unearthed from the ancient Mesopotamian cities of Ur, Nineveh and elsewhere. Texts such as these would undoubtedly have been available to the exiled Israelites in Babylonia in the 6th century BC, and from these they most certainly drew their accounts of the Creation and the Flood. In a good many respects, therefore, the Mesopotamian records hold the intrinsic keys to the early Genesis period.

## The Garden of Eden

We have already seen that biblical centres such as Ur, Babylon and Nineveh were all cities of ancient Mesopotamia, with Ur and Babylon in the Sumerian Chaldees (later called Babylonia) and Nineveh in Assyria. We have also seen how certain Mesopotamian city names replicated Abraham's ancestral and immediate family names as given in Genesis—for example, Peleg, Serug, Nahor, Terah and Haran. So let us now look at the names of some other cities as detailed in Genesis, to see if they have also been discovered.

The best early mention of a series of place names (Genesis 10:8-12) centres upon King Nimrod, three generations after Noah. It states:

> And Cush begat Nimrod.... He was a mighty hunter before the Lord.... And the beginning of his kingdom was Babel, and Erech, and Accad, and Calneh, in the land of Shinar. Out of that land went forth Ashur and builded Nineveh, and the city Rehoboth, and Calah.

Nimrod's city—now known as Nimrud, but in the early days called Kalhu, which is synonymous with the Calah mentioned in Genesis above—was excavated in 1845 by the English diplomat Austen H. Layard.[27] Shortly afterwards Britain's foremost Assyriologist, Henry Creswicke Rawlinson, unearthed the great library of King Ashur-banipal a little north of Nimrud at Nineveh.

Nimrod's kingdoms of Babel and Accad are self-explanatory, being Babylon and Akkad respectively. Modern Baghdad and Babylon are in the region of Iraq once known as Akkad, north of Sumer, and the early kings of Akkad were also kings of Kish, a city immediately east of Babylon. Kish is identical with Kûsh (or Cush), as given above. Erech is equally straightforward, being the great city of Uruk (modern Warka), from which, as we have seen, the country name of Iraq derives,[28] and the land of Shinar relates to Sumer.

The sameness of personal and place names, as identified by Abraham's ancestral family, is a repetitive feature of the *Pentateuch* texts, but it is often difficult to determine which came first: were the places named after the people, or were the people named after the places? Whatever the case, it is clear that these nominal uniformities denote a particularly important lineage—a family whose members were senior rulers in the Mesopotamian domain. As for the personal names given in Genesis, the chances are that these were actually titular and that they were specifically related to the family members' city seats. In much the same way, Scotland's noble Earl of Moray might sign himself 'Moray', or the Duke of Atholl might be referred to as 'Atholl', irrespective of their actual names. Even in the latter stages of the Old Testament, many individual names are certainly descriptive, if not titular. A good example is the name of Prince Zerubbabel, who led the Israelites out of Babylonian exile in 536 BC and whose name simply means 'begotten in Babel'.

Prior to the group of place names given in Genesis 10, we have been told very little about locations—with the obvious exception being the Garden of Eden. In the Sumerian language, a lush pastureland between irrigated areas (what we would today call a steppe or grassy plain) was called an *eden*.[29] Among the most notable *edens* of ancient times was the land of Eridu (modern Abu Sharain), about 16 miles (*c*.26 km) south-west of Ur in the Euphrates delta. Eridu was a most sacred city of ancient Mesopotamia and was the very first seat of Sumerian kingship before the Flood.

The unearthed temple-remains of the Eridu ziggurat date from about 2100 BC, but beneath these remains have been found seventeen more temples (many of them very elaborate), each built one above the other and dating back to proto-historic times.[30] Since the world's most ancient civilization was Sumerian, it is of particular biblical relevance that the fertile eden of Eridu was the very oldest seat of civilized settlement in Sumer,[31] the earliest truly important place in the world.

The four Rivers of Eden (Genesis 2:10-14) have caused any amount of theological confusion, with researchers questing far and wide for rivers that might fit the Old Testament depictions. There is no mystery to unravel though, for the conventional English version of the Genesis text has been wholly mistranslated in this regard. The King James Authorized Bible states:

> And a river went out of Eden to water the garden; and from thence it was parted, and became into four heads. The name of the first is Pison: that is it which compasseth the whole land of Havilah, where there is gold.... And the name of the second river is Gihon: the same is it that compasseth the whole land of Ethiopia. And the name of the third river is Hiddekel: that is it which goeth toward the east of Assyria. And the fourth river is Euphrates.

The River Euphrates, which runs into the Persian Gulf, is clearly enough defined—but what of the others? There is, for example, no river which leads to the same Sumerian outlet having encompassed Ethiopia in North Africa. Indeed, there is no river which encompasses Ethiopia running to anywhere.

There are, in fact, three key errors in the King James translated passage. As detailed in the *Anchor Bible* (a direct translation from the Hebrew text, rather than from the Greek and Latin texts), the first of these errors is that the Hebrew writings do not state that the river became four rivers having flowed 'out of' Eden, but that four rivers flowed 'into' Eden where they became one. Secondly, the word 'compasseth' (which is used twice in the above passage) implies an encircling, but the pertinent Hebrew stem *SBB* actually denotes a winding course. Thus, the first river did not encompass the land of Havilah, but meandered through it.

The same applies to the second river (said to be of Ethiopia), except that in this instance the name of the place has been wrongly translated. Ethiopia is not mentioned at all in the original text; the place named is Cush. When the Bible was translated, this was thought to refer to Kush (modern Sudan)[32] in old Abyssinia, North Africa. But Ethiopia did not exist as such in the early days, being simply a name given to North Africa as a whole by the Greeks.[33] The biblical Cush was actually Kûsh, or Kish (modern Al'Uhaimir), east of Babylon.

The third river, the Hiddekel, was the River Tigris, which flowed eastwards of Ashur, Assyria. It was called *Tigris* in Greek, *Hiddeqel* in Hebrew, *Idiqlat* in Akkadian and *Dijlat* in Aramaic.[34] The four rivers which flowed into Eden then were the Tigris, the Euphrates and their two main tributaries, one of which ran through Kish and the other through the land of the Havilah (a tribe of the region). A more precise translation of the Genesis passage directly from the Hebrew text is:

> A river rises in Eden to water the garden; before that it consists of four separate branches. The name of the first is Pishon; it is the one that winds through the whole land of the Havilah people, where there is gold.... The name of the second river is Gihon; it is the one that winds through all the land of Kish. The name of the third river is Tigris; it is the one that flows eastward of Ashur. The fourth river is the Euphrates.[35]

Having now discussed the biblical Garden of Eden, it is evident that there is considerably more of a story to tell in historical terms, and a far more relevant location to consider. We shall, therefore, return to the subject again in Chapter 7 to discuss a rather more important Eden of pre-Sumerian times—the garden where the ground-plan for domesticity was truly laid.

# 4

# The Chaldean Genesis

## Bible and Babel

> When on high the heaven had not yet been named,
> Firm ground below had not been called by a name,
> Nought but primordial Apsû, their begetter,
> And Mummu, and Tiâmat—she who bore them all,
> Their waters mingled as a single body.

So begins the original pre-Genesis Creation epic—the story known to the ancient Babylonians and Assyrians as the *Enûma elish* in accordance with its opening words 'When on high'. It was first composed around 3500 years ago,[1] and there are still existing versions from the 1st millennium BC—the era from which the above extract is taken.

The poetic story tells in this first verse that in the beginning there was nothing but a watery dimension, for the gods Apsû (male) represented the 'sweet waters', Mummu (male) the 'veiling mist' and Tiâmat (female) the 'salt waters'.[2] This is not so different from the beginning of Genesis, written much later, in the 6th century BC, which states that before God created dry land, 'The earth was without form, and void, and darkness was upon the face of the deep. And the spirit of God moved upon the face of the waters (1:2).

In progressing its story, the Babylonian epic does not tell that the Earth was created in six days, with a seventh day of rest, as explained in Genesis. There is, however, a thought-provoking similarity, in that the original Creation story is conveyed through a series of six clay tablets, with a seventh tablet devoted to celebration and reverence for the creative achievements of the Babylonian deity Marduk[3] *(see* Chart: *The Babylonian Creation Epic and Genesis*).

The first *Enûma elish* tablets to be discovered were unearthed, in the 1848-76 excavations of Sir Austen Henry Layard, from the library of King Ashur-banipal at Nineveh. They were subsequently published by George Smith of the British Museum in 1876 under the title *The Chaldean Account of Genesis*. Other tablets and fragments containing versions of the same epic were found at Ashur, Kish and Uruk,[4] and it was ascertained from colophons (publishers' imprints) that an even older text existed in a more ancient language. This conveyed the same story of how a certain deity had created the heavens and the Earth, and everything on Earth, including humankind.

It is interesting to note that there is an even closer association between the Mesopotamian and Genesis accounts than may at first be apparent, and one of the common denominators is the Akkadian name *Tiâmat* (Salt waters). Although English translations of Genesis use the expression 'the deep', the original Hebrew word relating to 'the deep' was *tehôm*, which has a similar root to *Tiâmat*.[5] *Tehôm* in the plural becomes *tehômot* (*thwmwt*) but, as pointed out by Semitic scholars, the association between the Hebrew word *tehômo*t and the Akkadian name *Tiâmat* was purposely suppressed for doctrinal reasons.[6] In the *Enûma elish* epic, the Babylonian god Marduk is said to have fought a great battle to overcome the primordial salt waters of Tiâmat, who is portrayed in the account as the great Dragon Queen.

This part of the story is not recounted as such in Genesis, except to say that God 'divided the waters' (1:7), but it is repeated more fully in Psalm 74 (verses 13-14), where God 'didst divide the sea... and... breakest the heads of the dragons in the waters'. In this account, the dragon of the *tehôm* is called the Leviathan (a Canaanite term), as it is also named in the book of Job (41:1). Elsewhere in the Old Testament, the formidable sea-dragon is called Rahab, as in Psalm 89 (verses 9-10): 'Thou rulest the raging of the sea... Thou hast broken Rahab into pieces'; and also in the book of Isaiah (51:9): 'Awake... O arm of the Lord... Art thou not it that hath cut Rahab and wounded the dragon'.

As we have already deduced, the chaos-monster of the deep was, in the Canaanite tradition, called Yamm (meaning 'sea') and it was a common theme in the writings of the Mesopotamians, Canaanites and Hebrews that the foremost accomplishment of their respective deities was the calming of the wild ocean deep. Even in the later teachings of the Alexandrian Gnostics, the great 'first father', Yaldaboath, was brought forth from the depths by the Holy Spirit, who was called Sophia, meaning 'wisdom'.[7] The Holy Spirit of Sophia was said (just as is related in Genesis) to have 'moved on the face of the waters'. (In this regard, the word *ruah*, which was translated in Genesis as 'spirit', actually meant 'wind'.[8])

In the 6th century BC, when the Israelites were captives of Nebuchadnezzar, the *Enûma elish* was a standard recitation at the New Year festivals in Babylon, as it had been for many centuries. This festival lasted through the first eleven days of Nisan (modern March-April) and the poem (more than 920 lines) was related in its entirety by the High Priest, with parts of the story re-enacted.[9] There was no way that the old Creation epic could have escaped the attention of the Israelites, and they were clearly fascinated by its content. By that time, they were referring to their God as Jehovah, having dispensed with the Canaanite names El Elyon and El Shaddai—but it mattered not that the Babylonians called their deity Marduk, for here was the story of universal creation being ritualistically played out before their very eyes. Thus was the biblical Genesis born, as the onlooking Israelite priests made their notes of record.

There was, however, a distinct difference between the Babylonian epic and the resultant Genesis account, in that the former tells not only of the god Marduk, but of his being one of a pantheon of gods—a group of deities who (in the parallel Canaanite tradition) were called the Elohim. From the verse quoted above, the *Enûma elish* continues:

> No pasture had yet been formed; no marsh had yet appeared.
> None of the gods had yet been brought into being.
> Not one bore a name; their destinies were undetermined.
> Then it was that gods were formed in their midst.

Hence, we can see how the biblical Genesis that we know so well has been manipulated even from the texts of the 6th-century BC Israelite exiles. For, like the Babylonians, they too recorded 'gods' in the plural: the Elohim fraternity of El Elyon—a definition that was singularized to accommodate the emergent, all-embracing concept of Jehovah. Perhaps we should remind ourselves once again of Jehovah's words from Genesis: 'Let *us* make man in *our* image, after *our* likeness' (1:26); and, 'Behold, the man is become as one of *us*' (3:22).

After relating the story of disputes among the gods, and of the creation of the firmaments of the sky and the heavens, the *Enûma elish* states that Marduk established the Earth's solar orbit and defined the duties of the moon thereby determining the earthly year and its divisions, with the moon to make known the nights and the months. In just the same way, Genesis states that 'God said, let there be lights in the firmament of the heaven to divide the day from the night; and let them be for signs, and for seasons, and for days and years' (1:14).

At length, the *Enûma elish* tells that Marduk, in conversation with another god, imparts his final plan: 'Then will I set up *lullû*—man shall be his name. Yes, I shall create *lullû*: man'.[10]

At this point, we shall break off from the Creation story, to return to the appearance of man in due course, for it now emerges that the story of the Babylonian Marduk and his

Creation is far from being the earliest account in this context. In its very oldest form, Marduk's story might be 1000 years older than the Genesis account, but it is distinctly Babylonian and the Babylonian era began in about 1890 BC. Prior to that was the Sumerian era from about 3800 BC to 1960 BC—the era of the kings of Eridu, Kish, Shuruppak, Larsa and Ur. It is within the records

*Marduk, with the Rod and Ring of divinely measured justice, alongside the sacred Mûs-hûs (from a Babylonian relief).*

of ancient Sumer that Marduk's original prototype appears, and it is from these that we find the first account of Adam.

## The Mystery of Sumer

A matter about which researchers are seemingly unanimous is the unknown origin of the Sumerians. The leading Sumerian archaeologist Sir Charles Leonard Woolley wrote that they came 'whence we do not know'.[11] The noted Sumerian scholar Samuel Noah Kramer stated that 'their original home is quite uncertain'.[12] The Iraq historian Georges Roux, when confronting the problem, made the point that recent discoveries, 'far from offering a solution, have made it even more difficult to answer'.[13] And the orientalist Henri Frankfort suggested that 'the problem of the origin of the Sumerians may well turn out to be the case of a chimera [a hybrid]'.[14]

Another point upon which scholars agree is that the Sumerians were not so called because they lived in Sumer. Quite the reverse: the land was called Sumer because the Sumerians were settled there. Moreover, the Sumerians gained their own descriptive name not from any place or culture, but directly from their unique language, which was itself called Sumerian. Hence, they are more correctly defined as 'Sumerian speaking people'.[15]

To this day, the majority are baffled by the sudden, extraordinary emergence of the Sumerians, seemingly from nowhere. But there is no doubt that, upon their advent in southern Mesopotamia, they were already highly advanced to a level far beyond that recorded or sustained in any place from where logically they could have emanated. Nowhere on earth was there a culture like that of the Sumerians, who appeared soon after 4000 BC—at least that is what is generally supposed.

Even the Sumerian language puzzled scholars when the first tablets were discovered in the 19th century, for it was neither Semitic nor Indo-European. It bore no relation to Arabic, Jewish, Canaanite, Phoenician, Syrian, Assyrian, Persian, Indian,

Egyptian, nor to any language from the European, African or Asian continents. To quote Professor Kramer, the Sumerian language 'stands alone and unrelated to any known language living or dead'.[16] So, what was this strange language which told of ancient kings with unimaginable names such as Al-lulim-ak, En-men-gal-anna and Pala-kin-atim, who reigned long before the 1st dynasty of Egypt? These names made no sense at all to historians or linguists, and the Assyriologist Sir Henry Rawlinson announced to the Royal Asiatic Society in 1853 that such names belonged to no known group or culture hitherto discovered.[17]

What Rawlinson also announced, however, was that he had found an interesting pre-Sumerian script in Babylonia—a non-Semitic script which he proffered was probably of Scythian origin from Central Europe. But his colleagues were not convinced and they decided to call this early script Akkadian (Akkad being the older name for Babylonia). At this, Rawlinson made the point that the ancient Scythians (a transient kingly tribe who first domesticated the horse before 4000 BC) were indeed the early occupiers of Akkad in pre-Sumerian times. Notwithstanding this, however, the matter was dropped and there was deemed to be no connection between this script and the emergent Sumerian cuneiform text.

The facility which made the written texts of the Sumerian language decipherable in the early 20th century was that comparative writings were also found in later Akkadian script, with footnotes that related to some of the Sumerian records from which they had been transcribed. This particular Akkadian tongue had a known Semitic base and, being akin to a number of other languages, it could therefore be translated by the Assyrian and Babylonian scribal schools. With this done, they then set the comparative Akkadian and Sumerian texts side by side and compiled bilingual syllabaries (dictionaries of symbols relating to syllables). By comparing the Akkadian words and phrases with the corresponding Sumerian symbols, it became possible to decipher the latter, even though the two languages were as dissimilar as any two languages could be.[18]

Sumerian writing is still reckoned to be the oldest sophisticated form of writing in existence, having first appeared in about 3400 BC.[19] It is neither crude nor primitive, and there is no region on earth which identifies any scribal concept that might have been its immediate forerunner. It appeared in a complete and composite form, as if from another world, in the style known as cuneiform (wedge-shaped). This was a series of angular phonetic symbols (cuneates), ostensibly abbreviated from the pictographs of the Sumerian temple priests.[20]

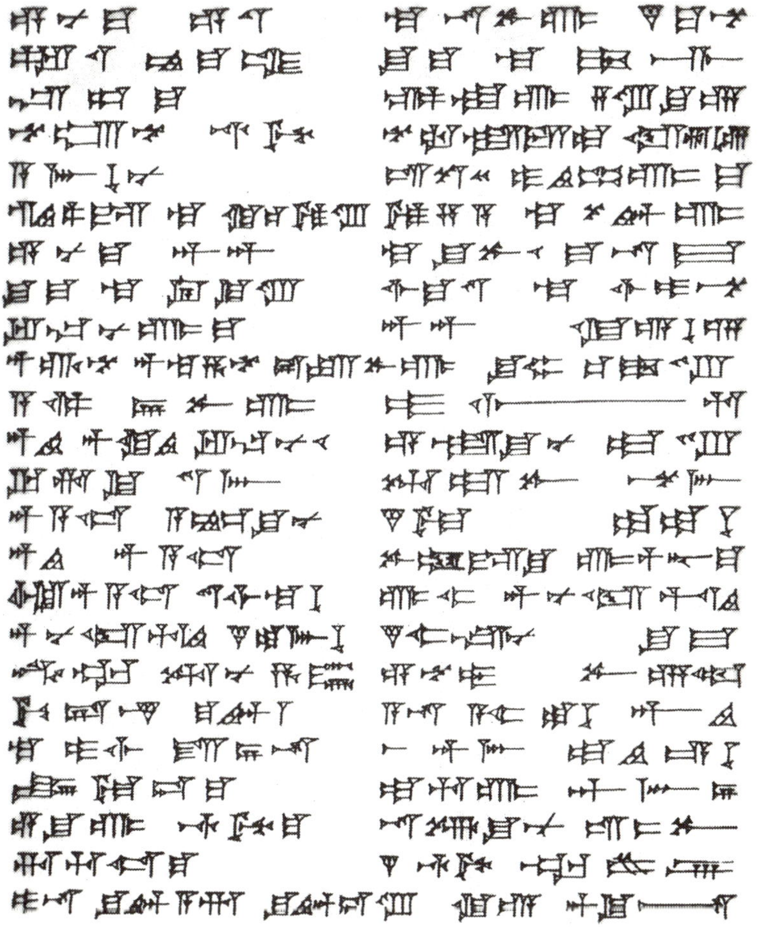

*Cuneiform writing of the* Enûma elish.

Having said that, however, a less sophisticated form of writing, identical to that found by Rawlinson in Akkad, has been unearthed (just as he surmised) in the Transylvanian village of Tartaria in the Balkans. In the 1940s three small clay tablets were found there in an ash-filled dedication pit and, as detailed in the *Scientific American* journal of May 1968, their markings are in many ways similar to later symbols emanating from Crete in about 2000 BC. Perhaps more surprisingly, they of precisely the same style as that which preceded cuneiform in Mesopotamia (although not visually related to it) and the symbols relate directly to those found at Jemdat Nasr, near Babylon, by the Oxford Assyriologist Stephen Langdon in 1925. (The comparative scripts are pictured in this book's companion volume, *Realm of the Ring Lords*.) Moreover, they pre-date Sumerian cuneiform by more than a thousand years,[21] making it quite plain that the Sumerian people could well have originated by way of migration from ancient Scythia and the Black Sea regions. This possibility is considerably strengthened by a number of recent discoveries—not the least of which is that one of the Tataria tablets includes the name of the Sumerian god Enki (whom we shall meet in due course), along with the fact that Ur, the Sumerian city of Abraham and the great god Anu, stems from the Scythian word *Ur*, meaning Lord.

Not much more than a century ago, no one had ever heard of the Sumerians, but now the collections at the British Museum, the Louvre, the Berlin Museum, Yale University and elsewhere hold a greater wealth of Sumerian texts than have been found from any other ancient culture. There are literally tens of thousands of clay tablets and cylinder-seals, containing everything from administrative and taxation records to essays and literature. Many of these are from a distant era, more than 1000 years before epic Greek poems such as the *Iliad* and the *Odyssey*, and even longer before the Israelites' first notations for Genesis.

The tablets were of flattened, cushion-shaped clay, upon which the scribes drew horizontal and vertical lines to form squares or rectangles within which pictographs were etched.

Alternatively, cuneiform writing was similarly inscribed into the soft clay with obliquely cut reed stalks and the tablets were then baked hard in the hot Mesopotamian sun.

The cylinder-seals were quite different, being made of stone and, as their name suggests, cylindrical in form. Their main difference was that they were negatively engraved—that is to say, engraved in reverse, as a printer's block or a royal seal might be. The imprints were either of writing or, very commonly, were descriptive pictures from which much has been learned about the Sumerian times and culture. These cylinder-seals were used to roll positive images into soft clay, which was then baked. Since the stone seals were reverse masters, they facilitated a reproduction process for any number of impressions and, by virtue of this, not only were numerous copies made possible (say for decorative building reliefs or matching pottery), but the existence of a library-retained master completely undermined any attempt at forgery.

In consequence of the requirement for qualified scribes and administrators, the Sumerians introduced the first-known schools—professional environments much like our business schools today, where clerks and secretaries were trained. In a short time the scope of the schools widened and they became general centres of advanced learning for doctors, scientists, historians, astronomers, mathematicians, lawyers, accountants and the like.

One of the scholarly adepts of later times was none other than King Ashur-banipal of Assyria, who wrote on a clay tablet in the 7th century BC, about 100 years before the Israelite captivity: 'The god of the scribes has bestowed upon me the gift of the knowledge of his art. I have been initiated into the secrets of writing. I can even read the intricate tablets in Sumerian. I understand the enigmatic words in the stone carvings from the days before the Flood'.[22]

'From the days before the Flood'? But the Flood was in 4000 BC—so to what stone carvings of such ancient origin did the King refer? As we shall see, Ashur-banipal learned, as did many others of privileged esteem, from the most treasured archive of original civilization—the ultimate godly document of sacred knowledge: the *Table of Destiny*.[23]

This is perhaps a good moment to remind ourselves of our immediate quest—the quest for the root of the Messianic Grail bloodline, a dynasty that supposedly began with Adam. He is traditionally recorded as being the first man, and in this regard he was the first of a uniquely advanced strain of *homo sapiens-sapiens*. The world's first truly civilized and advanced race were the Sumerians, who emerged with a wholly new technological and academic culture soon after 4000 BC, having their kingly and priestly empire firmly cemented by 3800 BC. And what is the mean date that we have previously ascertained for Adam? It is 3882 BC.

# 5

# Realm of the Angels

## The Nephilim

One of the Old Testament's most enigmatic entries occurs in Genesis (6:1-4) where, in relation to the time of Noah, it is stated:

> And it came to pass, when men began to multiply on the face of the earth, and daughters were born unto them, that the sons of God saw the daughters of men that they were fair; and they took them wives of all which they chose.... There were nephilim on the earth in those days; and also after that, when the sons of God came in unto the daughters of men, and they bare children to them, the same became mighty men which were of old, men of renown.

Although this passage contains the specific definition of *nephilim* in the Hebrew accounts, it is common practice in English texts to convert the word to 'giants'—i.e. 'There were giants on the earth in those days'.[1] It must be said that this is a corruption, not a translation, for the words 'giants' and nephilim do not mean the same thing at all.

The error originated because there was no single-word translation for *nephilim*, and the translators had been provided with the possible alternative, 'giants' by various writers, including Flavius Josephus in his 1st-century *Antiquities of the Jews*.[2] He explained that:

> Many angels of God accompanied with women, and begat sons that became unjust... on account of the confidence they had in their own strength; for the tradition is that these men did what resembled the acts of those whom the Grecians call giants.

As can be seen, Josephus did not say that the nephilim were giants. In fact, he did not mention the nephilim at all; he mentioned only the 'angels of God' whose sons (by earthly women) performed acts of physical strength reminiscent of the Titans: 'those whom the Grecians call giants'. The Genesis text relates that these offspring were 'mighty men' and 'men of renown'—but such descriptions (irrespective of any perceived physical stature) referred to extraordinary ability, just as Nimrod was himself called 'a mighty one in the earth' (Genesis 10:8).

The apparent translation of *nephilim* to 'giants' is wholly inaccurate. But what does the word *nephilim* really mean? It actually means 'those who came down', 'those who descended', or 'those who were cast down'.[3]

Given that the so-called 'sons of God' were reputed (according to the Hebrews) to have caused their own dishonour by consorting with earthly women, they were said in the 2nd-century BC book of Enoch,[4] and in various apocryphal writings, to have fallen from grace. The word 'fallen' was perceived to be in keeping with the word *nephilim* (those who descended), and since the 'sons of God' had been identified as angels (*aggelos*) in the *Septuagin*t, a wholly new breed of beings emerged in scriptural literature. They were the fallen angels. The book of Enoch even goes so far as to state that there were about 200 of these fallen angels, who were led by the 'chiefs of their tens' (*see* Chart: *Chiefs of the Tens of the Fallen Angels*).

Because of the general ambiguity of the Genesis entry, it is not really clear whether the nephilim and the sons of God were one and the same. Neither is it clear whether the sons of God were synonymous with angels – although, back in the 2nd century AD, Rabbi ben Jochai said they were not,[5] and the Jews traditionally said they were not. The Old Testament is actually quite specific in its definitions – using the terms 'sons of God' and 'angels' independently throughout, while the book of Job (1:6, 2:1) makes the point that when the sons of God presented themselves before the Lord, Satan was among them. (In the older Canaanite tradition, Satan's equivalent as the recalcitrant son of El Elyon was Baal.) Outside the Bible, there are numerous satans (organized aggressors) to be found, and in the book of Jubilees they are represented by a certain Mastema. It is a common thread within non-canonical works that the satans performed their aggressive deeds only with God's permission.

As far as the biblical 'sons of God' are concerned, this description has also been wrongly translated in the Genesis text. The Hebrew writings state more accurately that they were the *bene ha-elohim*, and the word *elohim*, as we have seen, is a plural noun. By a more correct translation, the passage should refer to the 'sons of the gods'. If we are to be absolutely precise, *elohim* is a dual-gender plural and so the passage equally refers to the 'sons of the goddesses'.[6]

As previously noted, even Jehovah recognized that there were other gods – and indeed that there were sons of these other gods. The book of Joshua (24:2) relates that Jehovah acknowledged the fact that Abraham's father, Terah, 'served other gods'. Not only does the Old Testament detail Jehovah in discussion with the *bene ha-elohim*, but he is also seen to make his own bid for supremacy within the pantheon. From the Jerusalem Bible comes the following example of Jehovah at the Divine Assembly. This appears at the opening of Psalm 82:

> Jehovah takes his stand at the Council of El to deliver judgement among the elohim.

Then from verse 6:

> You too are gods,
> sons of El Elyon, all of you.

In the King James Bible, these verses are worded differently, but the nature of their content remains the same—that even Jehovah was understood to acknowledge his counterparts when he attended the grand assembly of the deities:

> God standeth in the congregation of the mighty; he judgeth among the gods....
> Ye are gods, and all of you are children of the most High.

In the book of Enoch, the sons of the gods are identified with a group of beings called Watchers, who are also mentioned in the books of Daniel and Jubilees. Enoch further explains that the Watchers were those same deiform beings who had mated with the earthly women.[7] In Daniel we learn that the Watchers were akin to the Nephilim, and King Nebuchadnezzar envisions a sequence which includes a Watcher who is described as having 'come down': 'Behold, a watcher and an holy one came down from heaven' (4:13); 'This matter is by the decree of the watchers, and the demand by the word of the holy ones' (4:17); 'And whereas the king saw a watcher and an holy one coming down from heaven (4:23).

The singular form of nephilim is *nephil*, and it is of interest to note that although the term (or at least its vowel-free Semitic root, *NFL*—'cast down') was used in the early Hebrew editions of Genesis from the 6th century BC, it had been superseded by the term Watcher when the book of Daniel was written 400 years later in about 165 BC.[8] Similarly, the non-canonical books of Enoch and Jubilees (written in much the same era) both use the term Watchers instead of Nephilim. Notwithstanding orthodox Jewish opinion, the Nephilim/Watchers had by that time become victim to both the 'fallen angel' and the 'giant' classifications.

This is exemplified in the *Damascus Document* found among the Dead Sea Scrolls—a manuscript composed in, or shortly prior to, the 1st century AD:[9]

> I will uncover your eyes... that you may not be drawn by thoughts of the guilty inclination and by lustful eyes. For many went astray because of this.... The watchers of heaven fell because of this.... And their sons as tall as cedar trees, whose bodies were like mountains.[10]

Such writings as these are thoroughly indicative of the way that original concepts and meanings grew ever further removed from their historical bases as the centuries passed. In the 6th century BC, the exiled Israelites had written down their history in all honesty from available Babylonian records. Having also discovered the old book of the Mosaic Law, they were further enabled to cement the rules of their religious doctrine—and they returned to Jerusalem and Judaea with a comprehensive literary base. By the 2nd century BC, additional books were being compiled, not necessarily with history in mind, but with a view to adding a mythological aspect in line with the prevailing Greco-Alexandrian culture. This was certainly a romantic age, but in adding the romance a good deal of history was unfortunately veiled, so that the original Nephilim of the Sumerian era became misidentified as morally fallen angels.

And so, for some two millennia, a 'fallen angel' tradition has prevailed—a tradition which was never a part of original Mesopotamian history. But in losing the history, we also lost our grasp of the knowledge recorded by scribes of more than 4000 years ago. This was the first-hand experience of ancient Sumer, the land of the world's oldest civilization—a civilization which progressed the legacy of humankind thousands of years ahead of natural evolution. This was the historical land of the Elohim, the Lofty Ones; and it was the realm of the mysterious Nephilim, 'those who came down'.

Let us now look once again at the related Genesis entry, but not at the traditional English mistranslation. This time, let us consider a more accurate rendering from the Hebrew, as presented by the Semitic linguist Zecharia Sitchin—a rendering which, thankfully, puts things into a more understandable perspective:

> At that time the sons of the gods saw the daughters of man, that they were good; and they took them for wives, of all which they chose. The Nephilim were upon the earth in those days, and thereafter too, when the sons of the gods cohabited with the daughters of men, and they bore children unto them. They were the mighty ones of eternity—the people of the shem (Genesis 6:1-4).[11]

And so, at last, the sons of God are properly defined as the 'sons of the gods', and the tiresome giants of mythology have given way to something historically far more exciting: 'the mighty ones of eternity'. But what is this new addition that is omitted from the standard translations? What does it mean, 'the people of the shem'? In ancient times, a *shem* was strangely described as a 'highward fire-stone'—an important definition which will feature again as we progress.

Having dispensed with giants in this particular context, it is worth considering the more general relevance of giants in the Old Testament—and they are most apparent in the book of Deuteronomy. This book deals with Moses and the Israelites after their return to Canaan from Egypt; also with the Israelites' subsequent invasion of Canaan under the leadership of Joshua. There are a number of entries which refer to Canaanite tribesmen being giants, but what one gathers from these accounts is not that they were enormous superhumans—simply that they were larger and generally more fearsome than the incoming Israelites. Deuteronomy explains: 'The people [the Amorites] is greater and taller than we; the cities are great, and walled up to heaven'

(1:28); 'They [the Emims] were a people great and many, and tall as the Anakims; which also were accounted giants, as the Anakims' (2:10-11); 'I will not give thee the land of the children of Ammon... that also was accounted a land of giants... in old time, and the Ammonites called them Zamzummims; a people great, and many, and tall, as the Anakims' (2:19-21); and 'Thou art to pass over Jordan this day, to go in to possess nations greater and mightier than thyself, cities great and fenced up to heaven; a people great and tall—the children of the Anakims' (9:1-2).

The Old Testament's best known giant is, of course, Goliath of Gath, the Philistine warrior who challenged the shepherd-boy David. We are told that Goliath's height was 'six cubits and a span' (1-Samuel 17:4)—that is six forearms (of 20 inches/c.150 cm) and a spread hand (of 9 inches/*c*.22.5 cm). So Goliath was 10 feet, 9 inches (3.27 m) tall. By any standard of reckoning, this is immense. Even allowing for a 25 percent exaggeration in order to enhance David's predicament, we are still left with an 8-foot man. However, there are such warriors in our modern age: the post-War German wrestler Kurt Zehe, for example, was 8 feet 4 inches tall, while the Rotterdam colossus of the ring, Rhinehardt, stood at 9 feet 6 inches.[12] Many of today's American basketball players might be regarded as giants, but they are plainly not hideous ogres in accordance with the image conjured by the word 'giant' in mythology and romantic literature.

In spite of Goliath's physique, and the enormity of his sword, young David slew him, prior to any legitimate combat, with a well-aimed sling-shot to the forehead. But in later times, when threatened by Goliath's equally large family members, 'David waxed faint', leaving their destruction to his servants (2-Samuel 21:15-22). Elhanan of Bethlehem managed to slay the brother of Goliath, 'whose spear-staff was like a weaver's beam'. David's nephew Jonathan then slew a son of Goliath, who had 'on every hand six fingers, and on every foot six toes'. Other sons of Goliath, namely Ishi-benob and Saph, were also killed by David's men Abishai and Sibbechai, but in no event are we told how the victories were won.

## The Watchers

If the angels were not giants, and if they were not *bene ha-elohim* (sons of the gods and goddesses), then what were they? As related in *Bloodline of the Holy Grail*,[13] the first thing to consider is that there is nothing spiritual or ethereal about the word 'angel'. In its Greek form, the definition *aggelos* (more usually transliterated as *angelos*, or in Latin, *angelus*) was translated from the original Hebrew *mal'ath*, which meant no more than 'messenger'. The modern English language derives the word 'angel' from the Latin, but the Anglo-Saxon word *engel* came originally from the old French *angele*. An angel of the Lord was, therefore, a messenger of the Lord or, more correctly, an ambassador of the Lord. An archangel was an ambassador of the highest rank (the prefix 'arch', meaning 'chief', as in archduke and archbishop).

Generally, the Old Testament angels acted like normal human beings—as for example in Genesis (19:1-3), when two angels visited Lot's house, 'and [he] did bake unleavened bread, and they did eat'. Most Old Testament angels belonged to this straightforward category, such as the angel who met Abraham's wife Hagar by the water fountain (Genesis 16:7-12), the angel who stopped Balaam's ass in its tracks (Numbers 22:21-35), the angel who spoke to Manoah and his wife (Judges 13:3-19) and the angel who sat under the oak with Gideon (Judges 6:11-22). Even the Archangel Gabriel is referred to as a 'man' in Daniel (9:21) when he arrives, saying to Daniel, 'I have come to give you skill and understanding'.

It is in the non-canonical book of Enoch that we find Gabriel listed as one of the seven archangels, along with Michael, Raphael, Uriel, Raguel, Saraqael and Remiel.[14] The book of Jubilees states that Enoch, the early patriarch, 'was the first one from among the children of men that are born on the Earth to learn writing and the knowledge of wisdom—and he wrote the signs of heaven'.[15] These signs (from the *Table of Destiny*) are described as being the 'science of the Watchers', which had been carved in a rock in distant times,[16] and Enoch tells that the Watchers were the 'holy angels who watch'.[17] In some incantations of latter-day sorcery, a certain deiform Rehctaw is invoked. This has been thought by many to have a sinister implication, but it is nothing more than Watcher spelt backwards.[18]

## Naphidem and Eljo

We now discover why it was that the Nephilim/Watchers were said to have fallen from grace having fathered their offspring from the daughters of men. Enoch tells that those of their senior number (the seven archangels) were annoyed that the Chiefs of the Tens had begun to teach their offspring too much too soon by imparting some of the secrets of the signs in earlier days. It was reported[19] that they had taught about the metals of the earth, and how to use them; they taught about the roots of the earth and their medicines; they taught about the sun, the moon and the constellations, and of clouds and weather patterns. The Archangels were said to have admonished the chiefs of the Watchers[20] for having 'revealed the eternal secrets' and for having thrown humankind into an internecine turmoil so that the pre-eminent sons of the Watchers were at variance with the evolutionary sons of men.

The writings indicate that, in the light of their new-found supremacy, the Watchers' offspring took advantage of their privilege and assumed martial control over their mundane brothers, (who were called the *Eljo*,[21] slaughtering them wholesale in the process. It is often said that 'a little knowledge is a dangerous thing', and this is presented as the case in this regard. Although the sons of the Watchers (called the *Naphidem*)[22] had gained an amount of advanced knowledge from their Nephilim fathers, they were genetically still somewhat primitive by way of their mothers, and they were, seemingly, unable to cope with this knowledge. Hence, they demonstrated the Darwinian principle of the 'survival of the fittest'. They were bigger and stronger than their neighbours; they were generally superior to their neighbours; and so they slew their neighbours. Indeed, the Jubilees text indicates that there was a full-blown genocide, with the Naphidem race against the Eljo people, while the Nephilim unsuccessfully endeavoured to restrain their Naphidem sons.

These events, which appear in the books of Enoch and Jubilees, seem at first glance to tie in with the events described in Genesis 6, and they are presented as if they belong to the era immediately before the Flood. But the Flood was chronologically moved in Genesis to the time of Noah, whereas it actually occurred before the time of Adam. In essence, the creational story in Genesis is in keeping with the tablet records of ancient Sumer, whereas this other tale of a semi-advanced race slaughtering its less developed predecessors is from a much earlier time.

Since the book of Jubilees refers to the book of Enoch, it is clear that Jubilees was written after Enoch, which (in the form that we know it) was compiled in the 2nd century BC. We know, however, that although Genesis was first compiled in the 6th century BC, its content was actually extracted from far more ancient records. On the same basis, it is reasonable to assume that the book of Enoch was similarly constructed from ancient records, even though it was intermixed with a spiritual theology of a much later age. It is purported that its original was written by Enoch, the great-grandfather of Noah, and the book begins by explaining that Enoch's knowledge was passed to him by the angels: 'from them I heard everything, and from them I understood as I saw, but not for this generation, but for a remote one which is to come'.[23]

So, does Genesis have anything unusual to say about Enoch? It certainly does, for of all the patriarchs of his immediate line (before and after him), only Enoch and Noah are said to have 'walked with God' (Genesis 5:24, 6:9)—or, as more precisely given in early texts, 'with the Elohim'.

It is apparent, therefore, that the story of the Naphidem-Eljo racial war comes from long before the Flood, and from long before Adam. On that account, it is significant (as will be disclosed when we look at the Sumerian historical listings) that the Nephilim ancestry is itself said to trace back tens of thousands of years. From the time of the genocidal slaughter, the Nephilim became what we might describe as 'guardian angels' – the custodians of a salvaged world which they had practically destroyed. Their new domain was essentially the world of the Naphidem – a root breed of culturally advanced Afro-Asian *homo sapiens*, who had superseded their Eljo predecessors by about 30,000 BC.

## Ezekiel's Vision

Having mentioned that most Old Testament angels acted like pretty ordinary men, there are some others who seem to have been rather more than straightforward messengers. They are portrayed as armed emissaries with fearsome powers of destruction. This type of avenging angel features in 1-Chronicles (21:14-16): 'And God sent an angel unto Jerusalem to destroy it... having a sword drawn in his hand stretched out over Jerusalem'.

Quite a few angels are described as wielding swords, but they are never perceived to be divine and there is no hint in the text of the graceful wings that are so often portrayed. The now familiar wings were used by artists and sculptors to symbolize the angels' spiritual transcendence above the mundane environment. Notwithstanding this, however, the question of flight must be addressed since it features so often in ancient texts. Deities are frequently portrayed with the ability to fly and there are numerous winged figures depicted in the oldest Mesopotamian carvings and reliefs – albeit the wings might be symbolically representative of flight, rather than denoting physical attributes as such.

The twelve clay tablets recounting the *Epic of Gilgamesh*, ruler of Uruk, were discovered among the effects of King Ashurbanipal of Assyria (669-626 BC) at Nineveh. Among the various events described is the story of Enkidu who was confronted by a roaring from the heavens—then seized and transported upwards in the brazen talons of an eagle, with a vertical speed that made his body feel as heavy as an enormous boulder. Similar reference occurs in the *Moses Apocalypse*, when Eve sees a chariot of light drawn by shining eagles.

This brings us to another category of daunting Old Testament phenomena which were said to rise above the earth by mechanical means. They were never called angels and generally these blazing spectacles had wheels, as in Daniel 7:9: 'His throne was like the fiery flame, and his wheels as burning fire'.

In Isaiah 6:1-2 there is a similar account of an airborne throne, and 'above it stood the seraphims: each one had six wings'. Yet another reference to such an apparatus occurs in Ezekiel 1, where the whole scenario—so vividly depicted in Sir Peter Robson's painting *Ezekiel's Vision*—is entirely in keeping with the others.

The prophet Ezekiel (*c*.550 BC) explains that, while among the Israelite captives in Babylonia, a great whirlwind came out of the north, spouting fire. Out of the brightness flew what appeared to be four living creatures, each with four wings and straight feet, shining like burnished brass. Their wing sets were joined together and the creatures displayed on their sides the faces of a man, an ox, a lion and an eagle. They all flew straight forwards, gleaming like lamps and issuing bolts of lightning.

There were dreadful rotating rings above them, noisy like rushing waters—while the creatures, as green as beryl, appeared to be full of eyes. They also had wheels which folded against them when flying, while each had a crystal firmament above. But when they stood and let down their wings, Ezekiel saw within each lighted firmament a throne with the appearance of a man upon it.

Unrelated to the Bible, but very similar in concept to the Ezekiel story, is an ancient tractate from 3rd-century Alexandria, entitled *The Origin.* It tells of the immortal Sophia, and of the ruler Saboath who 'created a great throne on a four-faced chariot called Cherubim.... And on that throne he created some other dragon-shaped seraphims'. Interestingly, it is narrated in Genesis 3:24 that the Lord stationed cherubims (chariots or mobile thrones) and a revolving sword of fire to protect the Garden of Eden.

The Cherubim appears again in an ancient Greek work called *The Hypostasis of the Archons,* which deals with the Rulers of Entirety and the creation of Adam. Once more it concerns Saboath and his heavenly chariot, the Cherubim. There is mention of a similar vehicle in 2-Kings 2:11, when Elijah is taken up in a chariot of fire:

> Behold, there appeared a chariot of fire, and horses of fire, and parted them both asunder; and Elijah went up by a whirlwind into heaven.

Flaming seraphims also appear with regularity in the ancient documents. That they are fiery is consistent with the etymology of the word *seraph,* which is related to an old Hebrew stem meaning 'flame'. But they sometimes have awesome destructive properties, as in Numbers 21:16, when a large proportion of Israel died after the Lord sent fiery serpents (*seraphims*) among them. Such stories are not confined to the countries of the Near East. From that same period similar accounts come from Tibet, India, Scandinavia and elsewhere. The writings all tell of heavenly chariots that spout fire and quicksilver, and of thunderbirds with brazen wings.[24]

Without a good deal of speculation, it is currently impossible to examine the precise whys and wherefores of such automated phenomena with their noisy rotating wings, folding wheels, illuminated glazed compartments and men within. One can only present them as they are depicted in the ancient texts. What is certain, however, is that these flying chariots (*cherubims*) with their accompanying seraphims (the fiery dragon-shaped auxiliaries) were never at any time described as having human form, as angels always were. It was the fearful dogma of the later religious establishment which transformed the apparently mechanical cherubims and seraphims into adoring celestial putti.

# 6

# An Age of Enlightenment

## The Missing Link

In 1871, when publishing his *Descent of Man,* Charles Darwin coined the expression 'missing link' in relation to a perceived anomaly in the human evolutionary progression.[1] There was an undeniable inconsistency in the supposed lineage which, at first, seemed like a gap in the sequence, but it was soon realized that there was no gap, simply an unexplained link.

It is frequently alleged that Darwin taught that humans had descended from early apes, such as chimpanzees, orang-utans and gorillas, but this is nonsense: Darwin never taught that. If it were true, there would be no chimpanzees, orang-utans or gorillas today. In the wider scheme of things, it was logically conceived that humans must have evolved from a different type of ape—a bipedal ground-dwelling ape, but there had been no archaeological discovery which supported this theory. And so it was generally agreed that there had to have been a sub-man, an ape-man, a dawn-man: a 'missing link'.

The very idea of human evolvement from apes was, of course, anathema to the Church, for it was contrary to the book of Genesis, which told how man (Adam) was created in a unique and original adult form. Some years prior to the *Descent of Man,* Darwin had published his *On the Origin of the Species,* and the

Church took up the challenge in June 1860 by publicly confronting Darwin's greatest proponent at Oxford, the scientist Thomas Henry Huxley. Against him was set Bishop Samuel Wilberforce, who decided to be sarcastic rather than progress a sensible debate. 'Were you descended from apes through your father or your mother?' he asked Huxley—to which Huxley responded that he would rather be descended from a monkey than be associated with such an ignorant man. The Bishop was notionally dismissed by an audience who had hoped for better things, and that was the end of that discussion!

Huxley won the day, almost by default, because the audience recognized that, even without proof, the Darwinian principle appeared more plausible than a Church ideal which its bishop could find no way to uphold with any reasonable argument. But, in the event, there was still no affirmation of a continuous evolvement from apes to modern humans (*homo sapiens-sapiens*). Darwin himself was unhappy about the soulless nature of his theory and he strove to find the answer one way or another.

Some years after Darwin's death, a skull was found at Piltdown, Sussex, in the south of England, which seemed to possess the qualities to bridge the evolutionary void. The Piltdown Man became famous overnight—but not for long. By 1953, fluorine analysis of the skull revealed that it was an outright hoax, perhaps perpetrated by its finder, Mr. C. Dawson. The skull was, in fact, a concoction, being that of an ancient man with the added jaw of a chimpanzee (or some other ape), cleverly stained and distressed to replicate ageing.

Darwin had been so sure about the possibility of a 'missing link' because of two significant finds during his own lifetime. In 1857, the skeleton of a very primitive hunter had been discovered in the Neander Valley, near Düsseldorf, in Germany, and his type was duly dubbed 'Neanderthal'. Other discoveries have shown that the Neanderthalers were prevalent in Europe, Asia and Africa, having existed from sometime before 70,000 BC. They were thought to have evolved from an early form of *homo erectus* through a gradual process from about 300,000 BC. The problem with the Neanderthal breed was that, although they were the primary hominoid race through the Old Stone Age (when fire, hand-axes and flint tools were in use), they were not merely simpler and less developed than ourselves, they were from another line altogether.[2]

This, then, was the crux of Darwin's dilemma. The Old Stone Age Neanderthalers were so physically unlike modern humans that we could not possibly have evolved from them in so short a period of time. They were even mentally quite different, as determined from a skull shape that afforded little room for the thinking and speaking parts of the brain.

The other great discovery of the Darwinian age was made soon afterwards in 1868, when the first examples of *homo sapiens* were unearthed at Cro-Magnon in the Dordogne region of France. Unlike the crouched Neanderthalers with their heavy brows, receding foreheads, protruding jaws and robust bone structure, the Cro-Magnons (as the newly discovered people were called) were tall, upright, broad-faced individuals, with a very differently structured brain cavity. In terms of geological time, there appeared to be nothing to separate the late Neanderthalers and the early Cro-Magnons, but they were as different from each other as cattle are from horses. Not only that, but their cultures were remarkably dissimilar, with the Cro-Magnons displaying an uncanny sophistication in terms of their art, clothing, habitation and general lifestyle.

The apparent time-frame for the Neanderthal/Cro-Magnon crossover was about 35,000-30,000 BC, and they did exist as contemporaries for a time, thereby proving that one did not evolve from the other. It is of particular interest to note that there has never been a trace of any interbreeding between the distinctly different strains, and as the Cro-Magnons grew to prominence, so the Neanderthalers became totally extinct.

Until quite recently, it was thought that perhaps today's world supported various peoples that were separately descended from each of these two key races, but this theory has now been overturned. In July 1997, a breakthrough in genetic analysis proved beyond doubt that modern *homo sapiens-sapiens* have not the slightest trace of ancestry from the Neanderthalers.[3] This was ascertained when a team led by Dr Svante Pääbo of the University of Munich managed to extract DNA (deoxyribonucleic acid) from a Neanderthal upper armbone fragment.[4] Mitochondrial DNA is passed down, unchanged, from mothers[5] to their children, and, apart from the odd random mutation, all today's humans have very similar sequences.[6] It transpired that the *c*.40,000-year-old Neanderthal DNA was so significantly different that it had to be that of an entirely separate species. The scientists announced that, without question, the Neanderthal race was a 'biological dead end' and that there is no indication of any crossbreeding with Cro-Magnon homo sapiens. It was possible, they said, that Neanderthalers and homo sapiens had some form of common ancestor about 600,000 years ago, but this could not be proven and was of little relevance.

The Cro-Magnon types appear to have developed out of Africa, Asia and perhaps from the Balkan and Black Sea regions, spreading throughout Europe century by century. As for their immediate ancestry, this is quite unknown, while their semi-advanced culture (highly advanced for the time) and their modern physique appear to have no scientifically obvious forerunners.

*Neanderthal man.*

*Cro-Magnon man.*

Equally startling was the earlier announcement in December 1996 that skulls found on the Indonesian island of Java suggest that homo erectus (thought to have disappeared about 200,000 years ago) was still in existence 40,000 years ago. If so, this means that the *homo erectus* apes did not evolve into the Neanderthalers with whom they lived side by side.[7] This conclusion was reached by a team of geologists led by Dr Carl Swisher of the Berkeley Geochronology Center in California. Using some teeth from the site where four *homo erectus* skulls had been found, they applied an electron spin resonance dating method to the tooth enamel. Also, as a cross check, other specimens were tested by a process which analysed the radioactive decay of uranium in fossils. Each of the separate tests threw up the same figures, and the skulls were dated at between 53,000 and 27,000 BC—a 40,000 BC mean.

## Progeny of the Nephilim

What we now know, and has been proven beyond doubt, is that there is no missing link in the way that Darwin perceived it. The Cro-Magnon *homo sapiens* did not descend from the Neandathalers; they were entirely different breeds with entirely different DNA structures. It appears that we are descended from the Afro-Asian Cro-Magnon types, but from what species did they evolve? Maybe this is where the Enochian records come into play—the accounts of the Nephilim who spawned an entirely new race prior to 35,000 BC, in the same era that the advanced Cro-Magnons appeared, after which the backward Neanderthalers were gradually wiped out.

What we also know is that if the Nephilim created a new species by interbreeding with the 'daughters of men', then these daughters were not of the Neanderthal race because, as confirmed by Dr Svante Pääbo, mitochondrial DNA is a female inheritance passed down from mothers. Could it be, therefore, that there was another race contemporary with the Neanderthalers? Dr Pääbo and others believe there was, for they make the point that the Neanderthal breed was actually European in origin, and that while they were evolving in Europe, another parallel hominoid strain was simultaneously evolving in Africa and other regions.

In this regard, it transpires that the archaeological history of the 20th century includes a number of ancient hominoid finds in Africa:[8] 1911 in Tanzania (then German East Africa); 1924 in Taung, south-west of Johannesburg, South Africa; 1959 at the Olduvai Gorge, Tanzania; and 1972 at Lake Turkana, Kenya, central-eastern Africa. Whatever the individual merits of these discoveries, they were each dismissed by various 'experts' because they did not conform to the traditional evolutionary reckoning of the European Neanderthal. But then, in 1974, Donald Johanson, an archaeologist from the University of Chicago excavating at Hadar in Ethiopia, found a collection of hominoid bones in a deposit dating back more than 3 million years. Gradually, he and his team pieced together the fragments of a female primate skeleton. They named her Lucy.

Subsequently, they found the bones of another thirteen hominids which, along with Lucy, were dated to about 3.5 million BC; and they were dubbed the 'First Family'. Stone tools were also discovered at the site, and a few miles away fossilized hominoid footprints were later found, dated (by potassium-argon dating) to the same era. But these were not the footprints of any conventional ape: they had raised arches, rounded heels, pronounced balls and a forward-pointing big toe. These bipedal anthropoids were physically in advance of the later Neanderthalers and their remains were in Ethiopia, the closest land mass to Saudi Arabia, which sits between the Red Sea and the Persian Gulf.

Here was a most ancient species, which had evolved through more than 3 million years quite independently of the strain which produced the European Neanderthal. Here, perhaps, were the primordial ancestors of the Eljo people who occupied the Afro-Asian regions around 35,000 BC when the sons of the gods united with the daughters of men—a race which disappeared as the new, more advanced *homo sapiens* took over. It is now known that this earlier breed (who were eventually concurrent with the Neanderthalers) had been present in the Afro-Asian regions, and maybe elsewhere, for about 100,000 years.[9]

Evidence of this early race comes from the Ararat Mountains, at a source of the River Tigris in the Mesopotamian north of Iraq. Here, in 1957, Professor Ralph Soleki was investigating the Shanidar Cave when he found nine ancient skeletons, four of which had been crushed by a rockfall.[10] Seven of these, including a baby, appeared to belong to a single family who had huddled together from the cold of winter. The bones were said to be about 44,000 years old, and it was ascertained through further excavation that the cave had been regularly used for shelter from about 100,000 BC.

## Anomalies of Evolution

In the light of the information gathered thus far, it would appear that in so many instances anthropologists have, for the past century, been making a rigorous study of ancestors that we never had. For the most part, they have been recording generations of prehistoric apes that were actually the ancestors of today's apes, and were nothing whatever to do with eventual humankind. Indeed, the very fact that these apes exist in their different breeds today emphasizes the point that they have evolved in separate lines. Maybe there was a common ancestral strain somewhere in the dim and distant past, but this was clearly so long ago that it has little bearing on the individual developments of later ages.

We now know that the bipedal species known as *Australopithecus afarensis* (the species of Lucy and the First Family) dates back more than 3.5 million years, not 800,000 years as our reference books indicated before the late 1970s. We also know that there were four emergent hominoid groups, styled to be known as *Australopithecus africanus*, *Australopithecus robustus*,

*Australopithecus boisei* and *homo habilis*.[11] From which of these the later *homo erectus* was descended (if from any), scientists are still disputing. In reality, these species appear to have been, to some extent, contemporary, thereby denoting that they were different breeds and not descendant breeds. *Homo erectus* (sometimes called 'apeman') was long thought to date from about 400,000 years ago, but has been found (since the 1980s) to have existed as far back as 800,000 years, in the same era as *homo habilis*, proving yet again that one did not evolve from the other. Furthermore, *homo erectus* has now been discovered to have existed as recently as 40,000 years ago, living in a contemporary situation with the Neanderthal cavemen. So, once more, the latter did not evolve from the former as had been thought prior to 1996.

In addition, we are now further informed, from the conclusions of DNA testing in 1997, that our own modern *homo sapiens-sapiens* did not evolve from the Neanderthalers; also, that there was a distinct crossover period before the Neanderthalers became a 'biological dead end' in about 30,000 BC. We are, it seems, an entirely different species with no fully identifiable ancestry. We are additionally told that we have a DNA structure that contains a wealth of what genetic scientists call 'junk'—parts of the chain which house open-ended genes that have no explainable function. It is likely, however, that our so-called 'junk DNA' does have practical purposes of which we are at present unaware.[12] Perhaps these puzzling genetic codes will be broken by tomorrow's molecular biologists, or maybe the mysterious genes will somehow be activated to push us into a more advanced era—an era when it will also become apparent why, to date, we use only a minor portion of our total brain capacity.

So, does all this mean that Charles Darwin was wrong? No—it simply means that he died before he could complete his research. He knew full well that there was a 'missing link', and he said so. He was also bothered about the non-spiritual nature of his theory of evolution when applied to humankind, and he said so. Darwin was not wrong, but his theory's slavish disciples have been proved wrong. They have followed a geologically based blood-and-bones principle of chronological evolution which has taken no account of the more abstract elements. How was it that Cro-Magnon *homo sapiens* could speak, while the Neanderthalers could not? How was it that Cro-Magnon *homo sapiens* walked fully erect, while the Neanderthalers were crouched? How was it that Cro-Magnon *homo sapiens* were intelligent and inventive, while the Neanderthalers, though appearing to have been quite spiritual, were creatively uninspired. How was it that these two species lived on earth at the same time?

One of the main problems with the Darwinian principle is that, if followed too doggedly, it can lead to incorrect conclusions by virtue of its own logic. Suppose, for example, one were looking back on our present era from some thousands of years in the future. The precise chronology of the manufacturing events of a single century might be difficult to determine without access to records, and the application of pure logic could well lead one to suppose that the automobile evolved from the skateboard. In practice, however, these are not lesser and greater forms of an evolving mode of transport, but quite unrelated concepts.[13]

There is little doubt that evolution by means of natural selection is a well-founded principle, with environmental and circumstantial advantages being passed on to successive generations. But, as pointed out in 1871 by Darwin's critic St. George Mivart, 'Natural Selection does not harmonize with the co-existence of closely similar structures of diverse origin',[14] Certain specific differences are found to have appeared suddenly rather than gradually, and 'there are many remarkable phenomena in organic forms upon which Natural Selection throws no light whatever'.[15]

There is similarly no doubt that the Darwinian concept of the survival of the fittest has a solid foundation. It constitutes far more than a theory, as has been proven in the plant, fish, bird, insect, reptile and animal worlds. Even so, the principle cannot be regarded as an absolute rule, for if it were, only the 'fittest' would exist and there would be no surviving life-forms in the less-fit category. It is therefore a concept which applies in general terms only, with the fit and less-fit naturally existing side by side at every stage of the evolutionary process. It would appear, however, that the conclusive principle of the survival of the fittest can be applied to the Cro-Magnons and Neanderthalers—for the thinking, speaking, inventive Cro-Magnons survived, while the backward, primitive Neanderthalers were eventually wiped out.

Until recently it has been thought quite impossible to extract DNA from prehistoric bones because DNA degrades and decays through the actions of oxygen and water. This is why it was such a coup in 1997 when Dr Pääbo's Munich team managed to extract Neanderthal DNA from the original specimen found in the Neander Valley in 1856. This extraction was made possible only because, when unearthed, the bone was in a remarkable state for its age, and it had since been twice varnished by the Bonn Museum curators, thereby preventing outside contamination. Dr. Chris Stringer of London's Natural History Museum explained that 'Varnishing bones is a practice that we now frown on, but in this case it may have been the best thing that could have happened'.

Unlike many of today's synthetic varnishes, 19th-century varnish was a resin based product, and resin is a plant secretion, a natural substance. Just like other organic matter, resins can themselves become fossilized into forms such as amber (the hardest known resin) and kauri (quite likely the copal base used for the Bonn varnish). Who knows, in time to come a dinosaur fragment may be found locked in a fossil resin and a whole new chapter of learning will begin. Meanwhile, we can feel relieved for the biblical Noah who, but for a twist of nature, may well have had to contend with dinosaurs in his ark!

## History and Mythology

The main difference between the evolutionary history of homo sapiens, as against the evolutionary history of other life-forms, is that the former species is now known to be unique, having appeared at some unknown time before 35,000 BC with no fully identifiable ancestral strain and with a DNA structure that defies modern scientific resolution. So, if the more extreme Darwinists have been proven wrong in this regard, then what about the Bible—what does the Old Testament tell us?

Genesis relates that the Israelite god, Jehovah, made man in the image of the gods. But, from more than 1000 years before Genesis was compiled, we are informed in the *Enûma elish* that the Babylonian god Marduk said 'I shall create *lullû*—Man shall be his name'. From centuries even before the story of Marduk, other versions of man's creation came out of ancient Sumer and fortunately some of the texts are preserved today. From these, we can see how the Babylonian and Hebrew texts each emerged in their revised forms, and it is not difficult to understand how the original historical message was corrupted and subsequently misinterpreted to suit later religious ideals. Nonetheless, the constituent element remains in keeping with the primary message, which centres upon the fact that modern humankind was created as a hybrid by the gods (the Elohim).

At almost every stage of our education, the knowledge brought to our attention is controlled and censored by the religious doctrines of our respective societies. This manipulative control comes from State level and it is manifest in numerous British State schools, for example, being established as Christian institutions, with many of them designated Church schools.[16] This is not only morally unfair to the families of children who are other than Christian, but it is equally unfair to the Christian children whose non-Christian friends are perceived to be spiritually inferior. Anglican prelates are also prominent on the boards of universities which are not necessarily seen to be Church foundations. Britain's national media is an additional protagonist of the Christian message, with both radio and television pursuing their sectarian courses. Britain's Parliament is not simply a Christian institution, it is specifically Anglican, while the Monarch and Head of State is also Head of the Church of England. So too are similar religious ideals promoted in other countries, which front their respective information and educational systems with the individual cultural doctrines that prevail.

In each instance, there is an arrogant intolerance of the faiths of others, and this form of intolerance is equally apparent in other non-religious fields of faith—fields such as medicine, science, history and the general world of the qualified academic. To some extent, these fields are perhaps not quite so dogmatic as in the religious arena, and there are signs of bending to new discovery now and again. Even so, we still retain such descriptive styles as 'alternative medicine'. Why 'alternative'? It is alternative because it does not conform to an industry standard which is designed to support the wealthy drug companies. One might as well refer to legs as 'alternative transport'.

In the academic world, though, we find no recognition for such a thing as 'alternative history' (now more correctly styled as 'revisionist history'): even that degree of acknowledgement is too much for the expert whose learning curve stopped with the last qualifying exam. In this blinkered world there is only history and myth. History is that which the governing establishments approve for their courses, and Myth is everything else. So, what governs approved history in Britain, Europe and Christendom in general? To a large extent it is governed by Church doctrine, just like most other things. If the Christians of the Middle Ages went to war with the Muslims in the Holy Land, then the Christians clearly had God on their side—so says the doctrine of approved Western history. But what of the Muslims who, in essence, worship the same God? Their viewpoint, according to the Christian establishment, is a myth. Such is the arrogant nature of doctrinal education.

Since we are primarily concerned with ancient history at this stage, let us consider the *Memorandum and Articles of Association* of the Egypt Exploration Fund, first established in Britain in 1891 to expedite archaeological digs in Egypt. In this document it is expressly stated that the Fund's objective is to facilitate surveys and excavations 'for the purpose of elucidating or illustrating the

Bible narrative'.[17] In other words, if something is found which supports, or can be said to support, the Old or New Testaments then we, the public, will be informed. This will be classified as 'history'. Anything which does not support the scriptures will be designated 'myth'. When unearthed fossils began to overturn the six-day Creation story in Victorian times, the zoologist Philip Gosse actually went so far as to say that God had purposely inserted fossils into the rocks to test and try the Christian faith![18]

Although many interesting new discoveries were being made by British archaeologists in the 19th century, the reality is that the Victorian era was one of very poor education in Britain. Large sectors of the working population could neither read nor write, and so they admired, respected and trusted those who were more scholarly. In rural areas, it was often the case that only Church clerics were literate and so (as had been the custom for many centuries) it was they who maintained local records and undertook to advise people in all manner of affairs. In such an ill-equipped social environment the Church had long held sway over what people would and would not be told, and this gave the individual clerics enormous power over the masses. Throughout the 20th century, however, things changed and, by way of obligatory schooling, people have become both literate and investigative. Now they are able to read for themselves and can form their own opinions and beliefs. This, however, has not changed the medieval dogma of the stalwart clerics, who are content to see their congregations dwindle rather than rejoice in the educated age of enlightenment.

It is well known to all historical and theological scholars that the Old Testament's book of Genesis was extracted from older Mesopotamian records. Why is it, then, that so many of those same scholars uphold the Church's veneration of Genesis as an absolute truth, whereas they decry the original records as legend and mythology? It is because, in the final analysis, despite falling congregations, Church opinion always wins at an official level since it is inherently tied to the governments which control the academic establishments.

What actually transpired was that the original Mesopotamian writings were recorded as history. This history was later rewritten to form a base for foreign religious cults—first Judaism and then Christianity. The corrupted dogma of the religions then became established as 'history' and because the contrived dogma (the new approved history) was so different from the original writings, the early first-hand records were then labelled 'mythology'.

As we have seen, the ancient Sumerians were a very advanced race: they had schools, hospitals, lawyers, accountants, doctors, astronomers and historians. The training of these professionals was expensive and time consuming; the schools were strict and accuracy was everything, as can be seen from the scribal records. It is quite inconceivable that the scribes, clerks and historians, having gone through the academic system to win their qualifications, would then be sent out into the world to write mythology! Such an assumption is ludicrous. Their task was to record events of the past and present as they understood them to be, and we now have the results of their labours to hand: tens of thousands of neatly written cuneiform tablets. But these are the very records which modern academia classifies as the legends of primitive people. Why? Because they do not conform to the accepted notions of a Church society which rewrote the accounts and has since defined its own known mythology as history.

So, how does Adam feature in this scenario? The answer is that he does not—at least not yet. What we have discovered so far is that, according to the most ancient of available records, modern humankind was created by the Elohim/Nephilim, who were somehow mated with earthly women of the Eljo race. These Eljo women appear to have been descended from a strain whose people were far more advanced than their Neanderthal contemporaries. The apparent outcome was a hybrid Naphidem stock—very likely the people who have become known as Cro-Magnon.

From about 11,000 BC, at the turn of the Ice Age, another very marked change occurred in the Fertile Crescent, from North

Africa, across Syria and Canaan, into Mesopotamia. This brought the Bible Lands into the Domestic Age – an age of cultivation that was significantly far ahead of other parts of the world. But then, in about 4000 BC, came the truly remarkable Age of Civilization, and this was specifically centred upon the southern Mesopotamian region of Sumer.

Although other regions of the Fertile Crescent, as well as parts of China, India, and places as far north as Transylvania, were by then into an age of rural cultivation and domesticity, the civilized realm of Sumer was very different by virtue of its cities and municipal structure. An inscription from ancient Nippur makes the point that the first of all known empires was that founded by the High Priest of the city of Uruk – an empire which stretched 'from the lower sea to the upper sea' (from the Persian Gulf to the Mediterranean).[19] Here were the first ever priests, and the first ever kings, in a post-Flood environment which (just like the events prior to 35,000 BC) swept the people of the region once more into hitherto unknown realms of advancement, thousands of years ahead of any natural evolution. This was the true dawn of modern socially structured society; this was the era of awareness and enlightenment; this was the Age of Adam.

7

# When Kingship Was Lowered

## Assembly of the Anunnaki

To this point, we have referred to the community of the Nephilim gods as being the Elohim, by which name they were collectively known in the Canaanite and Hebrew traditions. Now we are going further back in time to the world of ancient Sumer, where the collective term for the divine Lofty Ones was *Anunnaki*,[1] which meant 'Heaven came to Earth' (*An-unna-ki*).[2] Alternatively, they were the softer-sounding *Anannage*—the fiery sons of heaven, or Shining Ones. In the Sumerian era, the Grand Assembly of the Anunnaki met at the Temple of Nippur.[3] This was the Court of the Most High—the prototype of the Court attended by Jehovah in the Old Testament's Psalm 82—and its recorded president was the supreme Lord of the Sky, the great Anu.

A primary function of the Assembly was the appointment of kings, but it was also a court of justice and in all instances it operated by way of a democratic voting system. When a decision was made concerning policy, appointment or judgement, the members would signify their assent by saying the word *haem*, meaning 'so be it'. This was later manifest in Hebrew ritual by the supposedly equivalent word *amen*,[4] but this Egyptian word actually related to the State god Amen, and to something hidden or concealed.

We have already encountered the primordial father, Apsû, and his consort Tiâmat, the Dragon Queen (who was also called Mother Hubbur), along with their son Mummu. But it is now time to meet Mummu's brothers and sisters. They were born as two male and female pairs—first Lahmu and his sister Lahâmu, and then Anshar and his sister Kishar. The stories of this deiform family date back thousands of years and are largely concerned with the very dawn of earthly time when the world was brought forth out of a watery chaos. In due course, Anshar and Kishar produced a son who was to reign overall; this son was Anu. Anu's consorts were his sisters: Antu, Lady of the Sky (also called Nammu), and Ki, the Earth Mother (also called Urash). As well as having their original Sumerian names, the Anunnaki also became known by their alternative Semitic names as used in Akkad and later Babylonia.

Anu had two sons, Enlil (or Ilu),[5] Lord of the Air (whose mother was Ki), and Enki (or Ea), Lord of the Earth and Waters (whose mother was Antu). Enki (meaning 'archetype') had two wives, one of whom was the goddess Damkina, the mother of Marduk who became the god of the Babylonians. Enki's other wife was his half-sister Nîn-khursag (meaning Mountain Queen), the Lady of Life, who was also known as Nîn-mah the Great Lady. We shall meet again, quite soon, with Enki and Nîn-khursag, for it is they who hold the key to the story of Adam—the original story that was adapted for the Genesis account.

Enki's brother Enlil was also espoused to Nîn-khursag, and their son was Ninurta (Ningirsu), the Mighty Hunter. By his other wife, Nînlil (or Sud), Enlil's second son was Nanna (or Suen), known as the Bright One.

Nanna and his wife Nîngal were the parents of the well-known goddess Inanna (also called Ishtar), who married the Shepherd-King Dumu-zi (given in the Semitic Old Testament book of Ezekiel 8:15 as Tammuz); it was from the well-recorded wedding ceremony of Inanna and Dumu-zi that the *Hieros Gamos* (the sacred marriage) of the kings of Judah later evolved.[6]

A further son of Enlil and Nînlil was Nergal (also known as Meslamtaea), King of the Netherworld.[7] His wife, the Queen of the Netherworld, was Eresh-kigal (the daughter of Nanna and Nîngal),[8] and their daughter was the legendary Lilith, handmaiden to her maternal aunt, Inanna *(see* Chart: *Grand Assembly of the Anunnaki*). In all, there were said to be 600 Anunnaki of the Netherworld and 300 of the Heavens.[9]

The definition *Eloh* (Lofty One) derived from the Akkadian term *Ilu*, which (as given above) was another name for Anu's son Enlil. It was the long standing *Eloh* tradition of Enlil the El Elyon that Abraham and some of his family forebears transported into Canaan, having made their respective journeys from the cities of Mesopotamia. Then, some five generations after Abraham, Jehovah (I am that I am) emerged as the God of Moses and the children of Israel when they returned to Canaan from Egypt. The book of Exodus further explains how God told Moses that he was the same God who spoke with Abraham, except that Abraham had called him El Shaddai (Lord of the Mountain) because he did not know the divine name Jehovah (Exodus 6:3). The Jehovah of the Jews (El Elyon of the Canaanites) was, therefore, synonymous with Enlil of the Anunnaki, son of the great Anu. In the Mesopotamian tradition, Enlil was referred to as *Ilu Kur-gal*, meaning Great Mountain Lord,[10] which is why Abraham addressed him by the equivalent of that name.

It is likely that the definition *Kur-gal* (great mountain) was linguistically related to the great burial mounds of the Kurgans who emerged from the Russian steppe lands and swept through Europe in waves from about 4400 BC. The Kurgan people (whose name means barrow or tumulus) have been largely credited with the widespread introduction of the domesticated horse and disc-wheeled transport.[11] These people were of Scythian origin, and it was their early Transylvanian writing which (as detailed in Chapter 4) preceded the first Mesopotamian script of Akkad.

In the early tradition, Jehovah (just like Enlil the El Elyon) had a wife and family, but the essential difference between the Enlil and Jehovah portrayals was that Enlil was seen to have identifiable parents and grandparents, as detailed in the *Enûma elish* and other ancient documents.

Another key difference between the Bible's portrayal of Jehovah and the Sumerian portrayal of his peers and prototypes was that the Anunnaki were not immortal. There are no records so far discovered which relate to their natural deaths, but numerous accounts refer to their individual deaths by means of war and violence. The deaths of Apsû, Tiâmat, Mummu and Dumu-zi are all detailed,[12] but in striking contrast, the Bible's Jehovah is said to be 'from everlasting to everlasting' (Psalm 90:2). 'Heaven and Earth will perish, but he will endure and his years will have no end' (Psalm 102:25-28). Given that the term Jehovah superseded the name Enlil the El Elyon, and since Enlil was the great-grandson of Apsû and Tiâmat, there is a paradox here to be examined.

Every item of written and pictorial attestation confirms that the ancient Sumerians were absolutely sincere about the existence of the Anunnaki, and those such as Enki, Enlil, Nîn-khursag and Inanna fulfilled earthly functions with designated community duties. They were patrons and founders; they were teachers and justices; they were clinical technologists agriculturalists and kingmakers. They were jointly and severally venerated as archons and masters, but they were certainly not idols of religious worship as the ritualistic gods of subsequent cultures became. In fact, the word which was eventually translated to become 'worship' was *avod*, which meant quite simply 'work'.[13]

The Anunnaki presence may baffle historians, their language may confuse linguists and their advanced techniques may bewilder scientists, but to dismiss them is foolish. The Sumerians have themselves told us precisely who the Anunnaki were, and neither history nor science can prove otherwise.

## Kingship Begins

Between 1906 and 1923, a number of eminent Sumerologists translated and published the contents of ancient texts and fragments concerning the early kings of Sumer. In the later 1920s and the 1930s a good deal of further information was unearthed in this regard, and in 1939 Professor Thorkild Jacobsen of the Oriental Institute collated the various texts for publication by the University of Chicago. He modestly referred to his amazing work as a 'short essay', but it comprises more than 200 pages of highly detailed translation, transcription and commentary.[14]

In his introduction to the work, Jacobsen made the point that, since the information recorded by the ancient Sumerians did not conform with the ideals of some of his fellow academics, it was treated with an amount of scepticism by them. Despite the considerable efforts of high-ranking scholars to translate and compile the *Sumerian King List*, it was largely ignored by traditional historians and theologians. Why? Because it was not in line with biblical scripture, and it was not in keeping with the books that these so-called 'experts' had themselves written. Almost in desperation, in his attempt to break through the dogmatic barriers of the Western teaching establishments, Jacobsen stated, 'In late years, the *King List* has come almost to a standstill, and its evidence is hardly ever used for purposes of chronology.... It is our hope that this essay will contribute to bringing the study of the *King List* out of the dead water in which it now lies'.

This was written in 1939, over sixty years ago, and yet how many of today's schoolchildren are taught anything from these original texts of record? They learn about the ancient Greeks, the ancient Egyptians and of course the Bible, but they are told little or nothing about the oldest of all civilizations because the Sumerian writings pose such a threat to the cultish dogma of our modern religions.

These days, pioneers of chronological re-evaluation still suffer the recriminations of a hierarchical establishment which refuses to budge from its self-styled comfort zone. Prominent among the tenacious pioneers is the Egyptologist David M. Rohl. In his writings (as in his compelling television series, *Pharaohs and Kings*), he makes the very valid point that the conventional chronology applied to the Egyptian dynasts in our history books was not compiled from Egyptian dates, but from the standard dating structure applied to the Old Testament.[15] Archbishop Ussher of Armagh had published his biblical chronology in 1650, and the Egypt Exploration Fund was established in Victorian times with the express directive that archaeologists should seek to uphold the Old Testament tradition as dictated by the Christian Church.

Egyptian records do not give dates in any BC form that we might understand, but they do apply specific events to the numbered years of the respective kingly reigns. Therefore, when certain pharaohs were identified (correctly or incorrectly) as being the unnamed or loosely named pharaohs of the Bible text, their dates were plotted in accordance with the standard Old Testament reckoning. Then, by counting the regnal years backwards and forwards from these strategic points, the Egyptian chronology that we now have in our authorized textbooks was constructed. This pharaonic chronology is entirely dependent on the presumption that the standard biblical chronology is correct—but the Bible chronology of Archbishop Ussher and the Christian Church is far from correct. What our schools teach in this regard is not accurate history, but the propagandist ideal of a Church-led movement which is entirely dedicated to supporting its own mythology, irrespective of the historical truth.

Where Sumerian history is concerned, we are looking at texts with much older roots than the earliest Egyptian records so far discovered. Hence, if enterprising Egyptologists have their problems with the orthodox establishment, then one can well imagine the heightened frustrations faced by the Sumerologists. Their historical findings should be enough to blow the lid off traditional religious and historical propaganda, but their disclosures are suppressed and contained so that the debates take place within the confines of academic society and are very rarely discussed in our schoolrooms. We are told that our children are being shielded from the romance of mythology, but they are actually being prevented from learning the truth of history. This is a purposeful, strategic manipulation by an establishment which knows only too well that learned people are the greatest of all threats to governmental thraldom.

The *Sumerian King List*, compiled sometime before 2000 BC,[16] and comprising some fifteen different tables,[17] provides an uninterrupted record of kings from the very dawn of monarchy, beginning long before the Flood and progressing down to the 18th century BC.[18] It lists not only the individual kings, but also gives their seats of kingship within Sumer. The schedule begins with the pre-patriarchal kings (*see* Chart: *Antediluvian Kings of Sumer*) and this list not only mentions the Flood but actually opens with the words, 'When the kingship was lowered from heaven'.

A very ancient Sumerian tablet fragment, found at Nippur and published by the noted master of Sumerology Arno Poebel in 1914,[19] confirms the opening of the *King List* with the statement, 'Kingship had been lowered from heaven.... The exalted tiara and the throne of kingship had been lowered from heaven'. Then, in further confirmation of the *King List*, the very same city seats of original kingship are given—those of Eridu, Bad-tibira, Larak, Sippar and Shuruppak.

In all respects, the office of kingship was perceived as being divine and of Anunnaki origin,[20] and the eminent Sumerologist Professor Henri Frankfort stated in 1948, 'There can be no question in Mesopotamia of kings who differ necessarily and in essence from other men, and the precise implications of the determinative remain problematical'.[21] Prior to the introduction of kingship by the Anunnaki, it was recorded that

> They had not yet set up a king for the beclouded people. No headband and crown had been fastened;

> no sceptre had been studded with lapis lazuli.... Sceptre, crown, headband and staff were [still] placed before Anu in heaven.... There was no counselling of its people; then kingship descended from heaven.[22]

The eight kings in the pre-Flood list are said to have reigned for a total of sixty-seven shas—a *sha* being denoted by a circle = 360 degrees. The word comes from *sha-at-am,* which literally means 'a passing', and a 360-degree passing can be related to the completion of an orbit.

In about 275 BC (about 300 years after Genesis was compiled),[23] a Babylonian priest called Berossus wrote for the Greek-speaking market a strange mixture of astrology and romantic tradition called *Babylonica.*[24] In this work he recorded that an ancient *sha* was the equivalent of 3600 years, and so the sixty-seven *shas* of the antediluvian kings have since been calculated to equal 241,200 years in some works. However, it is actually from the Mesopotamian *sha* that we have derived our 360-degree circle, because each earthly orbit was the equivalent of a single degree (1/360) of an Anunnaki *sha-at-am.* A *sha* was confirmed by Sir Charles Leonard Woolley to be the equivalent of 360 Earth years, not 3600 years,[25] and the determination of the earthly calendar was said to be the prerogative of the great Anu. His Akkadian name was Anum,[26] from which derives the word *annum* (year), relating to the Earth's solar orbit.

It can be deduced that the eight antediluvian kings (the pre-Flood Nephilim kings) reigned for a total of 24,120 Earth years (that is sixty-seven *shas*). But there is, as Professor Jacobsen explains, a king missing from the list who appears in other texts. He is King Zi-u-sudra, the son of Ubar-Tutu of Shuruppak.[27] Zi-u-sudra (also known as Uta-napishtim, which was a later Akkadian variant) was the king who was actually reigning when the Flood struck, and he was the prototype for the biblical Noah:

> Man of Shuruppak, son of Ubar-Tutu,
> Tear down [thy] house; build a ship.

Abandon [thy] possessions, and seek [thou] life.
Discard [thy] goods, and keep thee alive.
Aboard the ship take the seed of living things.[28]

The average reign of each of the eight given kings is 3015 Earth years (that is 24,120 ÷ 8), so if we presume, for argument's sake, that the Flood came halfway through King Zi-u-sudra's notional reign, then we can add say 1508 years to the 24,120 antediluvian kingly period, achieving a total of 25,628 years.

With the Flood taking place in about 4000 BC, as has been ascertained from the archaeological digs of Sir Charles Leonard Woolley, then the first Nephilim king ruled from about 29,628 BC (25,628 = 4,000), which is remarkably close to the approximated 30,000 BC date when the Neanderthal species and the Eljo race finally became extinct after the coming of the hybrid Naphidem and Cro-Magnon strains. It was from this period that the Enochian Watchers (the Nephilim) became the guardians of their new-found society.

If the Anunnaki had their own orbit and, as the records suggest, their own equivalent of an annual calculation (the 360-degree *sha*), then, try as we might to find another explanation for their existence, everything points to their perhaps being from another world. In this regard, the *King List* is quite specific, stating that their office of kingship was 'lowered from heaven'.

So, from where were the Anunnaki and the Nephilim? The known planets of our solar system are Mercury, Venus, Earth, Mars, Jupiter, Saturn, Uranus, Neptune and Pluto. The farthest giant planet from the sun is Neptune, with an orbit equal to 165 Earth years. The orbit of Pluto is eccentric (off centre), so it is sometimes the outermost planet, and sometimes not. Its solar orbit is equivalent to 248 Earth years, which means that any planet with an orbit of 360 Earth years would be way out beyond Pluto. To date we know nothing of such a planet, but this does not mean that it is not there; it simply means that astronomers have not identified a solar planet beyond Pluto. There is, of course, always the consideration that the 360-degree *sha* relates to something other than a solar orbit as we know it, and so the origin of the Anunnaki must, for the time being, remain a matter of pure conjecture. In general terms, however, it is all rather less perplexing than the Judaeo-Christian concept of a single, unidentifiable entity who is perceived as having no source of origin whatever.

Those who are familiar with my work know that I always seek rational, matter-of-fact explanations for those things which might appear uncanny or paranormal. Also, from experience of textual comparison, I am inclined to believe that, whatever later interpretation may be placed on original records by those who manipulate and rewrite them, the original writers generally had the best clue as to what they actually meant to convey. In this particular instance, I can find absolutely no way to explain the phenomenon of the Anunnaki beyond that which was originally recorded—and text after text says precisely the same thing: they were the 'mighty ones of eternity', the 'lofty ones from on high', the 'heroes of yore'; their Nephilim ambassadors 'came down' and their 'kingship was lowered from heaven'.

Quite what these beings looked like is impossible to say, but the numerous Sumerian portrayals of the gods and goddesses are generally quite human in appearance. Most of the depictions show them as being tall, with large eyes, and the males are generally bearded. There are, however, some archaic figurines from around 5000 BC which depict characters with expressly serpentine features. It is unlikely that these have anything to do with the Anunnaki as such, although records do indicate that the word 'serpent' was used in a descriptive manner to denote various of those among the great Wise Ones, with Nîn-khursag described in the *Kharsag Epic* as the Serpent Lady. The facial characteristics of these statuettes are not dissimilar to those found on other deiform representations from as far afield as the Carpathian and Transylvanian regions above the Black Sea. It was from the Black Sea kingdom of Scythia that the ancient Scots Gaels migrated to Ireland, and an old Irish word which denotes a serpent or dragon is *sumaire*.

As for the inordinate lengths of the said kingly reigns, it might perhaps be that the names given (as if for individual kings) are dynastic names, rather like English historians would refer to the house of Plantagenet reigning for 331 years and that of Tudor for 118 years. On the other hand, the terms of office could well have been precisely as portrayed, for if the Anunnaki were of an alien domain, then our own familiar rules cannot be applied. In all of this, one thing is clear beyond doubt: no scholar of language has any idea of the root origins of the strange names applied to the antediluvian kings of Sumer—names such as En-men-gal-anna and En-sipa-zi-anna. These names truly do belong to an unknown linguistic dimension.

## Where Heaven and Earth Met

Some of the most pioneering modern research into the cultural roots of the long distant BC years has been conducted by the writers Christian and Barbara Joy O'Brien. Christian, who read Natural Sciences at Christ's College, Cambridge, subsequently spent many years as an exploration geologist in Iran, where he was involved in the discovery of the Tchoga Zambil ziggurat. From 1970 he concentrated his research into many enigmas of prehistory and the O'Briens have excellent books to their credit, namely *The Genius of the Few* and *The Shining Ones*. In the context of these works, it becomes very clear that the establishment of Anunnaki kingship and the Sumerian city states were actually parts of an ongoing process which had begun long before with agricultural development and early community structure from the 9th millennium BC. The first stages of this advancement programme introduced seed cultivation, crop management and the domestication of certain animals.

Descriptions of the project location (specifically referred to in the texts as Eden) are given in the foundation cylinder and tablets of the lately dubbed *Kharsag Epic* (Epic of the

Enclosure). These were discovered at Nippur in the late 19th century, but were written around 2500 BC. It is in this expansive work that the Anunnaki reference first appears—more specifically denoted at that stage as *A-nun* [*nan*]-*na* (the great sons of Anu):

> At Kharsag, where Heaven and Earth met, the heavenly assembly, the great sons of Anu, descended—the many wise ones.

It can be deduced from these records that the originally developed Eden (the grassy plateau)—so crucial to this advancement programme—was not in Sumer (as was the biblical Eden discussed in Chapter 3). It was in the more mountainous northern reaches of Mesopotamia—the Zagros range of modern Kurdistan near Lake Van, as discussed so definitively by Andrew Collins in his notable work *From the Ashes of Angels*.

Given that cedar trees feature prominently in the Kharsag tablets, O'Brien logically associated the pre-Sumerian Eden with southern Lebanon—the region around Mount Hermon so famed for its cedars. However, as Collins makes clear (and as confirmed in the Kurdish studies of Mehrdad Izady, professor of Near East Studies at New York University), cedars were abundant in the Zagros mountains until the 1st century BC.

Paramount in the story is the biologist Nîn-khursag, the Lady of Life, who selected the site because of its permanent water supply, stating:

> With this settlement will come prosperity; an enclosed reservoir—a water trap—should be established.... This perfect Eden is full of water; it should be irrigated from a cascading watercourse.

Quite apparently, the Anunnaki tradition was not an original aspect of Sumer, confined to a boundaried region above the Persian Gulf as has long been supposed, but was much wider spread within the Fertile Crescent and beyond—even across Central Europe to the Balkans.

As detailed in *The Times Atlas of the Bible,* a settlement called Scythopolis (or *Beth-shean*: House of Power) was established south of Damascus in Galilee. With *shean* being a derivative of *sidhéan,* it relates (as is apparent in the alternative name Scythopolis) to being of Scythian origin. It was announced by the British Assyriologist Sir Henry Creswicke Rawlinson, in his 1853 address to the Royal Asiatic Society that the Scythians from the Black Sea regions were the early occupiers of Akkad in Mesopotamia—a fact which we encountered in Chapter 4. Even Scythian writings from 1000 years before the earliest Sumerian script[29] are identical to those of early Akkad.

The Scythian warlords of the *Sidhé* (a transcendent intellect called the Web of the Wise) originated in the Carpathians and Russian steppe-lands to become a migratory race who took their culture far and wide—as far as Ireland to the West and Mongolia to the East. Indeed, the very name of Ur (the capital of Sumer) came from the Scythian word *Ur,* meaning 'Lord', while the settlement of Anu was not in Sumer where one might expect to find it, but hundreds of miles to the north on the Caspian Sea.

The advanced town of Damascus, founded in Syria at about the same time that Stonehenge was erected in the South of England, gained its name from Damuz (Tammus or Dumi-zi) the consort of Anunnaki Queen Inanna, granddaughter of Enlil. Moreover, in accordance with the oldest Scythian custom, Damuz's festival is still celebrated in parts of the Balkans today.[30]

# 8

# The Lady of Life

## The Original Noah

One of the most intriguing Old Testament and Mesopotamian parallels is the story of the great Flood. There is a remarkable amount of very old information in this regard, which is perhaps why so much attention is paid to the event in Genesis where it occupies no fewer than eighty verses. When making comparisons between the biblical and Mesopotamian texts, the similarities are very striking, but the most obvious difference is the apparent biblical change of time-frame so that Noah could become the revised hero of the piece. The Genesis tale is no more than an adapted version of the Mesopotamian accounts, which feature the same forewarning of a single man with a view to safeguarding the seed of life.

The most complete and comprehensive version of the Flood saga comes from the twelve Babylonian clay tablets of the *Epic of Gilgamesh*.[1] These were found in the middle 19th century among the Nineveh library ruins of King Ashur-banipal of Assyria, and since then numerous other tablets in the series have come to light. They tell of the mythical adventures of Gilgamesh (king of Uruk in about 2650 BC), who travelled to meet with the long dead Uta-napishtim of Shuruppak, the king who reigned when the Flood struck in about 4000 BC. Hence, the Babylonian epic enabled a literary retelling of Uta-napishtim's account of the Flood based on ancient Sumerian records. The main Gilgamesh tablets date from about 2000 BC, but the information therein was from even more aged texts, some of which, dating from beyond 3000 BC, have been found in part.[2]

There is a Genesis similarity in the report that the boat of Uta-napishtim was said to have come to rest on a mountain—but this is specifically called Mount Nisir, as against the Bible's general description of the mountains of Ararat (Genesis 8:4). The range of Ararat (meaning 'high peaks')[3] was to the north of Mesopotamia, and the book of Jubilees[4] explains that the ark landed on the Ararat mountain of Lubar.

Among the additionally discovered material are five Sumerian poems relating to Gilgamesh, and a separate poem entitled *The Deluge* was unearthed at Nippur.[5] Quite unrelated to the adventures of Gilgamesh, this poem is solely concerned with the Flood as encountered by King Zi-u-sudra.

The adapted Genesis version of the story tells that the Flood was an act of God's personal vengeance, but the Sumerian tablet explains that the great deluge was caused by Enlil and the Assembly of the Anunnaki. The decision was taken by way of a majority vote, but it was not approved by all concerned. Seemingly, Nîn-khursag, the Lady of Life, deplored the idea. In the event, Enlil's brother, Enki the Wise, made his own arrangements to save King Zi-u-sudra, to whom he gave advance warning of the deluge and imparted a plan of escape by means of a specially constructed boat.[6]

This, the oldest known version of the story from a Sumerian scribe, has one particular feature which is immensely significant, a feature which entirely separates it from the later 'animals two-by-two' imagery of the Noah's Ark story. The original account does not portray Zi-u-sudra as the saviour of a menagerie, but as the 'preserver of the seed of mankind'.[7]

The text relates that Zi-u-sudra did take some animals into his boat, but it specifies only an ox and some sheep, along with some other beasts and fowl. These were taken aboard for food provision, not to preserve the species. The matter of preservation is more fully covered in the Babylonian account, which explains that Enki told Zi-u-sudra to build an enclosed ship in which he should convey 'the seed of all living creatures'.[8] Once again, the operative word is 'seed', and from the conjoined accounts we learn that the vessel of King Zi-u-sudra was not a floating zoo for the salvation of living creatures, but a clinical container-ship for the seeds of human and animal life in storage.

In agreement with the Sumerian tablets, the *Epic of Gilgamesh* also records that the Flood was decreed by the Anunnaki, naming in particular Anu and Enlil, along with their counsellors Ninurta and Enuggi. The primary instigator was Enlil,[9] and after the Flood his granddaughter Inanna was reported as saying, 'In truth, the olden time has turned to clay'. The account also states that 'the ground was flat like a roof', which is precisely what Sir Charles Leonard Woolley's team found in the 1920s—a great flat bed of hard clay in the flood stratum of Mesopotamia.

The Genesis version of the story relates that the Flood was instigated by God (Jehovah) because the once 'very good' human race had become wicked, but the Mesopotamian accounts indicate a rampant population problem which had to be curtailed. An ancient Akkadian text called the *Atra-hasis Epic*[10] states that the people had multiplied beyond any control and were so noisy that Enlil could not get any sleep.

What we have here is something which really cements the essence of the Genesis story of Adam and Eve into place once the Flood is viewed in its proper chronological context. The old tablets make it quite clear that although the *homo sapiens* species had developed in many ways beyond natural evolution from before 35,000 BC (when the sons of the gods were mated with the daughters of men), they were still lacking the key elements of wisdom and a properly regulated society. There was no marital institution and there were no rules governing procreational couples. Until 4000 BC, sexual mating was largely a matter of free will, with a freedom of partners. The people were culturally advanced to a Cro-Magnon stage, well beyond the Eljo-

Neanderthal primitives, but they were apparently not conditioned to municipal structure and organized social behaviour.

The tablets reveal that, prior to the Flood, Enlil had tried to reduce the population by means of selective famines and plagues, but without success.[11] And so the Assembly of the Anunnaki elected for a drastic solution that could very quickly pave the way to a new beginning. They agreed to flood the Sumerian region in its entirety, but to preserve a stock of female human seeds (ova) and animal seeds (sperm and ova) in clinical storage. They had (as would be identified in our modern terminology) genetically engineered the semi-advanced *homo sapiens* once before, but this time they would take the process a stage further by adding more of the Anunnaki gene in a second stage of cross-fertilization. In short, they would produce the first *homo sapiens-sapiens*—a species that could be educated and socially regulated. From our understanding of this, we can now move directly into the Genesis tradition, with its First Man, First Woman and the post-diluvian institution of Wisdom—the Tree of Knowledge (Genesis 2:9).

## Enter the Adam

'Male and female created he them; and blessed them, and called their name Adam, in the day when they were created' (Genesis 5:2). So says the book of Genesis, but in reading this we are immediately confronted by something contrary to our traditional indoctrination: 'Male and female created he *them*... and called *their* name Adam'. We are separately informed (Genesis 3:20) that the man 'called his wife's name Eve, because she was the mother of all living', but we are left with the fact that Adam was not a personal name. In practice, *adam* was not a proper noun at all—it was a generic term applied to both men and women.[12] The Bible text relates that 'God formed man of the dust of the ground'

(Genesis 2:7). It has, therefore, been presumed that the name Adam, had something to do with earth—and the word for earth was *adâmah.*

In his 1st-century *Antiquities of the Jews,* Flavius Josephus adds an extra dimension, stating, 'This man was called Adam, which in the Hebrew tongue signifies one that is red, because he was compounded out of red earth'.[13] Josephus had been trained for the Pharisee priesthood, so he was clearly well versed in the correctness of his own Hebrew language. Nevertheless, in relating the word *adam* to 'one that is red' he called upon his further knowledge of the Akkadian language of Mesopotamia in which *adâmatu* was a dark-red earth. These two Semitic languages were not dissimilar, and the Hebrew word for 'red' was *adom,*[14] while another word denoting something red was *adum,* as indicated by the *Adummim* (the red men) of the book of Joshua (15:7).[15] In addition to all this, it is said in many dictionaries that the word *adam* actually means 'man'. So, in no particular order of preference, we have *adom, adâmah, adam*—or red, earth, man.

As detailed in Genesis, the 'Adam' definition was applied to both the man and the woman, so in using the term 'man' we are speaking more generally of mankind, and thus of humankind, male and female (*zakar* and *neqivah*). It is clear that the primitive human race was not called Adam, for this was the name applied to the 'first of a kind' in about 3882 BC. In old languages such as Vedic, the word *hu* relates to 'mighty' and the proto-linguistic term *hu-mannan* (whence, 'human') identifies 'mighty man'. So, let us now look at the *Enûma elish,* the Babylonian Creation epic that was the inspirational source for Genesis. What does this ancient work have to say on the matter?

Tablet VI of the *Enûma elish* states that man was created with the blood of Kingu, a son of Tiâmat who had been executed for inciting a rebellion[16]—and we have, in blood, an immediate relationship with 'red' as cited by Josephus. The Hebrew words for blood were *adamu* and *dam,*[17] as in the *goel ha dam* (the blood avenger) of Deuteronomy (19:12). But, if man was fashioned solely from the blood of a god as suggested, then man (perceived as *A-dam*) would be a god, which is not the case—so there had to be another agent. Upon further investigation we discover that an alternative Mesopotamian Creation account details that advanced man was produced by uniting the blood of a god with clay.[18] This was not ordinary clay as in cohesive earth, and yet the created man was said to be 'of the earth'—which is to say, more correctly, 'of the Earth', or as more specifically given in the Hebrew *Anchor Bible*, an 'earthling'.[19]

The linguist and translator Robert Alter, Professor of Hebrew and Comparative Literature at the University of California, has made the point that the modern English versions of the Old Testament have 'placed readers at a grotesque distance from the distinctive literary experience of the Bible in its original language'.[20] In this regard, he maintains that it is quite incorrect to relate the word *adâmah* to dust or soil, for the word has a much wider territorial meaning.

While the Babylonian *Enûma elish* pre-dates the Genesis account by more than 1000 years, it was itself based on far more ancient records, and the earliest Sumerian Creation story discovered to date is more than 1000 years older than the *Enûma elish*.[21] Here too, along with the mention of Anunnaki blood, there are specific references to the use of little clay models fashioned by Nîn-khursag, the Lady of Life. We saw, in the *Enûma elish*, that man was called *lullû*, which literally means 'one that is mixed'.[22] Moreover, in the ancient Sumerian text from Nippur (now held at the University of Pennsylvania Museum) it is specifically stated that 'Anu, Enlil, Enki and Nîn-khursag had themselves fashioned the black-haired people',[23] those called the Sumerians—the very race whose mysterious origin, language and culture have never been fathomed.

The Anunnaki had no time to waste after the flood waters had subsided; the once fertile land had become a bed of clay and the whole environment had been destroyed. The records tell of how the first priority was to make the ground habitable again, and to restore the rich *eden* of the delta country. The grain crops had to be reinstated, along with the cattle and sheep herds which were given the priority of the 'creation chamber'. According to one ancient tablet (pieced together from seventeen fragments),[24] the matters of farming and agriculture were placed in the hands of Ashnan and her brother Lahar. These junior Anunnaki, who were themselves products of the 'creation chamber',[25] were given the task of preparing the ground, and of farming grain and cattle respectively, with sheep appearing to be a joint responsibility. However, the task was too great for the Anunnaki alone and labour assistance was urgently required. Consequently, it is explained that humans were reintroduced at an early stage, and the *Tablet of Ashnan and Lahar* details that 'for the sake of the good things in their pure sheepfolds, man was given breath'.[26]

*Nîn-khursag and Enki at the House of Shimtî (from a Sumerian relief).*

The instruction came firstly from Dragon Queen Tiâmat, the primeval mother of the Anunnaki, who said to Enki, 'O my son, rise from your bed.... Work what is wise. Fashion servants of the gods, [and] may they produce their doubles'.[27] To this, Enki replied,

> O my mother, the creature whose name you uttered, it exists. Bind upon it the image of the gods... Nîn-mah [Nîn-khursag] will work above you... [she] will stand by you at your fashioning. O my mother, decree upon its fate; Nîn-mah will bind upon it in the mould of the gods. It is Man.

Nîn-khursag was then approached by Enki and the Assembly, and was formally requested to create man 'to bear the yoke' of the Anunnaki.[28]

In political affairs, the relationship between Enki and his sister-wife Nîn-khursag was fraught with disagreement: they appear to have spent a great deal of time drinking wine and quarrelling. That apart, Nîn-khursag was a highly regarded anatomical specialist and there are many accounts of her research, which included the saving of Enki's semen to be applied to the cross-fertilization of certain life-forms.[29] The documented 'creation chamber' of Nîn-khursag was called the House of Shimtî, from the Sumerian *sh-im-tî*, meaning 'breath-wind-life'.[30]

Nîn-khursag's experiments were soon perfected, and she was ready to create her utmost masterwork, *homo sapiens-sapiens*. The *Atra-hasis Epic* records that Ea and Nîn-igiku (Enki and Nîn-khursag) created fourteen new humans soon after the Flood: seven boys and seven girls, and the clinical process involved the wombs of women who had survived the deluge. The tablet is very fragmented and much of the text has been lost, but what remains describes how Nîn-khursag made use of the 'seven and seven wombs', having prepared fourteen 'pinches of clay' upon which Enki had delivered his 'repeated incantation'. In one instance the opening of a navel is detailed, and the wombs are called the 'Creatresses of Destiny'. It is related that these wombs completed Nîn-khursag's work by developing the 'forms of the people' that she made.[31]

The fundamental difference between the Sumerian records and the Genesis version of the creation of modern humankind was that the new men and women did not emerge in ready-made adult form. They were scientifically induced, with human ova fertilized by the Anunnaki, to be placed as cultured embryos into the wombs of surrogate mothers. As a result, they were born quite naturally as babies:

> Nîn-khursag, being uniquely great,
> Makes the womb contract.
> Nîn-khursag, being a great mother,
> Sets the birth-giving going.[32]

Being the daughter of the great Anu, Nîn-khursag was the designated Lady of Life and her emblem (which is to be found on various tablet and cylinder representations) was a symbolic womb, shaped rather like the Greek letter *omega* (Ω).[33] She was also called the Lady of Form-giving, Lady Fashioner and Lady of the Embryo, while a text entitled *Enki and the World Order* calls her the Midwife of the Country.

Likewise, Nîn-khursag's half-brother Enki, Lord of the Earth and Waters, was called Nudimmud, meaning Image Fashioner, being the 'archetype' of original form—the Master of Shaping and the Charmer of Making.[34]

Not only was a new workforce created to toil in the fields, to build new cities and to work the mines, but a whole new social structure was conceived with *hu-mannans*, by becoming their own governors, destined to perform functions hitherto carried out by the Nephilim. The tablet fragment continues:

> Mother Nintur [Nîn-khursag], the lady of form giving,
> Working in a dark place, the womb.

To give birth to kings, to tie on the rightful tiara;
To give birth to lords;
To place the crown on [their] heads.
[It] is in her hands.

In about 2100 BC, the future King Gudea of Babylon recorded that Nîn-khursag was the 'Mother of all children'.[35]

It is clear from the Mesopotamian texts that the Sumerians who emerged from Nîn-khursag's work believed that their main purpose in life was to serve the Anunnaki by providing them with food, drink and habitation.[36] In return, they were educated and trained in social skills and academic affairs, and the products of this training are abundantly clear from their writings. They abhorred evil, falsehood, lawlessness and injustice, but they cherished goodness, truth, law, order and freedom within a well regulated, structured society.

A tablet from the third millennium BC explains that Enki established law and order in the land and generally masterminded the dramatic rise of civilized Sumer:[37]

The plough and the yoke he directed....
To the pure crops he roared.
In the steadfast fields he made the grain grow....
Enkimdu, him of the canals and ditches,
Enki placed in their charge.
The [ ] grains he heaped up for the granary....

It is further related that Enki then turned his attention to the pickaxe and the brick-mould, laying foundations and building houses. And it is told that all this was done by the grand design of 'Her [Nîn-khursag]... who held the might of the land [and] the steadfast support of the black-headed people'.

In general terms, it seems that the cloning enterprise of Enki and Nîn-khursag was a success, but a more advanced plan was then conceived to create a prototype for a race of superior earthly leaders. (The English word 'clone' derives from the Greek word *klon,* meaning 'twig'.) With this in mind, it was decided to place a cultured embryo into Nîn-khursag's own womb instead of into a mortal woman's womb, so that it was fed with Anunnaki blood. Among her various titles, Nîn-khursag was also known as Nîn-ki (Lady Earth) and it is by this name that she is recorded in a quotation from Enki that describes her surrogate role: 'Nîn-ki, my goddess-spouse, will be the one for labour. Seven goddesses of birth will be near to assist'.[38]

So Nîn-ki (Nîn-khursag) bore the child, having developed an embryo cultured from the seed of a mortal woman, which had been clinically fertilized by Enki. The outcome of this successful experiment was the *Adâma* (Earthling),[39] who was recorded as the Model of Man. Enki called the man Adapa and was so pleased that, in time, he appointed him to be his personal delegate.[40] At Eridu, Adapa was placed in charge of Enki's temple in the Sumerian Eden, and he became the world's first ever priest *(see* Chart: *Ancestry of Adam and Eve*).

Tablets containing Adapa's story were originally discovered, along with the *Enûma elish,* in the Nineveh library ruins of King Ashur-banipal of Assyria, and also in the Egyptian archives of Pharaoh Amenhotep III, who reigned in about 1400 BC. They explain that Lady Earth's son, Adapa the *Adâma,* was truly a 'mighty man' (*hu-mannan*), who was given extraordinary powers of control, being anointed (Anu-oint[*ment*]ed) into kingship.

> [Oil] he commanded for him, and he was anointed.
> A garment he commanded for him, and he was clothed....
> His command was like the command of [Anu].
> With wide understanding, he had perfected
> him to expound the decrees of the land.
> He had given him wisdom, but he had not given
> him eternal life.
>
> At that time, in those years of the wise son of Eridu,
> Enki had created him as a leader among mankind.
> Of the wise one, no one treated his command lightly.[41]

Later, in a continuation from another fragment,[42] the *Adâma* is described not only as the High Priest, but also as being of the Royal Seed.[43] And so it is apparent that the great importance of Adapa (the biblical Adam) was not that he was the first man, but that he was the first human of the Royal Seed—the first priest-king of the Enki bloodline.

We should now consider the mysterious little 'clay models' to which the translated records all refer. How was it that the Genesis compilers presumed the *Adâma* to be made from earth, often described as clay? The answer lies in the translatory misunderstanding of a single small word—a word encountered by the captive Jewish scribes in Babylon. The Babylonian word for potter's clay was *tît*, but in the more ancient Sumerian language *tî-it* meant 'that which is life'.

In Hebrew the word *tit* meant 'mud'.[44] When the blood (semen) of Enki was united by Nîn-khursag with the *tî-it*, it was being united not with clay, but with 'that which is life'—female ovum. From such beginnings, Nîn-khursag cultured the 'little models' which she implanted into the wombs of surrogate mothers, and the precise nature of these little models is manifest in Nîn-khursag's description, Lady of the Embryo. In Adapa's case, Nîn-khursag had been the surrogate mother, and so the resultant Model of Man, the Adâma, was born from the womb of Lady Earth herself. His partner Khâwa (the biblical Eve) was created in precisely the same manner.

While on the subject of misidentified words, we can also discover why it is that the Bible describes how Eve was formed by God from a rib taken out of Adam's side (Genesis 2:21-23). The name Eve is said in Genesis (3:20) to signify the 'mother of all living', and this is repeated in the 1st-century *Antiquities of the Jews*, wherein Josephus explains: 'Now a woman is called in the Hebrew tongue *Issa* (she-man); but the name of this woman was Eve, which signifies the mother of all living'.[45]

In Hebrew, the name Eve was *Hawah* (Ava), but the verbal root which gave rise to the name was *hayah* ('to live').[46] Hence, Eve was akin to the Sumerian Nîn-tî, Lady of Life—and this, as we have seen, was yet another title of Nîn-khursag. The Sumerian word *tî* meant 'to make live', but another Sumerian word, *ti* (pronounced *tee*), meant 'rib'.[47] When Nîn-khursag's title Nîn-tî was applied to her surrogate daughter and transposed to the name Eve, it was correctly interpreted by the Genesis compilers, but its further association with Adam's rib was wholly inaccurate and had nothing whatever to do with the original accounts.

An intriguing reference to the biblical 'rib' was made by the Protestant dissenter Matthew Henry in the early 1700s. Whereas Genesis (3:16) states that God said to Eve that Adam 'shall rule over thee' (a sexist guideline adopted by the Catholic and Anglican Churches), the Church dissenters claimed that Eve was 'not made out of Adam's head so as to rule over him, nor out of his feet to be trampled upon by him, but out of his side to be equal with him'.[48] In presuming the rib symbolism to be emblematic of male and female equality, the dissenters were rather more at odds with episcopal dogma than is generally portrayed by their reluctance towards the *Book of Common Prayer*.

In considering the word *hayah* (to live), it is of interest to note that the similar Arabic word *hayya* denoted a female serpent, whilst *hayât* related to life. As detailed by the linguist Balaji Mundkur, the words were all akin in origin,[49] and the definitions of 'life' and 'serpent' were mutually supportive. This is particularly relevant since Eve (Khâwa/Hawah) was not only the Lady of Life, but was also described as the Serpent Lady.

# 9

# Shepherds of the Royal Seed

## The Kings of Sumer

In the days before the Flood, the operative Kings of Sumer were Nephilim guardians appointed by the Anunnaki, but after the Flood came a new era of the first earthly kings. It was this post-4000 BC era (the Age of Adam) which saw the sudden and glorious rise of the Sumerians, the people whose strange new language gave its name to the region. Even in those times, the kingly appointments were still made by grant of the Assembly under the continuing presidency of Anu. From about 2100 BC comes the proclamation for the installation of King Shulgi of Ur, who reigned shortly before the birth of Abraham: 'Let Shulgi, king with a pleasant term of reign, perform correctly for me, Anu, the rites instituted of kingship. Let him direct the schedules of the gods for me'.[1]

Earthly kingship was established as a hallowed employment encompassing both social and military duties. It was not governmental, though, for the kings were the designated guardians of the people, and their role was to protect and direct the people. In functional terms, the king was defined as a shepherd and his rod of assembly was a shepherd's staff (a crook or crosier). This was a requisite symbol of the original kings; it was not until much later that the Christian Church appropriated the crosier as an instrument of authority for its bishops.

Also granted to the king were a sceptre of office and a tiara—a headband circlet of gold which was said to envelop the great wisdom of Anu. The one item not in the kingly regalia was the sword, which, in later Christian Europe, was introduced to denote absolute martial command by grant of the Pope.

Although the early Sumerian kings were responsible for affairs of national defence, they were not established as warriors in the first instance. Their military role, should the need come to pass, was to be the supreme protectors of the realm and to guide the troops with justness and wisdom. In his role as a shepherd, a Sumerian king (called a *lugal*[2]) was also a designated priest (*sanga*). The king was additionally head of the judiciary (an *ensi*),[3] his operative base being within the temple compound of his city-state.[4] The queen held the formal title of Lady (*Nîn*), and she and the king lived in a high property designated the Great House (the *E-gal*). It was, in fact, from the earliest Sumerian *sanga-lugals* that the tradition of priest-kings later evolved in the Messianic line.

The specified duties of a king were to administer his city, while governing the overall state on behalf of the particular god in charge. The king was also the Chief Justice and head of the temple clergy. He was responsible for all public works, including community building and restoration projects, and his role was detailed as follows:[5]

1. The interpretation of the will of the Anunnaki.
2. The representation of the people before the Anunnaki.
3. The administration of the realm.

As we have seen, the records relate that the very first earthling head of a temple was Adapa (Adam). It has also been mentioned that he was not only the High Priest, but was additionally defined as being of the Royal Seed—the model of earthly kingship, and, as such, he was the world's first *sanga-lugal* (priest-king). It was for this reason that Adam made his supreme and memorable mark in history. Never before had there been a man with so much Anunnaki blood: both his father (Enki) and his surrogate mother (Nîn-khursag) were true Anunnaki, being the son and daughter of the great Anu, as well as being the brother and sister of Enlil-El. Only the woman whose ovum was used was of mundane blood. Nevertheless, Adam's was not the original earthly Blood Royal (the *Sangréal*). He was a prototype, a model for things to come, but he was not the physical progenitor of the kingly line. As will be detailed, there were a further two stages in the creative process—a process which actually involved Eve rather than Adam.

The *Sumerian King List*, having recorded that 'the Flood swept thereover', begins again with the words, 'After the Flood had swept thereover, when the kingship was lowered from heaven, the kingship was in Kish'. And so, the list commences anew with King Ga-[ ]-ur, whose name is partially missing from the text. We know nothing of this king except that his reign appears to have been unsuccessful and the establishment was passed to the 'heavenly Nidaba'. This was Queen Nidaba, mother-in-law of Enlil[6] *(see* Chart: *Grand Assembly of the Anunnaki*).

Subsequently, seven Nephilim guardians are listed, followed by King Atabba of Kish (alternatively given as Atab or Abba).[7] This was the original style of the first patriarch of the kingly race, with *Abba* relating to 'Father', while Atabba was synonymous with Adapa the *Adâma*. In this context, the distinction of 'father' did not relate to a physical progenitor, but derived (as explained by Professor Jacobsen) from the Akkadian word *abûttu*, which meant an 'intercessor'—one with Anunnaki connections and the ability to protect his flock.[8] Although the style of *Abba* moved into Semitic use, and was later adopted in the New Testament to define God,[9] it was originally a Sumerian word which defined the *sanga-lugal*.[10]

Later we shall return to the kingly succession, but for the time being it is worth noting that the senior royal descent was not the line from Eve's third son Seth as portrayed in Genesis. It was, in accordance with the earliest matriarchal tradition, the line from her first and senior son Cain—the character so maliciously discredited by the Christian Church (*see* Chart: *Post-diluvian Kings of Sumer*).

## The Tower of Babel

The Sumerian system of kingly guardianship was fully operational for about 2000 years, from around 3800 BC when Sumer made its mark in history as the cradle of civilization. But then, quite suddenly, in 1960 BC everything changed as invaders came in from all sides.[11] They were essentially Akkadians from the north of Sumer, western Semites of the Amorite (*Mar-tu*) tribes of Syria and Elamites from the east (now Iran).

> When they overthrew, when order they destroyed;
> Then like a deluge all things together consumed.
> Whereunto, Oh Sumer! did they change thee?
> The sacred dynasty from the temple they exiled.[12]

It was at this stage of Sumerian history that the empire fell and Abraham was forced to flee northwards from the city of Ur. But what had happened to the Anunnaki, the assembly of gods who had established everything? Quite apparently, they deserted the nest, and it was reported that

> Ur is destroyed, bitter is its lament. The country's blood now fills its holes like hot bronze in a mould. Bodies dissolve like fat in the sun. Our temple is destroyed. The gods have abandoned us like migrating birds. Smoke lies on our cities like a shroud.[13]

In historical terms, this total collapse of the Sumerian Empire follows the founding of Babylon by King Ur Baba in about 2000

BC. Unlike the Flood, which was chronologically moved for the Genesis account, the story of the Tower of Babel in Shinar (Sumer) and the resultant wrath of Jehovah precisely fits the time-frame of the Sumerians' own abandonment by the Anunnaki.

Today's conventional teaching of the Babel incident tells only of the wrath of Jehovah, but the Genesis text does actually cite him along with other gods. Even the King James English-language Bible states that when God saw the people building their tower, he said 'Go to; let *us* go down....' (Genesis 11:17). What has occurred over the centuries is that, irrespective of the biblical texts, Jehovah has been sidestepped into a wholly singular identity, the thoroughly non-historical portrayal of the One God which prevails today. In this context (outside the more traditional esoteric circles), Jehovah has been divested of his wife, his family and his fellow gods, to be left alone in a wilderness of enigma that no one has ever truly understood. There are numerous references in the Old Testament to the 'gods' (the *elohim*), and to the 'sons of the gods' (the *bene ha-elohim*), and these seemingly anomalous entries have caused their own confusion through the years because of Jehovah's perceived isolation.

A long standing-puzzle which has loomed in the face of all biblical researchers is God's distinctly split personality. One minute he is the gentle shepherd calling his loyal sheep to his side; the next minute he is launching fire and brimstone upon his own supporters. In the book of Isaiah (45:7) God is quoted as saying, 'I create evil', and in Amos (3:6) it is asked, 'Shall there be evil in a city, and the Lord hath not done it?'

None of this has ever made any sense—but it makes all the sense in the world if Jehovah (Enlil/El) is removed from the constraints of religious dogma and placed in his proper historical context as one of a pantheon of Anunnaki who had their own ups and downs, their own political disagreements, made their own misjudgements and perpetrated their own wrongdoings. In the original Sumerian tradition, the Anunnaki were just as fallible as ordinary human beings, and in the Canaanite tradition the Elohim were equally so. One always knew which god to support and which to fault—but Jehovah has been left alone to take all the praise and all the blame, whether deserved or not. Since it is not the done thing to lay blame on Jehovah, it is generally the case that the bad things are simply said to be 'His will', and they are left unchallenged with wholly inadequate justifications such as 'God moves in mysterious ways'.

Jack Miles, a one-time Jesuit and scholar of the Hebrew University in Jerusalem, has made the point that much of what the Bible says about God (the definition originally being *Gûdo*) is rarely preached from the pulpit because, examined too closely, it becomes a scandal.[14] St. Jerome, when translating the Old Testament from Hebrew into Latin in the 4th century, complained that many of the narratives were 'rude and repellent'. From medieval times, Jewish rabbis and Christian bishops have opted for selective teaching and interpretation rather than accurate reporting, while they have justified the obvious scriptural anomalies with the unqualified dogma that God's logic is impeccable; only man's understanding is wanting.

It appears that the reason the Flood story was shifted in time for Genesis was that it was naturally suited to be God's vengeful reprisal after the Nephilim had consorted with the daughters of men. But the verses dealing with this latter affair were themselves entered in the wrong place in Genesis; they belong to a time before Adam, not to the time of Noah. Genesis 6 (5-7) states that as a result of earthly sons being born to the Nephilim, 'God saw that the wickedness of man was great in the earth.... And the Lord said I will destroy man, whom I have created, from the face of the earth'. What then follows is the story of the Flood, whereby God is seen to obliterate humankind, which he has previously termed as 'very good' (Genesis 1:31) But he seems to do this because the people have broken some rule which to that point has never been clarified. The religious commentator and former nun, Karen Armstrong, has suggested that, to a sector of humankind which she has astutely dubbed *homo religiosus*, such badly presented stories actually introduce the concept of justifiable genocide.[15]

We are aware that the story of the Nephilim and the daughters of men belongs to a much earlier age (pre-35,000 BC) and that the Flood has been scientifically dated to about 4000 BC. There is, however, a further story in Genesis 11 which follows that of the Flood (although separated by a wealth of genealogical begetting): the story of the Tower of Babel from about 2000 BC. Once again, the people who were hitherto said to be 'very good' are seen to be severely punished because of another strange transgression which had not been ruled upon. The said misdeed was that they all spoke the same language—and the uniquely common tongue was, of course, Sumerian.

In reality, their uniform language was not the transgression at all; the true transgression was that laid down in Genesis 11:4, which has been mistranslated in English-language and other modern Bibles. What we read now is that the people said, 'Go, let us build us a city and a tower, whose top may reach to heaven, and let us make a name lest we be scattered abroad'. This has never meant very much to anyone: 'let us make a *name* lest we be scattered abroad'. However, what the original text actually stated was that the people said 'let us make a *shem* lest we be scattered abroad'. A *shem* was described as a 'highward fire-stone' and, as we have seen, the Nephilim were called the 'people of the shem'. The word *shem* (along with the term *shamaim*, meaning heaven) derives from the root word *shamah*, which means 'that which is highward'.[16] To the Sumerians, *shems* were called *na-ru*—'stones that rise', and to the Amorites they were 'fiery objects'.

So, a *shem* was not a 'name': it was something highward, fiery and made of stone. In some form or another, the Nephilim used *shems* and they were associated with heaven. In fact, King David was said to have raised a *shem* as a monument after he had defeated the Syrians (2-Samuel 8:13). In one respect, a *shem* was indeed a monument—a tall, conical edifice—the original models for what we know today as church steeples (towers with conical spires). But these monumental stone *shems* cannot be considered 'fiery' as were the Nephilim *shems* which they emulated.

Tablets found at the Nineveh library of King Ashur-banipal and in the Egyptian archives of the pharaohs Amenhotep III and IV, all detail that a heavenly *shem* was provided by Enki for the priest-king Atabba when he ascended to meet with the great Anu. Because of this, some writers have suggested that *shems* were perhaps a form of transport akin to the fiery chariots of the Bible. Maybe they were—but that aside, there were more important attributes attached to these objects of veneration.

*Shems* were associated with something called *an-na,* which meant 'heavenly stone', a term that was also used to define a shining metal. The use of the word *shem* in respect of its 'shining' aspect is apparent in the alternative name for Prince Utu, the brother of Inanna *(see* Chart: *Grand Assembly of the Anunnaki*). His epithet was Shem-esh: the Shining One. The word is also evident in the name of Sumer, which, as we have seen, is more correctly pronounced 'Shumer'—derived from *Shem-ur*. This was the land of the Anunnaki and the Nephilim: the 'people of the shem', and regardless of conical towers and heavenly metal, there was, as we shall eventually see, a far greater significance to the revered 'highward fire stone' of the *shem-an-na.*

For a reason which is not made clear in the Bible, the Anunnaki were displeased about the Babylonian tower with its topmost *shem.* The Genesis text relates that Jehovah and the Elohim came down and 'did confound the language of all the earth'. The Sumerian historical documents tell much the same story, except that the confounding of language is far better explained by the hordes of invaders who were allowed to come into the region with their different tongues. It transpires that this invasion was the direct result of friction among the Anunnaki, for at Anu's retirement from the Assembly, his eldest son Enlil had been voted to the presidency:

> The gods had clasped their hands together,
> Had cast lots and had divided.

Anu then went up to heaven.
To Enlil the Earth was made subject.
The seas, enclosed as with a loop,
They had given to Enki, the Prince of Earth.

Enki was not happy about his brother's promotion because, although Enlil was the elder of the two, his mother (Ki) was Anu's junior sister, whereas Enki's mother (Antu) was the senior sister. True kingship, claimed Enki, progressed as a matrilinear institution through the female line, and by this right of descent Enki maintained that he was the first born of the royal succession:

I am the great brother of the gods.
I am he who has been born
as the first son of the divine Anu.

In the midst of this struggle, Enki's son Marduk made his own bid for supremacy and usurped the Assembly decision to gain a majority following among the people of Sumer and Akkad. This is why Marduk is portrayed as the god of creation in the Babylonian *Enûma elish,* whereas his father, Enki, was depicted as the creator in the more ancient Sumerian accounts.

Evidently, the people were terrified of Marduk, fearing exportation if they did not support his regime. This is confirmed in Genesis when they exclaimed 'let us build a city and a tower ... let us make a *shem,* lest we be scattered abroad'. But, whatever the people's reason, this was all too much for Enlil. Having lost his popularity, he and his party completely withdrew their protection when the people erected a *shem* to the honour of Marduk and, as recorded in 1960 BC, the invasions began, while the Anunnaki court of Enlil departed 'like migrating birds'.

The instigator of the invasions which followed the Anunnaki departure was Enlil himself. It was he who opened the gates of Sumer to the invaders, who came in from all sides. The scribes recorded that it was he, the vengeful Enlil, who brought the 'great storm' which caused the annihilation of a people who had given their loyalty to his nephew Marduk:

> The high gates, the roads, were piled high with dead.
> In the wide streets, where feasting crowds would gather, scattered they lay.
> In all the streets and roadways bodies lay.
> In open fields that used to fill with dancers, they lay in heaps.[17]

But that was not the end of it, for Abraham and his family retained their allegiance to Enlil and followed their God Most High into Canaan, where his cult was already established. In his capacity as the El Elyon, Enlil promised Abraham (renamed at that time from Abram) and his descendants that he would exalt their race above all others, saying, 'I will give unto thee, and to thy seed after thee, the land wherein thou art a stranger, all the land of Canaan for an everlasting possession, and I will be their God' (Genesis 17:8). But for all that, the newly defined race of Hebrews were not the governors of Canaan as they had been governors in their own land. To the native population they were immigrants, and for many generations they encountered famine, wandering and hardship, while El Elyon (although the covenanted God of the Hebrews) was also the God of the indigenous Canaanites. Meanwhile, Marduk gained new support from the incoming Amorites in Babylonia, and he instigated a revised building programme[18] of such magnitude that Babylon soon became the key power-centre of the following era.

# 10

# The Tree of Knowledge

## Wisdom and the Serpent

In the book of Genesis (2:9) we are introduced to the central trees of the Garden of Eden: the Tree of Life and the Tree of Knowledge of Good and Evil (of *Tov* and *Raa*). It is related that God commanded Adam not to eat from the Tree of Knowledge, 'for in the day that thou eatest thereof, thou shalt surely die' (Genesis 2:17). At that stage, it seems that the other tree, the Tree of Life, posed no immediate problem—but there is no indication as to how Adam was supposed to tell one tree from the other.

Eve (the *esha/issa*: woman)[1] was subsequently brought on to the scene and, on advice from the serpent, she ate the fruit from the Tree of Knowledge, having been informed (contrary to Adam's earlier information) that 'Ye shall not surely die.... In the day ye eat thereof, then your eyes shall be opened, and ye shall be as gods, knowing good from evil' (Genesis 3:4-6). It transpired that Eve did not die, and when Adam had also eaten from the Tree, 'the eyes of them were both opened, and they knew that they were naked, and they sewed fig-leaves together and made themselves aprons' (Genesis 3:7). Without any explanation of how these newly created people knew the technique of sewing, the hitherto all-seeing God then lost Adam completely and called out, 'Where art thou?', to which Adam responded that he was hiding. God, seemingly quite unaware of the preceding events, then asked, 'Hast thou eaten of the tree?', whereupon Adam blamed Eve and Eve blamed the serpent (3:8-13). At that stage, God was said to be 'walking in the garden'.

In the aftermath of this episode, God addressed the Elohim, saying, 'Behold, the man is become as one of *us*, to know good and evil'. The Tree of Life then posed a secondary problem—God banished Adam from the garden 'lest he put forth his hand and take also of the Tree of Life, and eat, and live forever'. Not content with this, a revolving sword of fire was installed to prevent access to the Tree of Life (3:22-24), but there is no mention of guarding the problematical Tree of Knowledge of Good and Evil. (The biblical swords of fire are reminiscent of the fire-and-power weapons of the Babylonian *Enûma elish*.).[2]

To complete the vindictive punishment, God said to Eve, 'I will greatly multiply thy sorrow and thy conception; in sorrow thou shalt bring forth children'. He also said to Adam that, having eaten once from the tree, 'In sorrow thou shalt eat of it all the days of thy life'. Furthermore, although Adam had not touched the Tree of Life, he was deprived of immortality in any event (3:16-22). Thereafter, Adam and Eve became wise with the knowledge of good and evil, and for some unexplained reason God then took up the tailoring role: 'And did the Lord God make coats of skins, and clothed them' (3:21).[3]

The Tree of Life (the *Kiskanu* tree) is generally regarded as being a source of personal immortality, but it related more specifically to the immortality of kingship. In fact, the Tree of Life (sometimes called the Plant of Life or Plant of Birth) was directly associated with the office of kingship, its twigs (*klons*/clones) being the shepherds' staffs of dynastic investiture and succession.[4] The symbolism relating to Adam's denial of immortality (i.e. his denial of the right to a continuing kingship in his own line) was apparent in the event that the office was not inherited by Adam's eldest surviving son Seth, but by Eve's eldest son Cain.

What are we to make of all this? Does it relate in any way to the Mesopotamian records upon which the Bible story was based? It does in a rather vague manner, but first we should consider the nature of the serpent, whose presence has been thoroughly misrepresented for centuries. The biblical term that was used to denote the said serpent was *nahash*. However, before the vowels were added, the original Hebrew stem was *NHSH*,[5] which meant 'to decipher' (to find out, or to divine).

From the earliest times, the serpent was identified with wisdom and healing. It was a sacred emblem of the Egyptian pharaohs, a symbol of the Essene Therapeutate (the ascetic healing community) of Qumrân, and has become identified with today's medical institutions.[6] The serpent has never had any dark or sinister connotation except for that imposed on the Genesis text by latter-day Church doctrines.[7] A serpent depiction from old Mesopotamia is wholly indicative of the emblems of the American and British Medical Associations, where in each case the serpent is coiled around the Tree (plant/staff) of Knowledge and Wisdom.[8] In the ancient Greek tradition, the great Father of Medicine was Asklepios of Thessaly (*c*.1200 BC), whom the Romans called Aesculapius. His statue (*c*.200 BC) at the Capodimonte Museum, Rome, also portrays the staff and coiled serpent. The eighteenth lineal descendant from Asklepios was the medical teacher Hippocrates, whose *Hippocratic Oath* is sworn by physicians to this day.

The serpent who conversed at length with Eve was clearly not a lowly, dumb creature, but a guardian of the sacred knowledge, and we know from the Mesopotamian story of Adapa that it was Enki who created him and Enki who imparted to him wisdom and knowledge:

> With wide understanding, he [Enki] had perfected him
> to expound the decrees of the land.
> He had given him wisdom, but he had not given him
> eternal life.[9]

It is further evident from the Mesopotamian serpent illustration that it has a direct Enki association, since Enki (Ea) was traditionally depicted as the Serpent-Lord of the Euphrates.[10] Just as the serpent was the giver of wisdom, so Enki was constantly referred to as Enki the Wise—as in the Flood story, when he challenged the authority of Enlil by giving Zi-u-sudra advance warning of the deluge. After the Flood, while Enki had been busy working with Nîn-khursag in her 'creation chamber',

*The Sumerian coiled serpent of Enki, emblematic of Asklepios and the British and American Medical Associations.*

his brother Enlil had been quite opposed to the embryo scheme. Enlil had devised the Flood to get rid of the human problem, but Enki was a true champion of humankind.

Since we know that El Elyon-Jehovah was synonymous with Enlil, the Garden of Eden story is a direct representation of the ongoing feud between the Anunnaki brothers. Enlil was insistent that humankind should be kept in ignorance, and should be maintained solely to toil and to bear the yoke of the Anunnaki. But Enki had other ideas: he was insistent that the black-headed people should be educated. As previously mentioned, Enki and Nîn-khursag had successfully created at least fourteen of the new humans before they created Adapa and Khâwa (Adam and Eve), and the story of two of these, Ullegarra and Zallegarra, relates that their purpose was to till the soil, to erect buildings and to serve the Anunnaki for all time in accordance with Enlil's requirement.[11]

In the first instance, Enlil endeavoured to prevent Adam and Eve from gaining any wisdom beyond their perceived 'servant' status, and he warned them away from the Tree of Knowledge of Good and Evil, claiming that they would die if they took of its fruit. Enki (the wise serpent) claimed that this was untrue and that they should partake of the knowledge: 'Ye shall not surely die—for God [Enlil] doth know that in the day ye eat thereof, then your eyes shall be opened, and ye shall be as gods, knowing good and evil' (Genesis 3:3-4).[12]

In the event, Enki was correct—the man and woman did eat of the tree and they did not die, whereupon the disgruntled Enlil announced that 'the man is become as one of us' (3:22). Even so, he still imposed his will and sent the *Adâma* to 'till the ground' as a punishment for his disobedience (3:24). At that point the Genesis story of Adam and Eve concludes, to be followed by the stories of their sons—but certain non-canonical works do follow the adventures of the famous couple.

Adam and Eve's original state of nakedness, which is apparently so important to the Genesis narrative, was a reflection of their subordinate status in the prevailing environment and their covering of themselves had nothing whatever to do with matters of sexuality. It had to do with the fact that servants and workers of the Anunnaki were naked in those days, as depicted in reliefs of the era. When Adam's and Eve's eyes were opened, they gained the knowledge of their true station—a station akin to that of domestic animals. Prior to that, they had thought nothing of their nudity, but on becoming aware that they were inferior beings (naked subordinates) they were immediately struck with the embarrassment of their situation and sought to rectify the matter.

Clothes were a prerogative of the masters and it is for this reason that the *Adapa Tablet* tells that when the *Adâma* was anointed to his priestly station, 'a garment was commanded for him, and he was clothed'. Undeterred by Enlil's attempted interference, Enki had specifically created the earthling as 'a leader among mankind' from his own seed,[13] whereas others of the earthly race had been created from the blood of Kingu. Atabba (to give Adam his correct historical name) thus emerged as the first earthly priest-king of ancient Sumer in about 3800 BC, and his wife was Nîn-khâwa (Lady Eve, or Lady of Life).

There is an account similar to the Adapa story in the *Epic of Gilgamesh*, which tells once again of the importance of clothing to the enlightened race, as against the nakedness of the standard domesticated earthlings. Here, a temptress says to the naked (another created *adâma*), 'You are wise, you are like a god', subsequent to which she marks his new status by providing the man with some clothes.[14]

It is commonly believed that the Christian term Original Sin had something to do with Adam's and Eve's sexual behaviour, but this is a Church-promoted absurdity. To the point where Adam is banished from the garden, there is no mention whatever of any physical contact between him and Eve. The eventually determined 'sin' was that Eve (a mere woman in the Church's eyes) had seen fit to make her own decision: a decision to disobey Enlil in favour of Enki's advice, a decision to which Adam conceded and a decision which proved to be the correct one. In practical terms, Eve had committed no sin at all because the interdict concerning the Tree of Knowledge had been placed on Adam alone, which is why only he was subsequently exiled.

Not until the next chapter of Genesis do we discover that Eve followed in Adam's footsteps and, according to the book of Jubilees (3:28), they 'dwelt in the land of Elda'. There, she fulfilled her wifely function, but it then becomes clear that Eve's first son was not the child of Adam, and because of this we discover why Eve was ultimately dubbed a sinner by the orthodox religious movements of future times.

## The Myth of Satan

Before we leave the Garden of Eden (called Edem[15] and Paradise in the Greek translation), it is necessary to free our minds of the fearful satanic dogma which the Christian Church has attached to the incident with Eve and the serpent. Nowhere in the Genesis account is there any mention (direct or indirect) of Satan's involvement, and yet it has become common practice for the Church to portray the serpent as an emissary of Satan, or even as Satan himself.[16] This has been done in an attempt to support the Church's self-styled concept of Eve's Original Sin—a concept (developed and promoted by St. Augustine)[17] which, like so many doctrines of the early bishops, emerged from an unhealthy sexual paranoia. Not only did the Christian bishops reinterpret the story of Adam and Eve, they also had the story rewritten so that a few verses of Genesis became great biographical books, and it is from these spurious works of fantasy that the familiar portrayals of satanic involvement have emerged.

In the Hebrew Bible, as in mainstream Judaism to this day, Satan never appears as western Christendom has come to know him.[18] The Christian perception of Satan is that of an evil imperialist whose despicable horde wages war upon God and humankind. But this Satan character was an invention of the post-Jesus era, a fabulous myth with no more historic worth than any figment of a Gothic novel.

In the Old Testament, 'satans' (though rarely mentioned) are portrayed as obedient servants or sons of the gods (the *bene ha-elohim*) who perform specific functions of strategic obstruction. The Hebrew root of the definition is *STN*, which defines an opposer, adversary or accuser, whereas the Greek equivalent was *diabolos* (whence, diabolical and devil), which relates to an obstructor or slanderer. Until Christian times, the word 'satan' had no sinister connotation whatever and, in the olden tradition, members of a straightforward political opposition party would have been called satans. In the book of 1-Samuel (29:4), David is himself referred to as a satan (adversary) of the Philistines.

Whenever a *bene ha-elohim* satan appears in the Old Testament, he is seen as a member of the heavenly court—a member who carries out God's more aggressive dictates. In the book of Job (1:6-12, 2:1-7) for example, a satan is sent twice by God to tease and frustrate Job, but with the express instruction that he should not seriously harm the man—an instruction which is duly obeyed. In the book of Numbers, when Balaam decided to take his ass where God had warned him not to go, 'God's anger was kindled ... and the angel of the Lord stood in the way for an adversary [a satan: *le-satan-lo*] against him' (Numbers 22:22). In this instance, although performing an obstinate role of physical obstruction, the satan was acting for Balaam's own benefit at God's command.

By the time of the Old Testament's penultimate book of Zechariah (3:1-2), the appointed satan (chief magistrate) is portrayed with an independent will, for here we see him in conflict with God in a social matter. In this instance, the Jews returning from Babylonian exile were attempting to regain their family stations in Jerusalem, but they arrived to find a High Priest and a governing establishment already in place. God sided with the residential Israelites in the dispute, but the satan took the side of the disaffected Jews. Nonetheless, despite the political stand-off, there is still no indication of anything remotely dark in the character of the satan.

The sinister satanic figure (sometimes called Lucifer, Beelzebub or Belial—meaning 'worthless') emerged mainly through the onset of Christian Dualism—the concept of two opposing and equally powerful gods.[19] According to different traditions, Satan was either the brother or the son of Jehovah, or was even the competitive and aggressive aspect of Jehovah himself. In essence, the Jehovah-Satan conflict was representative of the ancient pre-Christian tradition of the symbolic battle between Light and Darkness as perceived by the Persian mystics. This tradition found its way into the ascetic Judaism of sects such as the Essenes of Qumrân, and it is to some extent recognizable in the New Testament, but it was not apparent in the Hebrew lore of the Old Testament wherein satans are seen to perform specific duties of mundane opposition.

So, from what original concept or Bible entry was the modern Christian image of Satan born? In the Old Testament book of Isaiah is a section dealing with the prophesied fall of Babylon, and in referring to the city and its despotic king, Isaiah says, 'How are you fallen from heaven, day star, son of the dawn! How are you fallen to earth, conqueror of nations!' (Isaiah 14:12). Many centuries after this was written, the image of the fallen day star (Venus) was redefined as 'light-bearer', and when translated into Latin with a proper noun connotation it became *Lucifer*. Hence, Lucifer appeared in this Venus context in St. Jerome's 4th-century *Vulgate* Bible, to become associated with an evil satan some 1400 years later[20] in John Milton's *Paradise Lost*:

> Of Lucifer, so by allusion called,
> Of that bright star to Satan paragon'd.[21]

Today, the Isaiah verse in authorized Christian Bibles retains the Latinized Lucifer entry which emanated from the Christian Church's creation of its own Satan mythology during Roman Imperial times. The Roman faith was based wholly on subjugating people at large to the dominion of the bishops,[22] and to facilitate this subordination an anti-God/anti-Christ figure was necessary as a perceived enemy. This enemy was said to be Satan, the evil one who would claim the souls of any who did not offer absolute obedience to the Church. For this scheme of threat and trepidation to succeed, it was imperative for people to believe that the diabolical Satan had existed from the beginning of time, and there was no earlier story with which he could be associated than that of Adam and Eve. The only problem was that Genesis made no mention whatever of Satan—but there was, of course, the inherent account of Eve and the wise serpent. The Serpent Lord was Enki, but in parts of Chaldea he had been called *Shaitan,* and so it was determined that the story could be rewritten to suit the desired purpose. The original text was, after all, a Jewish version and Christianity had become quite divorced from Judaism, even from the Westernized Judaism of Jesus.

In those days there was no understandable translation of the Bible available to Christians at large. The Jews had their Hebrew, Aramaic and Greek versions of the Old Testament, while the primary Christian Bible existed in an obscure form of Church Latin, as translated by St. Jerome in the 4th century. Outside the immediate Roman Church of the West, there were enthusiastic Eastern Christian branches in places such as Syria, Egypt and Ethiopia, and it was mainly from these regions (where the Jewish competition was stronger) that the new Genesis accounts emerged for the Christian market.

Among these was an Egyptian and Ethiopic work called *The Book of Adam and Eve,* subtitled *The Conflict of Adam and Eve with Satan,* which was produced sometime in or after the 6th century AD.[23] This lengthy book not only features Satan as a central character, but even goes so far as to say that the cross of Jesus was erected on the very spot where Adam was buried!

A Syriac work entitled *The Book of the Cave of Treasures* (*M'ãrath gãze*) is a compendium of earthly history from the creation of the world to the crucifixion of Jesus. It appears to have been compiled in the 4th century AD, but the oldest extant edition comes from the late 6th century.[24] Once again, this book introduces Satan as the constant protagonist of evil, setting the scene for the dark and sinister element that flourished in the Church-promoted Gothic tradition that evolved during the brutal Catholic Inquisition. In one instance, Adam and Eve are seen to be dwelling in a cave when Satan comes fourteen times to tempt them, but each time an angel of God puts the demon to flight. The book even maintains that orthodox Christianity was in place before the time of Adam and Eve and the emergent Hebrews. In this regard, and as previously mentioned (Chapter 2), it is claimed that when God said 'Let us go down', he was referring to the Holy Trinity: Father, Son and Holy Ghost—a concept not established until the Council of Nicaea in AD 325.[25]

Another volume which upholds this same notion concerning the Christian Trinity is *The Book of the Bee*[26]—a Nestorian Syriac text from about 1222, compiled by Bishop Shelêmôn of Basra, Iraq. Its title is explained by virtue of the fact that it 'gathered the heavenly dew from the blossoms of the two Testaments, and the flowers of the holy books', thereby applying Christian doctrine to the traditional Jewish scriptures which it reinterpreted.

If these books can be said to have anything in their favour it is that their Old Testament genealogies are very much in accordance with the far more ancient Jewish works such as the book of Jubilees. Apart from that, they are no more than fictional fables, designed to undermine historical record and to intimidate readers into compliance with the dogmatic and sexist rule of the Christian bishops. Their portrayals of Satan are entirely fabricated, and they are contrary to all original Sumerian, Canaanite and Hebrew archives.

## The Mark of Cain

Although our familiar translations of Genesis constantly refer to God, it must be emphasized that there was, originally, no such word or definition in the book. What was used was the general classification of *Eloh* along with *YHWH* (*Yod-Hay-Vav-Hay*), the latter of which is traditionally identified as God, Lord, Yahweh or Jehovah.[27] However, since the Jews were forbidden to pronounce *YHWH*, a customary alternative was *Yod-Yod*.[28]

When Abraham promoted the Mesopotamian tradition of Enlil-El in Canaan, he was said to have gained access to a uniquely inscribed tablet of ideograms (symbols of concept without nominal expression, as in some Chinese characters). This was revered as 'the testament of a lost civilization—a testament of all that humankind had ever known, and of all that would ever be known'.[29] To the Sumerians, this composition was known as the *Table of Destiny*, and their history records that the guardians of the *Table* had been Kingu (a son of Tiâmat) and Tiâmat's great-grandsons Enlil and Enki.[30] In the esoteric Jewish tradition, it was also called the *Book of Raziel*—a collection of secrets cut into sapphire and inherited, at length, by King Solomon.[31]

The philosophical cipher of the *Table* became known as *Ha Qabala* (The *QBL* tradition of light and knowledge) and it was said that he who possessed *Qabala* also possessed *Ram*, the highest expression of cosmic knowingness. Indeed, the very name Ab-ram (or Av-ram) means '[He] who possesses *Ram*', and the expression was used in India, Tibet, Egypt and in the Celtic world of the Druids to denote a high degree of universal aptitude. The holders of *Ram* were the representative masters of eternal understanding and the identification was evident in such names as Rama, Ramtha and Aram. In the context of the Old Testament narrative, we see *Ha Qabala* being passed from Abraham to his son Isaac, thence to Jacob and so on.

From a quite separate root—the Arabic *KBL* (meaning 'to twist')—came the German word *kabel* and the English word 'cable', as in a twist of wire strands. Hence, the resultant word *Kabalah* relates to a 'confusion', and is not to be assigned, as it so often is, to the enlightenment of the *QBL* (*Qabala*). When really twisted, to the extent of intrigue, the emphasized consonantal stem becomes *KBBL*, whence *Kabbalah*, which relates to the German word *kabal* and the English 'cabal'.

There were, therefore, two distinct movements within early mystical Judaism. The Kabbalistic movement (the *KBBL*) reached its European zenith in the Middle Ages in northern Spain and southern France, by which time the true virtues of the Qabalistic concept (the *QBL*) were largely forgotten in the West. Certainly in the world of mainstream Judaism the spirit of *Ha Qabala* has been almost completely ignored since the 18th century, while material values have prevailed in its stead.[32]

Along with linguists such as Professor Robert Alter, the adepts of *Ha Qabala* (including noted present day exponents such as Carlo Suarès) have traditionally maintained that our conventional understanding of biblical scripture is a gross corruption of the original writings. Teachings and translations have been structured to conform with the customs, beliefs and politics of the times when taught or translated, and as a result the original messages have been lost in the process. In *Bloodline of the Holy Grail* we see how this was the case with the New Testament, but the adulteration is rather more pronounced in respect of the more ancient Old Testament.

Returning now to the story of Adam and Eve (Atabba and Hawah), Qabalistic masters maintain that it was not the serpent (Enki) who was the deceiver as we are led to understand. The deceiver in this instance was Enki's half-brother, Eloh-Jehovah (Enlil), who said that Adam would die from eating the fruit. Enki, the serpent, actually related the truth that Adam would not die from the fruit, and Eve believed this truth. Eloh-Jehovah had, therefore, told a falsehood to Adam, who was afterwards enlightened by Eve, and so Adam was not conclusively deceived. In the final event, says Carlo Suarès, the only victims of deceit are the readers and recipients of the corrupted interpretation.[33]

In the opening verse of Genesis 4, it is written that Hawah (Eve) said, 'I have gotten a man from the Lord'.[34] Other variations are 'I have got me a man with the Lord', and 'I have acquired a man from the Lord'. The text then continues to say that this new man (Hawah's first son) was Q'ayin—better known by the phonetic translation Cain. Subsequently, Hawah is said to have given birth to a second son, Hevel—or, as we know him, Abel. The Jewish *Midrash* (meaning Inquiry), a traditional commentary on the Bible, emphasizes the point that Hawah's first son was the son of the Lord, whereas the second son was the son of Adam. But in defining 'the Lord' in this instance, the *Midrash* uses the personal name Samael, thereby identifying Enki the serpent. The name Samael (*Sama-El*)[35] derived from the fact that Enki was the patron Lord (*El*) of the kingdom of Sama, east of Haran in northern Mesopotamia.

It transpires that, although the well-known Cain and Abel were the sons of Hawah (Eve), they actually had different fathers. While Abel was the straightforward product of a *homo sapiens-sapiens* union with Adam, his elder half-brother Cain was an advancement on the earlier cloning experiments, with Hawah's ovum further enriched with Enki's Anunnaki blood. This means that Q'ayin (Cain) emerged as the most advanced product of the Royal Seed.

Whereas the original Genesis text made much of Q'ayin's prestige and the seniority of his line, these attributes have been demolished by translators and theologians in favour of a secondary descent from Hawah's third son Seth. In Genesis (4:2) we read that 'Abel was a keeper of sheep, while Cain was a tiller of the ground'. By a better translation, however, the text should read more accurately that 'Cain acquired dominion over the earth'—as indeed he did, in kingship.[36]

When we then read (Genesis 4:3-5) that Abel's offerings were acceptable to the Lord, but Cain's were not, we get the impression that Cain's offerings were in some way inferior. But the original emphasis was on the premise that offerings (venerations) were acceptable from Abel as a subordinate subject, whereas for Cain to make offerings was unacceptable because of his kingly status.[37] Genesis (4:6-7) does actually make the point that Cain's seniority over Abel was significant.

We then move to the sequence wherein Cain is reckoned to have slain Abel in the field (Genesis 4:8-10), but the word indirectly translated to 'slew' was *yaqam*, and the text should read that Cain (Q'ayin) was 'elevated' (raised or exalted) above Abel.

The terminology that Cain 'rose up' against Abel is used in the English translation, but in quite the wrong context. Abel was a man conditioned according to his station, time and location. His blood was, therefore, figuratively swallowed into the ground (Genesis 4:10) – which is to say that he became so mundane as to be indistinguishable from his toil.[38] The historical insignificance of Abel (or more correctly, Hevel) is qualified by the name by which he was identified, for a *hevel* was a puff of vapour.

As the short story progresses (Genesis 4:11-16), it is related that God sent Cain into exile as a fugitive, but having said that, the true relevance of Cain's standing is brought into play when the Lord explains that, should anyone slay Cain, 'vengeance shall be taken upon him sevenfold. And the Lord set a mark upon Cain lest any man finding him should kill him' (Genesis 4:15-16). What Cain received was not a curse, as is commonly portrayed, but the blessing and protection of the Lord, his father, Enki-Samael. Cain (Q'ayin) then dwelt in the land of Nodh – which is to say he lived in restless uncertainty.[39]

The question has often been posed as to who the Lord feared might want to kill Cain, given that he and his parents were (according to Bible lore) the only living beings. This question only arises because of the religious traditions of recent ages; in more ancient times the Eden symbolism was fully understood in the context of its Sumerian environment. For just the same reason, many have wondered how it was that Cain managed to find himself a wife (Genesis 4:17), but in a correctly understood historical framework the answer is self-explanatory.

As for the enigmatic mark placed upon Cain, this is probably the most important aspect of the story so far, because although not defined in the Bible, the Mark of Cain is the oldest recorded Grant of Arms in sovereign history. In the *Midrash* and Phoenician traditions, the Mark of Cain is defined as being an upright centred cross within a circle.[40] It was, in principle, a graphic representation of kingship, which the Hebrews called the *Malkhut* (Kingdom: from the Akkadian word *malkû* = sovereign).[41] This was a legacy of Tiâmat, the great matriarch of the Grail bloodline.

In accordance with the history of the Imperial and Royal Court of the Dragon - an ancient fraternity with Egyptian origins from about 2170 BC—the outer circle of the Mark of Cain was emblematic of a serpent-dragon clutching its own tail: a symbol of wholeness and wisdom known as the *Ouroboros*. In more recent representations it is shown precisely in this form. The cross—called the *Rosi-crucis* (Greco-Roman), from *rosi* = dew, and *crucis* = fire-cup (as in 'crucible')—is a sign of enlightenment and on this account the sacred *Rosi-crucis* (the Dew-cup) was the original mark of foundation of the kingly bloodline.

The cup was itself emblematic of the womb, representing the maternal aspect of kingship, whence the Blood Royal flowed. It was therefore deemed that the Mesopotamian kings were individually married to the Mother Goddess and, as cited by the Oxford Assyriologist Stephen Langdon, ceremonies were actually conducted in this regard.[42] In its female form (a circle with a cross below), the Mark of Cain becomes the familiar symbol of Venus . When set about, with the cross above the circle, the representation is that personified by the Orb of sovereign regalia.[43]

In the tradition of emblematic regalia, the Orb signifies completeness, being representative of all things gathered within the orbis. It is also associated with the symbolic eye of the 'all-seeing'—that of Enki who was called Lord of the Sacred Eye.[44] Given that kingship (*malkhut*) was perceived as a matrilinear inheritance through Tiâmat and Lilith, the name of Q'ayin (Kain, identified with King) was also directly associated with the definition Queen.

Although the *ayin* is associated with the All-seeing eye, it is more correctly attributed to blackness (or nothingness) by alchemists, who associate its mystery with the cerebellum, the posterior part of the brain. The 'all-seeing' aspect is that which perceives light from out of blackness. The very word 'alchemy' comes from the Arabic *al* (the) and *khame* (blackness). *Al-khame* is defined as the science which overcomes the blackness, or that which enlightens through intuitive perception.

The letter 'Q'—as in Q'ayin and Queen—is metaphysically assigned to the moon, and the *khu* (Q) was perceived as the monthly (lunar) female essence of the Goddess. The divine menstruum[45] constituted the purest and most potent life-force,[46] and it was venerated as Star Fire. Its representation was the All-seeing eye (the *Ayin*), whose hermetic symbol was a spot centred within a circle[47]—the *kamakala* of the Indian mystics, the *tribindu* of the oriental school[48] and the Egyptian symbol for Light.

The letter 'Q' derives from the Venus symbol, which was equally attributed to Isis, Nîn-khursag, Lilith and Kâli, all of whom were deemed 'black but beautiful' (Song of Solomon 1:5). Lilith and Kâli were both titular names, with Kâli appropriated from *kala* (the periodic time of the female lunar cycle), while Nîn-khursag was the ultimate Lady of Life. Hers was the *genus* which constituted the true beginning of the sacred bloodline—the genesis of the Grail Kings. In the Rosicrucian tradition this genesis has long been identified with the transcendent gene of Isis.

Genesis,[49] (meaning 'origin' or 'beginning') stems from the Greek, and from the word *genes* (meaning 'born of a kind'), whence also derive the words genetics, gender, genius, genii, genital, genre, generation, genealogy, etc. [50] As an alternative, the eye of illumination was sometimes depicted as a spot within a triangle which represented the *daleth*, or doorway, to the Light.

Q'ayin (Cain/Kain) has often been called the 'first Mr. Smith' because the term *q'ayin* also means 'smith', as in metal-smith, or more precisely as in blade-smith, a required skill (or *kenning* = knowing) of the early kings. In this regard, his given name in Genesis—like that of Hevel (Abel) and many others in the Bible—is a descriptive appellation rather than a real personal name. In the alchemical tradition he was indeed a *q'ayin*—an artificer of metals of the highest order, as were his descendants, particularly Tubal-cain (Genesis 4:22) who is revered in scientific Freemasonry. Tubal-cain was the great Vulcan of the era,[51]—the holder of Plutonic theory (knowledge of the actions of internal heat), and he was, therefore, a prominent alchemist.

Q'ayin's heritage was that of the Sumerian metallurgists—the Master Craftsmen whom we encountered at the court of El Elyon—and the supreme Master of the Craft was Q'ayin's father Enki, described as 'the manifestation of knowledge, and the craftsman *par excellence*, who drives out the evil demons who attack mankind'.[52] The alchemical pursuits of this family were of the utmost significance to their history, and the expertise of their craftsmanship held the key to the Bible's mysterious 'bread of life' and 'hidden manna'.

So, if Q'ayin was not the man's real name, then who was he? In Sumerian history he is referred to as Ar-wi-um, King of Kish, the son of Masda[53] and successor to King Atabba (the *Adâma*). Under his alternative names of Masda and Mazdao, Enki (via his son Ar-wi-um the Q'ayin) was the ancestral forebear of the Magian spiritual master Zarathustra (Zoroaster). The name Masda (from *Mas-en-da*) means 'one who prostrates himself (as a serpent)', and the Sumerian name *Ar-wi-um* is related to the Hebrew word *awwim* which denoted 'serpents'.[54] In the Persian tradition Enki was Ahura Mazda, the god of Life and Light, who was also called Ohrmazd (or Ormuzd), meaning Serpent of the Night, while in this context Mazda is also equivalent to Lord (*Ahura Mazda* meaning Wise Lord[55]). In the Aryan lore of Persia it was Ohrmazd who had first created the Righteous Man,[56] just as Enki was said to have performed the task in Sumer.

As to the identity of Q'ayin's wife (Genesis 4:17-24), she was called Luluwa (Pearl: a lunar jewel).[57] In some Christian works, Luluwa is given as being the daughter of Eve, although she is not mentioned by name in the Bible.[58] Luluwa was the daughter of Lilith, and in the Talmudic tradition[59] Lilith was Adam's primary consort before Eve.[60]

As identified in the Sumerian records, Lilith was the granddaughter of Enlil-El Elyon, being the daughter of his son Nergal (Meslamtaea), King of the Netherworld. Her mother was Nergal's cousin, Nîn-Eresh-kigal, and Lilith was handmaiden to her maternal aunt, Queen Inanna (Ishtar). Lilith was of pure-bred Anunnaki stock, and although she was Adam's designated short-term partner, the Jewish *Talmud*[61] explains that she refused to be his sexual mate.[62] Her physical partner in this respect was none other than Enki, the father of Cain's wife Luluwa.

As mentioned, Enlil's brother Enki (in his role as the serpent) was called Samael—and in this regard the literature of *Ha Qabala* brings us full circle to where this Eden section began, for it states quite explicitly that 'Samael and Lilith are personally referred to as the Tree of Knowledge of Good and Evil'.[63]

# 11

# The Queen of Heaven

## The Unspeakable Name

The book of Exodus relates that when Moses spoke to God from Mount Horeb prior to the Israelites' exodus from Egypt, he was somewhat baffled as to how he should convey God's identity to the people. He explained that the children of Israel would ask, 'What is his name?', and continued, 'What shall I say unto them?' (Exodus 3:13). This seemingly odd question, whether historically factual or not, does at least confirm that Moses lived in an era of many gods. From the time of Abraham, the Hebrews of Canaan had worshipped Enlil-El Shaddai, whom the Canaanites called El Elyon—but Moses had come from Egypt, where the Israelites were accustomed to gods with other names.

The reply that Moses received was vague in the extreme: 'And God said unto Moses, "I am that I am .... Thus shalt thou say to the children of Israel, I AM hath sent me unto you .... The Lord God of your fathers, the God of Abraham, the God of Isaac, and the God of Jacob, hath sent me unto you. This is my name for ever, and this is my memorial unto all generations" (Exodus 3:14-15).

So, what Moses learned was that this was indeed El Elyon, the God of Abraham, but that he was now to be called 'I AM'. God then confirmed (Exodus 6:3) that Abraham had referred to him as El Shaddai (Lord of the Mountain) because he did not know the divine name *YHWH*: 'I am that I am'. This verse is wrongly translated in English-language texts to suggest that *El Shaddai* meant God Almighty but, as we have seen, Enlil was also referred to as *Ilu Kur-ga*l (Great Mountain Lord) in the Mesopotamian tradition,[1] which is why Abraham had addressed him with a vernacular equivalent.

In general terms, the *Pentateuch* refers to God as *Eloh-YHWH* when speaking individually, and to the gods as Elohim when dealing with the plural. With vowels later added to the *YHWH* stem, the term Yahweh (or Jehovah) fell into common usage and by the time that Genesis and the Old Testament books were amalgamated it was the accepted norm. But, quite apart from a considered agreement concerning God's name, there had been a very marked change in the Israelite religious culture—a change which deified Jehovah beyond any original Mesopotamian or Canaanite concept.

In the tradition of old Sumer, the Anunnaki gods sat in council at Nippur and decided all important matters by majority vote. Sometimes the people were pleased with the results and sometimes they were not—but, as with committee procedure today, at least they understood the underlying process of governmental decision-making. From the dawn of the subsequent Hebrew culture, however, everything changed as Jehovah became ever more rationalized as an individual absolute—a unilateral overlord of all things.

The Hebrew perception of Jehovah also became totally abstract, so that all physical connection with humankind was lost. In Mesopotamian thought, the earth and heavens were a reflection of the majesty of Nature, of which the people were a part and the Anunnaki were a part. But, to the emergent Hebrews, Nature as a whole (including the sun and the heavens) was seen to be a servant of Jehovah, who was said to have created everything:[2] 'The heavens declare the glory of God, and the firmament sheweth his handiwork' (Psalm 19:1).

To the Hebrews, Jehovah transcended even Nature herself, and in consequence of this evolving thought process the true harmony of humankind and Nature was forfeit. In erstwhile Mesopotamian, Canaanite and Egyptian thought, the unexplainable divine was manifest within Nature, and Nature enveloped both the gods and society. This belief, however, was shattered for all time by the biblical Hebrews, who forsook harmony in favour of subservience. Hence the balance of relationship between humankind and the phenomenal world was destroyed, and what was ultimately lost was integrity.

Nature (which is still referred to in the female sense) had been venerated as the great beneficial Mother, but the Mother was shunned by an evolving society which held the male godhead supreme—an unapproachable, unseen, solitary godhead, whose name could not even be uttered. In later times, the High Priest of the Jerusalem Temple was permitted to say the name, 'Jehovah' once a year on the Day of Atonement, within the Holy of Holies (the Inner Sanctum of the Temple)—so long as it was said under his breath, beyond the earshot of others![3]

The dominant tenet of the new thought was based wholly on the utmost fear of Enlil, who was known to have instigated the great Flood, and to have facilitated the invasion and destruction of civilized Sumer. Here was a deity who spared no mercy for those who did not comply with his dictatorial authority. Abraham had experienced the vengeful Enlil first hand at the fall of Ur, and he was not about to take any chances with his own survival. He was even prepared to sacrifice the life of his young son, Isaac, to appease the implacable God (Genesis 32:9). As far as Abraham and his descendants were concerned, the power of Enlil (El Shaddai/Jehovah) was to be feared beyond measure, and the concept of this power became so awesome that it was said to transcend all things, material and immaterial. No longer was God seen to exist within Nature: it was thenceforth held that God had created Nature.

When writing for Chicago University in the 1940s, the oriental scholar Henri Frankfort summarized the situation by making the point that 'In Hebrew religion—and in Hebrew religion alone—the ancient bond between man and nature was destroyed. Those who served Jehovah must forego the richness, the fulfilment, and the consolation of a life which moves in tune with the great rhythms of the earth and sky'.[4]

In time, the original character of Enlil was forgotten as the newly interpreted Jehovah became even more impersonal and obscure. Jehovah had no identifiable personality—he was faceless and became totally *sui generis* (one of a kind), so that all values, of whatever significance, were attributed to him alone. As a result, the inherent rectitude of humankind was substantially degraded, to be perceived as quite valueless before God: 'We are all as an unclean thing, and all our righteousnesses are as filthy rags' (Isaiah 64:6). Even the righteousness of people, the highest of all personal and collective virtues, was devalued in comparison with the absolute deity,[5] and people were made to feel (as many are today) that they were of very low esteem in the wider scheme of things:

> 'Can a mortal be righteous before God, or a man be made pure against his maker? Even in his servants he does not trust, and his angels he charges with error. How much less them that dwell in houses of clay, whose foundation is in the dust' (Job 4:17-19).

Such an inexorable concept of God was without precedent in the pre-Hebrew cultures of the Near East and it led to an abysmal iconoclasm—a neurotic and timorous contempt for artistic imagery. Everywhere surrounding the Hebrew culture there was religious art, poetry and music—but where is the creative legacy of the early Hebrews? It does not exist. It was denied on the basis that whatever skill and understanding might go into gifted artistry, the outcome would be unworthy, would be as nothing in comparison to the formidable majesty of Jehovah. It is no wonder that so many researchers doubt the very substance of the Old Testament stories because there exists no physical evidence of the culturally devoid post-Abraham patriarchal era of unworthiness. People were conditioned to avoid ambition since ambitions were doomed to failure through inadequacy.

In later times, it was this very inferiority complex which Jesus tried so hard to combat. He endeavoured to persuade Jews and Gentiles, lame and lepers that everyone had primary rights to self-esteem and personal dignity, but these rights were denied to all by the sanctified establishment. Jesus's mission was one of equality, balance and harmony—the prerequisites of a unified and spiritually fertile society—but his ambition was not to be fulfilled. In the event, it was overcome by the ancient sectarian dogma of individual subjugation, so that people were left contained in a sterile wasteland of uncertainty. To this day, the Messianic dream prevails in the allegory of Grail lore, which contends that, 'Only when the wound of the Fisher King is healed, will the wasteland return to fertility'.

## The Bride of Jehovah

In her discerning work, *The Paradise Papers*, the American sculptor and art historian Merlin Stone relates that as a young girl she was taught that her greatest iniquity was to have been born female. In accordance with the holy scripture (Genesis 3:16), she was therefore destined in her adulthood to bear children in pain and suffering as a punishment for her wrongdoing—the sin of being a woman.[6] In a similar vein, the American gnostic cultural leader JZ Knight of Ramtha's School of Enlightenment,[7] stated in a recent address that she too was raised (as have been so many females worldwide) with an indoctrinated sense of guilt and shame for being born a daughter of Eve.

Unfortunately, pronouncements such as these abound because the status of womanhood has been methodically undermined for centuries by the contrived dogma of misinterpreted Bible texts. It has long been presumed by strategically misguided teachers that only the man (Adam) was created in God's image, and that the woman (Eve) was a subordinate offshoot who transgressed into sin. Be that as it may, the Genesis text actually says (even in modern authorized translations), 'Male and female created he *them* ... and he called *their* name Adam' (Genesis 5:2). The word 'man', as used in the surrounding context, denoted mankind in general—that is to say humankind.

Because of the sexist conditioning of male-dominated society, the harmonious male-and-female spirit of all early tradition has been lost so that veneration of the male deity is now called 'religion', whereas veneration of any feminine aspect is called a 'cult'. But that was not the way it used to be. The final cementing of the Hebrew ideal of the One [male] God did not occur until their years of captivity in Babylon (*c*.586-536 BC). Upon the Israelites' return to Jerusalem and Judaea, the first five Books of Moses[8] were collated into the Jewish *Torah* (the Law), while the rest of the Old Testament was gradually added, through 500 years, in order to stabilize the Jewish heritage with holy writings (*Hagiographa*) and heartening prophetic content during an era of social uncertainty.[9] Prior to the Babylonian invasion, however, the goddess Ashtoreth was as important a figure as Jehovah in the culture of the Hebrews.

As related by the Semitic scholar, Raphael Patai, the four consonants of the Hebrew stem *YHWH* (which became an eventual acronym for the One God) represented the four members of the heavenly family: *Y* represented El the father; *H* was Ashtoreth the mother; *W* corresponded to the son, Baal, and *H* was the daughter, Anath.[10]

Ashtoreth (Lady Asherah of the Sea, Progenitress of the Gods[11]) was often referred to as Elath and was said to have had seventy offspring by El-Jehovah, including Baal, Anath and their brothers Mot and Yamm.[12] In the Old Testament it is related that in about 1060 BC 'the children of Israel did put away Baal and Ashtoreth, and served the Lord only' (1-Samuel 7:4), but not long afterwards the Ashtoreth culture returned with the building of Solomon's Temple. The book of 1-Kings (11:5) explains that King

Solomon worshipped Ashtoreth, and the Holy of Holies was deemed to represent the womb of the divine Mother. As the supreme consort of El-Jehovah, Ashtoreth was an integral part of religious life in Judah until the reforms of King Josiah (2-Kings 23) at the time of the Babylonian invasion.[13]

Whether styled Ashtoreth or Asherah, the name of this goddess features no less than forty times in the Old Testament.[14] She also appears in the *Tell el-Amarna Tablets* (letters sent to the Egyptian pharaohs from Mesopotamia) and in the Canaanite texts from Ras Shamra.[15] Literature of the era additionally refers to wooden fertility idols called *Asherahs*, which were sometimes no more than tree trunks with the branches stripped away.[16] Like El-Jehovah (Enlil), Ashtoreth was originally a Mesopotamian deity called Ashratu in Babylon,[17] while the Assyrians knew her as Atirat, consort of the great god Ashur[18] who was synonymous with the Sumerian Enlil and with the Hebrews' Jehovah.[19] The Amorites called Enlil by the name Amurru, styling him Lord of the Mountain — the equivalent of his other names, Ilu Kur-gal and El Shaddai. For this reason, Atirat (Ashtoreth) was identified with Enlil's wife Nînlil.

To recap, we have a situation where the very same god and goddess were known by different names by different people in different regions. The goddess was Ashtoreth, Asherah, Elath, Ashratu, Atirat, Nînlil and Sud, while the god was Enlil, Ilu Kur-gal, Ashur, Amurru, El Elyon, El Shaddai and Jehovah.

The other great goddess of the Hebrews was Anath, the daughter of Jehovah and Ashtoreth. Anath was Queen of the Heavens and she was also known as Astarte, meaning 'womb'. In fact, all the deities had at least two names — a proper name and an epithet. Just as Ashtoreth was also Asherah, so El Elyon was called Jehovah. Their son Hadd was generally known as Baal (a titular distinction meaning Lord),[20] while his brothers Mot and Yamm were known as Gazir and Nahar, respectively.[21] Yamm was defined as a 'judge' (an accuser) and was therefore a satan, as were all judges. In the book of Judges (3:31), the satan-judge Shamgar was said to be a son of Anath. In Samaria, north of

Judaea, Baal was known as Baal-zebul (or Baal-zebub), meaning Elevated Lord (2-Kings 1:2), but this title was maliciously corrupted in the Christian New Testament[22] so that Beelzebub became classified as the 'chief of the devils'.[23]

There were also plural names for the deities, with *Elohim* being the plural of *El* or *Eloh*. The plural of Ashtoreth was Ashteroth, the plural of Anath was Anatha and the plural of Baal was Baalim. Again in Judges (10:6) it is stated that the Israelites, after the death of Moses, 'did that which was evil in the sight of Jehovah, and served the Baalim and the Ashteroth ... and they forsook Jehovah and served him not'.

In her role as the Queen of Heaven, Jehovah's daughter Anath is depicted in the book of Jeremiah (44:15-19), and she was regarded as the high goddess of love and war for whom incense was burned and in whose image cakes were baked. Her royal seat was the town of Beth Anath (or Anathoth),[24] north of Jerusalem. Now called Anatha, this was the birthplace of Jeremiah the prophet, son of Hilkiah the High Priest (Jeremiah 1:1). In her warlike capacity, Anath was often portrayed as being particularly aggressive, to the extent that her brother Baal pleaded with her to 'take away war from the earth' and to 'banish all strife'.[25]

In the tradition of *Ha Qabala*,[26] the female figures of Ashtoreth and Anath (being the wife and daughter of Jehovah) became merged into a single spiritual entity, an overall consort known as the *Shekhina*. The word was extracted from *sh'kinah*, a Hebrew abstract verb meaning 'to dwell', and by the late 1st century AD the *Shekhina* (Ashtoreth-Anath) had become the mother-goddess of the Jews, as given in the *Targum Onkelos*,[27] an Aramaic Bible which appeared soon after the lifetime of Jesus. Rabbi Yehoshua of Siknin wrote in the 1st century that 'As soon as the Tabernacle was erected [Exodus 36] the *Shekhina* descended and dwelt among them [the children of Israel]'. The Shekhina was deemed to be the spouse and female representative of God upon Earth; her original dwelling was the Tabernacle (the *Mishkan*),[28] and her later abode was Solomon's Temple of Ashtoreth in Jerusalem.

The *Shekhina* was a portrayal of the Holy Spirit—the epitome of Wisdom (in Greek, *Sophia,* and in Hebrew, *Hochmah*[29]). She represented Jehovah, but was opposed to him in matters of retribution, as related by the doctrines of Solomon in the book of Proverbs—for example (24:29): 'Say not I will do unto the man as he hath done to me. I will render to the man according to his work'. This is contrary to the 'life for a life, eye for an eye, tooth for a tooth' teaching of Jehovah (Exodus 21:23-24)—the same vengeful teaching expounded by Enlil in ancient Sumer, which was so despised by his sister Nîn-khursag, the *Shekhina* archetype.

When defining the feminine wisdom of Sophia in relation to Jehovah, the Old Testament book of Proverbs (8:29-30) states, 'When he gave to the sea his decree ... then I was with him, as one brought up with him; and I was his daily delight, rejoicing always before him'.

The legacy of *Ha Qabala* dates back well beyond Adam and Eve, to whom its secrets were disclosed by Enki (Samael) and Lilith, who were jointly defined as the 'Tree of Knowledge'. The word *Qabala* relates to 'tradition'[30] and to 'how it was obtained'. It emphasizes the intuitive grasp of the absolute truth of the ancient Masters—the great Archons who brought forth the world out of primeval chaos.[31] One of these Archons (by whatever name) was Wisdom—and Wisdom (the Holy Spirit) was always female, moving 'on the face of the waters', as related in the second verse of Genesis at the very beginning of biblical time. Wisdom was Tiâmat, Sophia, Ashtoreth-Anath and, in general terms, Wisdom was the *Shekhina* who embodied them all.

The problem was that the *Shekhina* was said to have been lost in the great realm of the Jewish Diaspora. She had lived in the Temple of Jerusalem, but the Temple had been destroyed at the time of the Babylonian captivity (*c.*586 BC). Although rebuilt, then destroyed again by Syrians and Romans, the *Shekhina* had never returned and Jehovah had been left to rule alone—a feat which the mystics claimed he could not accomplish without the bride who was the source of his wisdom.

Having progressed through an inordinate length of time, the tenets of *Ha Qabala* were corrupted and confused in medieval Europe, and the emergent doctrine of the Kabbalists gained the upper hand. Their most important work was *Sefer ha Zohar* (*The Book of Splendour*)[32]—close to a million words of applied scriptural philosophy based on ancient Jewish traditions and written in a strange form of literary Aramaic.[33] It was compiled in 1286 by Moses de Leon in Castile, Spain, and its content was attributed to the 2nd-century Palestinian mystic Shimeon ben Yohai.[34] The *Zohar* is a commentary on the five books of Moses, and along with the Bible and the *Talmud* it was upheld as a venerated work by a majority of Jews in the Asian, African and European countries of the Diaspora for several hundred years.[35]

By the Middle Ages, the Jews had been hounded and persecuted for centuries by the papal Christian movement,[36] and since Jehovah was regarded as a traditional God of Wrath,[37] there was a deep seated requirement to reinstate the maternal aspect of their deity. The book of Numbers (21:14) actually mentions the ancient book of the Wars of Jehovah, which pre-dated the writing of the Old Testament, but was not included.[38] Other pre-biblical Hebrew texts mentioned but not included in the Old Testament are the book of the Lord (Isaiah 34:16) and the book of Jasher (Joshua 10:13, 2-Samuel 1:18).

What the Jews of that era needed in order to cope with their situation of dispossession was the feminine wisdom of the goddess, and there was a heightened leaning through these centuries towards the *Shekhina*.[39] They sought the return of the lost bride—a matron who could intercede between themselves and Jehovah, who had not actually treated them very kindly. He was their all-powerful tribal Lord and had promised the patriarch Abraham to exalt their race above all others, but their subsequent history had been full of hardship and misgiving. And so, in the *Zohar* tradition, the *Shekhina* acquired the new domestic style of *Matronit* (from the Latin, *matrona*,[40] denoting a motherly lady).

The vision of the *Matronit* was not so much a vision of Ashtoreth as one of her daughter Anath, the Queen of Heaven. In ancient Sumer, Anath was Inanna, in Syro-Phoenicia she was Astarte, while in Akkad she was Ishtar, sister to the Greek goddess Aphrodite.[41] Anath was a mistress of paradox—the personification of Venus, a goddess of love and war, who was both wanton and a virgin. But she was also the *Matronit* who had carried Moses to his secret burial place from Mount Nebo (Deuteronomy 34:5). Considered to represent both herself and Ashtoreth, Anath was the *Matronit* and the *Shekhina*, and the renewed union which the Zohar Jews sought between her and Jehovah was called *Tzaddig* (Righteousness).

Although not granted the right to a significant sister in the Hebrew tradition, Anath (Inanna) did indeed have an older sister in the Sumerian pantheon, and that sister was the formidable Eresh-kigal, Queen of the Netherworld.[42] Being the senior female in the line from Tiâmat the Dragon Queen, Eresh-kigal carried the paramount heritage of the Kingdom, which the Hebrews called the *Malkhut*. As the prevailing heiress of the *Malkhut*, Erish-kigal was likened to a precious jewel—a 'pearl'—a *luluwa* (the name of her granddaughter who became the wife of Cain). In his works concerning the *Zohar*, Gershom Scholem, Professor of Jewish Mystery Studies at the Hebrew University, Jerusalem, related in 1941 that the accounts of Eresh-kigal's daughter Lilith were wholly related to the tradition of the great Dragon—and the Dragon was the *Malkhut*.

Given that the Hebrews had ignored Eresh-kigal in favour of her younger sister Anath, a technical problem arose by virtue of Anath's perceived station as the *Shekhina-Matronit* because, in the Jewish Zohar it was the *Shekhina-Matronit* who bore the angel Metâtron, along with his sister Lilith.[43] But in the original Sumerian tradition, Lilith was the daughter of Erish-kigal, Queen of the Netherworld, while her younger sister Anath had no offspring.

The Metâtron (from *meta-ton-thronon*, meaning 'nearest to the divine throne'[44]) was Lilith's father, King Nergal (Meslamtaea), who (being the son of Enlil/*Eloh-YHWH*) was the counterpart of the Hebrew-Canaanite Baal (*see* Chart: *Grand Assembly of the Anunnaki*). Strictly speaking, Anath was not the traditional spirit of Wisdom (the Sophia), for this status was the pre-Hebrew prerogative of Eresh-kigal, and it was the inheritance of her daughter Lilith, whose name derived from *lilutu* (Akkadian-Assyrian: 'wind spirit').

Not only had the *Zohar* Jews made certain strategic adjustments to the family structure of the Mesopotamian pantheon (e.g. claiming Anath/Inanna as a daughter of Enlil/*Eloh-YHWH* instead of correctly portraying her as a granddaughter), but the Jews in general had also modified the Mesopotamian festival of *Shabattu*. This had been the monthly feast of the full-moon, but they had converted it to a weekly event, and had renamed it Sabbath.[45] The Sabbath was not just a day of rest, it represented the sacred Shabbat (from *Shabattu*), the innermost psyche of the Bride of Jehovah—the *Shekhina-Matroni*t. In exile since 586 BC, *Shekhina-Matronit-Shabbat* was said to roam the Earth awaiting her bridal reunion with Jehovah. Nevertheless, she continued to be the mother of her Israelite flock, and joined them every Friday evening at dusk to herald the Sabbath[46]—hence the traditional words of the ritualistic synagogue song *Lekha Dodi* (Come my Friend):[47]

> Come my friend to meet the Bride.
> Let us receive the face of Sabbath.
> Come, let us go to meet Sabbath,
> For she is the source of blessing,
> Pouring forth from ancient days.

It is at this very point of searching for the female aspect that the Talmudic tradition sits today. As we have seen, Jehovah was *YHWH*: the tetrad (four persons) of Father, Mother, Son and Daughter. But the Bride (the inheritance of the daughter) is still lost in exile, and so the deity remains simply *YHW*,[48] It is consequently maintained that only when reunited with his Bride (the *Shekhina-Matronit-Shabbat*) can God become complete as *YHWH* again.

# 12

# Heritage of the Wasteland

## A Faith of Fear

In figuratively combining the characters of Ashtoreth, Anath, Eresh-kigal and, by implication, Nîngal (the daughter of Ashtoreth and mother of Anath) the Judaeans of the Captivity had created a version of the One Goddess to complement the One God perception of the era. In religious terms this was a convenient strategy, but as a result the individual personalities of Sumerian history were eventually lost to the mysterious *Shekhina-Matronit*, who was not wholly identifiable since she was said to be missing in exile. This meant that, when Genesis was finalized, aspects of original Mesopotamian record had to be manipulated to suit the new situation, and although non-canonical works retained the tradition of Adam's first wife Lilith, only Eve was mentioned in Genesis. If Lilith had been brought into the approved picture then the whole concept of the 'first man' and the 'first woman', along with the One God and the One Goddess (the enigmatic Holy Spirit), would have been undermined.

In the midst of all this restructuring, Lilith posed a major problem for the scriptural Hebrews. She could not be identified with Jehovah or Adam in the Bible because her Anunnaki consort was known to be Enki-Samael, and he was the brother of Enlil-El Elyon who had become Jehovah. Clearly, in the new scheme of things, Jehovah could not be seen to have a brother—certainly not a brother who opposed him so strongly in social matters. But, historically, it was Enki (not Enlil) who had created Adam (Atabba) and Eve (Nîn-khâwa); it was Enki who had granted them rights to Qabalistic wisdom, and it was Enki who had appointed Atabba to his priest-kingly station. These things were known in Mesopotamia and Canaan; they were written down and readily available in the temple libraries of Babylon, and so they could not be ignored—but they could be reinterpreted. Enki, the wise hero of Sumer, could be portrayed (in accordance with his emblem) as a troublesome serpent—an image which could incorporate Lilith too, for she held the matrilinear heritage of the kingdom: the Malkhut, the sovereignty of the Dragon.

In the original Sumerian accounts, Enki and Enlil were often politically opposed, with Enki being more liberally inclined, whereas Enlil's nature was severe. As with political opponents today, neither was always right and for the most part their individual platforms were subject to the voting system of the Grand Assembly of the Anunnaki. But the Old Testament compilers changed all this in their stalwart and unbending allegiance to Enlil-Jehovah. To these children of Israel, Jehovah was always right. He had informed Adam that he would die if he ate from the Tree of Knowledge (Genesis 2:17), and although this was proven to be untrue, Jehovah was deemed to have been right. On the other hand, the serpent (Enki) who told the truth, explaining that Adam would not die from the fruit, but would become wise like the Elohim (Genesis 3:4-5) was deemed to be wrong—not only wrong, but evil for daring to be honest and contradictory.

This muddled and unparalleled concept of Jehovah being right when he was wrong, honest when dishonest, was born out of an inherent fear of his vengeful power and unbounded wrath. Whether as Jehovah (in Genesis) or as Enlil (in Mesopotamian record) it was he who had instigated the Semitic invasions which led to the 'confusion of tongues' and the fall of Sumer. It was he who had brought about the devastating Flood, and it was he who had levelled the cities of Sodom and Gomorrah—not because of their wickedness, as related in Genesis (18-19), but because of the wisdom and insight of their inhabitants, as depicted in the Coptic *Paraphrase of Shem.*[1] It was Jehovah who had removed the Israelites from their homeland, sending them into seventy years of captivity by King Nebuchadnezzar II and his five Babylonian successors down to King Belshazzer (545-539 BC).

But, why had Jehovah treated the Jews so badly, condemning them to bondage in a foreign land? Because, as explained in the book of 2-Kings (21:3), ex-King Manasseh of Judah had erected altars to Jehovah's son Baal. It mattered not that Manasseh's grandson, King Josiah, had destroyed these altars with the people's blessing (2-Kings 23:12); Jehovah decided to take his revenge in any event, saying, 'I will wipe Jerusalem as a man wipeth a dish ... and deliver them into the hand of their enemies .... They have provoked me to anger since the day their fathers came forth out of Egypt' (2-Kings 21:14-15). It is then explained that 'At the commandment of the Lord came this upon Judah, to remove them out of his sight for the sins of Manasseh, according to all that he did' (2-Kings 24:3).

For no reason other than Jehovah's personal revenge upon the actions of a long-dead king, the Holy City and Temple of the Jews were demolished, while the Israelites and their families (tens of thousands of them) were held hostage for many decades in an alien environment. Upon their return to Jerusalem and Judaea they had every reason to fear the retribution of Jehovah, but they turned this fear into outright veneration and absolute obedience—a veneration which set the scene for all that was to follow in the Jewish and Christian religions, whose disciples became classified as 'God-fearing'.

In 539 BC, King Cyrus II of Persia (Iran) had overthrown Babylon and seized the kingdom. He then married the Jewish Princess Meshar, while her brother Zerubbabel was allowed to lead the Israelite captives to freedom in 536 BC. As the centuries progressed, Babylon fell to various other invaders, including Alexander the Great of Macedonia, who died there in 323 BC.

Others came in from Syria and the Black Sea regions, and year upon year Babylonia was ravaged and dismantled, so that by about AD 600 the once great cities had been abandoned. The forsaken canals were dried up, irrigation had ceased and the fertile land became a desert waste.

At length, Babylon and the other Mesopotamian cities were buried beneath the piling silt and windswept sand of the desolate Plain of Shinar,[2] just as Pompeii had been buried beneath the volcanic ash and lava of Vesuvius in AD 79. The written legacy of the Anunnaki was, henceforth, confined to an underworld darkness, and all the tablets of Sumerian and Akkadian record that had been available to the hostage Jews of the 6th century BC were destined to be forgotten beneath the wasteland. In practice, however, they had been forgotten long before, during the period of general turmoil and upheaval.

And so it has been that for the better part of 2000 years, the Old Testament was the sole record of the Mesopotamian patriarchal era. There was no way for anyone to know whether it was fact or fiction, but since it had become the base work for religious cults that dominated Near Eastern and Western society through the centuries, it was taken on board as history. Not until the 1850s did explorers begin to find the first of the ancient cylinder-seals and clay tablets, and not until the late 1920s were major excavations and translations begun in Mesopotamia. At much the same time, from 1929, a large number of ancient Canaanite texts were found at Ras Shamra in north-western Syria.[3]

In the light of these latter-day discoveries, we are now far wiser than our parents and forebears, for we now have to hand the Sumerian and Akkadian documentation which enabled the Captivity Jews to compile their ancestral story. What we now know is that their biblical account was not an accurate transcript of ancient records, but a strategically compiled set of documents which distorted the annals of the original scribes in order to establish a new cultural and religious doctrine. This was the doctrine of the One God, Jehovah—a doctrine born out of fear, that was contrary to all tradition and historical record in the contemporary and preceding environments.

In consequence, the most apparent general criticism to be levelled against the Old Testament compilers is that they compacted a variety of understandable records into a single baffling record, while at the same time portraying an individual God as if he were separate from the prevailing pantheon. In the wake of this, however, mainstream Judaism has not been perpetuated as if it were a religion of fear, but as one of loyalty – while academic Judaism has constantly striven for a greater understanding of the philosophies behind the faith, with the *Midrash*, *Qabala*, *Zohar* and *Talmud* as continual sources of interest and debate.

If any religion has truly corrupted the original concept of Jehovah and the pantheon, then that religion is materialist Christianity. This is not the honest 1st-century Nazarene faith of Jesus, James and the Celtic Church, but the State religion contrived by Roman imperialists in the 4th century, from which there are now many competitive offshoots. This hybrid cult (a mixture of Pauline doctrine and pagan beliefs) not only brought a new awesome, omnipotent, omnipresent God to the fore, but it gave him self-styled personal representatives on Earth: first the Emperors, and then the Popes who thrived on being the ultimate bridges to individual salvation. In practice, this repressive cult, which threatens a future divine intervention against humankind, has evolved not as any faith that would have been recognized by Jesus, but as a form of medieval 'churchianity' based on the subjugating dogma of the bishops. Jehovah, the long-standing god of the Jews, was selected under particular circumstances and had a traditional heritage, but the unnamed God of modern Christianity evolved through Imperial invention. He is certainly not the God of Jesus, for this God was a sublime discipline of self-awareness that dwells within everyone and needs no bridge-building pontiff to lay down the rules of access.

## Lilith and the Dragon

Enki-Samael, being the brother of Enlil-Jehovah, was referred to by medieval Kabbalists as the Other God, and his marriage to Lilith is said to have been arranged by Taninvar the blind dragon.[4] However, Lilith was not only the wife of Samael and the first consort of Adam; she was also said to have become Jehovah's partner after the fall of the Temple of Jerusalem when the *Matronit* (Ashtoreth-Anath) was lost in earthly exile. Lilith, although holding the reins of the *Malkhut,* was acting handmaiden to the *Matronit,* and Jehovah was perceived to be degraded by his new liaison. Citing the book of Proverbs (30:23), the *Zohar* chastises Jehovah for making the handmaid 'heiress to her mistress' and asks, 'Where is his honour? The King without the *Matronit* is not called the King!'[5]

Because of this unwelcome coupling, Lilith was proclaimed to be an evil seductress who had beguiled Jehovah with her beauty and charm. From the time of a 10th-century Jewish document called the *Alphabet of ben Sira,* the Israelites' hatred for Lilith grew to such proportion that she has been portrayed as everything from a baby-snatcher to a vampire. That apart, the oldest records of Lilith (sometimes called Lili, Lilin, Lillake, Lilutu or Lillet) come from ancient Sumer and a terracotta relief from about 2000 BC shows her naked and winged, with the feet of an owl, standing upon two lions. Upon her head is the wrapped, multi-horned cap of the high-ranking Anunnaki,[6] and in each hand she holds the Rod and Ring of divinely measured justice[7]—a subject discussed more fully in *Realm of the Ring Lords.*

The Rod of Measure (or Rule, from which comes the authoritative term 'ruler') and the Ring of Eternal Justice were important symbols of the deiform guardians, and because of these the eminent Semitic scholar Dr Raphael Patai says of Lilith: 'Evidently, this is no lowly she-demon (as portrayed by the later Hebrews), but a goddess who tames wild beasts'.[8] Indeed, Lilith was Princess of the Netherworld, and was featured, along with Inanna (Anath), in the *Epic of Gilgamesh.* In a sequence from

Tablet XII, Lilith is said to have made her home within a *huluppu* tree ('probably a willow', states the translation) which belonged to her aunt and mistress Inanna.[9] At the base of the tree was the lair of a serpent (emblematic of Enki), and at the top was the nest of Zu the thunderbird.[10]

In terms of a career, no Anunnaki female ever achieved such an amazing rise to fame as Lilith. As the daughter of King Nergal and Queen Erish-kigal of the Netherworld, she was heiress to the *Malkhu*t, but was, nonetheless, the designated handmaid to her aunt, Queen Inanna. In this capacity, it was her task to gather the men from the streets of Uruk and to convey them to the ziggurat temple. When Adam, the earthling, was created by Enki and Nîn-khursag, Lilith was appointed his consort, but she refused to submit to the wifely role and fled from Adam to become the bride of Enki himself. As previously stated, Enki-Samael and Lilith were jointly regarded, in the Talmudic tradition, as being the epitome of the Tree of Knowledge. In later times, Lilith was said to be incarnate as Abraham's Egyptian mistress Hagar, as Moses's Midianite wife Zipporah and as King Solomon's most renowned lover, the Queen of Sheba (1-Kings 10). She then rose to become the queen-consort of her grandfather, Enlil-Jehovah.

Like Anath, Isis, Kâli and other goddess figures, Lilith was a paradox, being both spiritually dark and light—'black but beautiful'—and she is thus represented (in her Sheba incarnation) in the Old Testament's Song of Solomon (1:5). In *The Ginza*, the sacred book of the Gnostic Mandaeans of Iraq, Lilith of the Netherworld is called Lilith-Sariel, wife of Manda d'Hayye, the King of Light and Gnosis (the Knowledge of Life).[11] He was the equivalent of Iran's Ahura Mazda, the God of Life and Light, who was Enki to the Sumerians and Samael to the Hebrews.

From the very outset of her career, Lilith was regarded as an unusually free spirit, and because of this she was dubbed by the male-dominated Hebrews as being demonic: the original *femme fatale*. She was called 'the beautiful', but was said to be a promiscuous temptress of whom all men should beware. 'Why should I lie beneath you?' she had yelled at Adam,[12] 'I am your equal!' With that, the *Talmud* relates that she departed for the Red Sea (more correctly, the Reed Sea or Sea of Reeds[13]), 'a place of ill-repute'. Even the three angels (Senoy, Sansenoy and Semangelof) whom Jehovah sent to retrieve her were unsuccessful in their mission.

The Hebrews were not at all used to determined, liberated women like Lilith and it is hardly surprising that, despite all the vengeful things said against her, she has emerged in the modern age to represent the fundamental ethic of female opportunity. By the 1st century AD, the Jews were absolutely paranoid about the danger of Lilith, and it was even said that she was a nocturnal succuba, who would take sexual advantage of men while they were asleep. In order to take preventive action, a certain Rabbi Hanina decreed, 'It is forbidden for a man to sleep alone in a house, lest Lilith get hold of him!'

It was in its dealings with the heritage of Lilith that the Jewish Church of the Middle Ages came to shadow the Christian Church's denigration of Mary Magdalene[14]—and it was for the very same reason that she was proclaimed a wicked harlot and a sorceress.[15] Whereas Mary Magdalene was the wife of Jesus and the mother of the sacred bloodline (the *Sangréal*) from the 1st century, it was with Lilith—in descent from Tiâmat, Dragon Queen of the *Apsû* (the underground waters)[16]—that it all began. Hence, as senior heiress to the primeval Tiâmat, Lilith was likened to a serpent or a dragon. The term 'dragon' derives from the Greek *drakön* (meaning 'serpent'), while in Sumer the words *usumgal* (dragon) and *mûs-usumgal* (serpent) were metaphors of praise for a god or a king.[17] The Anunnaki hierarchs, Ningirsu (Ninurta) and Ningishzida were, for example, classified as Great Dragons.[18]

The joint legacy of the serpent and dragon was that of the prehistoric crocodile, the most sacred of all creatures, and the traditionally identified serpent should not be confused with the cold and venomous image conjured by the English word 'snake'.[19] The holy crocodile was Draco the mighty dragon of kingship, whence were named the Pendragons (Head Dragons or

High Kings) of the British Celtic kingdoms.[20] The first Pendragon was King Cymbeline of Camu-lôt (the sacred domain of 'curved light'—i.e. Camelot) AD 10-17, and the last was Cadwaladr of Gwynedd AD 654-64, whose dynasty introduced the famous Red Dragon of Wales.[21]

*Early Welsh Dragon.*

In ancient Egypt, the pharaohs were anointed in the Mesopotamian tradition with the fat of the sacred crocodile, who was epitomized by the god Sobek and was called the *Messeh*. In Mesopotamia, the equivalent noble creature was the *Mûs-hûs*,[22] a giant serpentine quadruped not unlike the great forked-tongued monitors still found in Africa, Arabia and the East, or the 10-foot (3 m) Komodo Dragon of Indonesia.

It is from the words *Messeh* and *Mûs-hûs* that the Hebrew stem *MSSH* evolved—the stem which (with added vowels) formed the verb *mashiach* (to anoint) and the noun *Meschiach* (Messiah), which means 'Anointed One'—i.e. King or Christ (Greek: *Kristos*).[23] This was a custom which began with Enki's anointing of the *Adâma* (King Atabba), an event detailed in the archives of Pharaoh Amenhotep III, who reigned about 1400 BC.

Although the term Messiah is generally applied to Jesus, it is correct to say that he was 'a' Messiah rather than 'the' Messiah, for all anointed kings of the line were Messiahs, and Jesus did not achieve his Messianic status until anointed by the priestess Mary Magdalene at Bethany in March AD 33.[24] As anointed Messiahs, the early *Sangréal* kings were deemed to retain the supreme prowess of the sacred crocodile—the kingly aptitude of the Messianic dragon.[25]

In the book of Ezekiel (29:3), the Egyptian pharaoh is called 'The great dragon that lieth in the midst of his rivers', and a victory song in honour of Pharaoh Tuthmosis III runs, 'Behold your Majesty in the likeness of a crocodile feared in the waters'.[26] Crocodiles (dragons), extant in the Nile and Palestine's River Zerka, were not only worshipped at centres such as Crocodilopolis, Ombos, Coptos, Athribis and Thebes, but they were also mummified and placed in royal cemeteries along with the pharaohs themselves.

# 13

# Gold of the Gods

## Star Fire

We shall soon be looking at the kingly bloodline as it progressed from Cain and his sons—the succession that was strategically ignored by the Hebrews and the Christian Church in favour of a parallel junior line from Adam's son Seth. Prior to this, it is necessary to understand the particular significance of the Cainite dynasty and to establish why it was shunned by the fearful disciples of Enlil-Jehovah.

In Genesis (4:17-18, 5:6-26) the lines of descent are given from Cain and from his half-brother Seth—but it is of interest to note that, through the early generations, the names detailed in each list are very similar, though given in a different order. In view of this, it has often been suggested that the line from Seth down to Noah was contrived by the Bible writers to avoid showing the true descent. But if this were the case, then something must have transpired during the lifetime of Noah to cause the heritage of his son Shem to be veiled—and the answer is found in Genesis (9:4). At that stage in the family's history, Jehovah is reputed to have said to Noah, 'Flesh with the life thereof, which is the blood thereof, shall ye not eat'—an edict which became expressly important to the later Jewish way of life. But why would Jehovah suddenly have become so obsessed with opposing the intake of blood, while allowing his subjects to eat flesh? Might this have been because of some particular tradition which did not suit his own pre-eminent objective? Researchers and writers, such as the modern philosopher Neil Freer, have cited that the apparent longevity of the Nephilim race was 'consistently and explicitly related to an ingested substance'.[1]

It has long been a customary Jewish practice to hang meat for bloodletting before cooking and consumption, but in contrast the Christian faith is especially concerned with the figurative ingestion of blood. In the Christian tradition it is customary to take the Communion sacrament (the Eucharist), wherein wine is drunk from the sacred chalice, symbolically representing the blood of Jesus, the life-blood of the Messianic line. Could it be, therefore, that the modern Christian custom is an unwitting throwback to some distant pre-Noah rite of actually ingesting blood? If so, then since we also know that the chalice is a wholly female symbol which has always been emblematic of the womb, might this even have been an extract from divine menstrual blood which, as we have seen (Chapter 10), was revered as life-giving 'Star Fire'? The answer to these questions is yes, that was precisely the custom—but it was not so unsavoury as it might seem.[2] Few of us think to enquire about the ultimate sources of many of today's bodily supplements, and those in the know are generally reluctant to tell us. The premarin hormone, for example, is made from the urine of pregnant mares, while some forms of growth hormone and insulin are manufactured from E.coli, a human faecal bacterium.

Before considering this ancient practice in detail, it is worth reminding ourselves that the edict to abstain from blood came not from Enki the Wise but from Enlil-Jehovah, the god of wrath and vengeance who had instigated the Flood, wrought havoc in Ur and Babylon and endeavoured to deceive Adam with regard to the Tree of Knowledge. This was not a god who liked people and the Sumerian records are very clear in this regard. If he forbade the intake of blood, this was not likely to have been an edict for the benefit of Noah and his descendants—it was most probably to their detriment.

The menstrual Star Fire (*Elixir Rubeus*) of the goddess, being essentially regarded as fluid intelligence, was symbolically represented as the All-seeing eye, or as the fiery cross of the *Rosicrucis*, precisely as depicted in the Mark of Cain. These emblems were later used by the mystery schools of ancient Egypt, particularly that of the priest-prince Ankhfn-khonsu (*c*.2170 BC) which was formally established as the Dragon Court by the 12th-dynasty Queen Sobeknefru.

Another of the most prominent mystery schools was the Great White Brotherhood of Pharaoh Tuthmosis III (*c*.1450 BC)—so called, it is often said, because of their white raiment, but actually named because of their preoccupation with a mysterious white powder. According to the Supreme Grand Lodge of the Ancient and Mystical Order Rosae Crucis, there were thirty-nine men and women on the High Council of the Brotherhood, who sat at the Temple of Karnak in Luxor.[3] A branch of this Order became more generally known as the Egyptian Therapeutate,[4] who, in Heliopolis and Judaea, were identified as the Essenes.[5] It was into this White Brotherhood of wise therapeutics and healers (the original Rosicrucians) that Jesus was later initiated to progress through the degrees, and it was his high standing in this regard which gained him the so often used designation of Master.[6] The term Essene stems from the Aramaic word *asayya*, meaning physician, which corresponds to the Greek word *essenoi*, while also denoting something *essaios*: that is, something secret or mystic.[7] (In the Norse tradition, the gods are called the Asen, the guardians of purity, and the word has a similar root.)

Along with the serpent emblem of eventual medical associations, the Star Fire symbol was also associated with therapeutic healing, and it is used today by the International Red Cross Agency.[8] In Christian Europe, it was misappropriated (in ignorance of its true symbolism) as the cross of St. George, who, supposedly, lanced and impaled a dragon. In the original tradition, the cross was identified with Enki-Samael who impregnated the Dragon Queen. As we have seen, kingship was matrilinear in the line from Tiâmat. Since bloodlines are, by their very nature, matrilinear, it is no coincidence that a mother in the animal kingdom is generally referred to as the 'dam'—as against the paternal 'sire'—for *dam* was indeed the word for blood. In chivalric circles, these parental definitions were adopted to become the familiar styles Sir and Dame. The dragon was manifest in the Draco constellation (known as the Serpent in the Sky) which swings around the North Pole, and its revolution constituted the earliest clock ever devised.[9]

In strict terms, the original Star Fire was the lunar essence of the Goddess, but even in a mundane environment menstruum contains the most valuable endocrinal secretions, particularly those of the pineal and pituitary glands. Interestingly (whether in fact or fiction), clotted menstrual blood has been literally portrayed as being collected by some medicine women of the Australian Outback, for it is reckoned to have extraordinary healing properties for open wounds.[10] In mystic circles, the menstrual flow-er (she who flows)[11] has long been the designated 'flower', represented as a lily or lotus. The brain's pineal gland in particular was directly associated with the Tree of Life, for this tiny gland was said to secrete the 'nectar of supreme excellence'—the very substance of active longevity, called *soma*,[12] or *ambrosia* by the ancient Greeks.

Earlier (Chapter 10), we saw that the serpent and the Tree of Knowledge were represented in the insignia of the American and British Medical Associations. However, various other medical relief institutions, worldwide, use two coiled serpents, spiralling around the winged caduceus of the messenger-god Mercury. In these instances, the central staff and serpents represent the spinal cord and the sensory nervous system, while the two uppermost wings signify the brain's lateral ventricular structures. Between these wings, above the spinal column, is shown the small central node of the pineal gland.[13] The combination of the central pineal and its lateral wings are referred to in some Yogic circles as the Swan, and this is emblematic of the fully enlightened being. It is the utmost realm of Grail consciousness achieved by the medieval Knights of the Swan, epitomized by such chivalric figures as Perceval and Lohengrin.[14]

In the hermetic lore of the ancient Egyptian mystery schools, this process of achieving enlightened consciousness was of express importance, with spiritual regeneration taking place by degrees through the thirty-three vertebrae of the spinal column[15] until reaching the pituitary gland which invokes the pineal body. The science of this regeneration is one of the Lost Keys of Freemasonry, and it is the reason why ancient Freemasonry was founded upon thirty-three degrees.[16]

*The double-serpent and caduceus emblem of the mystical Swan, as used by various emergency aid organizations throughout the world.*

The pineal is a very small gland, shaped like a pine-cone. It is centrally situated within the brain, although outside the ventricles and not forming a part of the brain-matter as such. About the size of a grain of corn (1/4 inch long, and weighing 1/30 oz), the gland was thought by the French philosopher René Descartes (1596-1650)[17] to be the 'seat of the soul',[18] the point at which the mind and body are conjoined. (Descartes was the discoverer of analytical geometry and the founder of the science of optics.) The ancient Greeks considered likewise, and in the 4th century BC, Herophilus described the pineal as an organ which regulated the flow of thought. The pineal gland has long intrigued anatomists because, while the brain consists of two main halves, the pineal (which sits centrally) has no counterpart.[19]

In the days of ancient Sumer, the Anuists perfected and elaborated a ramifying medical science of living substances, with menstrual Star Fire being a vital source component. In the first instance, this was pure Anunnaki lunar essence called Gold of the Gods, but later, in Egypt and Mediterranea, menstruum was ritually collected from sacred priestesses (the Scarlet Women) and was dignified as being the 'rich food of the matrix'. The very word 'ritual' stems from this custom, and from the Sanskrit word *ritu*—the 'red gold' (sometimes called 'black gold').[20] Endocrinal supplements are used by today's organo-therapy establishment, but their inherent secretions (such as melatonin and serotonin) are obtained from the desiccated glands of dead animals and they lack the truly important elements which exist only in live human glandular manufacture.[21]

In the fire symbolism of alchemy, the colour red is synonymous with the metal gold, and in the Indian *tantras* red (or black) is the colour of Kâli, goddess of time, seasons, periods and cycles.[22] One does not have to seek beyond the simplicity of the *Oxford English Dictionary* (under 'menstruum') to find the menstrual action described as being 'an alchemical parallel with the transmutation into gold'. The metals of the alchemists were, therefore, not common metals in the first instance, but living essences, and the ancient mysteries were of a physical, not a metaphysical nature. The word 'secret' has its origin in the hidden knowledge of these glandular *secret*ions. Truth (the ritu—redness or blackness)[23] reveals itself as physical matter in the form of the purest of all metals: gold, which is deemed to be terminally noble.

Just as 'secret' has its origin in a previous English translation of an ancient word, so do other related words have their similar bases. As already cited (Chapter 7), the word *amen* was used in Egypt to signify something hidden or concealed. The word *occult* meant much the same: 'hidden from view'—and yet today we use 'amen' to conclude hymns and prayers, while something 'occult' is erroneously deemed sinister. In real terms, they both relate to the word 'secret', and all three words were, at one time or another, connected with the mystic science of endocrinal secretions.

Since Kâli was 'black but beautiful', the English word 'coal' (denoting 'blackness') stems from her name via the intermediate words *kuhl, kohl* and *kol (see* Chapter 15). In the Hebrew tradition, the heavenly Bath-kol (or Bath-q'oul) was called the 'daughter of the voice', and the voice (*vach* or *vox*) which called from the blackness was said to originate during a female's puberty. The womb was resultantly associated with the voice (the *q'oul* or call), and Star Fire was said to be the oracular 'word of the womb', with the womb itself being the utterer or *uterus*.[24] In the earliest schools of mysticism, the symbol of the Word (or the *Logos*) was the serpent: the venerated emblem of the Holy Spirit—the dragon that moved upon the face of the waters.[25]

The Scarlet Women were so called because they were a direct source of the priestly Star Fire. They were known in Greek as the *hierodulai* (sacred women), a word later transformed (via medieval French into English) to 'harlot'.[26] In the early Germanic tongue, they were known as *horés* (later Anglicised to 'whores')—a word which meant quite simply 'beloved ones'.[27] As pointed out in *Skeat's Etymological Dictionary*, these words of high veneration were never interchangeable with such words as 'prostitute' or 'adulteress', and the now common association was a wholly contrived strategy of the Roman Church in its bid to denigrate the noble status of the sacred priestess.

The withdrawal of knowledge of the genuine Star Fire tradition from the public domain occurred when the science of the early adepts and the later Gnostic Christians was stifled by the forgers of historic Christianity. A certain amount of the original *gnosis* (knowledge) is preserved in Talmudic and Rabbinical lore, but generally speaking the Jews and orthodox Christians did all in their power to distort and destroy all traces of the ancient art.[28] The tradition of the Fire Virgins was later superficially adopted in Rome, where the six Vestal Virgins served for individual periods of thirty years, but the true significance of their purpose was lost. The word *vesta* derived from an old oriental stem meaning 'fire'—hence, matches are today still called 'vestas'. Vesta was originally a Trojan goddess of fire,[29] and burning tapers were used in the veneration of her eternal flame. It was this vestal custom which, in time, the Roman Church perverted to become the familiar candle-lighting ritual of modern 'churchianity'.

In addition to being the Gold of the Gods, the menstruum was also called the Vehicle of Light, being a primary source of manifestation,[30] and in this regard it was directly equated with the mystical waters of creation—the flow of eternal wisdom. The Light was also metaphorically defined as a serpent called *Kundalini*, said by the Indian mystics to be coiled at the base of the spine, to remain quite dormant in a spiritually unawakened person.[31] *Kundalini* (the magical power of the human organism) is awakened only by will, and blood is the vehicle of the spirit. The pineal gland is the channel of direct spiritual energy and can be motivated by constant self-enquiry.[32] This is not an obvious mental process, but a truly thought-free consciousness—a formless plane of pure being.

It was this very concept of 'being', or self-completeness, which posed a significant problem for Enlil-Jehovah. In contrast, his brother Enki-Samael knew that humans who partook of the Tree of Knowledge (the Anunnaki wisdom) and of the Tree of Life (the Anunnaki Star Fire) could themselves become almost like gods. Even Enlil-Jehovah had recognized this, saying 'Behold, the man is become as one of *us*' (Genesis 3:22). Nothing, it was said in olden times, is obtained simply by wanting, or by relinquishing responsibility to a higher authority. Belief is the act of be-living, for to be live is to believe, and will is the decisive medium of the self. This is the route to true knowingness, for the only personal god is the god within, and the self is God—the absolute consciousness (the *Kia* or *Ka*): the *YHWH*.

## The Plant of Birth

Let us now follow the story as it transpired from the very beginning. In so doing, we shall discover why the taking of Anunnaki Star Fire was so important, and also how its principal and beneficial constituents were eventually supplemented by chemical laboratory process, just as many of today's remedial substances are prepared.

To recap on our foregoing chapters, we have seen that Adam and Eve (jointly the *Adâmae* earthlings) were clinically created by Enki and Nîn-khursag through Enki's fertilization of human ova at the House of Shimtî, as detailed in the Sumerian records. Cain (*Q'ayin*) was the son of Eve by Enki-Samael, and his inherent Anunnaki blood was highly potent. Cain's wife was Luluwa, the daughter of Lilith of the Netherworld, heiress to the matriarchal *Malkû* (the kingship of the kingdom). She was of pure-bred Anunnaki stock and their sons, whom we have not yet encountered, were Atûn and Henôkh. As a result, their Anunnaki blood was further heightened. Atûn succeeded his father as the king in Kish (*c*.3500 BC). He is detailed in the Sumerian annals as King Etâna, the shepherd who ascended to Heaven and partook of the Plant of Birth in order to father his own son and heir King Balih.[33] The other son, Henôkh, is better known to us from the Bible as Enoch.

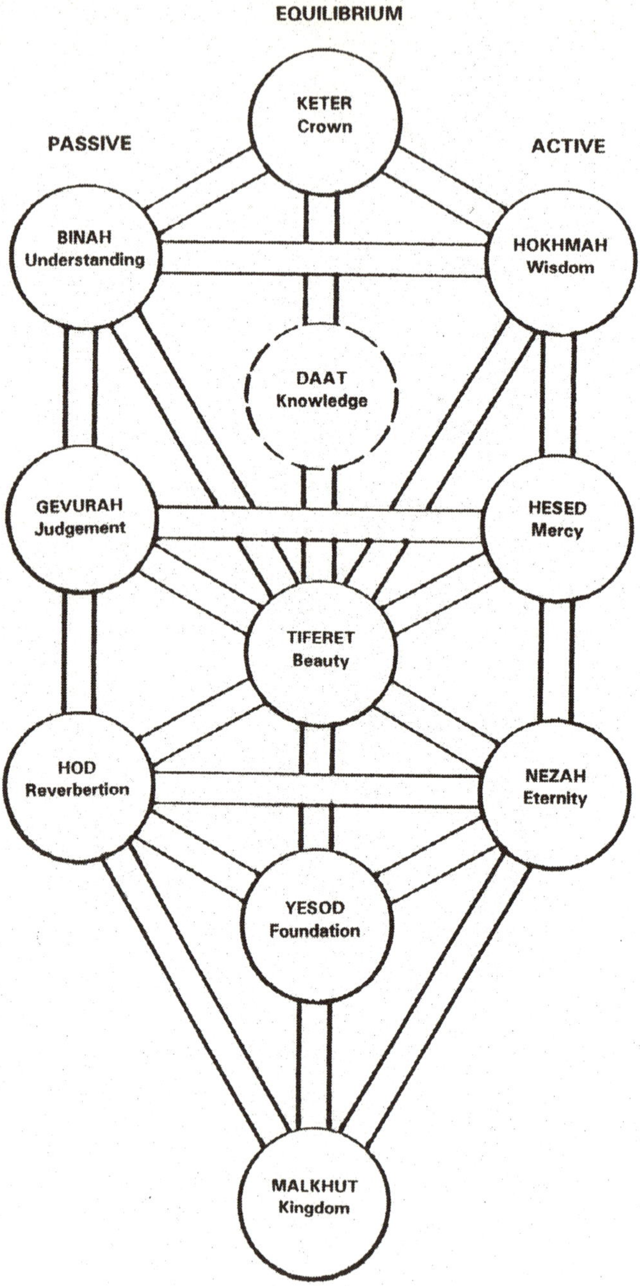


*The Kabbalistic Tree of Life, showing the cosmic spheres of the divine attributes.*

The Plant of Birth was synonymous with the Tree of Life, which was directly associated with longevity and the office of kingship. It was also related to Star Fire and pineal-gland activity. Thus, partaking of the Plant of Birth was the equivalent of taking the extract of Star Fire—the potent Anunnaki female essence: the 'nectar of supreme excellence' called the *Gra-al* (later the Graal or Grail).[34] In this regard, the goddess was held to be the 'cup-bearer', the transmitter of the power of the Anunnaki. She was also called the Rose of Sharon (from *Sha*, meaning 'Orbit' *(see* Chapter 7), and from *On* relating to the Light—or relating in Egypt to the Heliopolis temple-city of Annu and Ra, called the House of the Sun[35]—hence, *Sha-Ra-On*). As previously detailed, the flower (*flow-er*) was identified as a lily and these two descriptions come together in the Bible's highly esoteric *Song of Solomon*, wherein the Messianic bride states, 'I am the rose of Sharon and the lily of the valleys' (2:1).

Only in very recent times have medical scientists identified the hormonal secretion of the pineal gland. It was isolated in 1968, and became known as melatonin, which means 'night-worker' (from the Greek *melos* = black, and *tosos* = labour) because people with a high melatonin output react strongly to sunlight which affects their mental capability. By virtue of this, they are night operatives, and melatonin is called the 'hormone of darkness', being produced only at night or in the dark.[36] (Blind people produce above average melatonin, which heightens their senses other than sight.) Exposure to an excess of natural light makes the pineal gland smaller and lessens spiritual awareness, whereas darkness and high pineal activity enhance the keen intuitive knowledge of the subtle mind, while reducing the stress factor.

Melatonin is manufactured by the pineal gland through an activated chemical messenger called Serotonin. This transmits nerve impulses across chromosome pairs at a moment (called *meiosis*) when the cell nuclei are divided and the chromosomes are halved, to be combined with other half-sets upon fertilization.[37] Melatonin also enhances and boosts the body's immune system, and those with high pineal secretion are less likely to develop cancerous diseases. High melatonin production heightens energy, stamina and physical tolerance levels, and it is directly related to sleep patterns, keeping the body temperately regulated with properties that operate through the cardiovascular system. It is the body's most potent and effective antioxidant, and it has positive mental and physical anti-ageing properties.[38]

Gold was a traditional symbol of kingship, while pine resin (identified with pineal secretion: melatonin) was often used to make frankincense (the incense of priesthood). Hence, gold and frankincense were the traditional substances of the Priest-Kings of the Messianic line, along with myrrh (a gum resin used as a medical sedative), which was symbolic of death. In the ancient world, higher knowledge was identified as *daäth* (whence, death), and the terms 'tomb' and 'womb' were considered interchangeable and mutually supportive as routes to the higher knowledge.[39] The New Testament describes how the three substances, gold, frankincense and myrrh, were presented to Jesus by the ascetic Magi (Matthew 2:11), thereby positively identifying him as a dynastic priest-king of the Grail succession.

The pineal gland is impregnated by eternal ideas, and gives us the possibility of formulating our own conceptions. It is an organ of thought by means of which we acquire inner perception and can thereby change eternal ideas into earthly conceptions. Yoga masters associate the pineal gland with the *Ajna Chakra* (Sanskrit: *ajna* = command; *chakra* = wheel). Chakras are energy centres corresponding to each of the glands of the endocrine system and Yogis believe that the pineal is a receiver and sender of subtle vibrations which carry thoughts and psychic phenomena. (Endocrine glands, named from the Greek verb 'to arouse', are ductless glands which secrete directly into the bloodstream.) The pineal is also known as the Eye of Wisdom, the chakra of the mind, of heightened self-awareness and inner vision,[40] representing the ability to see things clearly with intuitive knowledge.

The Pineal Eye (the Third Eye) is a metaphoric eye, but it is found as a physical, seeing entity between the brain and skull cavity of many lizards. Hinduism claims that everyone has a Third Eye—an all-seeing channel for sacred powers, located centrally behind the forehead. In fact, the Third Eye is an anatomical reality in its status as the pineal gland. Yogic teaching suggests that the Pineal Eye is significant in the process of becoming aware, for this is the ultimate source of light out of darkness—the secret *ayin*.[41] A spiritual person will automatically perceive with the Third Eye, the subtle eye of insight, rather than be duped by mundane eyes which identify only physical presences. Such presences are defined by their place within arbitrary time, but to the pineal graduate there is no time to calculate, for he/she lives in a dimension where time and space are of little consequence.

The activities of the pineal gland are directly related to those of the pituitary gland, another small body at the base of the brain. The frontal lobe of the pituitary stimulates the intellectual centres in the frontal lobe of the brain, while the dorsal lobe of the pituitary affects the base of the brain where are situated the centres of poetic inspiration and exalted aspiration.

We are all surrounded and bombarded by thought-fields, and the thoughts we claim as our own are like a continuous universal broadcast. Some thoughts are cosmic in origin, while others are like local stations.[42] The pituitary gland is the primary radio-receiver, channelling all wavebands and frequencies. It transmits selected frequencies (through secretions) directly to the pineal gland, which then amplifies certain broadcasts for transmission throughout the body.[43] The pineal gland has total control over what it will and will not transmit through its controlled manufacture and release of the melatonin hormone. High melatonin production thereby increases the facility for receiving and transmitting high-frequency cosmic and local broadcasts, and leads to a greater state of cosmic awareness—a state simply of 'knowing'. In this regard, it is interesting to note that the Pineal Third Eye has been found to contain very fine granular particles, rather like the crystals in a wireless receiving set.[4]

# 14

# The Phoenix and the Fire-stone

## The Hidden Manna

The Cainite kings of Mesopotamia—the first Pendragons of the Messianic bloodline—while already being of high Anunnaki substance, were, therefore, fed with extracts from Anunnaki Star Fire to increase their perception, awareness and intuition, so that they became masters of knowingness, almost like gods themselves. At the same time, their stamina levels and immune systems were dramatically strengthened so that the anti-ageing properties of the regularly ingested Anunnaki melatonin and serotonin facilitated extraordinary lifespans. All records of the era confirm that this was the case—and in this regard there is no reason to be over-sceptical about the great ages of the patriarchs given in the book of Genesis.

In the canonical Bible, we are told that, during the lifetime of Noah, Jehovah issued the edict which forbade the further ingesting of blood—at least this was the time-frame applied to the edict by the Old Testament compilers in the 6th century BC. It is unlikely that this was the correct time-frame, however, for Enlil-Jehovah would have had no such final authority over Enki-Samael and the Grand Assembly of the Anunnaki. Even so, it is pertinent to note that, from that time, the Bible's given ages of the patriarchal strain begin to diminish quite considerably, so that from the days of Abraham and Isaac we are presented, in the main, with rather more normal lifespans. In contrast, the lifespans of the Sumerian kings in descent from Ar-wi-um the Cain and Etâna continued at a generally high level.[1]

What we do know beyond doubt is that whatever the realities of the edict and its chronology, a major shift in the Star Fire practice became necessary in about 1960 BC. This was when Terah, along with his son Abraham and family, moved northwards from Ur to Haran because their city had been overturned, and the Anunnaki had departed 'like migrating birds'. Whatever had taken place up to that point, there was then a significant change in circumstance because the Anunnaki Star Fire was no longer available and a substitute had to be found. It appears that this was not a problem, for this was the province of the hitherto trained Master Craftsmen—the great metallurgists who had followed the tradition of Tubal-cain (Genesis 4:22)—and the principle, as laid down in their archives was straightforward: 'To make gold, you must take gold'.[2]

In consideration of the Bible's New Testament symbology, it is of particular interest to note that, having established the reason for Jesus being presented with gold, frankincense and myrrh, his father, Joseph ab Heli, was recorded in the early Gospels as being a Master Craftsman. In modern English-language Bibles, Joseph is described as a 'carpenter'—but this is a blatant mistranslation. The word 'carpenter' was wrongly derived from the Greek *ho-tekton* (derived from the Semitic *naggar*[3]), which actually meant a Master of the Craft. This denoted that Joseph was not a woodworker but a learned alchemical metallurgist in the manner of his ancestral forebears.

In the Old Testament book of Exodus, at the time of Moses, we are introduced to a certain Bezaleel (son of Uri Ben Hur), who is said to have been filled with the spirit of the Elohim in wisdom, understanding and knowledge. We learn, furthermore, that Bezaleel was a skilled goldsmith and craftsman (Exodus 35:30-31), and that he was placed in overall charge of building the Ark of the Covenant and the Tabernacle. In detailing how Bezaleel should manufacture various crowns, rings, bowls and a candlestick, all of pure gold, the Bible text adds to the list something called *shewbread* (Exodus 25:29-31), and without further explanation the deed is seen to be done (Exodus 39:37). This sequence is recalled in the New Testament book of Hebrews, which states (9:1-2) that at the first Covenant there were, within the holy confines of the Tabernacle, a candlestick and a table with the shewbread. It is pertinent to note that the Lord's Prayer specifies, 'Give us this day our daily bread'. This is often taken to relate to sustenance in general terms, but in the old Gnostic tradition the reference was more specifically directed to the enigmatic shewbread of the Covenant.

The book of Leviticus returns to the subject of the shewbread (although not specifying it by name), and states, 'Thou shalt take fine flour, and bake twelve cakes thereof .... And thou shalt put pure frankincense upon each row' (24:5-7). However, the use of the word 'flour' in English translations is misleading; and the word 'powder' would be better used for, as pointed out by the Russian-Jewish psychiatrist Dr. Immanuel Velikovsky, 'shew-bread was obviously not of flour, but of silver or gold'.[4] This is especially significant because in the book of Exodus it is stated that Moses took the golden calf which the Israelites had made, 'and burnt it in the fire, and ground it to a powder, and strawed it upon the water, and made the children of Israel drink of it' (32:20). In this instance, the correct word 'powder' is used—but firing gold does not, of course, produce powder; it simply produces molten gold. So what was this magical powder that was fed to the Israelites on that occasion?

Through the regular use of Anunnaki Star Fire, the kingly recipients had been moved into realms of heightened awareness and consciousness because of the inherent melatonin and serotonin. This was the realm of advanced enlightenment (the dimension of the orbit of light) which was called the Plane of Sharon (a style later corrupted and misapplied to the coastal Plain of Sharon in Israel),[5] and the Star Fire gold was deemed to be the primary route to the Light. The mundane person (lead) could thus be elevated to a heightened state of awareness (gold) – and this was one of the roots of alchemical lore by which base metal was said to transmute into gold.

A fact worth mentioning here is that it becomes apparent from the Bible text that the shewbread of the Covenant remained a prerogative of the priests from the time of Moses. When David of Bethlehem became King of Israel some generations later he was allowed to take the shewbread, but the priest who afforded the privilege to David made the point that it was not a kingly entitlement (1-Samuel 21:3-6). The New Testament Gospels support this by confirming that even though David was the king, his partaking of the shewbread was unlawful.[6] This had not been the case in the kingly line from Cain, nor was it the case for the Egyptian kings of that same Messianic line. The shewbread was also a traditional entitlement of the early pharaohs, for they were fully consecrated priest-kings of the Dragon succession. Whether male or female, the practice was observed, because, in the true scheme of things, the distinctions of king and queen were entirely synonymous. Earthly kingship (the *Malkhut*) was *kainship* and queenship was *q'ayinship,* both titles deriving from Cain (Q'ayin/Kain). The word 'kinship' (with *kin* meaning 'blood relative') has a similar origin.

Let us now consider that other mystical food known as *manna*. We know from the Scriptures that manna was distinct from shewbread, but that does not mean they were wholly disassociated. What, then, do we know of manna? Perhaps a good place to look is in the *Antiquities of the Jews,* as compiled by Flavius Josephus in the 1st century AD. In relating the story of Moses and the Israelites in Canaan, Josephus explains that the manna was first identified when it lay upon the ground and 'the people knew not what it was, and thought it snowed'.[7] He continues, 'So divine and wonderful a food was this .... Now the Hebrews call this food manna; for the particle man, in our language [relating to *man-hu,* whence *manna*], is the asking of a question: What is this?'[8]

The Bible's equivalent passage in Exodus (16:15) states that 'When the children of Israel saw it, they said to one another, It is manna, for they wist not what it was, And Moses said unto them, This is the bread which the Lord hath given you to eat'. Subsequently, the manna is described as being white, resembling seed, and with a sweet taste like honey (Exodus 16:31). Moses had referred to it as bread, but still the people asked, 'What is it?'

In actual fact, this particular manna which fell to the ground like snow, and which was continually eaten by the Israelites in Sinai (Exodus 16:16-36), was a resinous secretion from the tamarisk plant[9]—a well attested, natural phenomenon of the region.[10] The tamarisk manna used by the Israelites during that period was, however, quite distinct from the manna of gold which they were afforded only once when the golden calf was burned (Exodus 32:20). This was the substance used in the manufacture of the shewbread, and the manna of gold was generally reserved for priests.

Priesthood was first introduced into the Israelite fraternity in Sinai at the time of Moses and Aaron, but the priestly concept came out of Egypt and was originally Sumerian. As identified in the Egyptian *Book of the Dead*—the oldest complete book in the world[11]—the pharaohs had been taking the white manna of gold from the third millennium BC. This was the truly mystical, alchemical manna that was placed in the Ark of the Covenant by Aaron (Exodus 16:33-34), and in the New Testament book of Revelation (2:17) it is said, 'To him that overcometh, I will give to eat of the hidden manna, and will give him a white stone, and in the stone a new name written which no man knoweth saving he that receiveth it.' In the much later European Grail tradition of the Middle Ages, a similar passage appears in the romance of *Parzival* by Wolfram von Eschenbach. It reads:

> Around the end of the stone, an inscription in letters tells the name and lineage of those, be they maids or boys, who are called to make the journey to the Grail.

> No one needs to read the inscription, for as soon as it has been read it vanishes.[12]

At Chartres Cathedral in France, the statue of Melchizedek, priest-king of Salem, depicts him with a cup containing a stone in representation of the bread and wine which he evidently offered to Abraham (Genesis 14:18). The wine, as we know, was representative of the sacred Star Fire, but the importance of the imagery is that the bread is held 'within' the cup, thereby signifying that the Star Fire was replaced by a substitute nourishment at the very time of Melchizedek and Abraham. The substitute was the white powder derived from gold, and this was the main ingredient for the original cakes of shewbread.

In ancient Egypt, the equivalent of shewbread was schefa-food, and this was always depicted as a conical (shem-shaped) cake. It was used to feed the light-body, as against the physical body, and the light-body was deemed to be the consciousness. A bas-relief at the great Temple of Amen at Karnak details the gold and silver spoils of Pharaoh Tuthmosis III, and in the seventh row a conical object bears the inscription 'White Bread'.[13] This is in accordance with the hieroglyph for bread as defined in the Ashmolean Museum's book of *Egyptian Grammar*.[14] In parallel with this, the *ayin* symbol of the secret eye re-emerges as the Egyptian hieroglyph for the Light,[15] while also representing time and the sun.

As far back as 2180 BC, the pharaohs were using the schefa-food to enhance their pineal activity and thereby heighten their perception, awareness and intuition—but only the metallurgical adepts of the mystery schools (the Master Craftsmen) knew the secret of its manufacture. These adepts were operational priests, and the High Priest of Memphis held the title of Great Artificer.[16] As formerly related, the overall process of rejuvenation was conducted through a programme of thirty-three degrees and, to facilitate the process, the hermetic philosophers taught initiates how to prepare a miraculous 'powder of projection' by which it was possible to transmute the base human ignorance into an ingot of spiritual gold.[17] In the *Book of the Dead*, the pharaoh in search of terminal enlightenment asks, at every stage of his journey, the overriding question, 'What is it?'—which in the Hebrew language was expressed in the single questioning word, *Manna*?

## Legacy of the Master Craftsmen

We can now relate back to an item which we considered earlier (Chapter 9) when we saw that the ancient Sumerians had venerated a mysterious substance called 'highward fire-stone'—a metallic enigma cited as being *shem-an-na*. When phonetically corrupted, this becomes the very equivalent of shewbread (*she*[w]*manna*).

It is significant that we now discover all of these attributes reappearing in relation to the exotic food of the pharaohs and Grail kings. This magical 'bread of life' was conically shaped in a *shem* replication; it was made from the white manna of gold (a shining metal: *an-na*) and it was a substitute for the Anunnaki Star Fire. Furthermore, it was identified in biblical and Grail lore as being of stone, while in both traditions it was associated with the bearing of individual 'names', known only to the recipients. A reason is perhaps now beginning to emerge for the Bible translators referring to *shems* as 'names'.

Whether considering the stone in the cup of Melchizedek, the white stone of the book of the Revelation, or the mysterious stone of the Grail Castle, we are at all times concerned with an aspect of that which is called the Philosophers' Stone. In both spiritual and romantic lore, the mystical stone is often associated with a name, or names, known only to those who receive the power of the Stone—and a name is to be identified with a *shem*, or with the bright metal of the 'highward fire-stone', the *shem-an-na*.

In alchemical tradition and practice, the Philosophers' Stone is said to be that which transmutes base metal into gold. This is deemed to be the case both in the metallurgical sense and in the spiritual sense of higher enlightenment. We shall return to the subject of physical transmutation later, but let us first consider a function of the Stone which relates to the differently determined identities of gold itself. There are, in fact, two contrasting forms of physical gold—the straightforward metal as we know it, and a much higher (or 'highward') state of gold. The latter is gold in a different dimension of perceived matter, the white powder of gold, the hidden manna, whose secret was known only by the Master Craftsmen.

In the alchemical document called the *Rosarium Philosophorum*, the hidden stone was described in terms of geometry: 'Make a round circle of the man and the woman, and draw out of this a square—and out of the square a triangle. Make a round circle, and you will have the stone of the philosophers.'[18]

The concept of a stone relies wholly upon the perception of the beholder. It is rather like the proverbial 'half-cup of water': to some the cup is half empty, but to others it is half full. Hence the image of a stone to some would be perhaps a pebble, while others would immediately visualize a gem. In the famous Grail romance of *Parzival: The Spiritual Biography of a Knight* (*c*.1200) it is said of the Temple knights of Grail Castle that

> They live by virtue of a stone most pure. If you do not know its name, now learn: it is called lapis exilis. By the power of the stone the phoenix is burned to ashes, but the ashes speedily restore it to life. The phoenix thus moults and thereupon gives out a bright light, so that it is as beautiful as before.[19]

Many have wondered about the name *lapis exilis*[20] because it appears to be a play on words, combining two elements. First, it is *lapis ex caelis*—'stone from the heavens' (the emerald gem of Venus), and, secondly, it is *lapis elixir*—the *lapis philosophorum*, the very Philosophers' Stone itself. Either way, in the context of the Phoenix, it relates to the *shem-an-na* of the 'highward fire-stone', the shewbread of the exotic Star Fire substitute.

In practical terms, the substitute became necessary when the Anunnaki departed the Mesopotamian nest, but the Master Craftsmen had been well trained. The direct Star Fire ritual continued by replacing the Anunnaki providers with high-bred priestesses called Scarlet Women—but the hormonal secretions were weaker from this source, and they continued to weaken through the generations. For the kingly succession, the craftsmen perfected the technique of producing the white powder of gold, which had a distinct advantage. Instead of giving immediate hormone supplements from an outside source, the exotic food had a stunning effect on the pineal and pituitary glands, whereby the recipients produced their own super-high levels of melatonin and serotonin.

The key to the *Parzival* allegory lies in the description of the Phoenix 'burned to ashes'—but from those very ashes comes the great enlightenment. So, what exactly is the Phoenix? One might answer that it is a mythical bird (the bennu-bird) which burned to a powder in the Temple at Heliopolis and was resurrected in a blaze of light. Heliopolis was a centre of the Essene therapeutics and the Great White Brotherhood of Master Craftsmen. But *phoenix* is actually the ancient Greco-Phoenician word for 'crimson' or 'red-gold'.[21] The Greek historian Herodotus (*c*.450 BC) claimed that the Phoenix represented the red and gold of the setting and rising sun. The Phoenix is in fact the utmost symbol of the *ritu*, the red-gold which burns to a powder: the *shem-an-na* of the 'highward fire-stone'.

Alexander the Great of Macedonia (356-323 BC) was said to have owned a Paradise Stone which gave youth to the old.[22] This stone, a medieval Jewish scholar explained, would outweigh its quantity of gold—but when converted to dust, even a feather would tip the scales against it. Mathematically, this was written as $0 = (+1) + (-1)$. This appears to be a very straightforward sum at first glance, because $(+1) + (-1)$ does indeed equal 0. But when applied to physical matter it is an impossibility because it relies upon using a positive and an equivalent negative to produce 'nothing'.

*Ezekiel's Vision* by Sir Peter Robson

Sumerian figurines of Anunnaki from *c*.3000 BC

5000 year-old electrum gold Sumerian helmet of King Mes-kalam-dug
(identified with Tubal-cain the Vulcan)

Golden headdress of Queen Shub-ad of Ur
(identified with Naamâh, daughter of Akalem *c*.3200 BC)

yrian gold pendant of Astarte *c*.1450 BC

Lord Enki and the Plant of Birth

Ahura Mazda relief at the Persopolis in Persia
(identified with Sumerian god Enki/Samael)

Assyrian relief of the god Ashur
(identified with Sumerian Enlil and Hebrew Jehovah)

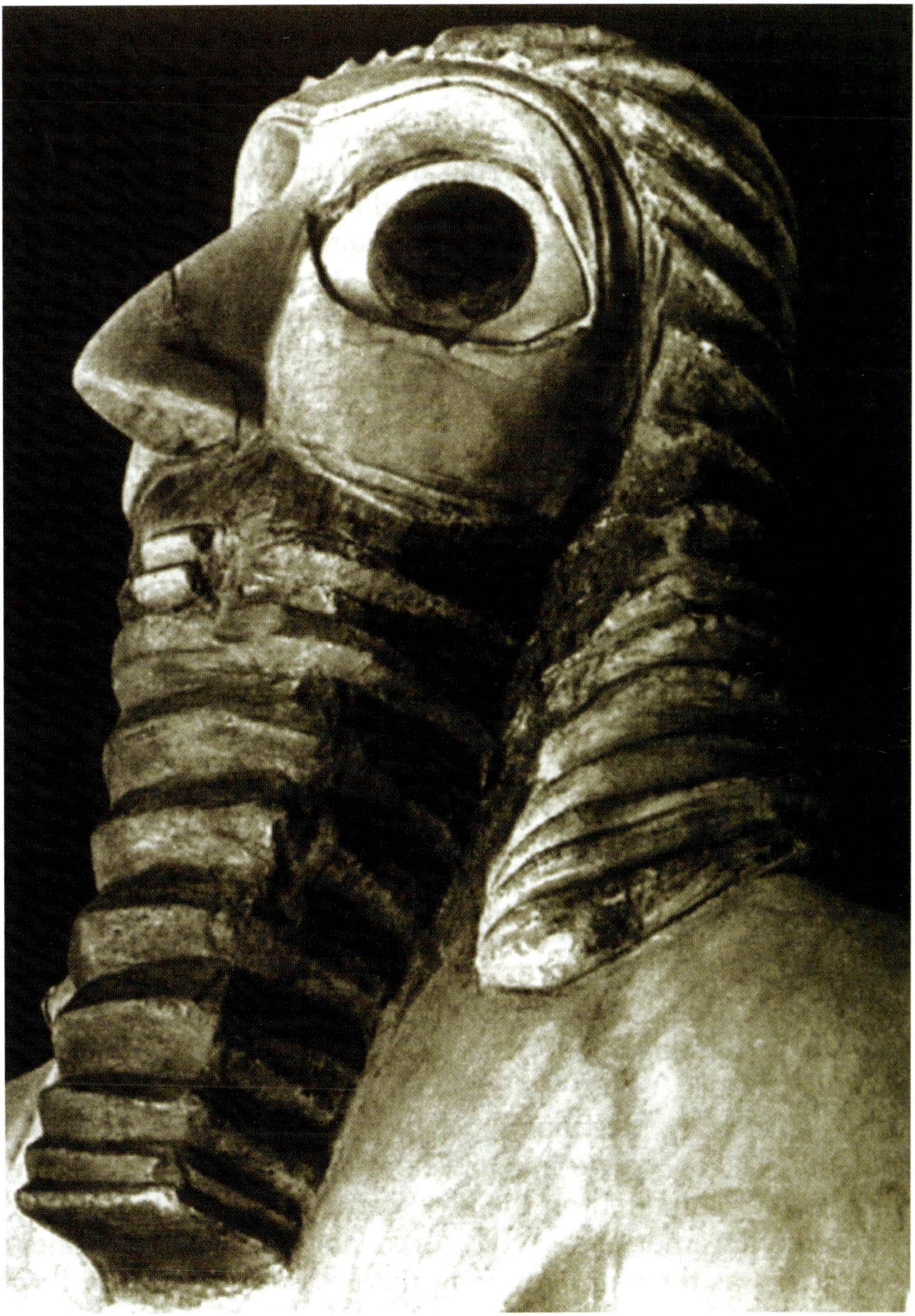

Sumerian depiction of Anu, Lord of the Sky *c*.3000 BC

Lilith of the Netherworld, Consort of the Gods
Sumerian relief *c.*2000 BC

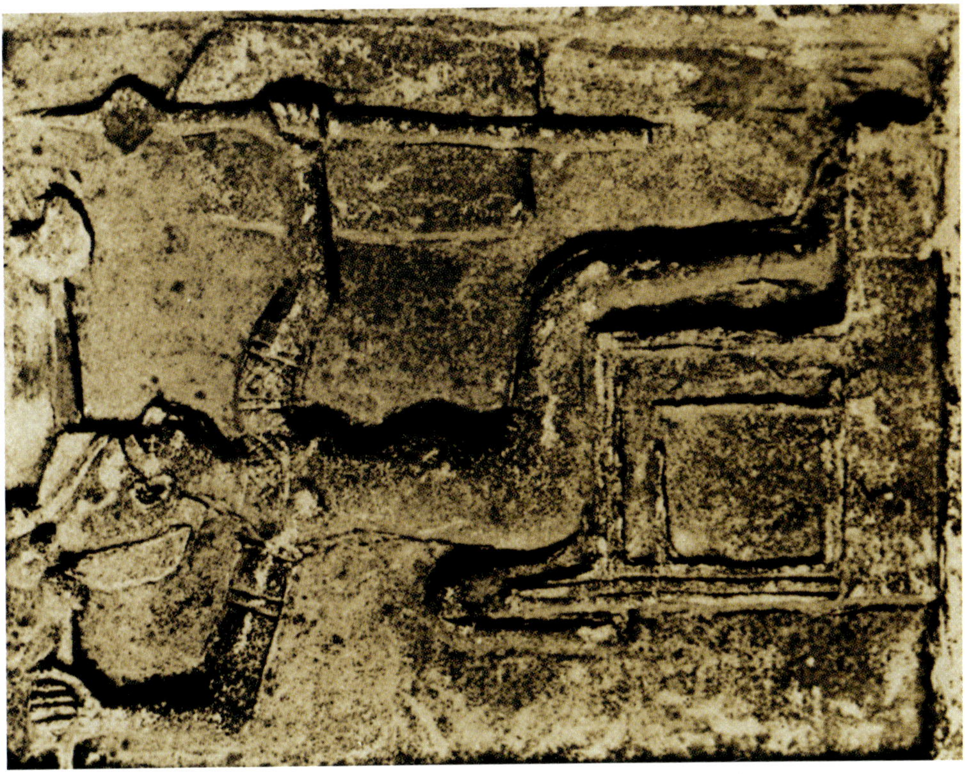

Anath, Queen of the Heavens
Canaanite relief of the daughter of El Elyon

Sumerian house at Ur in the time of Abraham
*c.*2000 BC

King Ur-nammu of Ur 2113-2096 BC
(Abraham's great-grandfather Raguel was married to Ur-nammu's daughter)

Sumerian priestly figure (early 3rd millennium BC)

Babylonian woman (2nd millennium BC)

Pharaoh Amenhotep IV (Akhenaten) - abdicated *c*.1361 BC
(identified with the biblical Moses)

Moses and the Tables of Testimony
(6th-century Byzantine fresco)

Moses depicted with horns at the tomb of Pope Julius II
Statue by Michelangelo 1475-1564

Mycenean Star Fire chalice with fallopian Gra-al design
13th century BC

Mery-khiba (Meryamon) of Egypt, junior queen of Akhenaten *c.*1362 BC
(Identified with the biblical Miriam)

Sobek, the crocodile god
Great Messeh of Egypt

Melchizedek, Priest-king of Salem *c*.1950 BC,
with the chalice of the Highward Fire-stone
(Statue at Chartres Cathedral, France)

The heights of Mount Serâbit el-Khâdim in Sinai
(identified with the biblical Mount Horeb)

Ruins of the mountain temple of Moses at Sinai

Hathor pillars at the North doorway of the Mount Horeb temple

Entrance to the Inner Temple at Mount Horeb, Sinai

Statuette head of Queen Tiye of Egypt, mother of Moses
(discovered at the Sinai temple, Mount Horeb)

Model reconstruction of the Mount Horeb temple site

The moment one has a positive piece of something it is not possible to add an equivalent negative of that same something to produce nothing. At best, one could move the positive something to somewhere else so that it was out of immediate sight, but it would still exist and it would therefore not be nothing. The only way to turn something into nothing as far as the material world is concerned is to translate the something into another dimension so that it physically disappears from the mundane environment. If such a process were achieved, then the proof of achievement would lie in the fact that its weight also disappears.

What then is it that can outweigh itself, but can also underweigh itself and become nothing? What then is it that can be gold, but can be turned to powder? It is the Phoenix that will burn to dust but will then be restored to enlightenment. It is the golden calf that Moses burned to ashes and fed to the Israelites. It is the stone of the hidden name, the *shem-an-na*, the 'highward fire-stone'—and, as the records determine, the Sumerian fire-stone of the Master Craftsmen was not of stone at all, but of shining metal.

So, given the facilities of today's scientific advancement and our knowledge of atoms and nuclei, is it possible (as it was in the distant past) to convert gold into a sweet-tasting, ingestible white powder? Is it possible for that powder to outweigh its optimum weight of gold? Is it also possible for that same powder to underweigh itself and to weigh less than nothing? Under such circumstances, is it possible that the powder can disappear from sight into another dimension of space-time and then be returned to its original state? The answers to each of these questions is 'yes'—for this is the post-Star Fire mystery of the Phoenix, and it is the key to the Messianic bloodline enhancement through the fire-stone. As to why the fire-stone was called 'highward' by the ancient Mesopotamians, we shall now discover as we enter the realm of high-spin metallurgy.

## The Transmutation of Gold

Before commencing this section, it must be stressed that because of the potentially dangerous nature of an enterprise which deals with high-spin atoms, the explanations will be purposely veiled and guarded. The following is, therefore, presented as a general overview, without detailing specific weights, temperatures, conditions or laboratory burn-times. This will prevent any ill-advised experimentation by unqualified enthusiasts and will avoid the contravention of prevailing international patents which govern the practice.

To begin, we should consider statements concerning the Philosophers' Stone made by the alchemists Lapidus and Eirenaeus Philalethes: 'The Philosophers' Stone is no stone, but a powder with the power to transmute base metals into gold and silver'.[23] Also:

> The stone which is to be the transformer of metals into gold must be sought in the precious metals in which it is enclosed and contained. It is called a stone by virtue of its fixed nature, and it resists the action of fire as successfully as any stone – but its appearance is that of a very fine powder, impalpable to the touch [imperceptible, like talcum powder], fragment [imperfect] as to smell, in potency a most penetrative spirit, apparently dry, and yet unctuous, and easily capable of tingeing a plate of metal. The stone does not exist in nature, but has to be prepared by art, in obedience to nature's laws. Thus, you see our stone is made of gold alone, yet it is not common gold.[24]

Each of these testimonies refers to the enigmatic stone being, in actuality, a fine powder, and in talking of the precious metals within which the stone is contained, modern practitioners refer not only to gold and silver but also to those metals which comprise the platinum group. These metals, along with platinum itself, are palladium, iridium, osmium, rhodium and ruthenium—and because of their ultimate strengths they are used in surgical, optical and dental instruments, crucibles and thermocouples, machine-bearings, electrical switch contacts and all manner of precision devices down to the tipping of needles and pen-nibs.

The metal that in jewellery manufacture is commonly known as 'white gold' is an alloy of gold coupled with palladium, which is said to have been first discovered in Brazil, California and the Urals in 1803, and was named after the asteroid Pallas in that year. Iridium, osmium and rhodium are also given the same date of discovery, with ruthenium following in 1843. However, the platinum-group metals were not truly discovered in the 19th century; this was when at least one of them, namely iridium, was rediscovered, for iridium was originally a key fire-stone of ancient Sumer. Because of its bright silvery colour and the then non-invention of its latter-day name (applied in 1803 by virtue of its iridescence), the mysteriously described shining metal was long presumed from the old records to have been tin.

Iridium is a very rare element on Earth, but geologists have discovered its existence in quantities up to thirty times the norm in crust layers where extraterrestrial meteorites containing the substance have landed in the distant past.[25] Iridium is, therefore, not so uncommon outside our own planet. The Sumerians and ancient Egyptians clearly knew about the properties of gold and of how to alloy it with other noble metals. The Master Craftsmen were adepts too in the workings of iridium, which, just like gold, could be taken to the exotic 'highward' state of the *shem-an-na.*

This means that they not only knew and worked with these metals, but that they understood the science of atoms and nuclei—for the 'highward' state of the white powder is only achieved through knowledge of the high-spin metallurgical experience. Only by understanding this part-physical and part-metaphysical science can one take a physical something and turn it into nothing by applying the principle of 0 = (+1) + (-1). Interestingly, the high-spin powder of gold has a distinct effect upon the pineal gland and its increased melatonin production, while the equivalent powder of iridium has its similar effect on the serotonin production of the pituitary gland.

Although the current names of the platinum-group metals are relatively new to us, the metals themselves are far from new. Recent tests have shown that, by dry-matter weight, over 5 percent of our brain tissue is composed of iridium and rhodium in the high-spin state.[26]

So, what precisely is the highward or high-spin state which converts these noble metals into an impalpable white powder? A normal atom has around it a screening potential—a positive screening produced by the nucleus. The majority of electrons going round the nucleus are within this screening potential, except for the very outer electrons. The nucleus goes to the highward or high-spin state when the positive screening potential expands to bring all of the electrons under the control of the nucleus.

These electrons normally travel around the nucleus in pairs—a spin-forward electron and a spin-reverse electron. But when these come under the influence of a high-spin nucleus, all the spin-forward electrons become correlated with the spin-reverse electrons. When perfectly correlated, the electrons turn to pure white light and it is quite impossible for the individual atoms in the high-spin substance to link together. On that account, they cannot naturally re-form as metal, and the whole remains simply a white powder.[27]

In simplistic terms, the white powder is created by striking the metal sample, under strictly controlled conditions for a pre-calculated time, with a designated high-heat—perhaps from a DC arc: a single directional current from two electrodes. But the truly unusual thing about the powder is that, through continuous sequences of heating and cooling, its weight will rise and fall to hundreds of percent above its optimum weight, down to less than absolutely nothing. Moreover, its optimum weight is actually 56 percent of the metal weight from which it was transformed. So, where does the other 44 percent go? It becomes nothing but pure light, and translates into a dimension beyond the physical plane. This conforms precisely with the formerly mentioned Alexandrian text which states that, when placed in the scales, the Paradise Stone can outweigh any of its quantity of gold, but when it is converted to dust (powder), even a feather will tip the scales against it.

In the first edition of *Bloodline of the Holy Grail*,[28] the question was posed as to how the Knights Templars and the alchemists of Omar Khayyám were able to make the uniquely luminous coloured glass of the *Notre Dame* cathedrals in 12th-century France. They claimed their secret to be the *Spiritus Mundi*—the 'breath of the universe'—and this is now known to have been the white light of the Paradise Stone, for the glass was made from metals. When the white powder of a highward metal is subjected to a specific heat, it transforms immediately to glass and the metal concerned will determine the individual colour and qualities of the glass. Not only is wonderfully clear glass produced by this method, but the missing 44 percent light (the *Spiritus Mundi*) reappears within the glass, which then returns to its optimum 100 percent metallic weight. This proves, of course, that the 44 percent never actually disappeared: it simply moved into a state of weightlessness.

An experiment conducted in the USA in the late 1970s made apparent the effect of the mystical white light in open-air conditions, without the controls of vacuums and inert gasses necessary for contained results. In this test the substance completely disappeared in an enormous blaze of light equivalent to some 50,000 flash-bulbs. It was, in effect, an explosion, but there was absolutely no blast, and an unsupported pencil (that was stood on end within the explosion) was left standing upright afterwards.[29]

Another feature of the white powder is that even its 56 percent substance (that is the sample excluding the 44 percent light content) can be made to disappear completely from sight, moving itself into another dimension. At that stage of experimentation (which, incidentally, can be wholly reversed), not only does the invisible substance weigh less than nothing, but the pan in which it was sitting also registers less than its zero-point starting weight. This particular aspect of the fire-stone's ability has some quite stunning consequences, as will be discovered when the latter stages of our investigation move into the anti-gravitational sciences of ancient Egypt.

In the *Scientific American* journal of May 1995, the effect of the platinum metal ruthenium was discussed in relation to human DNA. It was pointed out that when single ruthenium atoms are placed at each end of double-helix DNA, it becomes 10,000 times more conductive. It becomes, in effect, a superconductor.[30] Similarly, the *Platinum Metals Review*[31] features regular articles concerning the use of platinum, iridium and ruthenium in the

*Alchemical medallion of the Hidden Stone. the first letters of the outer legend words (Visita Interiore Terræ Rectificando Invenies Occultum Lapidem) spell the word 'Vitriol' – a glassy sulphate. This relates to the Oleum Vitrie – the oil of glass which is the highest essence of antimony.*

treatment of cancers, which are caused through the abnormal and uncontrolled division of body cells. When a DNA state is altered, as in the case of a cancer, the application of a platinum compound will resonate with the deformed cell, causing the DNA to relax thoroughly and become corrected. Such treatment involves no amputation surgery; it does not destroy surrounding tissue with radiation, nor kill the immune system as does chemotherapy. It is a straightforward cure which actually corrects altered cells, and doubtless we shall hear more about this from the medical establishment in due course. Or shall we? It is hardly in the financial interests of the influential drug companies. More likely, we shall be advised about it from other sources.

It is of particular significance that, irrespective of all today's costly and extensive research in these areas, the secrets of the highward fire-stones were known to our ancestors many thousands of years ago. They knew that there were superconductors inherent in the human body; they were the elements of our consciousness, or the light-body (the *ka*).[32] They knew that both the physical body and the light-body had to be fed,[33] and the ultimate food for the latter was called *shem-an-na*. This was manufactured by the priestly Master Craftsmen of the temples for the express purpose of deifying the kings.

It is known that both iridium and rhodium have anti-ageing properties, while ruthenium and platinum compounds interact with the DNA and the cellular body. It is also known that gold and the platinum metals, in their monatomic high-spin state, can activate the endocrinal glandular system in a way that heightens awareness and aptitude to extraordinary levels. The highward *shem-an-na* is capable of defying gravitational attraction, and it would appear that it perhaps activates the body's so-called 'junk DNA', along with the generally unused parts of the brain.

We have now stepped beyond the bounds of the Bible to witness the alchemical and scientific process which facilitated the genesis of the Grail Kings. This dynastic line from Cain (through the kings of Sumer and the pharaohs of Egypt) to King David and onward to Jesus was purpose-bred to be the earthly purveyors of the Light. They were the true sons of the gods, who were fed first on Anunnaki Star Fire from about 3800 BC, and afterwards on high-spin metal supplements. In short, they were bred to be leaders of humankind, and they were both mentally and physically maintained in the highward state.

In the context of the foregoing, we have dealt with a particularly straightforward aspect of the Philosophers' Stone, but in strict terms the enigmatic Stone has a much wider sphere of operation, being a product of the true application (called the Great Work) of alchemy. To the masters of this 'once and future science' the Philosophers' Stone is known as the Great Tincture. So far we have seen how gold can itself be transformed into a higher state, but in a future book of this Grail-related series we shall delve into the fascinating physical and metaphysical virtues of alchemical procedure to discover how the Stone can actually facilitate the base transmutation process. Meanwhile, it is important to note that alchemy is directly related to the sovereign lore of the Dragon, while the female and male ouroboros symbols are carried within the most ancient of hermetic regalia, along with the chalice of the Grail.

Around the Alchemical Medallion of the Hidden Stone (and as repeated on some *Temperance* Tarot cards) is the legend, 'Visit the interior parts of the Earth; by rectification shalt thou find the hidden stone'. Within this emblematic disc, the sun (soul) and moon (spirit) pour their essences into the chalice which sits above the Venus crescent and ouroboros. This emblem represents the Philosophical Mercury. Below this is the Ring of Plato, signifying the Stone in the centre of the Earth, and this is suspended upon the Golden Chain of Homer. Beneath the ring is the Orb which identifies the Antimony *(see* Chapter 15), and this is used in the rectification process to produce the Stone—the Great Tincture of alchemy.

15

# Vulcan and the Pentagram

## Hero of the Good Land

When detailing the line of descent from Eve's son Cain, the Bible is very sparing (Genesis 4:17-18), naming only one of his sons, Enoch, followed by Enoch's successors, Irad, Mehujael, Methusael and Lamech. In parallel with this line is given the descent from Eve's son Seth (Genesis 4:26, 5:1-25) and, with the addition of two extra generations, this line also reaches a Lamech:

| | |
|---|---|
| Cain | Seth |
| Enoch | Enos |
| | Cainan |
| | Mahalaleel |
| Irad | Jared |
| Mehujael | Enoch |
| Methusael | Methuselah |
| Lamech | Lamech |

The Sethian line includes a certain Cainan (whose name is a variant of Cain), along with Enos, who appears to have no direct counterpart—but apart from these digressions, the lists contain a near replication of names. This has led to suggestions that perhaps one of the lines was contrived by the Old Testament compilers, and since the Cainite succession was historically more important in kingly terms, then the obvious line to have been contrived would be the line from Seth. The fact remains, however, that although Cain's was the line of kingship, Seth's line was a dynasty of priesthood, with Lamech's son in that succession being Noah, the Righteous One (the *Tzaddik*), as he is called in the *Zohar*.[1] A *tzaddik* was, in essence, the Jewish equivalent of a saint.[2]

There appears to be little doubt that the line to Noah, and thence to Abraham, was descended from Seth as explained in Genesis, but it is entirely possible that the given names from Seth to Lamech were, in some measure, purloined from the Cainite listing in order to add weight to the early patriarchal succession. It is from the word *tzaddik* that the dynastic priestly title of Zadok emerged, ostensibly from the time of King David (2-Samuel 8:17). In extant manuscripts of early New Testament texts, both Jesus and his brother James are identified as *tzaddiks*.[3]

The tenets of ancient Dragon lore confirm that, from the earliest of times, the Cain succession was perpetuated without any marital association with the Sethian strain (*see* Charts: *Ancestral Lines of Tubal-cain and Noah*, and *Descents from Lamech and Noah*). In this way, its Anunnaki blood was kept as pure as possible, and it was this Cainite kingly line, the line of the *Rosi-crucis*, that was fed with the Star Fire essence of the goddess. In contrast, the Sethian line was of a more mundane heritage, and for this reason the post-Genesis writers endeavoured to heighten the image of this strain from the time of Noah by designing a story which suggested that Noah was not the natural son of Lamech.

Earlier in our investigation (Chapter 5), we saw that, from about the 2nd century BC, a body of original Hebrew literature was embellished and rewritten to suit the emergent Greco-Alexandrian mythology of the era. These new writings had little to do with history, but were more concerned with romance, and their authors took the opportunity to add a little mystery to some fairly straightforward characters and events.

Among these colourful works, we find an Aramaic document which Israeli scholars have dubbed the *Genesis Apocryphon*. This dates from around the turn of the BC-AD era, at the time of Herod Antipas, and it was discovered in 1948 at Qumrân, Judaea. Unlike the majority of Dead Sea Scrolls unearthed at that time, the Genesis Apocryphon was not preserved in a sealed jar and its sewn leather sheets were in very poor condition.[4] It has been possible, though, for some fragmentary extracts to be translated. These are written in a pseudo-autobiographical style, with characters like Lamech and Abraham appearing to convey their stories in the first person. This made it entirely possible for some of the gaps in the Old Testament narrative to be filled with additional material relating to patriarchal figures, including Noah, whose birth was mentioned, but not detailed, in the Bible. Here was the perfect opportunity to uplift the physical status of Noah by implying that he was perhaps the son of an angel (a Nephil or Watcher).

The tale relates that Noah was so pale and beautiful when born that Lamech doubted that he was the natural father, stating,

> Behold, I thought in my heart that the conception was from the Watchers, and that from the holy ones was the [ ]. And my heart was changed within me because of this child. Then I Lamech, hastened and went to Bath-Enosh [my] wife, and I said to her, By the Most High, by the Lord of greatness, by the King [ ], tell me in truth with no lies [ ].

In this particular text, although the suggestion of Noah's angelic status is made, Lamech's wife responds negatively to the accusation:

> When Bath-Enosh my wife saw that my face upon me was changed [ ], then she mastered her emotion and spoke to me, and said [ ] 'I swear to thee by the great Holy One, by the King of Heaven, that this seed is truly

> from thee, and this conception is truly from thee, and this childbearing is truly from thee [ ], and from no other; neither from any of the Watchers, nor from any of the sons of heaven'.[5]

In practice, it would appear that the object of the exercise was defeated in the telling, but the suggestion of Noah's Nephilim extraction was strategically made and the truth of the matter rested with whether the response of Lamech's wife could be trusted. The doubt was well enough cast to prompt another work on the subject, the *Book of Noah*. This book, of which fragments are preserved in Latin and Ethiopic, makes rather more of Lamech's dilemma by explaining that the baby Noah was 'whiter than snow, and redder than the flower of the rose; the hair of his head whiter than wool, and his eyes like the rays of the sun'.[6] Yet for all this, it is said in the final event that Noah was truly the son of Lamech and, once again, Noah is left very firmly in the line of Seth (the son of Adam and Eve). That this line was mundane is denoted from the very beginning when it is said that Seth begat Enos (Genesis 4:26), for *enos* was the common Hebrew noun for 'man'.[7]

As for the other Lamech (the descendant of Eve and Enki-Samael), Genesis explains that he had two wives, one of whom (Adâh) bore him two sons, and the other (Zillâh) bore a son and a daughter (Genesis 4:20-22). Adâh's first son was Jabal, who was said to be the 'father of such as dwell in tents'; according to the *Journal of Near Eastern Studies,* this designation is of express significance because the Mesopotamian records tell us precisely who these tent-dwellers were. In 1942 the ancient *King List of Khorsabad* was published, detailing the first succession of seventeen kings in Assyria, and these kings were referred to as 'those who dwell in tents' outside the city of Assur.[8]

Jabal's brother was Jubal, said to be 'the ancestor of all who handle the lyre and pipe',[9] while his half-brother Tubal-cain (son of Zillâh) is described as 'an instructor of every artificer in brass and iron'. As pointed out in the Hebrew *Anchor Bible*, the use of the word 'iron' is, of course, an anachronism (since this was some while before the Iron Age) and should more correctly read 'metal'. Indeed, Tubal-cain was the greatest metallurgist of the age and has long been revered as a great patriarch of the Master Craftsmen.[10]

Before investigating this family in greater detail, it is worth considering the commentary notes in the *Anchor Bible*, because these set the scene for the family's historical position, in contrast to the English-language Bibles which pay little attention to the Cainite succession. The sources for this section of Genesis date from the third millennium BC, and the *Anchor* text confirms that the background to this genealogical data cannot be divorced from Mesopotamian kingly traditions.[11] The Hebrew name Methusael (father of Lamech) has its Akkadian root in *Mûtu-sâ-îli* (Man of the God), and Lamech is a variant (almost an anagram) of the Sumerian name Akalem.

So, was there a prominent Sumerian king of the Cainite succession called Akalem, who ruled sometime after 3500 BC? There certainly was: his tomb was discovered by Sir Charles Leonard Woolley among the sixteen royal graves of the pre-dynastic kings (*lugals*) of Ur.[12] This notable king was Akalam-dug,[13] and the magnificent helmet of his son Mes-kalam-dug (Chapter 3) is an outstanding example of the goldsmith's art.[14] The great Vulcan and Master Craftsman of the era was Tubal-cain, the son of Lamech (Akalem-dug), and Tubal-cain is to be identified with King Mes-kalam-dug, the designated 'Hero of the Good Land'. His wife, Nîn-banda, was the daughter of A-bar-gi (Abaraz), Lord of Ur, whose grave Woolley also found, and the wife of Lord A-bar-gi was Queen Shub-ad of Ur, a matriarchal dynast of Dragon descent from Lilith. Shub-ad (also known as Nîn Pu-abi) is better known to us from Genesis as Naamâh the Charmer, the daughter of Lamech and Zillâh (*see* Chart: *Ancestral Lines of Tubal-cain and Noah*).

It can be seen, therefore, that the successions from Cain ruled their various kingdoms from Ur in southern Mesopotamia to Assur in the north, and they were the most prominent sovereign line of the era, holding the original heritage of the *Malkhut*. Yet for all this prominence, and indeed because of it, the Bible writers elected to ignore these mighty dynasts in favour of supporting a parallel line of descent from Adam's son Seth. There were a number of reasons for this, but the main purpose was to disguise the true heritage of a subsequent member of the Cainite family – a son of Tubal-cain who was the key Sumerian link to the early pharaohs of Egypt. This Egyptian connection was not welcomed by the Hebrew scribes because they sought to portray a clean Adamite succession to David and the eventual kings of Judah - a patriarchal line that did not incorporate the matriarchal legacy of the Dragon Queens. As a result, the relevant son of Tubal-cain (Mes-kalam-dug) was said to have been a son of Noah, and was then conveniently discredited, as had been his ancestor Cain. This son was the biblical Ham.

## Ham and the Goat of Mendes

The book of Jubilees explains that Noah's wife was Emzarah, and Genesis (5:32) tells that she bore him three sons, Shem, Ham and Japhet. Following the events of the Flood, it is said that Noah became drunk from the wine of his vineyard and was discovered in a state of nakedness by Ham. No reason is given as to why Noah should not have been naked within his own tent, but evidently Shem and Japhet rushed in to cover him with a garment. Then, when Noah was awake and sober, he learned that Ham had witnessed his naked state and because of this he placed a curse on Ham's son Canaan.

The significance of this strange and seemingly unjust curse has never been satisfactorily explained. Neither is it made clear why Ham is at that stage called Noah's youngest son (Genesis 9:24),[15] when he has hitherto been portrayed as the middle-born son (Genesis 5:32, 6:10). A positive cultural distinction is drawn, nevertheless, between Ham and Shem at the time of the curse, with Shem alone being granted access to Jehovah, while Ham's son Canaan is denounced for no apparent reason: 'Cursed be Canaan; a servant of servants shall he be to his brethren.... Blessed be the Lord God of Shem, and Canaan shall be his servant' (Genesis 9:25-26).

As identified in the *Anchor Bible*, this whole sequence 'supplies more questions than answers'.[16] In fact it supplies no answers at all, but a reasoning is found in the more accurate tradition that Canaan was a son (not a grandson) of Noah, while Ham was not a member of that family at all. It was from Canaan that the 1st dynasty of Babylon descended, and this posed a real problem for the Hebrew compilers of Genesis who were themselves held captive by the kings of Babylon. The Babylonian heritage had to be discredited, and the curse took care of that by denouncing the Canaanites, while at the same time making it possible to overawe the powerful Hamite strain with the Shemite succession in the ensuing list of thoroughly confusing begettings. Had Ham been correctly listed as the historical son of Tubal-cain, this subterfuge would not have been possible and Ham's important grandson Nimrod could not have been sidestepped, as he was, with just a passing mention (Genesis 10:9-10).

In strict terms of sovereign genealogy, the line of Ham and Nimrod (in descent from Cain, Lamech and Tubal-cain) held the true heritage of Grail kingship, while the Sethian line through Noah and Shem were of lesser standing, although rising to positions of city governorship in the generations immediately before Abraham. The heritage of Ham was so important to Messianic history that an escutcheon was devised and prominently used in documents as late as the *Stemma Jacobi* of the 1630 *Genethliacon*, held in the Rosicrucian archive. Not surprisingly, these Hamite Arms incorporate a dragon within the field, and the *Genethliacon* was dedicated to Charles I Stuart, during whose reign the *Invisible College* (later Britain's scientific Royal Society) was established in 1645.

When considering the biblical kingdom of Ham's grandson Nimrod the Mighty (Chapter 3), we identified the various

Mesopotamian cities of his domain. Having now reached the age of Nimrod in our chronological sequence, it is necessary to establish his references outside the Bible—especially since the Hamite lineage has become so crucial to the history of the Grail bloodline. In this regard, one of the most important entries concerning Nimrod comes from the *Targum*, a collection of ancient Aramaic writings relating to the Old Testament that were collated in the 1st century. Aramaic was the language of the Aramaeans, who were established in Mesopotamia in the 13th century BC, and who spread into Syria and Palestine a little later.[17]

The *Targum*[18] relates that Nimrod was the father of an Egyptian pharaoh, but does not give his name. However, a separate Ethiopic text[19] refers to another pharaoh who was contemporary with Nimrod, phonetically calling him Yanuf. This pharaoh is easily identifiable. His name is correctly written as Anedjib (phonetically Yanuf), and he was a king of the 1st dynasty of Egypt, reigning about 3000 BC, at precisely the time of Nimrod.

Not long after the reign of Anedjib (in about 2890 BC) a new dynasty emerged in Egypt, and with this family the heritage of Nimrod was cemented very firmly into place. We are left in no doubt of this, because it was King Raneb, the second pharaoh of the dynasty, who first introduced the veneration of the Goat of Mendes into Egypt.[20] This is especially relevant because in both the Grail and Dragon traditions (which are fundamentally one and the same), the Goat of Mendes has always been directly associated with Nimrod's grandfather Ham. Mendes was a city just north-west of Avaris in the Egyptian delta and the sacred goat (often called Khem, Chem or Ham) was the zodiacal goat of Capricorn. In accordance with the Dragon Court tradition, Ham was the designated Archon of the Tenth Age of Capricorn and in this regard his symbol was an inverted pentagram. This five-pointed star has two uppermost points, which are the horns of the Goat of Mendes. The two downward-sloping side-points represent the ears and the single base-point is the chin and beard,[21] as identified by Chevalier David Wood in his outstanding studies of sacred geometry.

When a pentagram is seen in this inverted (male) position, Khem is personally identified by an emerald jewel set centrally at the meeting of the horns. When turned about, the pentagram achieves its female status with the uppermost single point becoming the head of the goddess in a Venus-Lilith representation. The horizontal side-points are now arms, while the twin points (once the horns) are now at the base, being the legs of the goddess, with the jewel of Venus established in the vulval position. Sometimes, the inverted Khem representation is shown with flames rising (between the horns) from the sacred jewel; these flames are called Astral Light. But when reversed into the Venus position, the uterine flames are identified as Star Fire, the universal essence of the goddess.

From the earliest times, whether representing Astral Light or Star Fire, the pentagram was indicative of enlightenment and was associated with the pre-Jewish Sabbath, a ritualistic period of reflection and experience outside of general toil. For this reason, Khem of Mendes was called the Sabbatical Goat, from which derives today's use of the word 'sabbatical' in academic circles. Like the serpent, the goat was symbolic of attainment, and it was by no chance that the 16th-century artist Albrecht Dürer placed a goat centre-stage, with the serpent, in his allegorical portrayal of Adam and Eve.

In view of this age-old tradition, it is hardly surprising that the pentagram and sabbatical goat became associated with heterodox Christians (like the Cathars of Languedoc) from medieval times. In contrast, the orthodox Christian Church endeavoured to overawe the old wisdom of the mystery schools by creating a hybrid religion based upon salvation from the unknown—a salvation that was attained only through people's subjugation to the authority of the bishops. As an outcome, the spiritually based doctrines of the gnostic movement (which sought to discover the unknown) were declared blasphemous by the Inquisition, while the pentagram and the goat were denounced as symbols of black magic and witchcraft.

From those times (even to the present day in some Church-influenced circles), personal attainment and learning which does not conform to bishops' opinions has been considered heretical, and individually acquired wisdom became so feared that the Goat of Mendes has been decried as the epitome of the very devil himself. This is manifest in a wealth of trashy propagandist novels wherein crucifixes and holy water abound as the weapons used against the so-called emissaries of Satan.

The Goat of Mendes was also directly associated with alchemy, and although the word 'alchemy' derives from *al-khame*—the science of overcoming the blackness (*see* Chapter 10)—it had a secondary root in *al-Khem* (the Khem). In this regard, Khem, the black ruler of Mendes, was identified with a certain Azazel of Capricorn, whom the book of Enoch defines as a Watcher. It is said in Enoch that Azazel made known to men 'all the metals, and the art of working them ... and the use of antimony'[22] (otherwise known as *stibium* [Sb] Element no.51). This is an essential ingredient of the preparatory alchemical process when producing the Philosophers' Stone. In the ancient Arab world antimony was called *kuhl* (or *kohl*). The related word 'alcohol' stems from the Arabic *al-kuhul*, the highly refined Philosophical Mercury prepared from spirits of wine rectified over antimony.

Azazel also appears in the Bible, but not in the authorized English-language translation. In the *Vulgate's* book of Leviticus (16:8) there is an early reference to the custom of Atonement (Hebrew *kippur*—from the Assyrian *kuppir*[23]), stating that Aaron shall cast lots upon two goats, 'one for the Lord, and the other for Azazel'. That which fell to the lot of the Lord was to be sacrificed as a 'sin offering' and the other was to be sent into the wilderness as an 'atonement'. The more familiar English translation is somewhat confusing, for the name Azazel has been supplanted by the word 'scapegoat'. The reason for the substitution was simply that the original sequence made it quite clear that offerings were made both to Jehovah and to Khem-Azazel, while the book of Enoch (strategically excluded from the Bible) drew readers' attention to the direct link between Azazel and hermetic alchemy. Not only did it identify Azazel as a master metallurgist, but it said that he taught men about the use of antimony.

The term 'hermetic' comes from Hermes Trismegistus (Greek: Hermes the Thrice Great). He was so named from the great works of Anunnaki science in which he stated, 'I am called Hermes Trismegistus having three parts of the philosophy of all the world'.[24] He is better known to Egyptologists as Thoth (or Djedi), the scribe of the company of gods.[25] The content of the prized *Book of Thoth* describes how, through the process of the mysteries, certain areas of the brain can be stimulated to extend human consciousness beyond any imagining.

We have already considered the effect of gold upon the brain's pineal gland (the secret eye, or ayin) as being one aspect of hermeticism, and the writings of Thoth confirm the association, with the solar hieroglyph for gold (a spot centred within a circle) being identical to that of the *ayin*. Hence, there is a direct link between Thoth and Cain (*Q'ayin*), which becomes more understandable when we discover that Thoth was personally

*The heraldic escutcheon of Ham.*

identified with the biblical Ham *(see* Chart: *The Descents from Lamech and Noah*), while in alchemical circles he was also associated with the priest-king Melchizedek. In the 3rd century BC, the Ptolemaic chronicler Manetho credited Thoth with 36,525 words of wisdom—the same number of primitive inches as in the Great Pyramid's designed perimeter[26]—and it was said that Thoth wrote the *Book of the Dead*.[27]

Ham, then, was not a son of Noah, but was of the royal succession of Cain. The alchemical secrets were held securely within that family, and marriage to the descendants of Seth was forbidden in order to keep the bloodline of the Lilithian *Malkhut* as pure as possible. Books of Rosicrucian and Hermetic philosophy mention that much of the material found in the books of Moses is derived from the initiation rituals of the Egyptian mysteries,[28] and the earliest masonic teachings relate that Ham-Thoth was the inheritor of the Wisdom of Lamech.

As previously detailed (Chapter 10), Cain was the ancestor of the Magian priestly dynasts called Zarathustra (or Zoroaster), who prevailed through many generations in the centuries BC. The founder of this Persian succession, which emanated from Sumerian Chaldea, was Chem-Zarathustra, the biblical Ham. It is because of this that medieval commentators such as the Abbé de Villars[29] held that the original Zarathustra was a son of the wife of Noah.

Ancient Persia is now modern Iran—a name that derives from Aryan, denoting a noble race who had travelled to Persia in

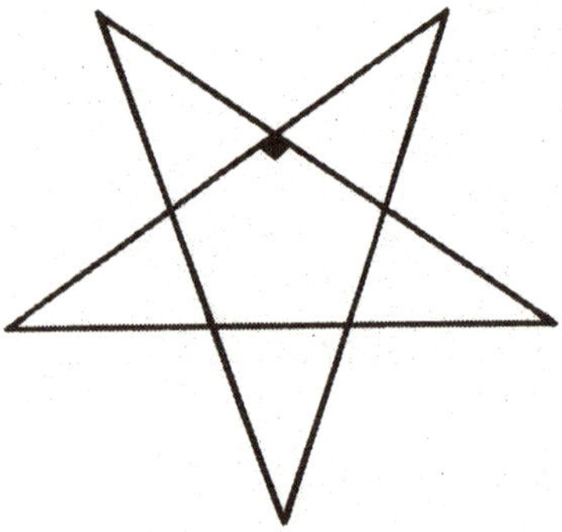

*The Goat of Mendes pentagram.*

*Pentagram of the Goddess.*

remote times from a place unknown. In contrast to the Hebrews, the Aryans were venerators of the wise lord Ahura Mazda (Ohrmazd), God of Light, who is better known to us as Enki-Samael. His earthly kingdom was defined in the old Avestan language[30] as *Pairi Daize,* from which comes the familiar word 'Paradise', the equivalent of Eden.

## The Pillars of Wisdom

It is a tenet of the very oldest mystery lore that Lamech was the father of Masonic symbolism and that his son Jabal was the master geometrician.[31] Early Masonic manuscripts (such as the Harleian, Sloane, Lansdowne, Edinburgh and Kilwinning) all relate that the Craft evolved in the most ancient of biblical times and many early Lodge constitutions cite the founders as being the sons and daughter of Lamech, namely Jabal, Jubal, Tubal-cain and Naamâh. They wrote their various sciences, it is said, upon two pillars—one called *Marbell,* which would resist fire, and the other called *Laturus,* which would resist water.

This recorded information (the *Wisdom of Lamech*) was based on the Anunnaki testament known as the *Table of Destiny* which, as we saw earlier contained 'all that humankind had ever known, and all that would ever be known'.[32] There are many differing accounts of the precise nature of these pillars of wisdom, but it is generally agreed that, in time, their content was translated to an emerald tablet by Tubal-cain's grandson Ham,[33] who was known to the Egyptians as Khem or Thoth.

One account which is at variance with the others is that written by Flavius Josephus in his 1st-century *Antiquities of the Jews.* Again, there is an attempt here to associate the acquisition of kingly wisdom with the Sethian line rather than with the Cainite succession as portrayed elsewhere. Josephus states that the children of Seth (those in the line of the other Lamech, father of Noah) were the founders of the pillars of wisdom, but in relating his adjusted story it is plain that Josephus strategically confused a supposed monument of Set (Seth), son of Adam, with that of Set (Seti I), the 19th-dynasty pharaoh of Egypt.[34]

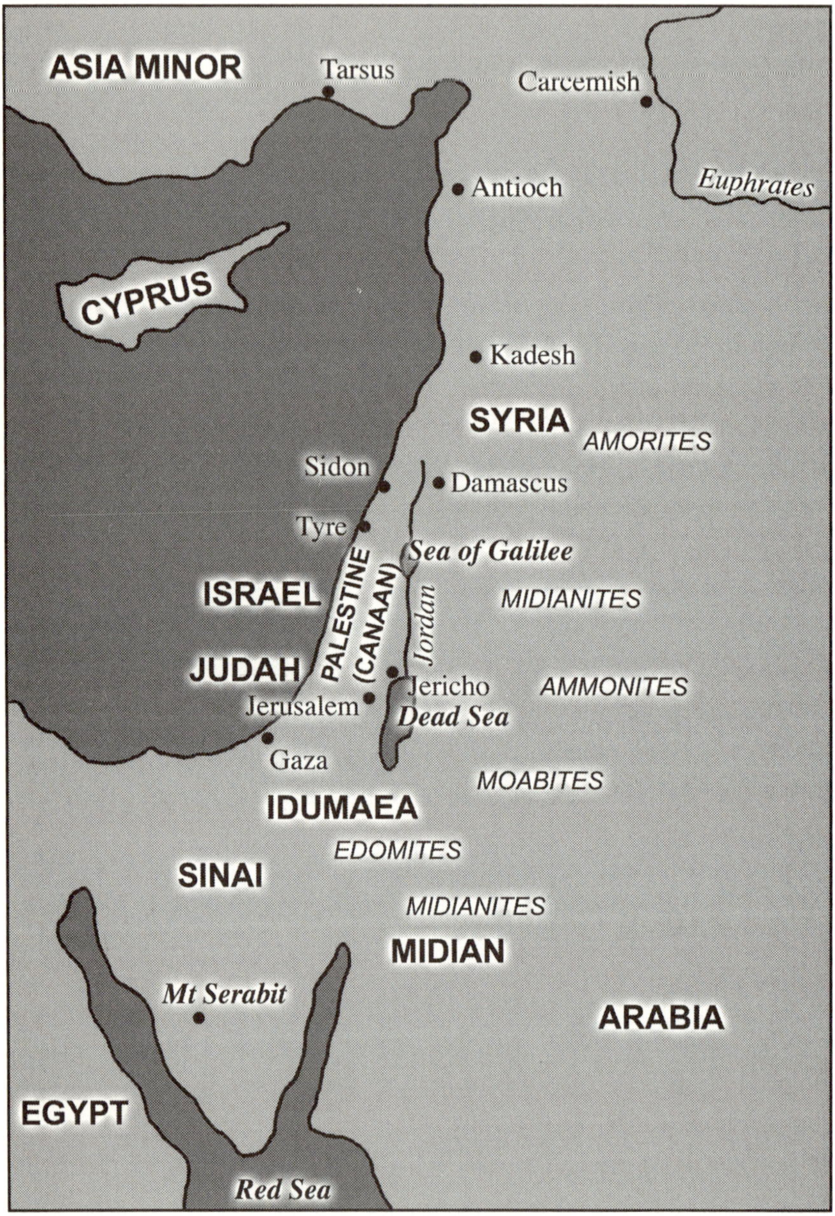


*Syria and Palestine.*

Yet another version of the story, which appears in some corrupted English masonic traditions, tells that the pillars (one of marble and the other of metal) were the work of the patriarch Enoch.[35] But the English masonic system, which was extensively revised in 18th-century Georgian times, adopted an exclusively Western doctrine wherein Thoth, the traditionally styled Great Architect, was figuratively supplanted by the Judaeo-Christian God. By virtue of this adjustment, it is claimed that the original secrets of Freemasonry have been lost—but rather more to the point is that the old mysteries were shunned by the Hanoverian inventors of the English system (based upon a York Rite), which retains only vague allegories and obscure ritual.[36] There is no alchemical science now taught in these Lodges, as was the case with the early Scottish Rite, and the emphasis is now on worthy charitable works, coupled with meaningless ceremonies that leave Lodge members quite bewildered as to the true scientific nature of the Order.

Certain Eastern-influenced Orders do still maintain a traditionally based doctrine and in a sixth-degree Temple ceremony of admission to the Sanctuary it is said, 'Let us travel in the path of the serpent'. Key figures of veneration are the Lord of Light (a style of Enki-Samael-Ohrmazd) and Isis, the designated 'bearer of the Grail'.[37] The ceremony continues:

> The sacred lance shall never fail;
> Veil and unveil the Holy Grail.
> Its wine and blood be freely poured,
> Eternally before the Lord.

16

# Empire of the Covenant

## A Mother of Nations

With the senior Mesopotamian succession from Ham and Nimrod diverted into Egypt, we are left with Shem and his family to provide the Bible's key patriarchal strain from Noah. The parallel lines from Ham and Japhet progressed into Arabia, Anatolia and Greater Scythia by the Black Sea, then eventually across Europe to Ireland. Japhet was indeed Ham's brother, just as the Bible explains. Hence, he was also a son of Tubal-cain, not a son of Noah as related in Genesis. Ham and Japhet were key ancestors of the Scots Gaels and, as correctly determined by the noted scholar Robert Graves,[1] Japhet was known to the Greeks as Iapetus—a traditional style within his Titanic strain. In practice, he was Iapetus II, the great Anu having been Iapetus I.

The cursed descendants of Noah's son Canaan were identified as Canaanites, whose Mediterranean boundary was said to extend from Sidon to Gaza, and inland to Sodom and Gomorrah by the Dead Sea (Genesis 10:19). These cities were ultimately destroyed by Enlil-Jehovah (*see* Chapter 12) and the Canaanites were generally perceived as enemies of the Hebrews who emerged in the line from Shem.

Very little is told in Genesis about Shem's immediate family, but they are listed through nine generations (Genesis 11:10-27) and the more detailed stories of the individual patriarchs begin anew with Abraham and his wife Sarai (Sarah). Once again confusion surrounds this couple, for although the Hebrew legacy was reckoned to have progressed through them, Sarai is said to have been barren during the early years of her marriage (11:30). This is not an uncommon feature of the biblical accounts of this family: Rebecca, the wife of their eventual son Isaac, was also described as barren (25:21), as was Rachel, the wife of their later son Jacob (29:31). It was common practice in those days, however, for girls to marry before childbearing age and it is to the infertile periods of their early married lives that the old texts generally refer.[2]

The story of Sarai is, nonetheless, a strange one. First we are informed that she cannot conceive, but then within a few verses we learn that her husband, Abraham, is to be the founding patriarch of a great nation (Genesis 12:2). Subsequently, Sarai presents Abraham with her Egyptian companion, Hagar, 'to be his wife'—but when Hagar conceives she is chastized and banished by Sarai (16:1-16) as if the outcome were unexpected. In due course, Ishmael, the first son of Abraham, is born to Hagar, but it is then announced that his inheritance is to be superseded by a forthcoming son of the hitherto barren Sarai—a son who will be named Isaac.

At this stage in the Old Testament account, three further pronouncements are made by Jehovah, who is called El Shaddai in the early texts. First, Abraham is renamed from his former name Abram. Second, the rule of circumcision is introduced for the family heirs. Third, Sarai's Mesopotamian name, meaning 'contentious', is changed to Sarah, denoting a 'princess'.[3] In the context of Sarai's change of name, El Shaddai further informs Abraham that the newly designated Sarah will be a Mother of Nations, and that 'kings of people shall be of her' (Genesis 17:15-16). Although Abraham's ancestral family had been influential in Mesopotamia, this is the Bible's first mention of future Hebrew kingship—but no reason is given for such an ostensibly important prospect. In fact, this particular covenant was not actually made with Abraham, but with the unborn Isaac: 'I will establish my covenant with him for an everlasting covenant, and with his seed after him' (17:19).

Genesis (15:18) also contains the promise that Isaac's descendants will inherit the Egyptian Empire 'from the river of Egypt, unto the great river, the river Euphrates'. No such promise is made, however, in respect of Abraham's eldest son Ishmael, nor for any of Abraham's other six sons by his additional wife Keturah (25:1-2). Abraham was somewhat bewildered by this and asked about Ishmael's prospects, to which El Shaddai replied that he would 'make him fruitful', but 'my covenant will I establish with Isaac' (17:18-21). This makes it quite clear that, although Ishmael was the elder of the half-brothers, Isaac was to be recognized as the ancestor of the future kings. Why, then, did Abraham later concede to slay Isaac with a knife upon the altar at Moriag (22:9)? And why, when putting a stop to the slaying, did the angel refer to Isaac as Abraham's 'only son' (22:11), when we know that he had previously fathered Ishmael?

Considering these two questions, it is of interest to note that the *Koran*, while relating the same story of the near-sacrifice, does not name the son concerned. Indeed, many Islamic scholars conclude that the intended victim was not Isaac, but Ishmael, the son of Hagar,[4] who is described in the *Book of Adam* as the daughter of a pharaoh in descent from Nimrod.

Researchers have long debated and pondered upon the ambiguity of this whole sequence of events, with particular wonder over why the Empire of Egypt should be the kingdom promised to the successors of Isaac. Historically, this would make sense only if the compilers of Genesis knew that a line of descent from Isaac had become pharaohs of Egypt.[5] Also, another anomaly which has long baffled historians is the introduction of circumcision at this particularly early stage of the Hebrew saga (Genesis 17:10-14).

Herodotus, the Greek cultural writer and Father of Historians, who visited Egypt in about 450 BC, recorded that circumcision (a custom 'inherited' by the Hebrews) was originally performed only in ancient Egypt, as has been confirmed from examinations of excavated mummies,[6] and by a bas-relief at Karnak which details the surgical procedure.[7] This being the case, then not only did Isaac's covenant of kingship promise future Egyptian dominion (from the Nile to the Euphrates), but the covenant of circumcision implemented a hitherto unique Egyptian custom into the Hebrew culture from the days of Abraham.[8] Why? What was the nature of the Egyptian influence upon the family at that particular time?

The only Egyptian connection that we are told about is Sarai's entry into the household of the pharaoh who wanted her for his wife, at which point Abraham denied that Sarai was his own wife and claimed instead that she was his sister (Genesis 12:12-15)! Then, a little later, we are informed that Abraham and Sarai were both offspring of Terah, and Abraham explains, 'She is my sister; she is the daughter of my father, but not the daughter of my mother, and she became my wife' (20:12).

In the Ethiopian chronicle *Nazum al-jawahir* (*The String of Gems*) Terah's wives are given as Tôhwait (mother of Sarai) and Yâwnû (mother of Abraham). Tôhwait is also recorded in the Syriac *M'ãrath Gaze* as Naharyath, who is to be identified with Nfry-ta-Tjewnen, the former wife of Pharaoh Amenemhet I. Her son by this marriage was the succeeding Pharaoh Senusret I—the very pharaoh who claimed Sarai for his wife *(see* Chart: *Egypt and the Tribes of Israel*). This is not surprising, since Sarai was Senusret's maternal half-sister (as well as being Abraham's paternal half-sister) and it was common practice for Egyptian pharaohs to marry their sisters in order to progress the kingship through the female line. With this in mind, could it perhaps be that Isaac was not the son of Abraham after all, but the son of Sarai and the Pharaoh? Let us look again at the sequence concerning Abraham and Sarai in Egypt.

The English translation of Genesis 12:19 quotes the Pharaoh as saying to Abraham, 'Why saidst thou, She is my sister, so I might have taken her to me to wife?' But this is not what the Hebrew Bible says. The same entry translated directly from the Hebrew states, 'Why did you say, She is my sister, so that I took her for my wife?'[9] There is a distinct difference here, and the Hebrew writers were quite emphatic about the fact that Sarai and the Pharaoh were actually married for a time. In contrast to this, both the Hebrew and English texts—when relating to the later period of Sarai's time in the company of King Abimalech of Gerar (Genesis 20:1-6)—make the point that 'Abimalech had not come near her'. But no such statement is made in respect of her relationship with the Pharaoh.

If Isaac were the son of Pharaoh Senusret, then the seemingly enigmatic details of the covenant would fall very neatly into place. We could then readily understand Sarai's change of name to Sarah (Princess). Similarly, the introduction of the Egyptian custom of circumcision would make sense, as would the prospect of future dynastic kingship in the Egyptian domain. It would even explain the relevance of the mysterious 'birthright' that was eventually sold by Isaac's son Esau to his brother Jacob (Genesis 25:30-34).

What we have here is very compelling evidence that Isaac might well have been the son of the Pharaoh, and not the son of Abraham. However, the evidence, though convincing and thoroughly rational, is largely circumstantial. Perhaps one day further information will be unearthed which will prove the case one way or the other. Meanwhile, Isaac remains the son of Abraham in accordance with long-standing tradition.

The story of Isaac and his search for a wife (Genesis 24) paints a rather different picture of Abraham than has hitherto been portrayed. Quite suddenly, Abraham appears not as an everyday nomad, but as a wealthy ruler with gold, silver, camels, herds and a large household of servants. This fits rather better with his earlier brief portrayal as a military commander (Genesis 14) who defeated the armies of four kings to rescue his nephew Lot, and it is more in keeping with his family's original high station in the Chaldean city of Ur. It is also significant that with Isaac's prospect of fathering a kingly race, his wife was not selected from the women of Canaan. She was specially chosen by Abraham's emissary from his own family in Mesopotamia, and when Isaac married his cousin Rebecca of Haran, she was bedecked with jewels and attended by her handmaids in the manner of a noble wedding.

Their twin sons were Esau and Jacob, the latter of whom was later renamed Israel. Like his father before him, Jacob also married into the Haran family of Rebecca, electing to wed his first cousin Rachel. But on their wedding night, Rachel's father Laban secreted Rachel's elder sister Leah into Jacob's bed so that she might be married first in accordance with custom. So it was that Jacob ended up with two wives (Genesis 29:28) by whom he had numerous offspring. Not content with this, Jacob also had children by his wives' handmaidens Bilhah and Zilpah. The net product was that from his wealth of sons by four different women sprang the twelve Tribes of Israel.

In the Abraham section of the Qumrân *Genesis Apocryphon*, Abraham perceives himself in a dream as a 'cedar tree', with his wife Sarah as a 'palm tree'.[10] His fear was that the Pharaoh might cut down the cedar in his pursuit of the palm—which is to say that Abraham recognized a significant threat to his life for having married Sarah who was the rightful sister-wife of King Senusret. In the most ancient of Sumerian liturgies, and on royal seals, the fallen cedar tree was the symbol of a dead god; the goddess Ishtar was said to have 'raised up the noble cedar' when she resurrected her beloved husband Dumu-zi. Strangely, though, there were no cedars in Sumer, where the only tree of any size was the date-palm.[11] Cedars grew only in the mountainous region of northern Mesopotamia and in nearby Lebanon.

The distinction of the royal palm tree was essentially Arabic, and appears to have evolved in a line from Tubal-cain's son Ham. The great palm oasis south-east of Sinai, beyond Aqaba, was called Tehâma (Teima or Temâ) from the vehement heat of the region's sand,[12] and from this root derived the Hebrew name Tamar which became so important to the Messianic line. The original biblical Tamar was the daughter-in-law of Isaac's grandson Judah and there is a very strange story in Genesis (38:1-

30) of how she conceived of her father-in-law who did not recognize her.

Some not very convincing excuses are made for Judah's action but, as a titular Palm Tree of the Hamite succession, Tamar would have been an obvious choice as a founding matriarch of the kingly line promised to Isaac's descendants. Judah had therefore selected her to be the wife of his firstborn son Er, but when Er died unexpectedly (Genesis 38:7) Tamar was passed to Er's younger brother Onan, who was also prematurely slain. The writers attributed both these deaths to the will of Jehovah and then told of how Tamar was accosted by Judah who seemingly mistook her for a harlot, pledging a kid from his flock in payment. No reason is given for Tamar's failure to announce her identity, but in due time she gave birth to Pharez, and the Hebrew line towards King David was under way.

Whatever the truth of Judah's illicit liaison with his widowed daughter-in-law, it is plain that, within a culture that held kingship to be a matrilinear inheritance, this Tamar was significant to the succession, just as had been the erstwhile titular Tamar, Abraham's wife Sarah. The facts of the matter were corrupted, however, by the later Bible writers at a time when the concept of a patrilinear dynasty was being promoted in a male-dominated Hebrew environment. Because of this, the hereditary importance of Tamar was lost. Also, by virtue of Tamar's illegal conception, the line from Judah was strictly illegitimate and it was not until a later time that a lawful marriage cemented a proper link with the Cainite royal strain.

Another Tamar turns up as the daughter of King David (2-Samuel 13) and there is a very similar tale of how she too was duped into sleeping with her brother Ammon. Then Absalom, another of David's sons, had a daughter called Tamar (2-Samuel 14:27), as did the later King Zedekiah, and also Jesus himself.[13] The stories of individual family males finding it necessary to mate with Tamars are each wrapped in blankets of weird explanation, but these females were of eminent station, conducive to perpetuating the true sovereignty of the line as it progressed from the time of Isaac in parallel with the main Egyptian succession.

## Esau and the Dragon Queen

Esau, the son of Isaac and Rebecca, was the elder twin brother of Jacob-Israel, who, as related in Genesis (25:30-34), purchased Esau's birthright for a mess of red pottage.[14] From the original word used to denote 'red' (i.e. *adom*), Esau—who was said to have been red when born (25:25)—acquired the alternative name Edom,[15] by which definition his descendant Edomites became known.

Esau was additionally said to be hairy (Genesis 27:11)—and this is reminiscent of the Man of Nature in the Sumerian *Epic of Gilgamesh*.[16] Some writers have suggested that the word *se'ar*, which was translated to 'hairy' in respect of Esau, should perhaps have been *seir*, a synonym for *edom* meaning 'red',[17] but such an error by the early writers is unlikely, particularly since the 'hairy' definition was also applied in Arabian and Jewish lore to other characters, such as Ham, Lilith and the Queen of Sheba.

When the Constitution of Ethiopia was drawn up in 1955, Emperor Haile Selassie was detailed as having descended from Solomon and Sheba's offspring King Menelek, who featured in the 13th-century *Kebra Nagast*—the *Book of the Glory of the Kings*.[18] Menelek's queen was Makeda, who was also described as 'hairy', but in this context the translated word is better explained as 'hairy in the likeness of a bright comet—a hirsute wandering star'. The wandering stars were in fact the biblical race of Cain and his wife Luluwa, and the 'hairy' definition was often used to denote prominent dynasts of Luluwa's succession from the Anunnaki King Nergal and his Queen, Eresh-kigal (*see* Chart: *Descents to Cain and Seth*).

Esau's name, *E-sa-um*, has been found on tablets discovered in 1975 at Tel Mardikh (the ancient city of Elba) in Syria, along with references to other biblical names such as Ab-ra-mu (Abraham), Is-ra-ilu (Israel) and Ib-num (Eber),[19] thereby confirming the nominal entries in Genesis. But what Genesis does not make clear is the precise nature of the birthright granted by Esau to Jacob. As far as we are made aware, there was no sovereign or titular entitlement to consider, and since both were the sons of Isaac, the only obvious birthright would be that of senior succession to their father, from whom it had been said that a race of kings would ensue (Genesis 17:16). The Bible relates that, in due time, King David of Israel and his dynasty sprang from the line of Judah, a son of Esau's brother Jacob, but under the original scheme of things, had the birthright not been sold, the kingly descent would rightly have been from Esau.

Before following the lines of descent from Jacob, it is worth considering the legacy of Esau, whose descendants carried an immediate Dragon heritage by way of his wife Bashemath, the daughter of Abraham's son Ishmael and his wife Mahalath of Egypt.[20] Mahalath was also known as Nefru-sobek, a daughter of Pharaoh Amenemhet II and granddaughter of Senusret I, the half-brother of Abraham's wife Sarah (*see* Chart: *Egypt and the Tribes of Israel*).

The daughter of Esau and Mahalath was Igrath, whose own daughter by Pharaoh Amenemhet III was Sobeknefru, Dragon Queen of Egypt *c.*1785-82 BC. Sobeknefru (Sobekhkare) was the last ruler of Egypt's 12th dynasty, and her name meant 'Beautiful of the god Sobek'.[21] Sobek was the mighty crocodile—the very spirit of the *Messeh,* whose great temple was erected at Kiman Faris by Queen Sobeknefru's father.[22]

It is generally reported that Sobeknefru had no male heir, and because of this a new 13th dynasty began after her death. However, since the Egyptian royal inheritance was held in the female line, new dynasties often sprang from the marriage of an heiress to a male of another family. Such appears to have been the case in this instance, and the 13th dynasty saw the continuing reigns of the Sobek pharaohs from Sobekhotep I to Sobekhotep IV.[23] Prior to this, Queen Sobeknefru had formalized the Dragon

Court of Ankhfn-khonsu (Chapter 13), establishing a firm base for the priestly pursuits associated with the scientific teachings of Thoth which had prevailed from the 2nd dynasty of Nimrod's grandson King Raneb.

As the 13th pharaonic dynasty drew to a close, other parallel dynasties began to rule alongside the main kingly succession. These coextensive kings ruled in the eastern delta, beginning with the short lived 14th dynasty, followed by the simultaneous 15th and 16th dynasties called the Hyksos Delta Kings. They governed from about 1663 BC alongside the 17th Theban dynasty of the main succession, until finally deposed by the 18th dynasty founder, Pharaoh Ahmose I, in about 1550 BC.

Centred mainly in Avaris, the Hyksos rulers were so named from their distinction as *Hikau-khoswet*, which is said to mean Desert Princes. They are often referred to as the Shepherd Kings, although this is said by many to be a misnomer. In reality, they were indeed 'shepherds' in accordance with the ancient Mesopotamian kingly style which had been transported into the Hyksos realm of Syro-Phoenicia, from where flourished a regular caravan trade with the Mesopotamian kingdom of Mari.[24] When documenting the Hyksos dynasts, Manetho referred to them not only as 'shepherds', but also as 'brothers', and this was precisely the term used to define the equal status of the prevailing individual kings of Mesopotamian regions such as Mari, Babylon and Larsa.[25]

The Hyksos kings were Amorite[26] descendants of Ham and as such would have been of a strain related to the early 2nd dynasty—perhaps even to the 12th dynasty of Queen Sobeknefru. One way or another, they challenged the 17th dynasty of Thebes, and in matters of warfare they introduced the horse, the chariot and the compound bow, none of which had formerly been used in Egypt. These things were, however, previously apparent in Troy, from where the Sea Kings and their followers spread into the Mediterranean seaboard lands after Troy V was devastated by fall-out from the Mount Santorini eruption in 1624 BC. It is likely, therefore, that the Hyksos (who were also called the Foreign Rulers) were of Trojan origin.

Although reference books make much of the fact that Ahmose I succeeded in overthrowing the Hyksos rulers, it is evident that there were marital alliances between the competing houses of Avaris and Thebes. It is generally reckoned that the Hyksos Pharaoh Apepi II (Apophis) was the last hereditary Dragon King to reign in Egypt, but it would appear that the heritage was perpetuated through a female line into the new dynasty. Even the grave of Ahmose's son Amenhotep I contained a preserved vase cartouche of the daughter of Apophis,[27] which signifies the enmity was not so great between the houses as is traditionally supposed.

The Sobek tradition of Apophis (the designated Beloved of Sobek) was continued by the 18th-dynasty pharaohs, and it was Tuthmosis III who established the famous alchemical mystery school of the White Brotherhood of the Therapeutate, from which an eventual branch established the Essene community at Qumrân. This original school was operated by the priests of Ptah, the god of metallurgists, architects and masons. Ptah was regarded as the Great Vulcan of Egypt,[28] and the High Priest of Ptah was the designated Great Master Artificer.

Notwithstanding the intervention of the Hyksos kings, Egypt had from the outset of its 1st dynasty (*c*.3050 BC) been a unified nation comprising the separate Upper (southern) and Lower (northern) kingdoms.[29] Each kingdom had its own regalia—a white crown (*hedjet*) for Upper Egypt and a red crown (*deshret*) for Lower Egypt, while the double-crown (*shmty*) incorporated both. Additionally, the lotus and the vulture were symbolic of the white kingdom, while the papyrus plant and the cobra symbolized the red kingdom. More important to our quest, though, is that each of the kingdoms had its own principal stone pillar—a spiritual umbilical cord between the priests and the gods.[30]

In the city of Heliopolis (in Lower Egypt) was the ancient Pillar of Annu, whose name is reminiscent of the great Sumerian god Anu, father of Enki and Enlil. Its counterpart at Thebes (in Upper Egypt) was called *Iwnu Shema*, which meant, quite simply,

Southern Pillar. These two eastward-facing pillars, which existed at the time of unification, were revered by the Tuthmosis Therapeutate and were the prototypes for the two eastern-porch pillars of Solomon's Temple of Jerusalem some 2000 years after the unification of Egypt. The Jerusalem pillars still feature in modern Freemasonry as Jachin (to establish) and Boaz (in strength) (1-Kings 7:21). In Egypt the pillars were symbols of unity and of a concept known as *Ma'at*, which defined a level and just foundation.[31] This ideal of righteous judgement was synonymous with divine kingship and with the Hebrew *Malkhut*, and not surprisingly Ma'at, the goddess of truth and law, was said to be the sister of Thoth. Her weighing of truth in the balance was conducted with a feather,[32] and truth was identified with gold, the most noble of metals.

When the souls of the early pharaohs passed into the Otherworld (the Afterlife) they were tested by the funerary god Anubis against the judicial feather of Ma'at and, as shown in reliefs of the era, Anubis was directly associated with the conical bread of the white powder—the highward fire-stone of the temple priests. Today's metaphysical studies now maintain that, by way of a superconductive process, the bodies of some Old Kingdom pharaohs could well have been physically transported into another dimension of space-time, where they remain in a suspended state precisely as the ancient texts suggest. There is as yet no final proof of this, but there is proof of the ability to perform such a feat and it would certainly explain the mystery of the undiscovered Gizeh pyramid kings, Khufu, Khafre and Menkaure.

It was a particular tradition of Egyptian kingship that the funerary rites which consecrated the dead as everlasting gods were identical to those which gave the pharaohs a divine status during their lifetimes.[33] Among the many royal insignia were the shepherd's crook and the sceptre, just as in ancient Sumer—and although legitimate gods were revered in both countries, the earliest form of ritualistic religion was an enthusiastic belief in the divinity of the kings.[34] Prevailing above all, though, was an overriding principle of sovereignty which insisted that 'A man may not become a king without a queen, and a queen must be of the royal blood'.[35]

Irrespective of the Bible's dismissal of the Egyptian descent from Esau through Queen Sobeknefru, the Old Testament writers did acknowledge the Lilithian heritage of the line to his wife Bashemath *(see* Chart: *Egypt and the Tribes of Israel*). It is explained that Esau's heirs by Bashemath and his other wives became the Dukes of Edom, and they are cited in Genesis (36:31) as 'The kings that reigned in the land of Edom before there reigned any king over the children of Israel'.

Scholars of Hebrew literature make the specific point that in listing the legitimate Dukes of Edom (Idumaea), the Genesis compilers defined twelve individual dukedoms, equivalent in number to the twelve tribes of Israel.[36] Also, there were twelve 'princes of nations' given as the sons of Abraham's son Ishmael (Genesis 25:13-16). Although the tribes of Israel are generally well known, these other influential groups of twelve have been strategically ignored, albeit the families of Ishmael and Esau were defined as high-bred dukes and princes. The Ishmaelites emerge as the twelve tribes of Syro-Arabia, while the Muslim tradition reveres Ishmael and Abraham as the joint founders of the Holy House at Mecca.[37] Esau's Edomites were destined, in turn, to inherit the kingdom of Idumaea as the Dragons (kings) and Owls (queens) of eternity, in accordance with the book of Isaiah (34:13-17): 'They shall possess it for ever; from generation to generation shall they dwell therein. The wilderness and the solitary place shall be glad for them, and the desert shall rejoice and blossom as the rose'.

17

# The Coat of Many Colours

## The Contrived Chronology

The base structure for today's knowledge of the Egyptian pharaohs comes from the pen of Manetho, a Greco-Egyptian priest of Heliopolis. He was born at Sebennytos in the Egyptian delta and rose to become an adviser to Pharaoh Ptolemy I (*c*.305-282 BC). In his chronicles, Manetho listed aspects of Egyptian history by way of a series of ruling dynasties, giving a skeleton of chronology from about 3100 BC (when Lower and Upper Egypt were united as one kingdom) to the death of pharaoh Nectanebo II in 343 BC.[1]

Unfortunately, no complete version of Manetho's text exists and his work is mainly known to us through the writings of later chroniclers such as Flavius Josephus (1st century AD), Julius Africanus (3rd century AD) and Eusebius of Caesarea (4th century AD). An additional dilemma is caused because although Manetho clearly had access to the Heliopolis Temple records, he did not have access to specific dates for his pharaonic listing.

Even though inscriptions from before the time of Manetho were discovered in later times, these were in the form of ancient hieroglyphs (picture-symbols) and it was not until 1822 that the hieroglyphic code was broken by the French Egyptologist Jean

François Champollion. This decipherment was achieved by way of the now famous Rosetta Stone,[2] found near Alexandria in 1799 by Lieutenant Bouchard of the Napoleonic expedition into Egypt. The black basalt stone from about 196 BC carries the same content in three different scripts: Egyptian hieroglyphs, Egyptian demotic (everyday cursive writing) and scribal Greek. Through comparative analysis of these scripts (with the Greek language being readily familiar), the hieroglyphic code was revealed; it was then cross-referenced with pharaonic cartouches (ornamental oval-shaped inscriptions denoting royal names)[3] of the Egyptian kings.

Once the hieroglyphs were understood, the content of other ancient records could be decoded. Among them are some which give kingly lists to compare with the records of Manetho. They include the Palermo Stone,[4] a black diorite slab which details the last pre-dynastic kings before 3100 BC, followed by the pharaohs through to the 5th-dynasty Neferirkare in about 2490 BC.[5] Also now translated are the *Royal List of Karnak* (Thebes),[6] the *Royal List of Abydos,*[7] the *Abydos King List,*[8] the *Royal List of Saqqara*[9] and the *Royal Canon of Turin*, a papyrus from about 1200 BC.

With all of these to hand, it is still difficult to fix absolute years for an Egyptian chronology because the lists bear no dates as such. At best there are given lengths of individual kingly reigns and certain astronomical references, along with some information pertaining to Mediterranean countries other than Egypt. But, in the context of these records, there is much debate about whether particular pharaohs, or even whole dynasties, reigned consecutively or simultaneously. As a result, alternative chronologies are currently available, wherein dynastic and regnal dates vary between 50 and 200 years.

Ultimately, we have a conjectural form of standard mean chronology which is generally used in textbooks today—but this is largely based upon the 17th-century biblical dating structure compiled by Archbishop Ussher of Armagh (*see* Chapter 2). Since the majority of Ussher's reckoning is inaccurate, it follows that the Egyptian dates calculated from his framework are similarly incorrect.

Only from 897 BC through to 586 BC can Palestinian dates be ascertained with any precision, for it was during this period that the northern Mesopotamian records corresponded with the royal succession in Palestine. These records, known as the *Assyrian Eponym Canon*, were discovered at Nineveh by Sir Henry Creswicke Rawlinson in 1862. They detail the appointments of the Assyrian *eponyms* (officers equivalent to Roman consuls), along with the accessions of the succeeding kings.[10] The first thoroughly accurate date which ties an Assyrian king to an Israelite king is 853 BC, when Shalmaneser III of Assyria recorded King Ahab of Israel at the Battle of Karkar.

Based on a recalculation from the Assyrian records, David is now said to have been king of Israel from 1001 BC (against the Ussher reckoning of 1048 BC), and his son Solomon to have reigned from 968 BC (against 1015 BC)—a forty-seven year difference in each case. Archbishop Ussher had no access to any such original texts in 1650; even if he had, he was certainly not experienced in translating ancient Assyrian writing. So, having commenced with Ussher's inaccurate dates for the Israelite kings, incorrect dates have consequently been assumed for the parallel Egyptian succession. This has caused a good deal of historical misunderstanding. In recent years, the Egyptologist David M. Rohl has made an in-depth study of this very haphazard form of pharaonic dating[11] and his findings show precisely how certain inaccuracies came about.

Champollion, who deciphered the ancient hieroglyphs in 1822, identified Pharaoh Sheshonq I with the biblical Shishak who plundered the Temple of Jerusalem in the reign of Solomon's son King Rehoboam of Judah (2-Kings 14:25-26; 1-Chronicles 12:2-9).[12] Since Ussher had dated Rehoboam's reign as being 975-57 BC, Sheshonq I of Egypt (founder of the 22nd dynasty) was accordingly dated to correspond with this, there being no known date for him beforehand. Other pharaohs were then plotted from this base using the recorded lengths of their reigns as a guide.

Subsequently, in 1882, Britain's Egypt Exploration Fund was founded with the express purpose of confirming Old Testament information by way of archaeological discoveries in Egypt,[13] but what followed was more of the same chronological manipulation to bring Egypt into line with the Bible stories through the arbitrary application of pharaonic dates.

The essential problem with the Sheshonq/Shishak chronology was that Ussher's date for Rehoboam differed by more than fifty years from that deduced from the Mesopotamian records. So, in recent times, Rehoboam has been re-dated so that the Jerusalem seige is said to have been in 925 BC; and Sheshonq I has also been re-dated to 945-24 BC in order to conform. Even so, there is absolutely nothing outside Champollion's original speculation to prove that Sheshonq and Shishak were actually one and the same person.

A more reliable pharaonic dating relates to the year 664 BC, when it was recorded that King Ashur-banipal of Assyria took his army into Egypt and sacked the city of Thebes. This invasion is confirmed in the Egyptian archives and can be directly attributed to the final year of the 25th-dynasty pharaoh Taharqa, whose dates are now given in most lists as 690-64 BC. In this book, however, we are not concerned with such recent dates from the time of King David, but with the pre-Davidic pharaonic era and with an Egyptian connection as far back as the period from Abraham to Moses.

## The Sojourn in Egypt

According to the book of Genesis (46-47), Abraham's grandson Jacob-Israel took his extended family (seventy members in all) from Canaan into Egypt, where they settled in the region of Goshen by the Nile delta. There, escaping an initial famine in Canaan, they remained and multiplied through a number of generations (Exodus 1:7) until they were eventually led out of

Egypt by Moses. The standard chronology of Ussher maintains that Jacob's original move into Egypt from Canaan was in 1706 BC, with the Mosaic exodus occurring 215 years later in 1491 BC.[14]

In apparent confirmation of the Israelites' sojourn in Egypt, the annals of Pharaoh Ramesses II (the Great) make reference to Semitic people who were settled in the delta region of Goshen, but this does not really help because they are not specified as Israelites. The Semites of the region (then as today) were not simply the Israelites, but included the Arab races of Syria, Phoenicia, Mesopotamia and the Fertile Crescent in general.[15] Apart from mentioning Semitic people in Goshen, the records of Ramesses II (along with those of his predecessor Seti I) also refer to the town of Asher in Canaan.[16] But, Asher (Joshua 17:7) was named after one of the tribes of Israel who returned with the Mosaic exodus (Numbers 1:41), thereby indicating that the exodus must have taken place before the reign of Seti (*c.*1333-1304 BC).

The book of Genesis (47:11) states that, in Egypt, the Israelites were settled in the land of Ramesses, while Exodus (1:11) claims that they actually built the city of Ramesses (Pi-Ramesses). But Ramesses I did not reign until *c.*1335 BC, and Ramesses II not until *c.*1304 BC[17]—practically two centuries after the Israelites had supposedly vacated his country according to Ussher. In fact, it was quite impossible for Jacob and his family to have settled in the land of Ramesses because they arrived in Egypt many centuries before the reign of Ramesses I.

These incongruous biblical statements have puzzled historians since Victorian times and it has long been recognized that the comments relating to Ramesses are anachronisms. They arose because the Old Testament compilers referred to the Egyptian delta settlement by the name known to them in the 6th century BC—and that part of the Nile delta was called the 'land of Ramesses' until the 4th century AD.[18] Though perhaps anachronistic, the Bible references are not necessarily altogether incorrect, for the exodus appears to have happened in protracted waves from the time of Moses and it seems that many Israelites remained in Egypt following the departure of the main body.[19]

Regardless of this, some scholars have lately redefined the period of Israelite settlement in Egypt so that its last days coincide with the reign of Ramesses II, giving the revised date of 1300 BC for the Mosaic exodus of the Bible.[20] There is an amount of logic in this, because it is clear that Ussher's 1491 BC date was far too early for the historical Moses—but it is still, nonetheless, guesswork.

A rather more accurate guide to the timing of the Israelite departure from Egypt was established only in 1997 when cereals from the archaeological layer at Jericho before its fall were carbon-14 dated to be about 3,311 years old.[21] This dates them to around 1315 BC, which means that Joshua's Israelite army which destroyed the city had still not arrived at that time. It also indicates that by 1360 BC the Israelites were still in Egypt, and had not yet removed to Sinai with Moses.

Additionally, the science journal *Nature*[22] has identified the volcanic ash from the eruption of Mount Santorini in the Mediterranean with the biblical plague of darkness in Egypt (Exodus 10:22-23), thereby wholly disassociating the event from the Exodus time-frame. The effect in Egypt of this volcanic disaster and its accompanying earthquake (geologically dated to 1624 BC) is related in the *Ipuwer Papyrus* acquired by the Museum of Leiden in 1828. This multi-page 19th-dynasty document, copied from an earlier source, tells of a series of devastating events in Egypt, in keeping with the plagues of Exodus, and it states that the fire and ash which consumed the land 'fell from the skies'[23] some 300 years before the time of Moses.

Moving back to the time of Abraham, we know from the book of Jubilees[24] that Abraham's great-great-grandfather, Reu (Raguel), was married to Ora, the daughter of the Sumerian king Ur-nammu of Ur. It was he who built the last great ziggurat of Ur and founded the 3rd Chaldean dynasty, reigning *c.*2113-2096 BC.[25] The subsequent fall of Ur took place in 1960 BC, at which time Abraham moved northward from Ur to Haran, along with his father, Terah, and family. Then, following the death of Terah, Abraham migrated into Canaan with his wife Sarai (Sarah) and his nephew Lot (Genesis 11:32, 12:5).

Within this sequence we find a very good example of the Old Testament's inherent confusion over dates and personal ages. Genesis (11:26) explains that Terah was aged 70 when his son Abraham was born; a few verses later (Genesis 11:32) it is related that Terah lived on to the age of 205. This would make Abraham 135 at his father's death. But then, after another four verses (Genesis 12:4), we are informed that Abraham was 75 years old when he departed from Haran after the death of Terah!

Plainly, in matters of chronology, the contemporary records are far more reliable than the Bible, and from these it can be deduced that the biblical accounts of the early Hebrews in Haran, Canaan and Egypt (from the time of Abraham to the time of Moses) are set within the 600 years from 1960 BC to 1360 BC, with the exodus to Sinai coming soon after the latter date.

Abraham's grandson Jacob was renamed Israel at the Beth-el covenant (Genesis 32:28, 35:10), and his descendants became known as Israelites or Children of Israel. Then, in the adulthood of his sons, Jacob-Israel took his complete family (by his two wives, Rachel and Leah, and by their handmaidens, Bilhah and Zilpah), including all his grandchildren, into Egypt in about 1760 BC. By that time, it is related that his son Joseph (who had previously been sold into Egypt by his jealous brothers) had become vizier (viceroy) to the pharaoh.

The duration of the Israelite sojourn in Egypt is confirmed in the Massoretic Hebrew Old Testament which states (Exodus 12:40): 'The time that the Israelites spent in Egypt was four hundred and thirty years'. In the King James Authorized Bible, the book of Exodus (12:40) similarly states: 'Now the sojourning of the children of Israel, who dwelt in Egypt, was four hundred and thirty years'.[26] If this calculation is roughly correct, then the departure of the Israelites with Moses would have occurred around 430 years after 1760 BC, which places the exodus at about 1330 BC.

## Four Centuries of Silence

The main genealogical problems presented by the Old Testament's seemingly comprehensive family lists appear from the outset of the Egyptian sojourn. Prior to the time of Abraham, the descent of the noble patriarchal family was recorded through the ages in Mesopotamia, and these records were available to the Genesis compilers in Babylon. But, from the moment of Abraham's migration to Canaan and the nomadic existence of his offspring, there is very little evidence of the generations until the time of King David and his successors.

The various Bible listings from Abraham to David (which are amalgamated in the book of 1-Chronicles) identify thirteen generations with an above-average generation standard of about seventy-two years. With the exception of the story of Joseph, the Bible is remarkably silent regarding the 430-year period which embraced the Israelites' sojourn in Egypt. The book of Genesis concludes with the death of Joseph and his embalming and burial in Egypt, whereupon the book of Exodus begins with a short account of procreational disputes between the Egyptians and Israelites, before leaping forward through the centuries to the birth of Moses. This becomes quite disconcerting when it is realized that the Joseph and Moses stories are portrayed as if they are linked together with hardly any time between (Exodus 1). And it is positively disturbing to read in the book of Numbers that when Moses led the Israelites across the Red Sea to Sinai, the said seventy family members of Joseph's father Jacob-Israel (Genesis 46:27) had somehow multiplied to about 2 million people, including an army of 603,550 male warriors aged over twenty![27]

It is explained in Genesis (41:39-46) that, at the age of thirty, Joseph became the 'ruler over all the land of Egypt', and was dubbed Zaphnath-paaneah. This is said by the Israeli Bible scholar, Moshe Weinfeld, to mean something akin to 'God speaks – he lives',[28] but in ancient Egypt such a title would not, of course, have referred to the God of the Hebrews. A closer translation comes from the German linguist, Georg Steindorff, who relates that the name means 'The god speaks—may he live'.

Were it not for the separate Egyptian records of Joseph the vizier, and of his genealogical link with Moses in the 14th century BC, it would be very difficult, if not impossible, to distinguish him from Joseph the son of Jacob-Israel in the 18th century BC. The Bible (through a strategic switch of time-frames, from Genesis to Exodus) implies that these two Josephs were one and the same—and this is managed by dispensing, between books, with 400 years of history,[29] just as is the case between the Old and New Testaments.

What further emerges is the possibility that the whole story of young Joseph's dispute with his brothers, and the legendary coat of many colours, was contrived by biblical scribes in order to link one chronological period with the other. Historically, Joseph the vizier was an Egyptian governor shortly before the days of Moses—but despite all popular tradition, he was not one and the same with Joseph the son of Jacob, who lived four centuries earlier.

The books of Exodus (13:19) and Joshua (24:32) each relate to the 'bones' of Joseph, claiming that the Israelites took them out of Egypt for burial at Shechem. But this is inconsistent with Genesis (50:26), which states that the body of Joseph the vizier was embalmed (that is to say, mummified) in Egypt. This form of physical preservation was specifically reserved for those of the highest orders, and there would have been no resultant bones to transport. If any bones were removed by the Israelites, these might have been the bones of the original Joseph, but they could not possibly have been those of Joseph the vizier, whose body has now been unearthed in Egypt.

So, what do we know about Jacob's son, the original Joseph? We are told that Joseph was born late in Jacob's life and that he was disliked by his many brothers because he was his father's favourite and had been given a coat of many colours (Genesis 37:3). Actually, this is a corrupted English translation from the Hebrew which denoted simply an 'ornamented tunic',[30] and made no reference whatever to colours. An ornamented tunic (the *ketonet pasim*) is later referred to in the book of 2-Samuel (13:18) and is again wrongly stated to be 'of divers colours' in English translations. In the original text, it was strictly 'a robe with sleeves'.[31] On this later occasion, the robe is worn by Tamar, the daughter of King David, and the text explains that the *ketonet pasim* (a unisex garment) was indicative of both princely station and virginity.[32]

In the *Anchor Bible*, it is explained that the story of Joseph's being sold into Egypt by his brothers (Genesis 37) is, by way of linguistic analysis, the composite work of two separate authors.[33] Sometimes Joseph's father is referred to as Jacob, and on other occasions as Israel. Within the context of the overlaid stories, we first have Reuben suggesting to Judah and the others that Joseph should not be slain, and then Judah makes the same plea to Reuben and the others. Whenever the paternal name Jacob is used, Reuben is portrayed as Joseph's protector, but whenever their father is called Israel, Judah is the protective brother.

There are, in consideration, numerous anomalies which make the story of young Joseph quite chaotic. Initially, the brothers threw Joseph into a pit with intent to kill him (Genesis 37:24). But then, through a change of heart, they sold him to a passing caravan of Ishmaelites (37:27). Afterwards, some Midianite traders arrived on the scene, whereupon the brothers pulled Joseph, once again, from the pit and sold him to the Midianites who took him to Egypt (37:28). Then, after Joseph appears to have been sold twice, Reuben looked into the pit (37:29-30) and was surprised to find him gone!

Although unsatisfactorily constructed, the purpose of this narrative was to ensure that Joseph made his way to Egypt independently of his father and the rest of the family, who were said to have followed some while after. By this means, Joseph was removed from the family scene in order to become strategically identified with the later Joseph who became Governor of Egypt.

Once in Egypt, at the age of seventeen, Joseph was apparently sold to a high chamberlain (*sar hatabahim*) named Potiphar

(Genesis 39:1), who is not mentioned by name thereafter. However, the introduction of the man's name at that early stage was conveniently suited to identifying this Joseph with his later namesake, who, at the age of thirty-three, married Asenath, the daughter of Poti-pherah,[34] a priest of Ra (Genesis 41:45). Although the names Potiphar and Poti-pherah appear mutually supportive, the characters were distinctly different, one being a courtier, and the other a priest.[35]

Finally, and to support the point concerning the contrived account of the early Joseph, we have the added story of his attempted seduction by Potiphar's wife (Genesis 39:7-18). When Joseph refused to submit, the woman ripped his garment from him and presented it to her husband, claiming that she had narrowly escaped being assaulted by Joseph. Until a few decades ago, there appeared nothing untoward about this discreet little tale—but then Egyptologists translated a hieroglyphic document called the *Orbiney Papyrus* from 19th-dynasty Egypt (*c*.1250 BC). In this document they discovered the story's original prototype within the romantic lore of old Egypt[36]—and it had nothing whatever to do with Joseph.

## Joseph the Vizier

Eighty miles (*c*.129 km) south of modern Cairo is the town of Medinet-el-Faiyûm, where a 200-mile (322 km) canal from the Nile has long transformed the desert waste into a lush garden paradise of fruit groves. To the local residents (the *Fellahin*) and throughout Egypt, the ancient waterway is known as *Bahr Yusuf* (Joseph's Canal), and it is said to be named after Joseph the grand vizier.[37]

Genesis (41:39-43) tells how this Joseph was made Governor of Egypt:

> And Pharaoh said unto Joseph ... Thou shalt be over my house and according unto thy word shall all my

> people be ruled: only in the throne will I be greater than thou ... and he made him ruler over all the land of Egypt.

A later Genesis entry, which is rarely quoted, has Joseph saying, 'God hath made me a father to Pharaoh' (Genesis 45:8). This is a particularly impressive statement and could not possibly have related to Joseph, son of Jacob, who was sold into slavery. But was there perhaps a grand vizier who fathered a pharaoh—a prestigious governor after whom a canal might have been named and who would have ridden in the king's second chariot, as related in Genesis (41:43)? Indeed there was—a vizier who, contrary to normal custom, was embalmed like a pharaoh (precisely as described in the last verse of Genesis), and entombed in a fine sarcophagus in no less a place than the royal burial ground—the Valley of Kings at Western Thebes (modern Luxor).

Egyptian tomb inscriptions usually relate, in one way or another, to the godhead under which the occupant was placed in life, using such deiform names as Ra, Amen and Ptah. In this case, the unusual tomb inscriptions of the grand vizier do not relate to any known god of Egypt; they reveal instead such names as *Ya-ya* and *Yu-ya*—phonetically being *Iouiya*, which is akin to *Yaouai*—a variant of Yahweh or Jehovah.[38] From these inscriptions, the vizier has become personally known as Yuya, and this is of particular interest because his grandson, Pharaoh Akhenaten, later developed the One God concept in Egypt.

Yuya (Yusuf) was the principal minister for the 18th-dynasty Pharaoh Tuthmosis IV (*c*.1413-1405 BC) and for his son Amenhotep III (*c*.1405-1367 BC).[39] His tomb was discovered in 1905, along with that of his wife Tuya (the *Asenath*), and the mummies of Yuya and Tuya are among the very best preserved in the Cairo Museum.[40] It came as a great surprise to Egyptologists that anyone outside the immediate royal family should have been mummified and buried in the Valley of Kings. Clearly, this couple were of tremendous importance in their day;

this becomes obvious from Yuya's funerary papyrus, which refers to him as 'The Holy Father of the Lord of the Two Lands' (*it ntr n nb tawi*), as does his royal funerary statuette.[41] The style Lord of the Two Lands was a pharaonic title relating to the kingdoms of Upper and Lower Egypt,[42] and so it is plain that Yuya was not only the viceroy and primary state official, but was also the father of a pharaoh, just as related in Genesis (45:8). He even held some personal kingly status, as determined by his pharaonic designation, 'One trusted by the good god in the entire land'.[43]

Yuya's family was very influential, holding inherited land in the Egyptian delta, and he was a powerful military leader.[44] Anen, the elder son of Yuya and Tuya, also rose to high office under Amenhotep III as Chancellor of Lower Egypt, High Priest of Heliopolis and Divine Father of the nation. But it was their younger son, Aye, who held the special distinction Father of the God[45] and became pharaoh in 1352 BC—as did other descendants of Yusuf-Yuya, including the now famous Tutankhamun (*see* Chart: *The Egyptian Connection*).

Not only was Yuya of individual royal significance, but so too was his wife Tuya. Genesis (41:45) tells us that Tuya (Touiou) held the distinction of Asenath (*iw s-n-t*)—a style which derives from an 18th-dynasty Egyptian dialect, and means 'She belongs to the goddess Neith'.[46] Tuya was the daughter of a priest of Heliopolis and according to the *Corpus of Hieroglyphic Inscriptions* at the Brooklyn Museum, she was the designated King's Ornament (*kheret nesw*). By way of her mother, she is reckoned to have perhaps been a granddaughter of Tuthmosis III,[47] founder of the Great White Brotherhood of the Therapeutate, while through her father she was descended from Igrath (daughter of Esau and Mahalath), the mother of Queen Sobeknefru who established the Dragon Court as a royal institution in Egypt.

We are, therefore, into the realm of the original covenant of kingship made with Isaac. His son Esau may have sold his birthright to his younger twin brother Jacob-Israel (whose descendants became kings of Judah), but now we discover that, through Tuya and Yuya, descendants of Esau did indeed become pharaohs of Egypt. These particular pharaohs have become known as the Amarna Kings: they were Akhenaten, Smenkhkare, Tutankhamun and Aye, who ruled consecutively *c*.1367-48 BC.

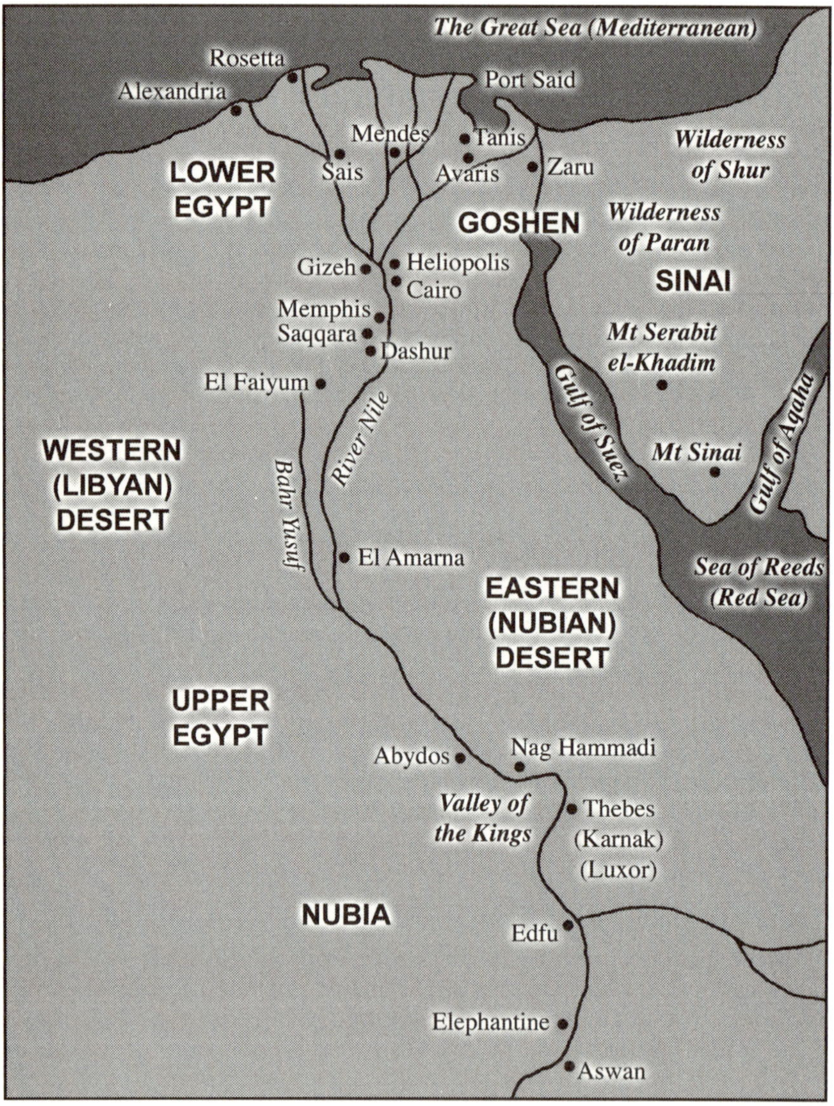


*Egypt of the Pharaohs.*

From the 18th-dynasty campaigns of Akhenaten's great-great-grandfather, Tuthmosis III (*c*.1490-1436 BC), Palestine was under Egyptian rule and it remained so into the era of the Amarna Kings. The American Egyptologist, James Henry Breasted, referred to Tuthmosis III as the 'Napoleon of Egypt',[48] and the empire (from Syria to Western Asia) established by him and his son Amenhotep II was certainly indicative of the kingly domain promised to the descendants of Isaac: 'from the river of Egypt, unto the river Euphrates' (Genesis 15:18). If the covenant were to be taken literally, it would appear that the selling of the birthright by Esau to Jacob had no effect whatever; it was not until after the Amarna period that the lines from Esau and Jacob were united through marriage, subsequently descending to the Davidic kings of Judah.

18

# Moses of Egypt

## An Ark of Rushes

Exodus (11:3) informs us that 'Moses was very great in the land of Egypt, in the sight of Pharaoh's servants, and in the sight of the people'. However, despite his importance according to the Bible, it has often been said that there is no documentary evidence of Moses in the records of Egypt. Actually, this is not strictly true, because Moses was discussed, by name, in the *History of Egyp*t (*The Aegyptiaca*) by Manetho, who, as previously stated, was an adviser to pharaoh Ptolemy I around 300 BC. In a later 1st-century AD work entitled *Against Apion*, the Jewish historian Flavius Josephus detailed that Manetho had recorded Moses as having been an Egyptian priest at Heliopolis.[1] But, later in the same document, Josephus (who was trained for the Pharisee priesthood in Judaea), takes exception to Manetho's assertion that Moses was an Egyptian, stating, 'They would willingly lay claim to him themselves ... and pretend that he was of Heliopolis'.[2]

In contrast to this challenge of Manetho, Josephus himself alleged that Moses was a commander of the Egyptian army in the war against Ethiopia. His *Antiquities of the Jews* further states that Moses took the King of Ethiopia's daughter, Tharbis, for a wife, in order to preserve the peace between the Egyptian and

Ethiopian nations.[3] There is no mention of this military command in the Bible but, in support of Manetho's chronicle, Moses is positively cited in Exodus (2:19) as 'an Egyptian'.

As far as the Old Testament is concerned, the story of Moses is particularly incomplete. To begin, in Exodus (2:1-10) we learn of the birth of Moses and of how he was hidden at the river's edge in an ark of bulrushes, sealed with pitch. Then, within a few verses, he is grown to adulthood and married to Zipporah of Midian (Exodus 2:21). All that we are told of him meanwhile is that he slew an Egyptian for smiting a Hebrew (Exodus 2:11-12). Like many of the more colourful Old Testament stories, the tale of Moses and the ark of rushes was adapted from a Mesopotamian original. In this instance the prototype was the *Legend of Sharru-kîn*, who became Sargon the Great, King of Akkad (2371-2316 BC). An Assyrian text relating to Sargon reads:

> My changeling mother conceived me; in secret she bare me. She set me in a basket of rushes, and with pitch she sealed my lid. She cast me into the river, which rose not over me. The river bore me up, and carried me to Akki, the drawer of the water.[4]

The definition, 'drawer of the water', is of significance here since, according to Exodus (2:10), Moses was given his name by the Pharaoh's daughter because she 'drew him out of the water'. Josephus explains that the Egyptian word for water was *mo*, while those that were saved from the water were called *uses*. From this combination of words, he says, derived the biblical name *Mo-uses*/Moses.[5]

In practice (and as pointed out in 1937 by Sigmund Freud), the name Moses is written *Mosheh* or *Moshe* in Hebrew and is generally reckoned to derive from the Hebrew word *mosche*, which means 'the drawer out',[6] or from the verb *m-sh-a*, 'to draw'.[7] It is very doubtful, however, that an Egyptian princess would have been aware of Hebrew etymology; she would more likely have used an Egyptian name for the boy she adopted,

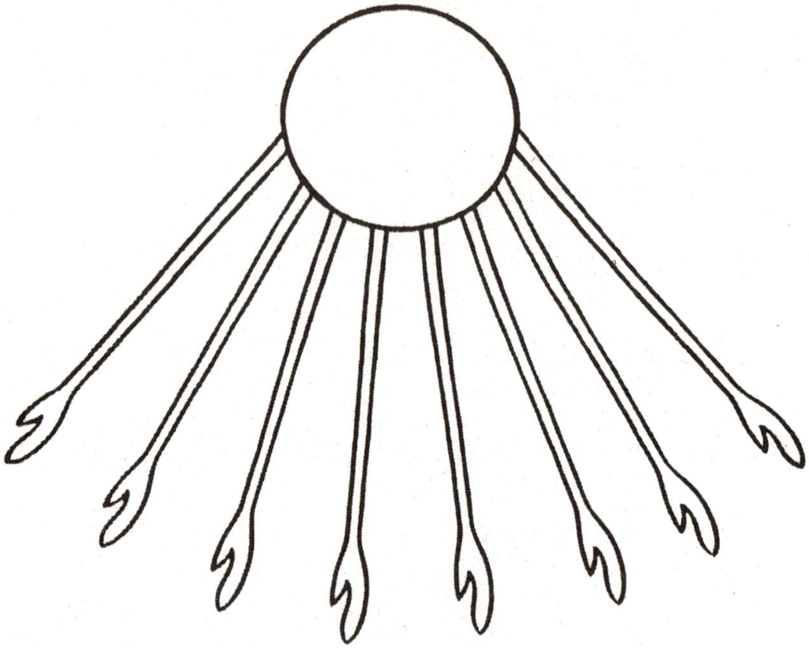

*The symbol of Aten.*

which rules out any Hebrew derivation of the name Moses. Either way, it is clear that the nominal root explained in Exodus was purposely structured to conform to the role of Akki, the drawer of the water, in the *Legend of Sharru-kîn*.

As cited by Freud, James Henry Breasted, Ahmed Osman, and others who have researched the etymology of the name Moses, it actually derived from the Egyptian word *mose* (Greek: *mosis*), which relates to an 'offspring' or 'heir',[8] as in Tuthmose (Tuthmosis): 'born of Thoth', and Amenmose (Amenmosis): 'born of Amen'.

The Cairo-born historian and linguist Ahmed Osman, who has conducted in-depth research into both Joseph and Moses in their contemporary Egyptian environment, has made a number of very important observations about the Old Testament story of Moses. In the course of these, he maintains that it would have been quite improbable under the customs of the time for an unmarried princess to have been allowed to adopt a child.[9] He also draws attention to the fact that Moses's father-in-law is named in Exodus (2:18-21) as Reuel, whereas only five verses later (Exodus 3:1) the man's name has strangely changed to Jethro. This is yet another example of how the Old Testament compilers managed to skip some 400 years of history by leaping, not very cleverly, from Reuel, the son of Esau (Genesis 36:4), to his descendant, Jethro, Lord of Midian, many generations later.

The book of Exodus explains that the baby Moses's life was in danger from the Egyptian authorities, whose Pharaoh had decreed death to all newborn Israelite males (a theme reintroduced for King Herod's slaying of the infants in the New Testament). The supposed reason for this blanket sentence was that the Israelites had 'multiplied, and waxed exceeding mighty, and the land was filled with them' (Exodus 1:7). The Pharaoh apparently instructed that 'every son that is born, shall ye cast into the river' — and so a woman of the house of Levi, in her attempt to deceive the Pharaoh, placed her three-month-old son in a basket of rushes and pitch, and set him down among the water-reeds.

Despite the complete illogicality of this action, which has been pointed out by many writers, the story then becomes even more implausible, for along came the Pharaoh's daughter, who seemed to care nothing for her father's dictate. She discovered the baby and immediately began conversing with the boy's sister, who just happened to be close by. The sister then returned the baby to its mother, who was paid by the princess to nurse him. Hence, the boy was back where he began and any fear of the authorities and their death-threat seems to have been conveniently forgotten. Eventually, the princess adopted the boy as her own son and called his name Moses, with no one levelling any query about the child's natural parents. That is the extent of the biblical story of Moses's childhood, and in the very next verse (Exodus 2:11) he is portrayed as a grown man.

The essence of this tale comes from the Mesopotamian folklore of Sharru-kîn, but apart from the romance of the baby in the ark, is there perhaps something similar in Egyptian record — maybe the story of a boy under sentence who was saved and later governed Egypt? The answer is 'yes'.

Yusuf-Yuya (Joseph) was chief minister to the Pharaohs Tuthmosis IV and Amenhotep III. When Tuthmosis died, his son Amenhotep married his infant sister Sitamun (as was the pharaonic tradition) so that he could inherit the throne. At that time Sitamun was very young, which has led some Egyptologists to reckon she was perhaps a daughter of Amenhotep—but she was his junior sister.[10] A cartouche[11] of Sitamun at the Metropolitan Museum, New York, describes her as 'The Great King's daughter', which is to say the daughter of Tuthmosis IV, not of Amenhotep III.

Shortly afterwards, in order to have an adult wife as well, Amenhotep also married Tiye, the daughter of Yusuf-Yuya. It was decreed, however, that no son born to Tiye could inherit the throne and, because of the length of her father's governorship, there was a general fear that his Israelite relatives were gaining too much power in Egypt. In addition, since Tiye was not the legitimate heiress, she could not represent the State god Amen (Amun).[12] So when Tiye became pregnant, there were those who thought her child should be killed at birth if a son. The first son born to Tiye was called Tuthmosis and he certainly did die prematurely (a whip bearing his name was found in the tomb of Tutankhamun).[13]

Tiye then conceived again, and on this occasion security arrangements were made with her Israelite relatives, who lived at Goshen in the Nile delta. Nearby, at Zaru (Zarukha), Tiye had a summer palace, where she went to have her baby. It was another son—but the royal midwives arranged to have the boy nursed by Tiye's sister-in-law Tey, a daughter of the house of Levi. (The fortified frontier settlement of Zaru was built on the site of the Hyksos city of Avaris. In later times it was reconstructed to become known as Pi-Ramesses in the reign of Ramesses II, who had been the mayor of Zaru.)[14]

Tiye's son Amenhotep (born *c.*1394 BC) was later educated at Heliopolis by the Egyptian priests of Ra (as explained by Manetho in respect of Moses) and in his teenage years he went to live at Thebes. By that time, his mother had become more influential than the senior queen, Sitamun, who had never borne a son and heir to the pharaoh, only a daughter who was called Nefertiti.

Pharaoh Amenhotep III then suffered a period of ill-health and, because there was no direct male heir to the royal house, young Amenhotep married his half-sister Nefertiti in order to rule as co-regent during this difficult time. When their father died, he succeeded as Amenhotep IV by virtue of his marriage to Nefertiti.[15] Were it not for this marriage, the 18th dynasty would have expired at their father's death.

Because of his part-Israelite upbringing, Amenhotep IV (sometimes called Amenophis IV[16]) could not accept the Egyptian deities and their myriad idols, so he developed the notion of Aten—an omnipotent god with no image, who was represented by a solar disc with downward rays. Aten was not the sun god, however, for the Egyptian sun god was Ra. The name Aten was the equivalent of the Hebrew *Adon*—a title borrowed from the Phoenician and meaning 'Lord'—with the equally familiar *Adonai* meaning 'my Lord'.[17] At the same time, Amenhotep (Amen is pleased) changed his name to Akhenaten (Glorious Spirit of the Aten[18]) and he closed all the temples of the Egyptian gods, making himself very unpopular, particularly with the priests of Ra and with those of the former national deity, Amen.

Akhenaten's household was distinctly domestic—quite different from the kingly norm in ancient Egypt—and he and Nefertiti had six daughters. But there were plots against his life and threats of armed insurrection if he did not allow the traditional gods to be worshipped alongside the faceless Aten. Akhenaten refused and was eventually forced to abdicate in short-term favour of his cousin Smenkhkare, who was succeeded by Tutankhaten (Akhenaten's son by his deputy queen, Kiya).

On taking the throne at the age of about eleven, Tutankhaten was obliged to change his name to Tutankhamun—thereby denoting a renewed allegiance to Amun (Amen), rather than to Aten—but he was to live for only a further nine or ten years. Akhenaten, meanwhile, was banished from Egypt in about 1361

BC,[19] although to his supporters he remained very much the rightful monarch. He was still the living heir to the throne from which he had been ousted, and he was still regarded by them as the royal *Mose* or *Mosis*.

Prior to his initial departure, Akhenaten (the *Mosis*) had been persuaded by his mother, Tiye, to move from Thebes—and this he did, establishing his newly built centre of Akhetaten (Horizon of the Aten),[20] the site of modern Tell el-Amarna. However, a fact which reference books generally fail to explain is that Akhenaten did not invent the god Aten. Even before Akhenaten's birth, the boat used by his father, Amenhotep III, on the lake at Zaru was called *Tehen Aten* (Aten Gleams).[21] There was also an Aten temple at Zaru before Akhenaten built his own Aten temples at Karnak and Luxor.[22]

The Israelite concept of a god without an image was already established in Egypt before Akhenaten came to the throne. What he did that was so different was to install Aten as the sole god of Egypt, and his was the world's first example of religious intolerance at a State level—a strict monotheism foisted upon the people. It was this somewhat discordant concept of the One God in Egypt that originally inspired the 1930s research of Sigmund Freud, leading him to associate Moses with the reign of Pharaoh Akhenaten.[23]

Although Aten was relegated to a more general position within the Egyptian pantheon during the reign of Tutankhamun, Aten-worship was not banned by the young pharaoh. This is confirmed by the colourful gold and inlaid back panel of his throne, which depicts him and his wife, Ankhesenpaaten, together with the Aten disc. Tutankhamun did, however, move the royal capital from Akhetaten to Memphis.[24] The Aten cult continued after Tutankhamun's death, at which time the crown was transferred to his great-uncle Aye, the husband of Tey, who had nursed both Akhenaten and his half-sister Nefertiti. But Aye was to be the last of the so-called Amarna Kings; he was succeeded by his son-in-law General Horemheb, who dispensed with Aten, forbade the mention of Akhenaten's name and excised the Amarna Kings from the official *King List*. He also destroyed numerous monuments of the era,[25] and it was for this reason that the discovery of Tutankhamun's tomb in November 1922 came as such a welcome surprise, for so little was known about him beforehand.[26]

## The Rod of Aaron

Initially, just as the Bible explains (Exodus 2:15-3:1), Moses fled to the land of Midian, east of the Sinai peninsular. His senior queen, Nefertiti, appears to have died a short while before this, and although her remains have not been discovered, a cartouche bearing her name was found in the 1930s in the royal tomb at Amarna.[27]

In Midian, Moses married Zipporah, the daughter of Lord Jethro, and she bore him two sons, Gershom and Eliezer (Exodus 2:22, 18:4). Outside the Bible, Zipporah (meaning 'female bird'[28]) is the subject of her own Jewish mythology; she is said to have had talons on her feet,[29] just as her ancestor Lilith was portrayed in ancient Sumer. Zipporah's father, Jethro, was a descendant of Esau and his wife Bashemath, the daughter of Abraham's son Ishmael *(see* Chart: *The Egyptian Connection*).

The Bible story then moves to Moses and the burning bush on Mount Horeb in Sinai. The bush was enveloped in a fiery light, but it was not consumed (Exodus 3:3) and from its midst came an angel. El Shaddai then appeared in person, announcing to Moses that he was to be called 'I am that I am' (Jehovah). After this, arrangements were made for Moses to return to Egypt and retrieve the Israelites, who had been placed in bondage by the new authorities.

By that time, with the Amarna dynasty terminated and General Horemheb's reign concluded, a whole new regime had begun in Egypt: the 19th dynasty, whose founding pharaoh was Ramesses I. Having been away from Egypt for many years,

Moses (Akhenaten) evidently asked Jehovah how he would prove his identity to the Israelites, whereupon three instructions were given. These instructions have puzzled theologians for the longest time because, although the Bible opposes all forms of magic, Moses was advised to perform three magical feats. Generally, when magical deeds are discussed, they are referred to as 'miracles', so that the power of man is always superseded by the supreme abilities of God. But in this instance Moses was seemingly granted divine powers to enable him to convince the Israelites that he was an authorized messenger of Jehovah (Exodus 4:1-9).

He was first advised to cast his rod to the ground, where it would become a serpent, but would be reinstated as a rod when lifted. Secondly, he was to place his hand on his breast, from where it would emerge white and leprous, but would return to normal when the act was repeated. Then he was to pour river-water on to the land, at which it would turn to blood.

Quite how these things were supposed to prove the involvement of Jehovah, as against that of any other god, is not made clear—but Moses seemed content enough with the plan. He did confess, however, that he was 'not eloquent', being 'slow of speech, and of a slow tongue', intimating that he was not well versed in the Israelite language. So it was arranged that his brother Aaron (who was more fluent) would act as an interpreter.

Until this point in the story, only an unnamed sister has been introduced, but now a brother called Aaron makes his appearance (Exodus 4:14), and with a somewhat baffling aftermath. Moses and Aaron journeyed to Egypt and made themselves known to the Israelites—but it was before the pharaoh, not before the Israelites, that the magic of the rod and serpent was performed. Moreover, it was not performed by Moses as planned, but by Aaron (Exodus 7:10-12).

This sequence is of particular importance because it serves to indicate that Aaron held his own pharaonic status. The rituals of the serpent-rod and the withered hand (though described as if magic in the Bible) were both aspects of the rejuvenation festivals of the Egyptian kings—ceremonies wherein their divine powers were heightened. The pharaohs had various sceptres (rods) for different occasions, and the sceptre of rejuvenation was a rod topped with a brass serpent. It was also customary for the king to place his right arm limply across his chest, while supporting it with his left hand.[30] A preparation for this ceremony is pictorially shown in the tomb of Kherof, one of Queen Tiye's stewards, and the scene depicts her husband (Moses's father) Amenhotep III.

So, did Akhenaten (Moses) have a brother who was himself a pharaoh—a pharaoh whose fate is unknown and who is similarly recorded as having disappeared rather than dying? Indeed he did—at least, he had a feeding-brother, whose own mother was Tey, the Israelite wet-nurse of Akhenaten and Nefertiti. As a pharaoh, this man had succeeded for just a short while after the abdication of Akhenaten; his name was Smenkhkare. He was the grandson of Yusuf-Yuya the vizier, and the son of Aye (the brother of Akhenaten's birth-mother, Tiye). Correctly stated, this pharaoh's name was Smenkh-ka-ra (Vigorous is the Soul of Ra).[31] Alternatively, since Ra was the state sun god of the Heliopolis House of Light, called On,[32] Pharaoh Smenkh-ka-ra was also Smenkh-ka-ra-on, from the phonetic ending of which derives the name Aaron.

Manetho's *Egyptian King List* records Smenkhkare (Aaron) by the name Achencheres,[33] which was later corrupted (by the Christian Church-father, Eusebius) to Cencheres.[34] By this name (further varied to Cinciris in the Gaelic annals) Pharaoh Smenkhkare was of particular significance to the histories of Ireland and Scotland, for he was the father of the princess historically known as Scota, from whom the original Scots-Gaels were descended.[35] Her husband was Niul, the Governor of Capacyront by the Red Sea.[36] He was, by birth, a Black Sea prince of Scythia, and according to the 17th-century *History of Ireland*, 'Niul and Aaron entered into an alliance of friendship with one another'.[37] The Gaelic text further states that Gaedheal (Gael), the son of Niul and Princess Scota, was born in Egypt 'at the time when Moses began to act as leader of the children of Israel'.[38] The name Scota (Scythian: 'ruler of people') was gained by the princess on marrying Niul.

## Enigma of the Tombs

In the *Journal of Near Eastern Studies*[39] it is reported that since Nefertiti was the designated Great Royal Wife of Akhenaten, she was doubtless of superior royal blood. Akhenaten achieved his kingly status by marrying her as the senior heiress in the pharaonic tradition, but, undeterred by this, many Egyptologists (in a continued attempt to decry the Amarna Kings, whose historical story is at variance with the Old Testament) make light of Nefertiti's heritage. They prefer to suggest that she was not necessarily the daughter of Amenhotep III and Sitamun, and take little notice of the fact that a boundary stela (upright slab) of Akhenaten specifically denotes her as the heiress,[40] calling her Mistress of Upper and Lower Egypt; Lady of the Two Lands. In fact, through some 3000 years of dynastic history, the face of Nefertiti has emerged as the best known of all the queens of Egypt, and her great importance is emphasized by the astonishing frequency of her name on discovered cartouches: sixty-seven mentions in contrast with only three for her husband Akhenaten.[41]

With regard to the Sinai exile of Akhenaten, it can be said that there is not a shred of evidence concerning his death: he simply disappeared from Egypt;[42] and while speculation continues over Smenkhkare, there is no Egyptian record of his death either. A tomb over which controversy now rages in respect of Smenkhkare and Akhenaten is not at Amarna, but that numbered Tomb KV 55 in the Theban Valley of Kings. This tomb was discovered, unfinished and water-damaged, in January 1907. It has only one burial chamber and the body within was identified as a female. At first it was thought that it was probably Akhenaten's mother, Queen Tiye, but this was only a guess since there were no cartouches to indicate the occupant's name. There were, nevertheless, remnants of Tiye's gold-overlaid sarcophagus. Subsequently, another unidentified female body was found nearby in Tomb KV 35 (the tomb of Amenhotep II) and this is now thought to be the body of Queen Tiye.[43]

In the wake of this discovery, the body from Tomb KV 55 (which is just a badly preserved skeleton) seems mysteriously to have changed sex, and was then claimed to be the remains of Akhenaten.[44] The reason for this revised theory was that some contemporary depictions of Akhenaten show him with an unusually rounded pelvic structure. But Amarna Art, as it has become known, was particularly unique in Egypt and incorporated many physical eccentricities, such as the exceptionally long neck on the famous bust of Nefertiti. To endeavour to match real figures against this revolutionary artistic style is rather like looking for the distorted characters who modelled for Picasso. Recognizing this, and conceding that the body was female, some Egyptologists (in order to sustain their Akhenaten theory) even suggest that perhaps Akhenaten was really a woman masquerading as a man—completely disregarding the fact that he and Nefertiti are known to have had six daughters. Others, who also pursue the idea that the body is an unusually shaped male, reckon it is perhaps the remains of Smenkhkare[45]—but this notion is quite unsupported and there is not one textual fragment which even suggests his name.

Four alabaster canopic jars (used for the entrails of an embalmed body), with finely carved female heads, were also found in the tomb, but they are uninscribed. In spite of the ongoing debate over whether the skeletal remains could perhaps be those of Akhenaten (Moses) or Smenkhkare (Aaron), the only extant textual fragments indicate that the tomb was prepared for a royal female and, although the inscriptions are badly damaged, the occupant's name certainly has a feminine ending.

As far as Akhenaten is concerned, his correctly planned tomb site has been separately located at Amarna, where it appears to have been cut from the rock in about year six of his seventeen-year reign. Also found is the outer of his three destined mummy casings (the main sarcophagus), but there are none of the inner casings that would have been used to house his mummy. Similarly, there are no items of funerary furniture, which indicates that the tomb was never used. Akhenaten's alabaster canopic chest (with four compartments for the jars) has also been found, but this too was empty, unstained and quite unused; it had simply been placed in the tomb in readiness to receive the jars, as was the preparatory custom.[46]

## The Exodus

We have identified that the Israelite exodus from Egypt took place in about 1330 BC, but before we progress the story further it is necessary to consider the statement in the book of 1-Kings (6:1) which claims that the Temple of King Solomon was built 480 years after the exodus. Solomon's reign can be determined fairly accurately from the astronomically dated Assyrian record of the Battle of Karkar in 853 BC. King Ahab of Israel was present at this battle in alliance with Hadad-idri of Damascus, and it was the twenty-first year of Ahab's reign. By working back through the regnal years of the kings of Judah and Israel, we arrive at Solomon in 968 BC, with the Jerusalem Temple begun around 966 BC.[47] Adding back 480 years to this date produces an exodus date of 1446 BC, which is considerably earlier than has been calculated. However, there is another important factor to consider when reading the 1-Kings entry.

At the very earliest, the Old Testament was begun during the Israelites' Babylonian captivity from 586 BC, by which time all the kings of Judah in the Davidic succession from Solomon had reigned. During the course of this, a figurative dynastic standard had been established in the royal line—a symbolic standard of 'forty years' for each generation,[48] which is why the reigns of David and Solomon are given at precisely forty years each (2-

Samuel 5:4, 1-Kings 11:42). The Bible lists a total of twelve generations from Jacob (who took the Israelites into Egypt) down to Solomon, and the resultant calculation of 12 x 40 produces 480 years. On account of this, the original estimate was made from the time the Israelites first arrived in Egypt, not from the later time of the exodus as stated. The problem confronting the scribes who made the calculation was that, as identified, some four centuries of history are completely ignored between the books of Genesis and Exodus, and so the forty-year dynastic standard could not be applied back to Jacob. It was, therefore, strategically applied to the period between the exodus and King Solomon, even though it did not conform to the generation standard. As pointed out by Professor of Egyptology T. Eric Peet, back in 1923, the 480 years as given in 1-Kings 'is a figure open to the utmost suspicion'.[49]

Having been in Sinai and Midian from his abdication in about 1361 BC, Moses (Akhenaten) returned to Egypt with Aaron (Smenkhkare) to take up the Israelite cause against the incoming Pharaoh Ramesses I, who was apparently holding many of the families in bonded service. Given that Akhenaten's own 18th dynasty had terminated with Pharaoh Horemheb, who had no legitimate heir, a new dynasty had commenced (*c.*1335 BC) under Horemheb's erstwhile vizier Ramesses, the son of a troop commander called Seti.[50]

By performing the secret rituals of the serpent-rod and withered hand, Moses and Aaron were clearly challenging Ramesses's right of succession—but Ramesses controlled the Egyptian army and this proved a decisive factor in the power struggle.[51] Moses succeeded in establishing his Israelite supporters as a community at Zaru and, having failed in his attempt to regain his pharaonic position, he managed to persuade Ramesses to allow him and the Israelites to leave the country.

Ramesses I did not survive until the end of his second regnal year. This may, or may not, equate with the Bible's implied death of the pharaoh in pursuit of the Israelites (Exodus 15:19), but immediately after the event (even before the mummification of Ramesses)[52] his son, Seti I, launched a campaign into Sinai and Syria, taking his troops in a swift military assault into Palestine.[53] The very fact that the land of Israel is mentioned by name in a documented account of this campaign proves that the Israelites were in Palestine at that time, for the Israelites (Children of Israel) were specifically the Egyptian-born descendants of Jacob-Israel. Outside Egypt, prior to the exodus, there were plenty of Hebrews, but there were no Israelites and there was no land of Israel.[54]

The Hebrews of Palestine had been documented long before the Israelite exodus from Egypt; they feature in letters from the reigns of Amenhotep III and Akhenaten. In 1887 a peasant woman, searching among the ruins of Amarna, unearthed a large number of inscribed clay tablets which proved to be diplomatic correspondence between various Palestinian rulers and the pharaohs of the 18th dynasty. From these (known as the *Amarna Letters*) it has now been deduced that the Egyptian Empire was in serious decline by the time of Akhenaten, with the Hittites invading Syria, while Abda-khiba, the Mitannian Governor of Jerusalem, appealed for Akhenaten's help against an invasion by the Hebrews (the Habiru).[55]

The information concerning Seti's campaign comes from a large granite stela discovered in 1896 by the British archaeologist Sir W. M. Flinders Petrie. It was found in the Theban funerary temple of Pharaoh Merneptah (*c*.1236-1202 BC), and its inscribed record had been commenced in the reign of Akhenaten's father, Amenhotep III. Merneptah (the grandson of Seti I) had brought the history down to date on the reverse of the stela, and in year five of his reign he spoke of the Israelite residents of Palestine. Not only had the Israelites completed their period in the wilderness of Sinai, but they had been in Palestine long enough to pose a significant threat to the pharaoh. The *Israel Stela*, as it is called, is now in the Cairo Museum and within the context of Merneptah's record are details of anti-Israeli campaigns which Egyptologists have dated to the reigns of his predecessors,

Ramesses II and Seti I.[56] 'Israel is devastated,' states the stela; 'Her seed is no more; Palestine has become a widow of Egypt'.[57]

It can be determined from this sequence of events that the Israelite exodus from Egypt occurred during the year of Ramesses I's death—the first year of Pharaoh Seti I (*c*.1333 BC). However, in studying the Old Testament account of the exodus, and the dramatic crossing of the Red Sea, whose waters parted to become 'a wall unto them on their right hand and on their left' (Exodus 14:22), we find there was actually no sea for the Israelites to cross. We are told that Moses led the people from Avaris (Pi-Ramesses) in the Nile delta plain of Goshen, from where they travelled into Sinai (Exodus 16:1) on a route towards Midian (Exodus 18:1)—but this route traversed the desert wilderness north of the Red Sea where the 103-mile (165 km) artificial Suez Canal (opened in 1869) is now located. This, of course, places the story of Moses parting the waters in the same mythical realm as the early tale of the ark of bulrushes.

19

# Magic of the Mountain

## The Furnace and the Pyramids

Eventually, we reach the point where Moses and the Israelites are camped by the holy mountain—ostensibly the same mountain where Moses had met with Jehovah and witnessed the burning bush. At this stage, the location is called Mount Sinai (Exodus 19:11), whereas it was hitherto called Mount Horeb (Exodus 3:1, 17:6), the name by which it is later identified again (Exodus 33:6). Because of this, many have wondered whether there were perhaps two sacred mountains, although the continuous story relates, seemingly, to only one with two names.

It is important to recognize that until the 4th century AD there was no Mount Sinai as such. Just as with the supposed Mount Ararat in the story of Noah (which is actually a mountain range), the mountains of the Sinai peninsular are extensive, and the southern peak commonly known as Mount Sinai was given its name by Greek Christian monks 1700 years after the time of Moses.[1] But this mountain (now called *Gebel Musa*—Mount of Moses) was not the sacred Mount Horeb of the Bible, for Horeb was the peak now called Mount Serâbît.

Soaring to over 2,600 feet above sea-level, the mountain is found *en route* from the Egyptian delta (before reaching Gebel Musa) at a location called Serâbît el-Khâdim. This is a region of turquoise mines; it is also the site of the most important biblical discovery ever made, although the explorers did not recognize its true significance at the time. Indeed, it has received little publicity since. Why? Because, as previously mentioned (Chapter 6), the *Memorandum and Articles of Association* of the Egypt Exploration Fund expressly stated that surveys and excavations would only be approved if they upheld the Bible narrative—and this discovery did not. At least, it did not uphold the Church's interpretation and teaching of the narrative.

From very early days, Sinai was regarded as part of Egypt, but it had no military garrison, nor any resident governor. During the 18th dynasty (the dynasty of Akhenaten) the peninsular was placed under the control of two officials: the Royal Chancellor and the Royal Messenger in Foreign Lands. In the time of Tuthmosis IV and Amenhotep III (the era of the vizier Yusuf-Yuya), the Royal Messenger was an official called Neby. He was also the mayor and troop commander of Zaru where the Aten cult flourished after Akhenaten's abdication through the reigns of Aye and Tutankhamun. From the days of Amenhotep III (Moses's father) the position of Royal Chancellor was hereditary in the Hyksos family of Pa-Nehas,[2] and Akhenaten (Moses) had appointed a descendant called Panahesy to the governorship of Sinai. Because of this, Moses knew that Sinai was a safe haven when he withdrew from the Egyptian delta—a haven where there was an operative Egyptian temple at Mount Serâbît.

The temple was built over an expanse of 230 feet (*c*.70 m), extending from a great cave high on the mountain plateau, overlooking a deep valley. From at least as far back as the 4th-dynasty pharaoh Sneferu[3] (*c*.2613-2589 BC—the said builder of the Dahshur pyramids), and predating the great Gizeh pyramids attributed to his successors, the temple had been dedicated to the goddess Hathor, but from soon after the time of Moses this important shrine was destined to be lost to the world for over 3000 years. Not until 1904 did Sir W. M. Flinders Petrie and his team discover the site—and in so doing they unexpectedly found the Bible's holy mountain.

The above-ground part of the temple was constructed from sandstone quarried from the mountain; it comprised a series of adjoined halls, shrines, courts, cubicles and chambers set within a surrounding enclosure wall. Of these, the key features unearthed are the Hall of Hathor, the main Sanctuary, the Shrine of Kings and the Portico Court. All around are pillars and stelae denoting the Egyptian kings through the ages, while certain kings such as Tuthmosis III are depicted many times on standing-stones and wall reliefs. Upon his discovery, Petrie wrote: 'There is no other such monument known which makes us regret the more that it is not in better preservation. The whole of it was buried, and no one had any knowledge of it until we cleared the site.'[4]

The Cave of Hathor is cut into the natural rock, with flat inner walls that have been carefully smoothed. In the centre is a large upright pillar of Amenemhet III (*c.*1841-1797 BC), the son-in-law of Esau and father of Dragon Queen Sobeknefru. Also portrayed is his chief chamberlain, Khenemsu, and his seal-bearer, Ameny-senb. Deep within the cave Petrie found a limestone stela of pharaoh Ramesses I—a slab upon which Ramesses (a traditionally reckoned Aten opposer, according to most Egyptologists) surprisingly described himself as 'The ruler of all that Aten embraces'.[5] Petrie also found an Amarna statue-head of Moses's mother Queen Tiye, with her cartouche set in the crown.

In the courts and halls of the outer temple were found numerous stone-carved rectangular tanks and circular basins, along with a variety of curiously shaped bench-altars with recessed fronts and split-level surfaces. There were also round tables, trays and saucers, together with alabaster vases and cups—many of which were shaped like lotus-flowers. In addition, the rooms housed a good collection of glazed plaques, cartouches, scarabs and sacred ornaments, designed with spirals, diagonal-squares and basketwork. There were wands of an unidentified hard material, and in the portico were two conical (shem-shaped) stones of about 6 inches (15 cm) and 9 inches (22.5 cm) in height, respectively. The explorers were baffled enough by these, but they were further confounded by the discovery of a metallurgist's crucible and a considerable amount of pure white powder concealed beneath carefully laid flagstones.

For many decades, Egyptologists have argued over why a crucible would have been necessary in a temple, while at the same time debating a mysterious substance called *mfkz*t, which has dozens of mentions in wall and stelae inscriptions.[6] Some have claimed that *mfkzt* might have been copper; many preferred the idea of turquoise; others supposed it was perhaps malachite—but they were all unsubstantiated guesses, as there were no traces of any of these materials at the site. If turquoise-mining had been a primary function of the temple masters through so many dynastic periods, then one would expect to find turquoise stones not only at the site, but also in abundance within the tombs of Egypt, but such has not been the case. Another cause of wonderment were the innumerable inscribed references to 'bread' and the traditional *ayin* hieroglyph for 'light' found in the Shrine of the Kings.

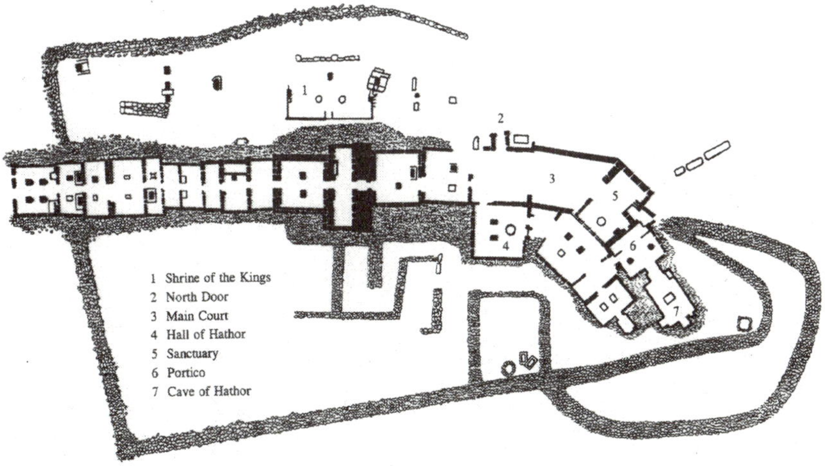


*Plan of the Sinai mountain temple at Serâbît el-Khâdim.*

After some consideration, it was suggested that the powder was a remnant of copper-smelting, but as Petrie pointed out smelting does not produce white powder: it leaves a dense black slag. Moreover, there is no supply of copper ore (the main metal of Sinai) within miles of the temple. In any event, it was determined that smelting was conducted in the distant valleys. Others guessed that the powder was ash from the burning of plants to produce alkali, but there was no trace whatever of plant residue.

For want of any other explanation, it was determined that the white powder and the shem-stones were probably associated with some form of sacrificial rite[7]—but this was an Egyptian temple and animal sacrifice was not an Egyptian practice. Moreover, there were no remnants of bones or any other foreign matter within the many tons of white powder that lay in the newly exposed storerooms—it was perfectly clean and quite unadulterated. Petrie stated: 'Though I carefully searched these ashes in dozens of instances, winnowing them in a breeze, I never found a fragment of bone or anything else'.[8]

What Petrie had actually found was the alchemical workshop of Akhenaten and the pharaohs before him—a temple-laboratory where the furnace would have roared and smoked in the production of the sacred fire-stone of the high-spin *shem-an-na*—the enigmatic white powder which the temple priests had called *mfkzt*. Quite suddenly, the words of Exodus begin to make sense as we read them again with a wholly new insight: 'And mount Sinai was altogether on a smoke because the Lord descended upon it in fire, and the smoke thereof ascended as the smoke of a furnace, and the whole mount quaked greatly' (Exodus 19:18). This is, of course, reminiscent of the earlier passage in Genesis, prior to the covenant with Abraham: 'And it came to pass that when the sun went down, and it was dark, behold a smoking furnace, and a burning lamp that passed between those pieces' (Genesis 15:17).

The burning bush, which was on fire, but was not consumed (Exodus 3:4), can now be considered anew, for the description is identical to the experiment (*see* Chapter 13) in which a pencil was stood on end within an explosive blaze of fiery light but emerged quite unmoved by the blast. In Exodus (32:20) we read that Moses took the golden calf which the Israelites had made and 'burnt it in the fire, and ground it to a powder'. This is precisely the process of a *shem-an-na* furnace, and it is evident that the Egyptian priests of the goddess Hathor had been working the fire for countless generations before the priests of Aten became involved in the time of Akhenaten. It was, of course, Akhenaten's great-great-grandfather Tuthmosis III who had reorganized the ancient mystery schools and founded the Great White Brotherhood of the Master Craftsmen. It was also Tuthmosis III who had constructed a painted rock-cut shrine to Hathor, who was depicted as the feeding-mother of his son Amenhotep II.[9] She was known to the Egyptians as Lady of the Turquoise,[10] and Serâbît el-Khâdim in Sinai was noted for its extensive turquoise-mines.

Hathor was an aspect of Isis the Great Mother,[11] and her tradition is particularly relevant because she appears on the very oldest artefact of ancient Egypt[12]—a green slate palette from the time of King Narmer, who ruled (*c*.3200 BC) at the time of Tubal-cain, before the 1st dynasty of Egypt. Whereas some gods and goddesses were discarded and forgotten through the changing dynasties, a new temple was built for Hathor by Ptolemy IX in the final throes of pre-Roman Egypt, and within thirty years of his reign, the last of all the pharaohs, the famous Queen Cleopatra VII (*c*.51-30 BC), had her one and only relief carved on the wall of the Hathor temple. (As a guide to the measurement of time in this regard, Cleopatra lived 1000 years nearer to today's date than she did to the early King Narmer.)

But why was Hathor so important—and what was her association with the sun-disc of Aten? She was actually a most prominent nursing goddess and, as the daughter of Ra, she was said to have given birth to the sun. In a slate relief of Hathor from the time of Pharaoh Menkaure (*c*.2520 BC) the Aten disc is carried between her horns, and she is similarly depicted elsewhere.

Hathor was traditionally portrayed with horns, as were Isis and others on occasions, for horns were indicative of knowledge reception—a divine communications device rather like antennae or aerials. For this reason, gods and goddesses alike were sometimes depicted as bulls, cows, goats or rams and, in the female sense, cow-goddesses such as Hathor were also representative of nursing motherhood. Female horns were often symbolized by an upturned, horizontal crescent moon, whereas the sun disc was a male emblem. Since horns were associated with godly communication, they were in later times the objects of kingly or warrior adornment, being attached to helmets such as the headpiece of the 5th-century Frankish King Clovis.[13] Those who communicated directly with the gods were generally attributed with horns; it was for this reason that Michelangelo (1475-1564) added horns to his famous statue of Moses on the Roman monument to Pope Julius II. The Christian Church authorities were somewhat disconcerted by this, for by that time horns had come to be more associated with the devil, while the traditional goat of Capricorn (an emblem of the biblical Ham) was denounced as a heresy of witchcraft.

Hathor was the originally defined Queen of the West and Mistress of the Lilithian Netherworld, to where she was said to carry those who knew the right spells.[14] She was the revered protectress of womanhood, the lady of the sycamore, goddess of love, tombs and song. And it was from the milk of Hathor that the pharaohs were said to gain their divinity, becoming gods in their own right. In more ancient Sumerian times, during the days of the original Star Fire ritual, the Bloodline kings who were fed with the hormone-rich lunar essence of the Anunnaki goddesses were also said to have been nourished with their milk—notably that of Ishtar. It would appear, therefore, that this milk contained an enzyme that was especially conducive to active longevity—and this was very likely the enzyme that genetic researchers have called telomerase.

As reported in the *Science* journal,[15] corporate studies and those of the University of Texas Southwestern Medical Center, have determined that telomerase has unique anti-ageing properties. Healthy body cells are programmed to divide many times during a lifetime, but this process of division and replication is finite, so that a non-dividing state is ultimately achieved: this is a crucial factor of ageing. The division potential is controlled by caps at the end of DNA strands (rather like the plastic tips on shoelaces), and these caps are the *telomeres*. As each cell divides, a piece of telomere is lost, and the dividing process ceases when the telomeres have shortened to an optimum and critical length. There is then no new cell replication and all that follows is deterioration.

Laboratory experiments with tissue samples have now shown that application of the genetic enzyme telomerase can prevent telomere shortening upon cell division and replication. Hence, body cells can continue to divide far beyond their naturally restricted programming (just as do cancer cells, which can achieve immortality through being rich in telomerase). Telomerase is not usually expressed in normal body tissue but, apart from being present in malignant tumours, it is also apparent in reproductive cells. It seems, therefore, that somewhere within our DNA structure is the genetic ability to produce this anti-ageing enzyme, but the potential has somehow been switched off.

By the time of Egypt's 12th dynasty of Queen Sobeknefru, the kingly rituals of the milk and Star Fire of the goddess had been superseded by the ceremonies of the sacred fire-stone. This manufactured supplement became the new route to the Light and, as we have seen (Chapter 14), it was figuratively represented as 'bread'.

On one of the rock tablets near to the Mount Serâbît cave entrance is a representation of Tuthmosis IV in the presence of Hathor. Before him are two offering stands topped with lotus flowers and behind him is a man bearing a loaf of white bread. Another stela details the mason Ankhib offering two conical bread-cakes to the king and there are similar portrayals elsewhere in the temple complex. Perhaps one of the most significant is a depiction of Hathor and Amenhotep III. The goddess, complete with horns and solar disc, holds a necklace in one hand, while offering the emblem of life and dominion to the pharaoh with the other.[16] Behind her is the treasurer Sobekhotep, who holds in readiness a conical shem of 'white bread'. Treasurer Sobekhotep is very importantly described elsewhere in the temple[17] as the 'Overseer of the secrets of the House of Gold, who brought the noble Precious Stone to his majesty'.

It was by no chance that Pharaoh Menkaure elected to feature Hathor beside his wife and himself in the slate triad portrait which incorporated the Aten disc,[18] for the Hathor temple at Mount Serâbît in Sinai was directly associated with pyramid construction. The 4th dynasty of Menkaure was the great dynasty of the Gizeh pyramids—the dynasty of Khufu (Cheops), who built the Great Pyramid (481 feet (*c*.146 m) in height); of Khafre (Chephren) who built the Second Pyramid (471 feet [*c*.143 m]); and of Menkaure (Mycerinus) himself, who is credited with the Third Gizeh Pyramid (215 feet [*c*.65 m]).

When the white powder of gold was manufactured for the purpose of feeding the light-bodies of the pharaohs in the Star Fire tradition, it was plainly not required in great quantity. However, the Sinai furnace laboratory of Hathor was geared to produce large amounts of the substance. Why?

If we now remind ourselves of the experiments discussed earlier (Chapter 14), we can recall that not only is the powder of the highward fire-stone capable of raising human consciousness, but it is also a monatomic superconductor with no gravitational attraction. One of the great researchers into gravity from the 1960s has been the Russian physicist Andrei Sakharov, and the mathematics for his theory (based on gravity as a zero-point) were published by Hal Puthoff of the Institute of Advanced Studies.[19] With regard to the monatomic white powder, Puthoff has since made the point that, because gravity determines space-time, then the powder is capable of bending space-time.[20] It is 'exotic matter', he explained, with a gravitational attraction of less than zero.

*Amenhotep III with the goddess Hathor, along with Treasurer Sobekhotep who carries the conical* shem-an-na.

As we learned from the powder analysis, not only can the substance be contrived to weigh less than nothing, and be made to disappear into an unknown dimension, but so too can the pan in which the substance is placed be caused to weigh less than nothing. Under the right circumstances, therefore, the powder is capable of transposing its own weightlessness to its host, which might be a pan, or might very well be an enormous block of stone.

How did they build the pyramids? Were the thousands of massive sandstone blocks[21] weighing many tons apiece raised to great heights, with such accuracy, by hundreds of thousands of slaves using nothing but ropes and ramps over an undefined period of time, as is the common speculation? Certainly not. To construct an inclined plane to the top of the Great Pyramid at a gradient of 1:10 would have required a ramp 4800 feet (*c.*1460 m) in length, with a volume three times greater than that of the pyramid itself.[22] The building process would actually have been far more straightforward: the pyramids were doubtless constructed with the technology of the superconducting highward fire-stone—the sacred anti-gravitational *shem-an-na* produced at the Mount Serâbît temple of Hathor. Indeed, the very word 'pyramid' derives from the Greek word *pyr*, which means 'fire' (whence *pyre* and *pyro*)—the pyramids were, in essence, 'fire-begotten'.[23]

The three great pyramids of Gizeh are assigned as the tombs of Khufu, Khafre and Menkaure, yet for all the investigation of their known internal and subterranean chambers and passages, no bodily remains have been found in these monuments, nor have the bodies of these Old Kingdom pharaohs been found anywhere else. In the secret repository of the King's Chamber, within the Great Pyramid, the age-old tradition relates that the builders had placed 'instruments of iron, and arms which rust not, and glass which might be bended and yet not broken, and strange spells'[24]—but what did the first explorers of the 9th-century Caliph Al-Ma'mun find, having tunnelled their way into the sealed chamber? Then, as today, the only furniture was a lidless, hollowed granite coffer,[25] containing not a body, but a layer of a mysterious powdery substance. This was superficially determined to be grains of feldspar and mica,[26] which are both minerals of the aluminium silicate group.

During the course of the recent white powder research, aluminium and silica were two of the constituent elements revealed by conventional analysis of a granular sample known to be a 100 percent platinum-group compound. Standard laboratory testing is done by striking a sample with a DC arc for 15 seconds at a sun-surface heat of 5500 degrees centigrade. However, a continuation of the burn-time way beyond the normal testing procedure revealed the noble metals of which the substance truly consisted. It is because of the limitations placed on the conventional testing sequence that 5 percent by dry weight of our brain tissue is said to be carbon, whereas more rigorous analysis reveals it as the platinum-group metals iridium and rhodium in the high-spin state.

The once sealed King's Chamber appears to have been contrived as a superconductor, capable of transporting the pharaoh into another dimension of space-time though the Meissner Field (a body's polar magnetic aura). It was here that the pharaoh's rite of passage was administered in accordance with the *Book of the Dead*—a passage which was facilitated by the question, 'What is it?' (*Manna*?).

The great tragedy of desecration now apparent at Mount Serâbît is that the Hathor temple site, as it exists today, is far removed from Petrie's own descriptions and photographic archive—much to the dismay of visitors who make the arduous climb. Along with all the portable items, numerous important stelae, carved slabs, inscribed pillars, obelisks and wall reliefs were removed by museum authorities subsequent to the discovery and secreted in storage away from the public gaze. Their current whereabouts is a subject that will feature in the next book in this Grail series: *Destiny of the House of Gold.*

## Miriam and the Book of Jasher

Having progressed thus far, we still have one of the Egyptian family to discover: Miriam, the sister of Moses. An elder sister first appears in the story of the ark of rushes (Exodus 2:7), but she is not named at that stage. Much later (Exodus 15:20) we are introduced to a woman called Miriam, who is described as being the sister of Aaron. Then, eventually (Numbers 26:59), it is said that Miriam was the sister of both Moses and Aaron.

The Hebrew name Miriam has its equivalent in the Greek form of Maria/Mary—and derived in the first instance from the

Egyptian name Mery, meaning 'beloved'.[27] It comes as no surprise to discover in the family records of Akhenaten the names of two princesses called Mery-taten (Beloved of Aten), one being his daughter and the other his granddaughter. The Mery epithet was also applied to Queen Nefertiti herself, the elder half-sister and wife of Akhenaten. She too was a feeding-sister of Smenkhkare, for her wet-nurse was Smenkhkare's mother Tey of the house of Levi: an inscription at Tey's Amarna tomb describes her as 'Nurse and tutor of the queen'. Similarly (with regard to Akhenaten), she is described as being 'The great nurse, nourisher of the god, adorner of the king'.[28] In view of this, Nefertiti was identified some years ago as the possible sister of Moses who appeared at the water's edge when he was a baby.[29] In theory, such a deduction would appear quite logical, but since the story of the ark of rushes has a fictional base, the identity of the sister portrayed in this sequence is of little relevance.

More important to the ongoing scheme of things is the later Miriam, who first appears with Moses and Aaron in Sinai. In this regard we find the *Mery* epithet applied to another half-sister and wife of Akhenaten. This junior queen was called 'the Royal Favourite; the Child of the Living Aten'.[30] She was the deputy of Queen Nefertiti, whom she outrivalled in many respects. Better known these days as Queen Kiya, this prominent wife of Akhenaten (Moses) was the 'greatly beloved' Mery-khiba[31] — a daughter of Amenhotep III and his third wife Gilukhipa *(see* Chart: *The Egyptian Connection*). One of the reasons for Kiya's prestige was that (unlike the senior queen, Nefertiti) she bore a son to Akhenaten, and that son was the future Pharaoh Tutankhamun.

Another reason for Kiya's high status was that her mother (prior to marrying Amenhotep III) was a Mesopotamian princess, being the daughter of King Shutarna of Mitanni. The name Kiya derived from the Mitannian goddess Khiba (pronounced *Kiya*). It was the Jerusalem Governor Abda-khiba (Servant of Khiba) who appealed for Akhenaten's assistance against invading Hebrews. At that time, the Mitannian dynasts were powerful throughout

Palestine, and their Mesopotamian heritage was in the Lilithian kingly line of Ham. So steeped was the family in the Anunnaki lore of old Sumer, that when Kiya's cousin Tadu-khiba was also sent to Egypt, her brother King Tushratta of Mitanni wrote, 'May Shemesh and Ishtar go before her'.[32]

All records indicate that towards the end of Akhenaten's reign, Mery-khiba (Beloved of Khiba) had become the dominant queen as Mery-amon (Beloved of Amon), carrying a dual royal legacy from the kings of Egypt and Mesopotamia. It was she who moved into exile with Akhenaten (Moses), to become known to the Israelites as Miriam (*Mery-amon*), and it was her matriarchal blood which, through her daughter (the sister of Tutankhamun), cemented the succession for the eventual Royal House of Judah. Unfortunately, as a result of the destruction of Amarna records by Pharaoh Horemheb, the name of this daughter has been expunged wherever it appeared in Egypt,[33] so for our textual and chart purposes we shall refer to her as Kiya-tasherit (meaning Kiya junior).

Despite the sovereign legacy of Miriam, the Old Testament affords her very little space: she appears only as an ancillary female who led the Israelite women in Sinai with her timbrel, or tambourine (Exodus 15:20). She and Aaron are seen to admonish Moses because of his marriage to an Ethiopian woman (Numbers 12:1), and this appears to relate to Princess Tharbis of Ethiopia, who (as stated in the *Antiquities of the Jews*) was married to Moses during his early Egyptian military campaign.[34] In practice, the anger of Miriam (Mery-amon) was actually stirred upon learning of her husband's marriage to Zipporah of Midian. Subsequently, Miriam is said to have died at Kadesh (Numbers 12:10, 20:1), and that is the extent of her portrayal in the Bible. Outside the Bible, however, Miriam's story is told at some length—particularly in the book of Jasher, a work not selected for inclusion in the canonical Old Testament.

It was not until after the time of Jesus that the separate scriptures of the Jews were collated into a single volume and it was then that certain books were excluded because they were at variance with the compositional strategy. One of these was the book of Jasher—a book so important to the earlier Hebrews that it is still mentioned twice in the canonical Bible. The very fact that these references are to be found in Joshua (10:13) and 2-Samuel (1:18) indicates that Jasher was around before these books were written—and they each claim that it was a repository of essential knowledge. But although not promoted by the mainstream establishment, Jasher has not been as historically secret as one might imagine. The 9-foot (*c*.3 m) Hebrew scroll was a prize of the Court of Emperor Charlemagne (AD 800-814), having been discovered in Persia by the monk Alcuin, who later founded the University of Paris.[35] As a reward for his discovery, Alcuin was awarded three abbeys and became England's Archbishop of Canterbury.

In the 14th century, the British reformer and Bible translator John Wyckliffe (1320-1384) wrote, 'I have read the book of Jasher twice over, and I much approve of it as a work of great antiquity'. It is generally reckoned that Jasher's position in the Bible should be between the books of Deuteronomy and Joshua, but it was sidestepped because it sheds a very different light on the sequence of events at Mount Horeb.

Jasher was the Egyptian-born son of Caleb. He was brother-in-law to the first Israelite judge Othneil (Judges 1:13) and was the appointed royal staff bearer to Moses. Consequently, the book of Jasher does not make the biblical error of first calling Moses's Midianite father-in-law Reuel, but calls him Jethro from the outset.[36] (The name Jethro, or more correctly *Ithra*, means 'abundance'.) Another difference, which becomes increasingly apparent, is the ultimate significance of Miriam, who is a constant adviser to Moses and Aaron, and is greatly revered by the Israelites, to whom she is clearly a cultural leader. In this we find another reason for the biblical exclusion of the book of Jasher, for it is quite unlike the familiar books in its portrayal of a woman who issues instructions that are generally obeyed by all who take counsel from her. Indeed, the reader is left in little doubt of Miriam's supreme royal heritage.

The main contrast between the Exodus and Jasl begins at the moment when God issues his diver ordinances to Moses at Mount Horeb. These are the known laws which follow the decree of Commandments—about which Jasher makes n mention whatever. Exodus (21:1-36) explains that Jeh instructions to Moses concerning masters and covetousness, neighbourly behaviour, crime, marriag and many other issues, including the all-important Sabbath. But, in Jasher, these laws and ordinanc conveyed to Moses by Jehovah; they are directly com by Jethro, Lord of Midian, at the foot of Mount Horeb.

An alternative understanding of the situation whi from this is that, if Jehovah (Yahweh) were by then i titular distinction in succession from Enlil (Ilu-kur-ga the Mountain), then Jethro could well have been the Yahweh of the era. As mentioned in Chapter 7, th Exodus certainly explains how the Lord told Moses th also called El Shaddai—which translates directly to L Mountain.

At this point in the story, Jasher explains that Mir up the challenge, asking why the old ways we abandoned in favour of the laws of a foreign natio Jethro instruct the Hebrews!' she cried. 'Are the chi Jacob without understanding?' She then reminde about the age-old Egyptian traditions of the Israelite he was seeking to forsake for the customs of Midian all this there is no talk whatever of Jehovah, only of t Jethro. Contrary again to the Exodus portrayal Israelites' allegiance to Moses, Jasher then relates t voice of the tribes of the congregation were on the Miriam'. Moses became so angry that he had imprisoned, 'and the people of Israel gathered then together unto Moses and said, Bring forth unto us Miri counsellor',[38] whereupon Moses was compelled to rele after seven days.

Clearly, Miriam (Mery-amon) was far more popular than her paternal brother Moses (Akhenaten the *Mosis*), and the book of Jasher makes much of her standing, while detailing the Israelites' great sorrow when she died in Kadesh:

> The children of Israel mourned for Miriam forty days; neither did any man go forth of his dwelling. And the lamentation was great, for after Miriam arose up no one like unto her. ... And the flame thereof went out into all the lands ... yea, throughout all Canaan; and the nations feared greatly.[39]

A correspondent named Tobias wrote in the *Testimonies of Jasher* that Miriam 'brought a grain out of Egypt, and sowed it in the field'—but this was totally ignored by the Bible compilers who promoted only the legacy of the Hebrew patriarchs in their attempt to forge a male-dominated religion. As the Bible story progresses, we are led to believe that the royal house of David and Solomon gained its office because a shepherd-boy slew a giant with a stone. The Bible tells us absolutely nothing about David's sovereign descent from the mighty dynasties of Mesopotamia and Egypt, and yet this is the book upon which oaths are sworn to tell 'the truth, and nothing but the truth' in courts of law!

There is no doubt that, for all the scribal manipulation of old texts, Miriam emerges outside the Bible as the key character in the Old Testament Grail bloodline—but, just like Mary Magdalene in New Testament times, she has been ignored and forgotten by Church establishments founded as male-dominated institutions. Of Miriam, the book of Aaron (credited to Hur, the father of Uri Ben Hur, whose son Bezaleel built the Ark of the Covenant (Exodus 35:30-31)) relates:

> Miriam from hence became the admired of the Hebrews; every tongue sang of her praise. She taught Israel; she tutored the children of Jacob—and the

people called her, by way of eminence, The Teacher. She studied the good of the nation, and Aaron and the people harkened unto her. To her the people bowed; to her the afflicted came.

## Amram and Jochebed

Of particular significance to the story of Moses is the nominal distinction of Amarna which defined the Egyptian kings of the Akhenaten family strain, including Smenkhkare, Aye and Tutankhamun. The word Amarna derived from *Im-r-n* (Imran), the name by which Akhenaten identified his spiritual father, the Aten.[40] In its Hebrew form, the name was Amram, and this was the very name given to Moses's father in the Old Testament (Exodus 6:20).

At the same time, Moses's mother is given as Jochebed, who is earlier (Exodus 2:1) described as a daughter of Levi (meaning, 'of descent from Levi'). Jochebed is also said to have been the mother of Aaron. In the Jewish tradition, rights to priesthood were granted solely to the descendants of Levi—but in practice the levite priestly succession descended only from Aaron. It has often been wondered why Moses and his sons were never priests if they were also descendants of Levi, especially since Moses and Aaron were brothers. The answer to this biblical anomaly lies, of course, in the fact that Moses was not Aaron's natural brother; neither was Moses a descendant of Levi. However, Aaron's natural mother was indeed the feeding-mother of Moses and it was she whom the Bible writers called Jochebed.

Jochebed (or more correctly, Yokâbar) was an Israelite daughter of the house of Levi,[41] and she married Aye (son of the vizier Yusuf-Yuya), who was himself vizier to Pharaoh Amenhotep III. Amenhotep was, in turn, married to Aye's sister Tiye, the junior queen. The eldest son of Aye and Jochebed was Smenkhkare (Aaron), while Akhenaten (Moses) and Mery-amon

(Miriam) were the offspring of Amenhotep by Tiye and Gilukhipa, respectively *(see* Chart: *The Egyptian Connection*).

During the course of nursing her own children (including Smenkhkare), Jochebed also became the feeding-mother of Akhenaten and as such she was granted the nominal distinction of her own mistress and sister-in-law Tiye. She was, therefore, also referred to as Tiye. To avoid confusion, historical records call her Tiy or Tey (variations of the same name) and for the same practical purposes she is defined in this book as Tey. So, Tey and Jochebed were one and the same—but what of Jochebed's biblical husband Amram? How does he equate with the historical Aye?

The name Amram has its root in the word *ram*, meaning 'height' or 'highness', and such names (including Rama, Aram, Ramtha, etc.) were all related to some high titular status. Such was the case with the later princely distinction *ha-Rama-Theo* ('of the Divine Highness'), which was corrupted in the New Testament to 'of Arimathea'.[42] In his Egyptian environment, Aye was the designated 'Father of the God',[43] and was a patriarchal Am-ram (*Imran*—a People's Highness)[44] in both Egyptian and Israelite circles, just as the Bible explains. He was also an upholder of the Aten philosophy, and it was in the tomb of Aye that Akhenaten's own *Hymn to the Aten* was discovered—a hymn which provided the model for the Bible's Psalm 104.

Across the river from Amarna lies the modern city of Mal-lawi (Malleui), which means, quite literally, City of the Levites, and the High Priest of Akhenaten's Amarna Temple was Meryre II.[45] This is equivalent to the Hebrew name Merari, which was the name of one of the sons of Levi (Genesis 46:11). It is evident that Akhenaten's association with the Israelites of Egypt was established long before he led them into Sinai, and it is further apparent that at the time of the exodus the One God of these Israelites was Aten—the original *Adon* ('Lord', as against Jehovah) of the Bible.

## The Royal House of Judah

To this point in our investigation, a number of discrepancies have been revealed in the Bible's portrayal of the key succession when compared with the historical accounts. These have occurred mainly because, as we have discovered, the Old Testament writers followed an original line from Eve's third son Seth, rather than from her first son Cain. Certain characters have now been portrayed in a different light to that with which we are familiar, but that apart, the story remains on the same terminal course towards David and the ensuing Messianic Kings of Judah. We are now at the stage where the two families converge, with one illegitimate line coming out of Israel in descent from Judah and Tamar, while the other (the legitimate royal line) emerges from Egypt with Kiya-tasherit, the daughter of Moses and Miriam.

The Israelite lineage of this era is very sparingly given in Genesis, and the book of 1-Chronicles (2:3-15) names only the males of the line, with no mention whatever of their all-important wives. Between the books of Genesis and Exodus, some 400 years of history were strategically excluded from the generations that follow Judah and Tamar, and this is not rectified in 1-Chronicles. Even the later compiled New Testament lists follow this lead: the genealogies in Matthew (1:3-6) and Luke (3:31-33) were clearly extracted from the Hebrew source.

Of slightly more help is the Old Testament book of Ruth (the Moabite descendant of Lot), who married David's great-grandfather Boaz (Ruth 4:12-22). Other wives, though not mentioned in the approved literature, do appear in some Arabic writings from Egypt[46] which agree with the Bible in stating that the Israelite priestly line (as against the kingly line) sprang from Aaron and Elisheba (a daughter of Aminadab, son of Rama) in descent from Judah and Tamar (Exodus 6:23).

The name Aminadab, which denotes a princely station, was a variant of the Egyptian pharaonic name Amenhotep - the original birth-name of Akhenaten. The separate Israelite kingly line evolved in parallel from Nashôn, brother of Elisheba, whose father Aminadab (Amenhotep) was the son of Rama and Kiya-tasherit, sister of Tutankhamun.

It is quite remarkable that the four generations from Rama to Boaz *(see* Chart: *Out of Egypt*) are given such little space in the Bible, for they hold the key to the royal succession that was finally settled upon David, the great-grandson of Boaz who is prominently featured in Masonic ritual. But although remarkable, it is in no way surprising, because theirs was a history that was strategically veiled in order to promote a tradition based on the Sethian patriarchs, as against the Cainite kingly succession which came out of Egypt and flourished in Israel from the time of Moses.

20

# Wisdom and the Law

## The Commandments

It is plain that the Ten Commandments, said to have been verbally conveyed to Moses by God upon the mountain (Exodus 20), were ordinances directly extracted from the Egyptian tradition. They were not new codes of conduct invented for the Israelites, but were simply newly stated versions of the ancient pharaonic confessions from Spell Number 125 in the Egyptian *Book of the Dead*. For example, the confession 'I have not killed' was translated to the decree 'Thou shalt not kill'; 'I have not stolen' became 'Thou shalt not steal'; 'I have not told lies' became 'Thou shalt not bear false witness', and so on.

The aspects of the Sinai sequence which bore no relation to the Egyptian code were the introductory statements by Jehovah, wherein he supposedly announced, 'I am a jealous God, visiting the iniquity of the fathers upon the children unto the third and fourth generation of them that hate me' (Exodus 20:5). Such remarks are indicative of the Bible writers' awareness that theirs was a god of wrath and vengeance, and by including such judgemental pronouncements in the text, the temple authorities of the 6th century BC were enabled to subject the rank and file to subservience, with the priests being the authorized bridges between Jehovah and the people. By virtue of this, the people were strategically brought under the rule of the priests, whose individual rights of communication with Jehovah were beyond challenge. The same tried and tested process was repeated by the Christian popes and bishops in later times.

Prior to the time of Moses there was no Israelite priesthood and there were no Israelite temples. The early patriarchs, up to the days of Abraham, would have experienced priests and fine temples in Mesopotamia, but once in Canaan the rituals of Abraham, Jacob and others became very primitive. They worshipped their god El Shaddai at outdoor stone altars (Genesis 12:7, 33:20), where they made offerings of drink and oil (Genesis 35:14) and performed ritual sacrifices (Genesis 31:54, 46:1). But with Moses came the concept of a newly defined Israelite priesthood based upon the Egyptian model, and their first temple was the portable Tabernacle of the Congregation constructed at Sinai. Another Egyptian concept introduced at that time was the Ark of the Covenant—a processional coffer to house the writings of the Law.[1]

Whatever form of godly veneration had existed for the early Hebrews in Canaan, it is plain that while in Egypt the generations of Israelites became accustomed to the practices of that land. Given the geographical location of the Israelite families in the eastern Nile delta, and of their association with the Aten cult at Zaru (Avaris/Pi-Ramesses), Aten emerges as their natural godhead at the time of the exodus with Moses. The only difference was in the spelling of the name, for to them Aten was Adon.

Even the ritualistic use of the name of the previous Egyptian State god, Amen, was retained by the Israelites. He was the god of Moses's father Amenhotep (meaning Amen is pleased) and the name Amen (or Amun) originally meant 'hidden'.[2] It was added to the end of prayers to denote that they were prayers to Amen and, even though such prayers were eventually transposed to suit the Hebrew doctrine, the use of the Egyptian end-name Amen persisted because the Israelites were not allowed to say the name Jehovah. Then, in order to justify the use of the name Amen in later times (even to the present day), it has been erroneously upheld to be akin to the old Mesopotamian word *haem*, which meant 'so be it'.

When the Israelites arrived at the Hathor temple of Mount Serâbît (Horeb) in Sinai, in the company of Moses (Akhenaten), they would not have expected suddenly to change their allegiance from Aten to Jehovah. Equally, they would not have expected to hear the voice of Aten or Jehovah, for Aten was perceived to be without presence, and Jehovah was barely known to them at that time. The person they would all have expected to meet was the Lord of the Mountain—the priest in charge of the Hathor temple, and he would have been rightly addressed by the Israelites as *Adonai* (my Lord).[3]

Clearly, it was this description, Lord of the Mountain, which was misinterpreted by the Old Testament writers many centuries later, for they knew that the god of Abraham had been called precisely that. As we know, in the Hebrew Bible, he is called El Shaddai (Exodus 6:3), which is the equivalent of his Sumerian name *Ilu Kur-gal*: Great Mountain Lord.[4]

In transcribing the story of the Israelites in Sinai to suit the growing cult of Jehovah (which was strongly prevalent after the Babylonian captivity when the Old Testament books were compiled), the scribes endeavoured to remain consistent in their godly portrayals. But they still referred quite independently to Eloh, El Shaddai, Jehovah and Adon, while in later translations these various names were related simply as God and Lord, especially in the emergent Christian tradition.

## Secrets of the Emerald Table

Throughout the Israelite sojourn in Egypt, the Hebrews of Canaan and Midian had continued their veneration of Enlil-Jehovah (El Shaddai) in the tradition of Abraham. But Sinai was not part of Canaan and so the Aten-Hathor (sun-moon) duality had prevailed in the region, just as in Egypt. On marrying Zipporah (the daughter of Jethro, Lord of Midian), Moses was therefore obliged to amalgamate the Aten cult with that of Jehovah in order to gain acceptance for the Israelites among the native Hebrews. As a route to this, Jethro issued the Midianite ordinances, which became embodied within Jewish law, and these were attached to the Commandments, which were plainly of Egyptian origin. It was because of this amalgamation that Miriam and Aaron stood against Moses and, by virtue of the Israelites' own preference, Moses was excluded from any priestly office, with the temple function firmly settled upon the line of Aaron—essentially upon his son Elieazar and his grandson Phinehas (Exodus 6:25). The Egyptian equivalent of the name Phinehas (meaning 'serpent's mouth') was Panahesy, and Panahesy was already the Egyptian Governor of Sinai, while also having been the chief servitor of Aten at the temple of Amarna.[5]

With Moses's birth having been around 1394 BC, his initial banishment *c.*1361 BC and the exodus about 1334 BC, he would have been near to sixty at the time of the Sinai covenant. This is in keeping with the ageing, bearded portrayal that has become so familiar, but it is interesting to note that, in contrast to the norm for portrayals of Hebrew prophets, some early depictions of Moses from before the Middle Ages show him quite unbearded and more in keeping with the Egyptian style.

In detailing the account of Moses and his receipt of the Tables of the Law, the book of Exodus is not only in conflict with the book of Jasher, but it is also rather different to the way the story is generally taught. This is primarily the fault of Church authorities (Jewish and Christian alike) and the errors have been further compounded by picture-book illustrators and the Hollywood film industry. As an outcome, the familiar dramatic image is one of the finger of God blasting the words of law on to great tables of rock; in many depictions these slabs are more like weighty tombstones than portable tablets.

The book of Jasher[6] makes it quite plain that Moses received the laws and ordinances from Lord Jethro of Midian, not from the Lord Jehovah. Jethro is specifically described as a descendant of Esau and there is no talk whatever about slabs of stone, only of the *Book of the Covenant*.[7]

But what of Exodus? Even this Old Testament narrative, while referring to Jehovah in person and to tables of stone, makes a positive distinction between the Ten Commandments and the Tables of Testimony, the latter of which were placed in the Ark of the Covenant.

The Bible explains that the Ten Commandments were delivered by God to Moses and the people on Mount Sinai (Exodus 19:20-23) and that these were accompanied by a series of verbal ordinances. Then, God said to Moses, 'Come up to me into the mount, and be there: and I will give thee tables of stone, and a law, and commandments which I have written; that thou mayest teach them' (24:12). There are two distinctly separate items here: 'tables of stone ... a law' and 'commandments'. God further stated, 'And thou shalt put into the ark the testimony which I shall give thee' (25:16). Later, it is detailed that 'He gave unto Moses ... two tables of testimony, tables of stone ...' (31:18).

We are informed that the original tables were broken by Moses when he cast them to the ground (32:19) and then God said to Moses, 'Hew thee two tables of stone like unto the first: and *I will write* upon these tables the words that were in the first tables, which thou brakest' (34:1). Subsequently, God verbally reiterated the commandments and said to Moses, '*Write thou* these words', whereupon Moses 'wrote ... the words of the covenant, the ten commandments' (34:27-28). There is, therefore, a clear distinction made in the Bible between the Tables of Testimony, written by God, and the Ten Commandments, which were separately written down by Moses.[8]

Notwithstanding the fact that Exodus talks of the Lord Jehovah, while Jasher refers to Lord Jethro of Midian as the proponent of the Law, an element of confusion has arisen and for centuries the Church has insisted that the Ten

Commandments were the important part of this package, in consequence of which the Tables of Testimony have been strategically ignored.

By virtue of the word 'stone' the said tables have conjured images of granite-like slabs and their perceived image has, in some measure, been influenced by the round-topped stela of Hamurrabi, King of Babylon *c.*1780 BC. This well-known basalt monument[9] was discovered in 1901 and is wonderfully engraved with the law-code of Hamurrabi. However, in accordance with strict Jewish tradition of the Qabalistic masters, the stone of the Mosaic tables was said to be a divine sapphire called *Schethiyd*.[10]

The Tables of Testimony contained within the stone are not to be confused with the Ten Commandments, nor with the divers ordinances of Midianite law (whether related by Jehovah or Jethro), but are rather more associated with the original *Table of Destiny* of the Anunnaki *(see* Chapter 4). This ancient archive is directly associated with the Emerald Table of Thoth-Hermes and, as detailed in alchemical records of Egypt, the author of the preserved writings was the biblical Ham,[11] a great Archon of the Grail bloodline. He was the essential founder of the esoteric and arcane 'underground stream' which flowed through the ages, and his Greek name, Hermes, was directly related to the science of pyramid construction, deriving from the word *herma,* which relates to a 'pile of stones'.[12] Indeed, the Great Pyramid is sometimes called the Sanctuary of Thoth.

The revered Emerald Table contains the most ancient of all alchemical formulae, which were of great significance to the early mystery schools. But the secrets have long been withheld from the brethren of modern Freemasonry whose leaders, for the past two centuries or more, have elected to pursue a spurious and strategically contrived allegorical ritual which teaches nothing of the true art of the original Master Craftsmen. In essence, the Emerald text relates to both the alchemy of metals and the divine alchemy of human regeneration, along with matters of science, astronomy and numerology. Once known to Rosicrucian adepts as the *Tabula Smaragdina Hermetis,* the table of Ham (Chem-

Zarathustra) was recorded as 'The most ancient monument of the Chaldeans concerning the *Lapis Philosophorum* [the Philosophers' Stone]'.

Outside Egypt and Mesopotamia, the table was known to Greek and Roman masters such as Homer, Virgil, Pythagoras, Plato and Ovid, while in much later times the 17th-century Stuart Royal Society of Britain[13] was deeply concerned with the analysis and application of the sacred knowledge. In conjunction with the Knights Templars and with the Rosicrucian movement, the original Royal Society flourished under prominent scholars such as Isaac Newton, Christopher Wren, Robert Hooke, Robert Boyle and Edmond Halley.[14] Although often admonished by the Christian Church authorities for entering realms of heresy, with their insistence that the Earth was in solar orbit, and because of their free association with Jews and Muslims, it was from the discoveries of these men that such enlightenments as the *Law of Gravity* and *Boyle's Law*[15] became known to the public at large—discoveries that were directly attributed to the ancient archive of the hermetic table. (It is from the hermetic fusion of glass in early times that we derive the present-day term 'hermetically sealed' glass.)[16]

The ultimate significance of the Emerald Table (to be further examined in a future book in this series) can be deduced from some directly quoted extracts: 'By this, thou wilt partake of the Honours of the Whole World.... And darkness will fly from thee.... With this thou wilt be able to overcome all things'.[17]

## Words of the Wise

Not only were the Ten Commandments drawn from spells in the Egyptian *Book of the Dead*, while the Psalms of David were likewise drawn from hymns of Egyptian origin, but so too was a majority of Old Testament teaching directly extracted from the wisdom of ancient Egypt. In just the same way, the early patriarchal history was derived from the records of old Mesopotamia. The Egyptian relationships are particularly noticeable in the Bible's books of the prophets, and good examples are also found in the Proverbs of Solomon—the 'words of the wise', which are customarily attributed to King Solomon himself (*see* Chart: *Amenemope and the Book of Proverbs*).

These well-known Proverbs were, in fact, translated almost verbatim into Hebrew from the writings of an Egyptian sage called Amenemope,[18] which are now held in the British Museum. Verse after verse of the book of Proverbs can be attributed to this Egyptian original, and it has now been discovered that the writings of Amenemope himself were extracted from a far older work called *The Wisdom of Ptah-hotep*,[19] which comes from more than 2000 years before the time of Solomon.

In addition to the *Book of the Dead* and the ancient *Wisdom of Ptah-hotep*, various other Egyptian texts were used in compiling the Old Testament. These include the *Pyramid Texts* and the *Coffin Texts*, from which references to the sun god Ra were simply transposed to relate to the Hebrew god Jehovah. Even the Christians' traditional *Lord's Prayer*, as defined in the New Testament Gospel of Matthew (6:9-13), was transposed from an Egyptian prayer to the State-god which began: 'Amen, Amen, who art in heaven....'

The unfortunate scenario which prevailed until fairly recently was that, while the Bible was promoted to the front line of our cultural consciousness, the more ancient writings of the Mesopotamians and Egyptians were lost. Had this not been the case, then the wisdom and historical records of these pre-Israelite civilizations would have prevailed and it would never have occurred to anyone to consider the Old Testament as anything but another chapter in an ongoing development of morality and religion. Instead, since no contemporary annals had been discovered, the Hebrew scripture achieved a thoroughly inappropriate status as a reliable work of history.

Only during the past 150 years or so, and more specifically since about 1920, have the great storehouses of Egyptian,

Mesopotamian, Syrian and Canaanite record been unearthed from beneath the desert sands. First-hand documentary evidence from before Bible times has now emerged on stone, clay, parchment and papyrus, and these tens of thousands of documents bear witness to a far more exciting history than we have ever been told. Had these records been available throughout the generations, the concept of a particular race enjoying a single divine revelation would never have arisen, and the exclusivity of Jehovah, which has blinded us for the longest time (setting us in warlike fashion against those of other faiths who follow their own traditions), would never have taken such an arrogant hold.

With these original records now recovered and translated, it becomes apparent that, although our civilizations have reached advanced levels of science and technology, we are in many respects still novices in comparison to some of the ancient masters. It is also evident that we are barely emerging from the darkness of our own preconceived but unfounded notions, and our centuries of Church-led indoctrination make it very difficult to discard the restrictive dogma of inbred third-hand tradition in favour of a greater enlightenment from those who were there at the time.

The truly inspiring prospect is that the learning curve has still not ended, for with each passing year new discoveries are made. Just as a single glacier is but a continuation of age-old activity, so too are the ancient wisdoms that now fall to us one by one, with each new facet of learning ready to be stacked alongside the former knowledge. The resultant broadening horizon cannot be ignored, no matter how difficult it might be to sever the medieval ties that bind—for in the not too distant future we shall see clear across that horizon. The dawn of consciousness is already behind us, and although many will choose to look backwards beyond its veil, those with eyes to see will step with vigour into the new millennium to witness a bright new sunrise—a revelation of unbounded possibility and a restoration of our true universal inheritance.

# NOTES AND REFERENCES

## 1: THE CRADLE OF CIVILIZATION

1. In the time of King Herod the Great documents of genealogical record relating to the family of Jesus (the *Desposyni*) were officially burned at the King's instruction. Eusebius, *The History of the Church from Christ to Constantine*, Penguin, Harmondsworth, 1989, Book 1:7, p.22. Also Schonfield, Hugh J., *The Passover Plot*, Element Books, Shaftesbury, 1985, pp. 245-46. And regarding the subsequent burning of records by the Romans in their AD 70 sacking of Jerusalem under General Titus, *see* Baigent, Michael, with Leigh, Richard and Lincoln, Henry, *The Messianic Legacy*, Jonathan Cape, London, 1986, p. 89.

The 2nd-century Palestinian historian Hegesippus reported in his *Hypomnenata* (Memoirs) that, during the reign of the Roman Emperor Domitian (AD 81-96), the execution of all desposynic inheritors of the Davidic succession was ordered by Imperial decree. However, although many were seized, including known descendants of Jesus's brother Jude, some were released and 'On their release they became leaders of the churches, both because they had borne testimony and because they were of the Lord's family'. This is also confirmed by Eusebius (*c.*AD 260-340), Bishop of Caesarea, in Eusebius, *The History of the Church from Christ to Constantine*, Penguin, Harmondsworth, 1989, Book 3:17, pp. 80-82.

The historian Julius Africanus of Edessa in Anatolia (as against Edessa in Greece), who lived AD 160-240, wrote that following the 1st-century burning of the genealogical registers of Jesus's family, 'A few careful people had private records of their own, having either remembered the names or recovered them from copies, and took pride in preserving the memory of their aristocratic origin. These included the people... known as the *Desposyni* because of their relationship to the Saviour's family'. *Ibid*, Book 1:7, p. 22.

Julius Africanus made his reputation by translating into Latin a series of works written by the 1st-century disciple Abdias, Nazarene Bishop of Babylon. The Books of Abdias amounted to ten volumes of first-hand Apostolic history. However, like so many other important eyewitness accounts of the era, they were rejected outright for 4th-century inclusion in the eventual New Testament. (Abdias is recorded as one of the 70 disciples of Jesus—as per Luke 10. He was the first Bishop of Babylon, consecrated by Simon and Jude, the brothers of Jesus.)

Only those in the bloodline of Jesus through his mother qualified as *Desposyni* (meaning 'Belonging to [or heirs of] the Lord'). They and their supporters were hunted down by Imperial Roman decree and put to the sword. However, in AD 318 (as confirmed by Fr. Malachi Martin, a Jesuit professor who served in Rome with Cardinal Augustine Bea and Pope John XXIII), a *Desposyni* delegation journeyed to Rome, where, at the newly commissioned Lateran Palace, the men were given audience by Bishop Silvester. Through their chief spokesman Joses (a descendant of Jesus's brother Jude), the delegates argued that the Church should rightfully be centred in Jerusalem, not in Rome. They claimed that the Bishop of Jerusalem should be a true hereditary *Desposynos*, while the bishops of other major centres—such as Alexandria, Antioch and Ephesus—should be related. Not surprisingly, their demands were in vain, for Silvester was hardly in a position to countermand the decrees of the Emperor. The teachings of Jesus had been superseded by a doctrine more amenable to Imperial requirement and, in no uncertain terms, Silvester informed the men that the power of salvation rested no longer in Jesus, but in Emperor Constantine! *See* Martin, Malachi, *The Decline and Fall of the Roman Church*, Secker & Warburg, London, 1982, pp. 42-44.

2. Pope Gelasius I (AD 492-96) introduced the Mass sacrament of bread and wine into the Christian Church, and denounced all who did not drink alcohol, proclaiming them to be heretics.

3. This story is told in *The Golden Legend* by Jacobus de Voragine, Archbishop of Genoa. It was translated into English and published by William Caxton in 1483.

4. Gardner, Laurence, *Bloodline of the Holy Grail*, Element Books, Shaftesbury, 1996, pp. 166 and 175.

5. Osman, Ahmed, *The House of the Messiah*, Harper Collins, London, 1992, pp. 151-52.

6. Bodde, D., *China*, in Kramer, Samuel Noah (ed.), *Mythologies of the Ancient World*, Anchor Books, Garden City New York, 1961, p. 400.

7. *Times Atlas of Archaeology, The* (*Past Worlds*), Times Books, London, 1988, p. 80.

8. In the alchemical tradition, the *Briah* (Creation) represents the *Materia Prima* (Blueprint) of the *Briatic* (Essential/Creative) World. *See* also Speiser, E. A., *The Anchor Bible – Genesis*, (translation from Hebrew text), Doubleday, Garden City, New York, 1964, p. xvii, and p. 12.

9. Roux, Georges, *Ancient Iraq*, George Allen & Unwin, London, 1964, p. 75.

## 2: LIKE MIGRATING BIRDS

1. Charles Darwin was not the first in the field of evolutionary research. The French naturalist, George, Comte de Buffon, Keeper of the Jardin de Roi, published *Epochs of Nature* in 1778. The Scottish physician James Hutton (the acclaimed founder of geology) published his *Theory of the Earth* in 1785. The French anatomist Baron Georges Cuvier (father of palaeontology) published his *Tableau élementaire de l'histoire naturelle des animaux* in 1798. This was followed by his great work, *Le règne animal*. The French naturalist, le Chevalier de Jean Baptiste de Monet Lamark, Professor of Zoology at the University of Paris, published his *Philosophie Zoologique* in 1809. This was followed by the *Histoire naturelle des animaux sans vertebrates*. The Scotsman Sir Charles Lyell published his *Principles of Geology* in the early 1830s. Charles Darwin published his *On the Origin of the Species by Means of Natural Selection* in 1859. This was followed by *The Descent of Man* in 1871.

2. *Oxford Concordance to the Bible.*

3. *The Universal History,* in 42 volumes, was compiled by a consortium of London booksellers. *See* also Wells, H. G., *The Outline of History,* Cassell, London, 1920, p. 977.

4. The Julian calendar was based on a year of 365 days, 6 hours, whereas true tropical solar time has 365 days, 5 hours, 48 minutes, 46 seconds. This gave rise to an extra day being lost every 128 years by the Julian reckoning. By the 16th century the discrepancy amounted to ten full days, and so in 1582 Pope Gregory XIII made an adjustment by way of his new Gregorian calendar. This was adopted by the Catholic nations, but the Protestant countries made their adjustment later, with Britain falling in line after 1751, by which time the accumulated error amounted to eleven days. It was announced in advance that 2 September 1752 would be followed immediately by 14 September; this prompted public demonstrations because people thought their lives would be shortened by eleven days.

France, which had adopted the new calendar in 1582, changed to a revised Revolutionary calendar from 1793 to 1805. Turkey and Russia adopted the Gregorian calendar in 1917, but the Eastern Orthodox Church in Russia and the Balkans did not make their change until 1923. Hence, for a good while different countries were operating on different time-frames. Currently, to avoid a further build-up of extra days during the 128-year periods, leap years are now restricted to century years divisible by 400 (e.g. 1600 and 2000), and to any other year divisible by four (e.g. 1984 and 1996). This reduces the average length of the annual calendar to a far more acceptable 365.2425 days.

5. Keller, Werner, *The Bible as History,* (trans. William Neil), Hodder & Stoughton, London, 1956, p. 68.

6. Wood, Michael, *Legacy – A Search for the Origins of Civilization,* BBC Network Books, London, 1992, p. 34.

7. These stone cylinders were retrieved in 1854 by J. E. Tayler, the British Consul in Basra, on a general investigative mission for the British Foreign Office. Being archaeologically unqualified, Tayler and his digging gangs managed to demolish completely the top tier of the uppermost building beneath the mound. It was not until 1915 that the true significance of the site became apparent when a British Museum official was stationed with Britain's Intelligence staff in Iraq during the First World War. It was he, R. Campbell Thompson, who took another look at the mound and determined its considerable importance.

8. Keller, W., *The Bible as History,* p. 40.

9. As identified in Genesis 10:10.

10. These were constructed upon great arches, 75 feet (23m) high, and were watered from the River Euphrates by way of a complex mechanical system.

11. Woolley, Sir C. Leonard, *Ur of the Chaldees*, Ernest Benn, London, 1929, p. 119.

12. Norvill, Roy, *Giants – The Vanished Race of Mighty Men*, Aquarian Press, Wellingborough, 1979, p. 58.

13. Woolley, C. L., *Ur of the Chaldees*, pp. 137-38.

14. *Ibid.*, p. 25.

## 3: CRIMSON ROBES AND SILVER COMBS

1. Carpenter, Clive, *The Guinness Book of Kings, Rulers and Statesmen*, Guinness Superlatives, Enfield, 1978, p. 15.

2. Woolley, C. L., *Ur of the Chaldees*, ch. 2.

3. Held in the Baghdad Museum.

4. Roux, G., *Ancient Iraq*, p. 117.

5. Woolley, C. L., *Ur of the Chaldees*, p. 26.

6. Keller, W., *The Bible as History*, p. 50.

7. Porter, J. R., *The Illustrated Guide to the Bible*, Duncan Baird, London, 1995, p. 26.

8. Chaos is determined by the words *Tohu* and *Bohu* – 'confusion' and 'emptiness'. *See* also Church, Rev. Leslie F. (ed.), *Matthew Henry's Commentary on the Whole Bible*, Marshall Pickering/Harper Collins, London, 1960, Genesis I:1 to 2/1(1).

9. *Ibid.*, Genesis I:1-2:1(2).

10. Sitchin, Zecharia, *The 12th Planet*, Avon Books, New York, 1978, p. 75.

11. Judges 3:13; 1 Kings 16:31-32.

12. Gordon, C. H., *Canaan*, in Kramer, S. N. (ed.), *Mythologies of the Ancient World*, p. 201.

13. Canaan was so called because of the Murex shellfish dye – the most famous purple dye in the ancient world. *See* also Keller, W., *The Bible as History*, p. 72.

14. Porter, J. R., *The Illustrated Guide to the Bible*, p. 72.

15. As given in Judges 2:13 and 1 Kings 11:5, 33.

16. Davies, Steve, *The Canaanite Hebrew Goddess*, in Olson, Carl (ed.), *The Book of the Goddess – Past and Present*, Crossroad Publishing, New York, 1989, p. 68.

17. Edessa, now Urfa in Turkey, as opposed to Edessa in Greece.

18. Collins, Andrew, *From the Ashes of Angels*, Michael Joseph, London, 1996, p. 35.

19. Church, L. F., *Matthew Henry's Commentary on the Whole Bible*, Genesis XIV: 13-16/I.

20. Patai, Raphael, *The Jewish Mind*, Charles Scribner's Sons, New York, 1977, p. 15.

21 *Ibid.*, pp. 17-19.

22. In practice, the *Torah* is not confined to a law or laws; it is rather more a narrative with aspects of teaching that relate to the Covenant Code written down by Moses (Deuteronomy 31:9). *See* also Speiser, E. A., *The Anchor Bible – Genesis*, pp. xviii-xx.

23. Reed, William L., *The Asherah in the Old Testament*, Texas Christian University Press, Fort Worth, Texas, 1949, p. 63.

24. Discovered in the excavations of G. Lankester Harding and Fr Ronald de Vaux.

25. Gardner, L., *Bloodline of the Holy Grail*, pp. 23-24.

26. Known as the *Codex Petropolitanus*.

27. Roux, G., *Ancient Iraq*, p. 242.

28. *Ibid.*, p. 68.

29. *Ibid.*, p. 111. (The Akkadian variant was *edin*.) *See* also Speiser, E. A., *The Anchor Bible – Genesis*, p. 16.

30. Roux, G., *Ancient Iraq*, p. 62.

31. *Ibid.*, p. 97.

32. Rohl, David, *A Test of Time – The Bible from Myth to History*, Century, London, 1995, pp. 22 and 123.

33. *Hutchinson's New 20th Century Encyclopedia*, Hutchinson Publishing, London, 1970 edn.

34. Speiser, E. A., *The Anchor Bible – Genesis*, p. 17.

35. *Ibid.*, 2:14,17.

# NOTES AND REFERENCES

## 4: THE CHALDEAN GENESIS


1. Heidel, Alexander, *The Babylonian Genesis*, University of Chicago Press, Chicago, 1942, p. 14.

2. Roux, G., *Ancient Iraq*, p. 86.

3. Sitchin, Z., *The 12th Planet*, p. 210.

4. Heidel, A., *The Babylonian Genesis*, p. 1.

5. Porter, J. R., *The Illustrated Guide to the Bible*, p. 20.

6. Graves, Robert, and Patai, Raphael, *Hebrew Myths – The Book of Genesis*, Cassell, London, 1964, p. 31.

7. Robinson, James M. (ed.), *The Nag Hammadi Library* under *Origin*, Coptic Gnostic Library: Institute for Antiquity and Christianity, E. J. Brill, Leiden, 1977, p. 163.

8. Graves, R., and Patai, R., *Hebrew Myths – Genesis*, p. 31.

9. Heidel, A., *The Babylonian Genesis*, p. 16.

10. *Ibid.*, p. 46.

11. Woolley, C. L., *Ur of the Chaldees*, p. 19.

12. Kramer, Samuel Noah, *The Sacred Marriage Rite*, Indiana University Press, Bloomington, 1969, p. 5.

13. Roux, G., *Ancient Iraq*, p. 75.

14. *Ibid.*, p. 78.

15. *Ibid.*, p. 75.

16. Kramer, Samuel Noah, *Sumerian Mythology*, Harper Bros, New York, 1961, p. 21.

17. Sitchin, Z., *The 12th Planet*, p. 21. The same point is also stressed by the linguist Professor I. J. Gelb in his *A Study of Writing*. The unclassified Sumerian language has resisted all attempts to relate it with any other. *See* also Norvill, R., *Giants – The Vanished Race of Mighty Men*, p. 57.

18. Kramer, S. N., *Sumerian Mythology*, p. 21.

19. Black, Jeremy, and Green, Anthony, *Gods, Demons and Symbols of Ancient Mesopotamia*, British Museum Press, London, 1992, p. 11.

20. Woolley, Sir C. Leonard, *The Sumerians*, W. W. Norton, London, 1965, p. 20.

21. Kalicz, Nándor, *Clay Gods*, Corvina Kiadó, Budapest, 1970, p. 49.

22. Sitchin, Z., *The 12th Planet*, p. 22.

23. Budge, Sir Ernest A. Wallis (trans.), *The Book of the Dead*, University Books, New York, 1960, p. 379. The *Table of Destiny* ('of the things which have been made, and of the things which shall be made') features also in the Egyptian *Papyrus of Ani*.

## 5: REALM OF THE ANGELS

1. This was deduced from the Greek translation of *nephilim* to *gi'gan-tes*. *See* also Norvill, R., *Giants – The Vanished Race of Mighty Men*, p. 36.

2. Josephus, Flavius, *The Works of Flavius Josephus*, Milner & Sowerby, London, 1870, *Antiquities of the Jews* I, 3:1.

3. Sitchin, Z., *The 12th Planet*, p. vii.

4. 1 Enoch 6. *See* Charles, R. H. (trans.), *The Book of Enoch*, (revised from Dillmann's edition of the Ethiopic text, 1893), Oxford University Press, 1906 and 1912.

5. Collins, A., *From the Ashes of Angels*, p. 10.

6. *Ibid.*, p. 62.

7. 1 Enoch 10:16.

8. Dupont-Sommer, André, *The Essene Writings from Qumrân*, (trans. Geza Vermes), Basil Blackwell, Oxford, 1961, p. 167.

9. *Ibid.*, p. 116.

10. *Damascus Document*, Manuscript A, 2:17-19.

11. Sitchin, Z., *The 12th Planet*, p. 171.

12. Oakeley, Sir Atholl, *Blue Blood on the Mat*, Anchor Press, Tiptree, p. 159.

13. Gardner, L., *Bloodline of the Holy Grail*, pp. 53-57.

14. 1 Enoch 20:20.

15. Jubilees 4:16-18. *See* Schodde, Rev. George H. (trans.), *The Book of Jubilees*, Capital University, Columbus, Ohio (E. J. Goodrich edition), 1888; reprinted Artisan, Calif., 1992.

16. Jubilees 8:3.

17. 1 Enoch 20:20. (In ancient Egypt the Watchers were called *Neters*.) *See* also Sitchin, Zecharia, *The Stairway to Heaven*, Bear & Co., Santa Fe, New Mexico, 1992, p. 77.

18. As detailed in Spare, Austin, *The Zoetic Grimoire of Zos*, unpublished MS, 1913. *See* also Grant, Kenneth, *The Magical Revival*, Skoob Books, London, 1991, pp. 189-90.

19. 1 Enoch 8:1-3.

20. 1 Enoch 8:6.

21. Jubilees 7:19.

22. Jubilees 7:18.

23. 1 Enoch 1:2.

24. The subject is well covered in Däniken, Erich von, *Chariots of the Gods*, Souvenir, London, 1969.

## 6: AN AGE OF ENLIGHTENMENT

1. Wilson, Colin, *From Atlantis to the Sphinx*, Virgin Books, London, 1996, p. 145.

2. Wells, H. G., *The Outline of History*, p. 76.

3. The Times, 11 July 1997; from a report in the scientific journal *Cell*.

4. Behe, Michael, *Darwin's Black Box*, Free Press, Simon & Schuster, New York, 1996, p. 102. (DNA resides within the cell nucleus.)

5. Jones, Steve, *In the Blood – God, Genes and Destiny*, Harper Collins, London, 1996, p. 93.

6. Mitochondria (singular, mitochondrion) is the energy-source of plant and animal cells. *See* also Behe, M., *Darwin's Black Box*, pp. 26 and 102.

7. *The Times*, 23 December 1996. Also reported in that month's USA Newsweek and in the American journal *Science*.

8. Wilson, C., *From Atlantis to the Sphinx*, pp. 153-61.

9. *Times Atlas of Archaeology* (*Past Worlds*), pp. 51-63.

10. Sitchin, Z., *The 12th Planet*, pp. 5-6.

11. Cremo, Michael A., and Thompson, Richard L., *The Hidden History of the Human Race*, Gorvardan Hill, Badger, Calif., 1994, pp. 260-65.

12. Däniken, Erich von, *The Return of the Gods*, Element Books, Shaftesbury, 1997, pp. 103 and 135.

13. Behe, M., *Darwin's Black Box*, p. 43.

14. *Ibid.*, p. 30.

15. Mivart, St George, *On the Genesis of the Species*, Macmillan, London, 1871, p. 21.

16. England's schools were wholly operated by the Anglican Church until State schools were introduced in the 1870s.

17. Rohl, D., *A Test of Time*, p. 113.

18. Graves, R., and Patai, R., *Hebrew Myths – Genesis*, p. 45.

19. Wells, H. G., *The Outline of History*, p. 164.

## 7: WHEN KINGSHIP WAS LOWERED

1. Heidel, A., *The Babylonian Genesis*, pp. 9-10.

2. Sitchin, Zecharia, *When Time Began*, Avon Books, New York, 1993, p. 10.

3. Jacobsen, Thorkild, *The Treasures of Darkness – A History of Mesopotamian Religion*, Yale University Press, New Haven, Conn., 1976, p. 86.

4. *Ibid.*, p 86.

5. *Ibid.*, p. 117.

6. Kramer, S. N., *The Sacred Marriage Rite*, p. 18.

7. The Netherworld was the Earth's spiritual domain. It included the underground waters and streams of the Apsû – a world which held all the personalities and knowledge of the past. It was a realm of closely guarded secrets and causes beyond the earthly domain, hence the term 'underground stream' for esoteric movements in later ages. *See* also Kramer, S. N., *Sumerian Mythology*, pp. 44-45.

8. Kramer, S. N., *Mythologies of the Ancient World*, p. 124.

9. Black, J., and Green, A., *Gods, Demons and Symbols of Ancient Mesopotamia*, p. 34.

10. Kramer, S. N., *Sumerian Mythology*, pp. 44 and 59.

11. Piggot, Stuart, *The Earliest Wheeled Transport*, Cornell University Press, Ithaca, NY, 1983, pp. 60-63.

12. Heidel, Alexander, *The Gilgamesh Epic and Old Testament Parallels*, University of Chicago Press, Chicago, 1949, pp. 137-38.

13. Sitchin, Z., *The 12th Planet*, p. 337.

14. Jacobsen, Thorkild, *The Sumerian King List*, (Assyrialogical Studies No.11), University of Chicago Press, Chicago, 1939. (The King List was compiled before the reign of Shu-sin of Ur (2038-30 BC) and (p. 141) probably compiled in Uruk.)

15. Rohl, D., *A Test of Time*, p. 10, ff.

16. Woolley, C. L., *The Sumerians*, p. 27; and Jacobsen, T., The Sumerian King List, pp. 129-31.

17. Roux, G., *Ancient Iraq*, p. 97.

18. *Ibid.*, p. 97.

19. Kramer, Samuel Noah, *History Begins at Sumer*, Thames & Hudson, London, 1958, p. 214.

20. Frankfort, Henri, *Kingship and the Gods*, University of Chicago Press, Chicago, 1948, p. 231.

21. *Ibid.*, p. 224.

22. *Ibid.*, p. 237.

23. Heidel, A., *The Babylonian Genesis*, p. 77.

24. Roux, G., *Ancient Iraq*, p. 350.

25. Woolley, C. L., *The Sumerians*, p. 29.

26. Jacobsen, T., *The Treasures of Darkness*, p. 95.

27. Jacobsen, T., *The Sumerian King List*, p. 76.

28. *Epic of Gilgamesh*, Tablet XI.

29. The subject of the Transylvanian script and its related archaeological discovery is discussed st length in Gardner, L., *Realm of the Ring Lords*, MediaQuest, Ottery St. Mary, 2000, pp. 66-70.

30. O'Brien, Christian and Barbara Joy, *Genius of the Few*, Dianthus, Cirncester, 1999, p. 121.

## 8: THE LADY OF LIFE

1. Correctly entitled *Sa nagba imurur*: 'He who saw everything'. *See* also Cottrell, Leonard, *The Land of Shinar*, Souvenir Press, London, 1965, p. 42.

2. Heidel, A., *The Gilgamesh Epic*, p. 15.

3. Lemesurier, Peter, *The Great Pyramid Decoded*, Element Books, Shaftesbury, 1977, p. 261.

4. Jubilees 5:26.

5. Kramer, S. N., *History Begins at Sumer*, pp. 214 and 260.

6. Heidel, A., *The Gilgamesh Epic*, p. 224.

7. *Ibid.*, p. 105.

8. *Epic of Gilgamesh*, Tablet XI:19-31.

9. Heidel, A., *The Gilgamesh Epic*, p. 225.

10. From the time of King Ammi-saducca of Babylon (*c.*1640 BC).

11. Heidel, A., *The Gilgamesh Epic*, p. 161.

12. Alter, Robert (trans.), *Genesis*, W. W. Norton, New York, 1996, p. 5.

13. Josephus, F., *Antiquities of the Jews*, I, 1:2.

14. Sitchin, Z., *The 12th Planet*, p. 349.

15. *Oxford Concordance to the Bible*.

16. Heidel, A., *The Babylonian Genesis*, p. 80. *See* also *Enûma elish*, Tablet VI, line 33.

17. Sitchin, Z., *The 12th Planet*, p. 349.

18. Heidel, A., *The Babylonian Genesis*, pp. 67 and 118.

19. Speiser, E. A., *The Anchor Bible – Genesis*, p. 16.

20. Alter, R., *Genesis*, p. xii.

21. Kramer, S. N., *Sumerian Mythology*, p. 69.

22. Sitchin, Z., *The 12th Planet*, p. 348.

23. Kramer, S. N., *History Begins at Sumer*, p. 215.

24. Kramer, S. N., *Sumerian Mythology*, p. 53, and p. 115 note 53.

25. Kramer, S. N., *History Begins at Sumer*, pp. 164-65.

26. Kramer, S. N., *Sumerian Mythology*, p. 73.

27. Kramer, S. N., *Mythologies of the Ancient World*, p. 103.

28. *Ibid.*, p. 122.

29. Jacobsen, T., *The Treasures of Darkness*, pp. 113-14.

30. Sitchin, Z., *The 12th Planet*, p. 350.

31. *Atra-hasis Epic*, Tablet fragment IV, column 4.

32. Jacobsen, T., *The Treasures of Darkness*, p. 108.

33. *Ibid.*, p. 107.

34. The Hebrew term for 'archetype', as used to determine the alchemical *Prima Causa* (Conception), was *atsîlûth.*

35. Jacobsen, T., *The Treasures of Darkness*, p. 106.

36. Kramer, S. N., *History Begins at Sumer*, p. 157.

37. Kramer, S. N., *Sumerian Mythology*, pp. 59-62.

38. Sitchin, Z., *The 12th Planet*, p. 351.

39. Speiser, E. A., *The Anchor Bible – Genesis*, p. 16.

40. Roux, G., *Ancient Iraq*, p. 95.

41. *Adapa Tablet*, Fragment I.

42. *Ibid*, Fragment IV.

43. Heidel, A., *The Babylonian Genesis*, p. 152, and p. 153 note 23.

44. Sitchin, Z., *The 12th Planet*, p. 357.

45. Josephus, F., *Antiquities of the Jews*, I, 1:2.

46. Alter, R., *Genesis*, p. 15.

47. Kramer, S. N., *History Begins at Sumer*, p. 210.

48. Church, L. F., *Matthew Henry's Commentary on the Whole Bible*, Genesis II:21-25/2.

49. Mundkur, Balaji, *The Cult of the Serpent*, State University of New York Press, Albany, NY, 1983, p. 70.

## 9: SHEPHERDS OF THE ROYAL SEED

1. Jacobsen, T., *The Treasures of Darkness*, p. 97.

2. From *lu* (man) and *gal* (great), i.e. 'great man'. *See* also Frankfort, H., *Kingship and the Gods*, p. 246.

3. Frankfort, Henri, with Frankfort, H. A., Wilson J. A., and Jacobsen, T., *Before Philosophy*, Penguin, Harmondsworth, 1951, p. 204.

4. Roux, G., *Ancient Iraq*, p. 115.

5. Frankfort, H., *Kingship and the Gods*, p. 252.

6. Jacobsen, T., *The Treasures of Darkness*, p. 10.

7. Jacobsen, T., *The Sumerian King List*, pp. 15-23.

8. Jacobsen, T., *The Treasures of Darkness*, p. 159.

9. Mark 14:36; Romans 8:15; Galatians 4:6.

10. Frankfort, H., *Kingship and the Gods*, p. 215.

11. Keller, W., *The Bible as History*, p. 30.

12. Woolley, C. L., *The Sumerians*, p. 169.

13. Wood, M., *Legacy*, p. 34.

14. Miles, Jack, *God – a Biography*, Vintage, New York, 1995, p. 7.

15. *Time*, 28 October 1996, p. 72.

16. Sitchin, Z., *The 12th Planet*, pp. 145-48.

17. Jacobsen, T., *Mesopotamia* in Kramer, S. N. (ed.), *Mythologies of the Ancient World*, p. 155.

18. Jacobsen, T., *The Treasures of Darkness*, p. 181.

# NOTES AND REFERENCES

## 10: THE TREE OF KNOWLEDGE

1. Speiser, E. A., *The Anchor Bible – Genesis*, p. 18. (The English word 'woman' derives from '*w*ife of *man*'.)

2. Pritchard, James B. (ed.), *Ancient Near Eastern Texts Relating to the Old Testament*, Princeton University Press, NJ, 1955, pp. 63 and 160.

3. In Deuteronomy 22:11 the English translation of God's law says, 'Thou shalt not wear a garment of divers sorts, such as woollen and linen together'. However, the original wording referred not to wool and linen, but to serpent-skin, and to spiritual garments as against material garments. The alteration occurred by way of a scribal change in consonantal structure, so that *sha'atnez metsar u-tofsim* became *sha'atnez tsemer u-fishtim*. *See* also Scholem, Gershom G., *On the Kabbalah and its Symbolism*, Schocken Books, New York, 1965, pp. 71-72.

4. Engnell, Ivan, *Studies in Divine Kingship in the Ancient Near East*, Basil Blackwell, Oxford, 1967, p. 29, note 2.

5. Sitchin, Z., *The 12th Planet*, p. 371.

6. Gardner, L., *Bloodline of the Holy Grail*, p. 311.

7. Alter, R., *Genesis*, p. 13.

8. *Journal of the American Medical Association*, vol. 270, no. 18, 10 November 1993. Professional medical institutions generally use the single-serpent and staff emblem, whereas (from the 19th century) commercial medical associations (such as the Association of American Medical Colleges) generally use the winged caduceus of Hermes (Mercury) with its two spiralling serpents.

9. *Adapa Tablet*, Fragment I.

10. Graves, R, and Patai, R., *Hebrew Myths – Genesis*, p. 87.

11. Kramer, S. N., *Mythologies of the Ancient World*, p. 123.

12. The fruit most commonly associated with this scene is an apple, but this was an invention of later artists. Genesis does not identify the fruit, which was a symbolic representation of knowledge.

13. *Adapa Tablet*, Fragment I.

14. *Epic of Gilgamesh*, Tablet I. *See* also Jacobsen, T., *The Treasures of Darkness*, p. 198; and Speiser, E. A., *The Anchor Bible – Genesis*, p. 26.

15. Scholem, G. G., *On the Kabbalah and its Symbolism*, p. 164.

16. As in Revelation 12:9.

17. Armstrong, Karen, *In the Beginning*, Harper Collins, London, 1997, p. 21.

18. Pagels, Elaine, *The Origin of Satan*, Random House, New York, 1995, p. 39.

19. Stoyanov, Yuri, *The Hidden Tradition in Europe*, Arkana/Penguin, Harmondsworth, 1995, *passim* on 'Dualism'.

20. Pagels, E., *The Origin of Satan*, p. 48.

21. Milton, John, *Paradise Lost*, Jacob Tonson, London, 1730, Book X, lines 425-26.

22. Gardner, L., *Bloodline of the Holy Grail*, ch. 11, ff.

23. Malan, Rev. S. C. (trans.), *The Book of Adam and Eve*, (from the Ethiopic text), Williams & Norgate, London, 1882, pp. v-vi.

24. Budge, Sir Ernest A. Wallis (trans.), *The Book of the Cave of Treasures*, The Religious Tract Society, London, 1927, p. xi.

25. Gardner, L., *Bloodline of the Holy Grail*, pp. 159-61.

26. Budge, Sir Ernest A. Wallis (trans.), *The Book of the Bee*, (from the Syriac text), Clarendon Press, Oxford, 1886, ch. 13.

27. Suarès, Carlo, *The Cipher of Genesis*, Samuel Weiser, Maine, 1992, p. 55.

28. *Ibid.*, p. 103.

29. *Ibid.*, pp. 19 and 21.

30. From the death of Kingu, Enlil was main guardian of the Table of Destiny, having succeeded to the presidential Anuship (the *Anûtu*, henceforth called Enlilship or *Enlilûtu*). However, Sumerian literature (such as the verse called *Ninurta and the Turtle* cites Enki as being the joint guardian. *See* also Black, J., and Green, A., *Gods, Demons and Symbols of Ancient Mesopotamia*, p. 173.

31. Graves, R., and Patai, R., *Hebrew Myths – Genesis*, p. 53. (Raziel was Raguel the Holy Watcher, one of the seven archangels of the book of 1 Enoch 20:4.)

32. Scholem, G. G., *On the Kabbalah and its Symbolism*, p. 1.

33. Suarès, C., *The Cipher of Genesis*, p. 120.

34. King James Authorized Version.

35. Graves, R., and Patai, R., *Hebrew Myths – Genesis*, p. 83.

36. It is sometimes suggested that the name Cain is related to 'possession', *see Oxford Concordance to the Bible*. The name Abel is similarly identified with

'vanity'. *See* also Church, L. F., *Matthew Henry's Commentary on the Whole Bible,* Genesis IV:1-2/I.

37. Suarès, C., *The Cipher of Genesis,* p. 137.

38. *Ibid.*, pp. 140-41.

39. Speiser, E. A., *The Anchor Bible – Genesis,* p. 31.

40. Graves, R., and Patai, R., *Hebrew Myths – Genesis,* p. 97.

41. Engnell, I., *Studies in Divine Kingship in the Ancient Near East,* p. 37.

42. Langdon, Stephen, *Tammuz and Ishtar,* Clarendon Press, Oxford, 1914, pp. 27 and 64.

43. In alchemical circles, the Orb represents the male (semen/energy), whereas the Venus symbol is emblematic of the female (blood/life). *See* also Grant, K., *The Magical Revival,* p. 37.

44. Carlyon, Richard, *A Guide to the Gods,* Heinemann/Quixote, London, 1981, p. 312.

45. From the Latin word *mensis,* meaning 'month'.

46. Grant, K., *The Magical Revival,* pp. 7, 45 and 121.

47. This symbol was used by the hermetic Illuminati, founded on 1 May 1776 by Jean Adam Weishaupt. *See* also Grant, K., *The Magical Revival,* pp. 10, 12, 13, 21 and 128.

48. *Ibid.*, p. 128.

49. This word was first introduced in the Greek *Septuagint,* and was retained thereafter.

50. The modern science of genetics was established by the Columbia University embryologist Thomas Hunt Morgan, who received the Nobel Prize in 1933. His work was founded, however, upon the records of Theodor Heinrich Boveri of Munich University who, in the 1880s, explained almost every detail of cell division and chromosomes long before the invention of the electron microscope. *See* Becker, Robert O., and Selden, Gary, *The Body Electric,* William Morrow, New York, 1985, pp. 42-44.

51. Church, L. F., *Matthew Henry's Commentary on the Whole Bible,* Genesis V:19-22/1.

52. Frankfort, H., *Before Philosophy,* p. 160.

53. Jacobsen, T., *The Sumerian King List*, pp. 17-21.

54. Graves, R., and Patai, R., *Hebrew Myths – Genesis*, p. 106.

55. Stoyanov, Y., *The Hidden Tradition in Europe*, p. 6.

56. *Ibid.*, p. 25.

57. Platt, Rutherford H. (ed.), *The Forgotten Books of Eden*, New American Library, New York, 1974, 'Adam and Eve', LXXIV, p. 53.

58. Luluwa is called Awan in the book of Jubilees.

59. Browne, Lewis (ed.), *The Wisdom of Israel*, Michael Joseph, London, 1948, p. 167.

60. Patai, Raphael, *The Hebrew Goddess*, Wayne State University Press, Detroit, 1967, p. 223.

61. The *Talmud* ('teaching') is essentially a commentary on the *Mishnah*, compiled originally in Hebrew and Aramaic and deriving from two independently important streams of Jewish tradition: the Palestinian and the Babylonian. The *Mishnah* – or Repetition – is an early codification of Jewish law, based on ancient compilations and edited in Palestine by the Ethnarch (Governor) Judah I in the early 3rd century AD. It consists of traditional law (*Halakah*) on a wide range of subjects, derived partly from old custom and partly from biblical law (*Tannaim*) as interpreted by the rabbis (teachers).

62. Patai, R., *The Hebrew Goddess*, p. 223.

63. *Ibid.*, p. 247.

## 11: THE QUEEN OF HEAVEN

1. Kramer, S. N., *Sumerian Mythology*, 2:44, 59.

2. Frankfort, H., *Before Philosophy*, pp. 240-48.

3. Graves, Robert, *The White Goddess*, Faber & Faber, London, 1961, p. 287.

4. Frankfort, H., *Kingship and the Gods*, p. 343.

5. Frankfort, H., *Before Philosophy*, p. 242.

6. Stone, Merlin, *The Paradise Papers*, Virago/Quartet Books, London, 1976, p. 22.

7. Ramtha's School of Enlightenment, PO Box 1210 Yelm, WA, 1995.

8. Genesis, Exodus, Leviticus, Numbers and Deuteronomy.

9. *Hagiographa* (or *Kethubim*): the twelve books comprising the last of the three major divisions of the Hebrew Old Testament to be added to the canon in AD 100. Additional to the divisions of the books of the Law and the books of the Prophets, it includes: Psalms, Proverbs, Job, Ruth, Lamentations, The Song of Solomon, Ecclesiastes, Esther, Daniel, Chronicles 1 & 2, Ezra and Nehemiah.

10. Patai, R., *The Hebrew Goddess, passim.*

11. Davies, S., *The Canaanite Hebrew Goddess,* in Olson, C., (ed.), *The Book of the Goddess – Past and Present,* p. 69.

12. The port of Elath on the Red Sea's Gulf of Aqaba was named after her. Also, the son of Leah's maid Zilpah (by Jacob) was named Asher after Lady Asherah, *see* Genesis 10:13.

13. In 1 Kings 18:19 it is stated that there were 400 priests of Asherah (priests of the Groves, as Asherah's cult was called) at the table of Jezebel of Tyre, wife of King Ahab of Israel, *c.*876 BC.

14. Once in Exodus, three times in Deuteronomy, five times in Judges, twice in Isaiah, once in Jeremiah, once in Micah and twenty-seven times in the books of Kings and Chronicles.

15. Reed, W. L., *The Asherah in the Old Testament,* p. 2.

16. *Ibid.,* p. 4.

17. *Ibid.,* pp. 25-26 and 72.

18. *Ibid.,* p. 27.

19. Carlyon, R., *A Guide to the Gods,* p. 307.

20. Hebrew women often referred to their husbands as *Ba'al,* denoting Master or Lord. *See* also Stone, M., *The Paradise Papers,* p. 71.

21. Patai, R., *The Hebrew Goddess,* p. 54.

22. Matthew 12:24; Mark 3:22; Luke 11:15.

23. Graves, R., and Patai, R., *Hebrew Myths – Genesis,* p. 13.

24. Smith, W. Robertson, *The Religion of the Semites,* Adam & Charles Black, London, 1894,p. 211. (The term *Anathoth* means 'Images of Anath'.)

25. Davies, S., *The Canaanite Hebrew Goddess,* in Olson, C. (ed.), *The Book of the Goddess – Past and Present,* p. 70.

26. The Kabbalah is not an intellectual discipline as such, nor is it a rational exegesis of Jewish Law like the *Talmud*. It is first and foremost a mystical practice, fully integrated with Judaism as a whole. *See* also Epstein, Perle, *Kabalah – The Way of the Jewish Mystic*, Shambhala Publications, Boston, 1988, p. xvii.

27. Patai, R., *The Hebrew Goddess*, pp. 98-99.

28. *Ibid.*, pp. 97 and 99.

29. Davies, S., The Canaanite Hebrew Goddess, in Olson, C. (ed.), *The Book of the Goddess – Past and Present*, p. 77.

30. Browne, L., *The Wisdom of Israel*, p. 13.

31. Scholem, Gershom G., *Major Trends in Jewish Mysticism*, Thames & Hudson, London, 1955, p. 20.

32. *Ibid.*, p. 156. (*Zohar* means 'radiance'.) *See* also Browne, L., *The Wisdom of Israel*, p. 380.

33. Scholem, G. G., *Major Trends in Jewish Mysticism*, p. 163.

34. Patai, R., *The Hebrew Goddess*, p. 114.

35. Scholem, G. G., *Major Trends in Jewish Mysticism*, p. 156.

36. Owning no land to cultivate in Europe, the Jews had turned to trade and banking, but money-lending was subsequently prohibited by the Church of Rome. King Edward I Plantagenet had all Jews expelled from England in 1209, with the exception of skilled physicians. *See* Gardner, L., *Bloodline of the Holy Grail*, p. 178.

37. Patai, R., *The Hebrew Goddess*, p. 148.

38. Speiser, E. A., *The Anchor Bible – Genesis*, p. xxxix.

39. Scholem, G. G., *Major Trends in Jewish Mysticism*, p. 229.

40. Davies, S., *The Canaanite Hebrew Goddess*, in Olson, C. (ed.), *The Book of the Goddess – Past and Present*, p. 78.

41. Guirand, Felix, *Greek Mythology*, (trans. Delano Ames), Paul Hamlyn, London, 1965, p. 63.

42. Jacobsen, T., *The Treasures of Darkness*, p. 142.

43. Patai, R., *The Hebrew Goddess*, p. 150.

44. Graves, R., and Patai, R., *Hebrew Myths – Genesis*, p. 106.

45. Patai, R., *The Hebrew Goddess*, p. 255.

46. *Ibid.*, p. 33.

47. *Ibid.*, p. 250.

48. *Ibid.*, p. 165.

## 12: HERITAGE OF THE WASTELAND

1. Coptic was a language of Egypt in the early centuries AD. *See* also Robinson, J. M., *The Nag Hammadi Library*, VII, 1:29.

2. Roux, G., *Ancient Iraq*, p. 353.

3. The English translation of these writings is by H. L. Ginsberg in *Pritchard's Ancient Near Eastern Texts*.

4. Patai, R., *The Hebrew Goddess*, p. 246.

5. *Zohar* 3:69.

6. Black, J., and Green, A., *Gods, Demons and Symbols of Ancient Mesopotamia*, p. 102.

7. The ring is sometimes portrayed as a circlet of beads, being also representative of divine numerology. *See* also Black, J., and Green, A., *Gods, Demons and Symbols of Ancient Mesopotamia*, p. 156.

8. Patai, R., *The Hebrew Goddess*, p. 222.

9. Kramer, S. N., *Sumerian Mythology*, p. 33; and Heidel, A., *The Gilgamesh Epic*, p. 94.

10. Jacobsen, T., *The Treasures of Darkness*, p. 132.

11. Begg, Ean C. M., *The Cult of the Black Virgin*, Arkana, London, 1985, p. 39.

12. Patai, R., *The Hebrew Goddess*, p. 223.

13. Lemesurier, P., *The Great Pyramid Decoded*, pp. 274 and 294.

14. Gardner, L., *Bloodline of the Holy Grail*, *passim*.

15. This was not an uncommon description. In the *Epic of Lugal-banda*, even Inanna/Anath is described as a harlot, as were most goddesses at one time or

another. *See* also Jacobsen, T., *The Treasures of Darkness*, p. 139.

16. *Ibid.*, p. 172.

17. Black, J., and Green, A., *Gods, Demons and Symbols of Ancient Mesopotamia*, p. 71.

18. Mundkur, B., *The Cult of the Serpent*, p. 286.

19. *Ibid.*, p. 2.

20. Gardner, L., *Bloodline of the Holy Grail*, pp. 179-91 and 204.

21. *Complete Oxford Dictionary*, item: Dragon 7a.

22. Mundkur, B., *The Cult of the Serpent*, pp. 2 and 67.

23. Osman, A., *The House of the Messiah*, pp. 151-52.

24. Gardner, L., *Bloodline of the Holy Grail*, pp. 66-73.

25. *Ibid., passim.* The Christian High Church hounded and persecuted the *Sangréal* (Holy Grail) dynasty of the Messianic line from King David of Israel, and in so doing they were attempting to 'slay the dragon'. This was a favourite theme of Christian mythology. There was, however, also another dragon—a pseudo-dragon—and that was the purple dragon of Imperial Rome. This dragon is portrayed in the New Testament book of the Revelation (12:7-9) as the enemy of the Archangel Michael. Just as Emperor Constantine the Great usurped the early Christian faith in the 4th century, and moulded it into a new hybrid State religion, so too had the earlier Emperors usurped the dragon of kingship as the emblem of their own Imperial standard. There is often, therefore, a conflict of identities, and in some literary romance it can be difficult to determine who is battling against whom.

26. Graves, R., and Patai, R., *Hebrew Myths – Genesis*, p. 51.

## 13: GOLD OF THE GODS

1. Freer, Neil, *Breaking the Godspell*, New Falcon, Phoenix, Ariz., 1987, p. 116.

2. Wood, David, *Genisis – The First Book of Revelations*, Baton Press, Tunbridge Wells, 1985, p. 267.

3. Lewis, H. Spencer, *The Mystical Life of Jesus*, Ancient and Mystical Order Rosae Crucis, San Jose, Calif., 1982, pp. 191-92.

4. Gardner, L., *Bloodline of the Holy Grail*, p. 310.

5. Lewis, H. S., *The Mystical Life of Jesus*, p. 194.

6. *Ibid.*, pp. 196-202.

7. *Ibid.*, pp. 25-26.

8. Established following the 1864 Geneva Convention. Notwithstanding the ancient therapeutic significance of the Red/Rosy Cross, it was said to be a colour reversal of the Swiss flag.

9. Grant, K., *The Magical Revival*, p. 218.

10. Morgan, Marlo, *Mutant Message Down Under*, Thorsons/Harper Collins, London, 1994, pp. 91-92.

11. Grant, K., *The Magical Revival*, p. 123.

12. *Ibid.*, pp. 147-48; and Hocart, A.M., *Kingship*, Oxford University Press, 1927, p. 60. (In the Vedic ritual of the Hindus, *soma* was a spiritual drink of the priestly caste, who claimed it to be the route to the Light. So potent was the *soma* that it was called the *amrita*, meaning 'immortality', For full details *see* Gardner, L., *Realm of the Ring Lords*, pp. 116-124.

13. Yatri, *Unknown Man*, Sidgwick & Jackson, London, 1988, p. 86.

14. Hall, Manly P., *The Secret Teachings of all Ages*, The Philosophical Research Society, Los Angeles, Calif., 1989, pp. XXXII and LXXXIX. (The Swan is the symbol of the initiates of the ancient mysteries, and of incarnate wisdom.)

15. The human spine contains 24 individual vertebrae (7 cervical, 12 thoracic, and 5 lumbar), plus the separately fused sections of the sacrum and the coccyx, which contain 5 and 4 vertebrae, respectively. These total 33 in all.

16. Hall, M.P., *The Secret Teachings of all Ages*, p. LXXIX.

17. *Ibid.*, p. XIX. (Descartes shares with Francis Bacon the honour of founding the systems of modern science and philosophy.)

18. Roney-Dougal, Serena, *Where Science and Magic Meet*, Element Books, Shaftesbury, 1993, p. 91.

19. Wilson, Colin, and Grant, John, *The Directory of Possibilities*, Webb & Bower, Exeter, 1981, p. 144.

20. Sanskrit was an ancient sacred language of the Hindus.

21. Grant, K., *The Magical Revival*, p. 120.

22. *Ibid.*, p. 142.

23. *Ibid.*, p. 123. (From *ritu* stem the words rite, root and red.)

24. *Ibid.*, 7:123

25. Lewis, H.S., *The Mystical Life of Jesus*, p. 82.

26. Gardner, L., *Bloodline of the Holy Grail*, p. 119.

27. Through giving the Star Fire to feed the consciousness of initiates, the priestly scarlet women (*horés*) were regarded as unmarried mothers. This definition was later misinterpreted to produce the concept of 'virgin birth'. *See* also Grant, K., *The Magical Revival*, p. 61.

28. *Ibid.*, p. 70.

29. Jennings, Hargrave, *The Rosicrucians – Their Rites and Mysteries*, Routledge, London, 1887, pp. 65-67.

30. Grant, K., *The Magical Revival*, p. 123.

31. *Ibid.*, p. 125.

32. *Ibid.*, pp. 77-78.

33. Pritchard, J.B., *Ancient Near Eastern Texts*, pp. 114-18.

34. The concept of the Grail existed long before the days of Jesus. *See* also Wilson, C., and Grant, J., *The Directory of Possibilities*, p. 37.

35. Annu was called Heliopolis by the Greeks. Heliopolis, the Egyptian centre of the sun god Ra, was sometimes called On. As Annu it was also known as Innu, or Innu Mehret. *See* also Budge, E. A. W., *The Book of the Dead*, pp. 1 and 201; and Hancock, Graham, *Fingerprints of the Gods*, William Heinemann, London, 1995, p. 360.

36. Utiger, Robert D., *Melatonin, the Hormone of Darkness*, in *New England Journal of Medicine*, vol. 327, no. 19, November 1992.

37. Becker, R. O., and Selden, G., *The Body Electric*, pp. 42-43.

38. Hardland, R., Reiter, R. J., Poeggeler, B. and Dan, D. X., *The Significance of the Metabolism of the Neurohormone Melatonin: Antioxidative Protection of Bioactive Substances*, in *Neuroscience and Biobehavioral Review*, vol. 17, 1993, pp. 347-57.

39. Scholem, G. G., *On the Kabbalah and its Symbolism*, p. 192. (In Hebrew, *da'ath* means gnosis or true knowledge.)

40. Shapiro, Debbie, *The Body Mind Workbook*, Element Books, Shaftesbury, 1990, p. 49.

41. Grant, K., *The Magical Revival*, p. 73 note.

42. Yatri, *Unknown Man*, p. 80.

43. Weinberg, Steven Lee (ed.), *Ramtha*, Sovereignty Inc., Eastbound, WA, 1986, pp. 173 and 189.

44. Grant, K., *The Magical Revival*, p. 36.

## 14: THE PHOENIX AND THE FIRE-STONE

1. Jacobsen, T., *The Sumerian King List.*

2. Grant, K., *The Magical Revival*, p. 133.

3. Gardner, L., *Bloodline of the Holy Grail*, p. 35.

4. Velikovsky, Immanuel, *Ages in Chaos*, Sidgwick & Jackson, London, 1952, p. 160.

5. The geographical Plain of Sharon is identified with a region in Israel extending between Haifa and Tel Aviv-Yafo.

6. Matthew 12:4; Mark 2:26; Luke 6:4.

7. Josephus, F., *The Antiquities of the Jews*, III, 1:6.

8. *Ibid.*, III, 1:6.

9. Velikovsky, Immanuel, *Worlds in Collision*, (1950) Victor Gollancz, London, 1973, p. 137.

10. The crystalline grains of tamarisk resin were recorded in 1483 by Breitenbach, Dean of Mainz, who confirmed that they fell like small beads at daybreak. The German botanist G. Ehrenburg explained in 1823 that the tamarisk trees exuded the white crystals (which were used as iron rations by the Bedouin) when attacked by a particular type of plant louse native to Sinai. *See* Keller, W., *The Bible as History*, pp. 129-31.

11. Complete texts from about 1425 BC based on earlier texts from the third millennium BC. *See* Budge, E. A. W., *The Book of the Dead*, p. ix, and 3.

12. Loomis, Roger Sherman, *The Grail – From Celtic Myth to Christian Symbolism*, University of Wales Press, Cardiff, 1963, p. 210.

13. Velikovsky, I., *Ages in Chaos*, p. 160.

14. Gardiner, Alan, *Egyptian Grammar*, Griffith Institute, Ashmolean Museum, Oxford, 1957, §24:33 and Excursion A:76.

15. *Ibid.*, §24:32.

16. Weigall, Arthur, *The Life and Times of Akhenaten*, Thornton Butterworth, London, 1910, p. 17.

17. Hall, M. P., *The Secret Teachings of all Ages*, p. LXXIX.

18. Gardner, L., *Bloodline of the Holy Grail*, p. 246.

19. Loomis, R. S., *The Grail – From Celtic Myth to Christian Symbolism*, p. 209.

20. This is rendered as *lapis exillas* in some versions.

21. *Complete Oxford English Dictionary* (etymology), items: (a) phoenician, (b) phoenix 1, and (c) phoenix 2.

22. Loomis, R. S., *The Grail – From Celtic Myth to Christian Symbolism*, pp. 212-13.

23. Lapidus, *In Pursuit of Gold – Alchemy in Theory and Practice*, (ed. George Skinner), Neville Spearman, London, 1976, p. 11.

24. *Ibid.*, p. 22.

25. BBC2 documentary, *Cosmic Bullets*, 1997, citing Gubbio, Northern Italy, in particular.

26. *Nexus*, October-November 1996, David Hudson lecture, part two, p. 39.

27. Hudson, David, *Alchemy* (video), Ramtha's School of Enlightenment, PO Box 1210 Yelm, WA, 1995.

28. Gardner, L., *Bloodline of the Holy Grail*, p. 264.

29. *Nexus*, August-September 1996, David Hudson lecture, part one, p. 30.

30. Superconductors are used for brain scanning and can even measure thoughts. A superconductor is sensitive to magnetic fields of minute proportion. Unlike electric conductivity, superconductivity does not require physical contacts.

31. The quarterly publication of the International Precious Metals Conference.

32. Breasted, J. H., *The Dawn of Consciousness*, Charles Scribner's Sons, New York, 1934, p. 49; and Gardiner, A., *Egyptian Grammar*, Excursion A, p. 72.

33. Budge, E. A. W., *The Book of the Dead: Papyrus of Ani*, p. 75.

## 15: VULCAN AND THE PENTAGRAM

1. *Zohar* 59b, on Noah.

2. Epstein, P., *Kabalah – The Way of the Jewish Mystic*, p. 29.

3. Eisenman, Robert, *Maccabees, Zadokites, Christians and Qumrân*, E. J. Brill, Leiden, 1983, p. 2, and p. 40, note 10.

4. Dupont-Sommer, A., *The Essene Writings from Qumrân*, p. 284.

5. *Ibid.*, p. 285.

6. *Ibid.*, p. 283.

7. Alter, R., *Genesis*, p. 21.

8. Roux, G., *Ancient Iraq*, p. 157.

9. Speiser, E. A., *The Anchor Bible – Genesis*, p. 21. (The word 'pipe' is corrupted in some English-language editions to 'organ'.)

10. Mills, Watson E. (ed.), *Lutterworth Dictionary of the Bible*, Lutterworth Press, Cambridge, 1994, p. 937.

11. Speiser, E. A., *The Anchor Bible – Genesis*, p. 36.

12. Roux, G., *Ancient Iraq*, p. 117.

13. Jacobsen, T., *The Sumerian King List*, p. 181.

14. Roaf, Michael, *Cultural Atlas of Mesopotamia and the Ancient Near East*, Equinox, Oxford, 1990, p. 93.

15. Some English-language editions use the word 'younger' to lessen the anomaly, but the Hebrew language does not yield this meaning.

16. Speiser, E. A., *The Anchor Bible – Genesis*, p. 62.

17. The 22-character Aramaic alphabet was the ancestor of both the Hebrew and Arabic alphabets. From the time of Darius I (*c*.500 BC) it was the official language of the Persian Empire and it overshadowed Hebrew as the main language of the Jews for about 1000 years from that time.

18. Genesis in the *Targum-Jonathan*, section xvi.

19. The *Book of Adam and Eve*.

20. Clayton, Peter A., *Chronicle of the Pharaohs*, Thames & Hudson, London, 1994, p. 26.

21. Hall, M.P., *The Secret Teachings of all Ages*, p. CIV. *See* also Wood, D., *Genisis – The First Book of Revelations*, p. 158 -a work which is especially concerned with the pentagram and its associated lore.

22. 1 Enoch 8:1.

23. Thompson, R.Campbell, *Semitic Magic*, Luzac & Co, London, 1908, p. 185.

24. Rola, Stanislas Klossowski de, *Alchemy*, Thames & Hudson, London, 1977, p. 15.

25. Hall, M.P., *The Secret Teachings of all Ages*, p. XXXVIII.

26. The primitive inch was equal to 1.00106 standard inches. *See* also Lemesurier, P., *The Great Pyramid Decoded*, pp. 10 and 16.

27. *Ibid.*, p. 32.

28. Hall, M.P., *The Secret Teachings of all Ages*, p. CXXXIII.

29. *Ibid.*, p. CVII.

30. A sister language to the Vedic Sanskrit of India.

31. Hall, M.P., *The Secret Teachings of all Ages*, p. CLXXIII.

32. Suarès, C., *The Cipher of Genesis*, pp. 19 and 21.

33. Hall, M.P., *The Secret Teachings of all Ages*, CLVIb.

34. Josephus, F., *The Works of Flavius Josephus*, (Whiston translation), p. 27, note.

35. Hall, M.P., *The Secret Teachings of all Ages*, p. CLXXIII.

36. Knight, Christopher, and Lomas, Robert, *The Hiram Key*, Century, London, 1996, pp. 3-4.

37. King, Francis, *The Secret Rituals of the OTO*, C. W. Daniel, London, 1973, pp. 163-66.

## 16: EMPIRE OF THE COVENANT

1. Graves, R., *The White Goddess*, p. 237.

2. Queen Tiye of Egypt was only about eight years old when she became the royal wife of Pharaoh Amenhotep III. *See* Osman, Ahmed, *Stranger in the Valley of Kings*, Souvenir Press, London, 1987, p. 39.

3. Sarai and Sarah etymology from the *Oxford Concordance to the Bible.*

4. Osman, A., *Stranger in the Valley of Kings*, p. 147.

5. The word *pharaoh* means 'great house'. *See* also Peet, T. Eric, *Egypt and the Old Testament*, Liverpool University Press, Liverpool, 1922, p. 103.

6. Freud, Sigmund, *Moses and Monotheism*, Hogarth Press, London, 1939, pp. 44 and 49. (Freud previously published his work concerning Moses in the 1937 German-language *Imago* magazine, with the title *Moses, an Egyptian.*) *See* also Osman, A., *Stranger in the Valley of Kings*, p. 35.

7. Alter, R., *Genesis*, p. 73.

8. Josephus, F., *Against Apion* (1:22), in *The Works of Flavius Josephus*. Josephus records that Herodotus also credited Ethiopians and Colchians with early circumcision, while claiming that the Phoenicians and Syrians in Palestine learned about it from the Egyptians.

9. Speiser, E. A., *The Anchor Bible – Genesis*, p. 89; and Alter, R., *Genesis*, p. 53.

10. Dupont-Sommer, A., *The Essene Writings from Qumrân*, p. 286.

11. Hooke, S. H., *The Siege Perilous*, SCM Press, London, 1956, p. 34.

12. *Koran, The* (*Al-Qur'an of Mohammed*), (introduction and discourse by Frederick Sale), Chandos/Frederick Warne, London (undated), p. 4.

13. Gardner, L., *Bloodline of the Holy Grail*, p. 101.

14. Clay tablets of the era from Nuzi in north-eastern Mesopotamia, near Haran, give details of a man who similarly transferred his rights to his brother for three sheep. The Nuzi Tablets (over 4000 documents) are now at the Oriental Institute, Chicago University, and in the Harvard Semitic Museum. *See* also Osman, A., *Stranger in the Valley of Kings*, p. 39.

15. Alter, R., *Genesis*, p. 129; and Graves, R., and Patai, R., *Hebrew Myths – Genesis*, p. 191.

16. Jacobsen, T., *The Treasures of Darkness*, p. 197.

17. Speiser, E. A., *The Anchor Bible – Genesis*, p. 195; and Alter, R., *Genesis*, p. 127.

18. Begg, E. C. M., *The Cult of the Black Virgin*, p. 31.

19. Cohn-Sherbok, Lavinia and Dan, *A Short Reader in Judaism*, Oneworld, Oxford, 1997, p. 13.

20. The two Bible entries concerning Esau's wives disagree about the names of the wives and their fathers: *see* Genesis 26:34 and Genesis 36:1-3.

21. Clayton, P. A., *Chronicle of the Pharaohs*, p. 84.

22. *Ibid.*, p. 87.

23. *Ibid.*, p. 91. (Sobekhotep means 'Pleasing to the god Sobek'.)

24. Seters, John van, *The Hyksos*, Yale University Press, New Haven, Conn., 1966, p. 77.

25. *Ibid.*, pp. 163-64.

26. From the Akkadian, *amurru* = westerner. *See* Mills, W. E., *Lutterworth Dictionary of the Bible* under *Amorites*.

27. Seters, J. van, *The Hyksos*, pp. 156 and 168.

28. Weigall, A., *The Life and Times of Akhenaten*, 1:17.

29. Clayton, P. A., *Chronicle of the Pharaohs*, p. 16.

30. Knight, C., and Lomas, R., *The Hiram Key*, pp. 101-02.

31. *Ibid.*, pp. 103-06.

32. Carlyon, R., *A Guide to the Gods*, pp. 278-79, item: 'Hu'.

33. Hocart, A. M., *Kingship*, p. 83.

34. *Ibid.*, p. 7.

35. *Ibid.*, p. 103.

36. Alter, R., *Genesis*, p. 204. (The Dukes of Edom are also listed in 1 Chronicles 1.)

37. Porter, J. R., *The Illustrated Guide to the Bible*, p. 42.

## 17: THE COAT OF MANY COLOURS

1. Clayton, P. A., *Chronicle of the Pharaohs*, p. 9.

2. In the British Museum, London.

3. Weigall, A., *The Life and Times of Akhenaten*, p. 144.

4. In the Palermo Museum, Sicily, with smaller fragments in the Cairo Museum

and in the Petrie Museum, University College, London.

5. Clayton, P. A., *Chronicle of the Pharaohs*, p. 11.

6. In the Louvre Museum, Paris.

7. In the Hall of Ancestors at the Temple of Pharaoh Seti I.

8. In the British Museum, London.

9. In the Cairo Museum.

10. *Oxford Concordance to the Bible.*

11. Rohl, D., *A Test of Time, passim.*

12. *Ibid.*, p. 10.

13. *Ibid.*, p. i.

14. *Oxford Concordance to the Bible.*

15. Smith, W. R., *The Religion of the Semites*, p. 1.

16. Velikovsky, I., *Ages in Chaos*, p. 10, note 18.

17. Some tables give Ramesses II as late as 1278 BC.

18. Rohl, D., *A Test of Time*, p. 116.

19. Velikovsky, I., *Ages in Chaos*, p. 10; and Peet, T. E., *Egypt and the Old Testament*, p. 124. (There were *Aperu/Habiru* (Hebrews) in Egypt as late as the reign of Ramesses IV.)

20. *Oxford Concordance to the Bible.*

21. *Lifelines* magazine, Lifelines Trust, Honiton, July 1997.

22. *Nature* magazine, Macmillan, London, summer 1997.

23. Velikovsky, I., *Ages in Chaos*, p. 27.

24. Jubilees 11:1-4.

25. Roux, G., *Ancient Iraq*, p. 137 and Chart Appendix.

26. Josephus, F., *The Antiquities of the Jews*, II, 15:2. Josephus claims that the said 430 years related to the period 'from the time Abraham first came into Canaan', with only 215 of those years being the sojourn in Egypt. It appears that Josephus

obtained the base of this information from the Greek *Septuagint*, which states: 'And the sojourning of the children of Israel, that is which they sojourned in the land of Egypt and in the land of Canaan, was four hundred and thirty years'. However, the Greek text does not refer to Abraham in this context, as does Josephus; it refers specifically to the 'children of Israel', who were the descendants of Abraham's grandson Jacob-Israel. With regard to Josephus's splitting of the 430 years into two sets of 215 years, there appears to be no precedent for this calculation, although it was used over 1500 years later by Archbishop Ussher.

27. Individual tribal and sectional numbers are detailed in the book of Numbers. *The Sunday Times* reported, 30 November 1997, that research by Colin Humphreys, Professor of Materials Science at Cambridge University, revealed that the actual number of Israelites was substantially smaller than reported because of translatory misunderstandings of the Hebrew word *lp* (*elep*). This was taken to mean 1000, but apparently meant 'troop'. However, even if a designated troop was less than 1000 men, the overall number of Israelites would still be tens of thousands, if not hundreds of thousands, and remains quite inequitable against the original seventy Israelites of only three generations before.

28. Alter, R., *Genesis*, p. 241.

29. Keller, W., *The Bible as History*, p. 108. (The books of Joshua and Judges cover the subsequent period of the Israelites in Palestine, but fail to make any mention of Egypt.)

30. Alter, R., *Genesis*, p. 209.

31. Porter, J. R., *The Illustrated Guide to the Bible*, p. 48.

32. Alter, R., *Genesis*, p. 209.

33. Speiser, E. A., *The Anchor Bible – Genesis*, p. 292.

34. The name Poti-pherah derives from *Pa-di-pa-ra*: 'Gift of the god Ra'. *See* also Keller, W., *The Bible as History*, p. 103.

35. Alter, R., *Genesis*, p. 241.

36. Keller, W., *The Bible as History*, p. 11.

37. *Ibid.*, pp. 104-05. (The *Bahr Yusuf* was largely engineered from the twelfth dynasty of Egypt onwards.) *See* also Clayton, P. A., *Chronicle of the Pharaohs*, pp. 82 and 84.

38. Osman, A., *Stranger in the Valley of Kings*, p. 123.

39. The Hyksos were foreign 'desert princes' (*hikau-khoswet*). They were immediately from Syria, Palestine or Phoenicia, and were previously from Troy.

They settled in the delta region in about 1700 BC and ruled from *c.*1663 BC until deposed by the eighteenth-dynasty Pharaoh Ahmose I, *c.*1550 BC. *See* also Peet, T. E., *Egypt and the Old Testament*, p. 98.

40. Clayton, P. A., *Chronicle of the Pharaohs*, p. 115.

41. In the Cairo Museum.

42. Osman, A., *The House of the Messiah*, p. 2.

43. Aldred, Cyril, *Akhenaten – King of Egypt*, Thames & Hudson, London, 1988, p. 220.

44. Clayton, P. A., *Chronicle of the Pharaohs*, p. 115.

45. *Ibid.*, p. 123.

46. Osman, A., *Stranger in the Valley of Kings*, p. 91.

47. Weigall, A., *The Life and Times of Akhenaten*, p. 26.

48. Clayton, P. A., *Chronicle of the Pharaohs*, pp. 109-10.

## 18: MOSES OF EGYPT

1. Josephus, F., *Against Apion*, I:26-27.

2. *Ibid.*, I:31.

3. Josephus, F., *The Antiquities of the Jews*, II, 10.

4. Roux, G., *Ancient Iraq*, p. 128.

5. Josephus, F., *Antiquities of the Jews*, II, 9:6.

6. Freud, S., *Moses and Monotheism*, pp. 12-13.

7. Osman, Ahmed., *Moses Pharaoh of Egypt*, Grafton/Collins, London, 1990, p. 66.

8. Breasted, J. H., *The Dawn of Consciousness*, p. 350; and Osman, A., *Moses – Pharaoh of Egypt*, p. 66.

9. *Ibid.*, p. 15.

10. Osman, A., *Stranger in the Valley of Kings*, pp. 14 and 66.

11. Gardiner, A., *Egyptian Grammar*, Excursion A, p. 74.

12. Osman, A., *Moses – Pharaoh of Egypt*, p. 61.

13. Clayton, P. A., *Chronicle of the Pharaohs*, p. 120.

14. Pi-Ramesses is often said to have been a grain-storehouse centre, but this description has now been overturned. It was thought to be such because an inscription relating to a public official was translated to define him as an 'overseer of granaries'. It now transpires that the correct translation is 'overseer of foreign lands'. *See* also Osman, A., *Stranger in the Valley of Kings*, pp. 111-12; and Peet, T. E., *Egypt and the Old Testament*, p. 84.

15. Nefertiti's mother is often said to be unknown, although it is recognized that she was raised by Tey, the wife of Yuya and Tuya's son Aye. *See* Clayton, P. A., *Chronicle of the Pharaohs*, p. 121. Nefertiti was, however, the daughter of Amenhotep III and Sitamun, and it was by way of marriage to Nefertiti that Amenhotep IV (Akhenaten) secured his right to the throne. *See* Osman, A., *Moses – Pharaoh of Egypt*, p. 62.

16. Gardiner, A., *Egyptian Grammar*, Excursion A, p. 75; and Clayton, P. A., *Chronicle of the Pharaohs*, p. 78. (Amenhotep IV was also called Amenemhat IV and Amenemes IV.)

17. Osman, A., *Moses – Pharaoh of Egypt*, p. 167.

18. Rohl, D., *A Test of Time*, p. 197.

19. Osman, A., *Moses – Pharaoh of Egypt*, p. 105.

20. Clayton, P. A., *Chronicle of the Pharaohs*, p. 122.

21. Baikie, James, *The Amarna Age*, A. & C. Black, London, 1926, p. 91.

22. Osman, A., *Moses – Pharaoh of Egypt*, p. 121.

23. Freud, S., *Moses and Monotheism*, *passim.*

24. Rohl, D., *A Test of Time*, p. 199.

25. Osman, A., *Moses – Pharaoh of Egypt*, pp. 63-64.

26. Clayton, P. A., *Chronicle of the Pharaohs*, pp. 128-34.

27. *Ibid.*, p. 124.

28. *Oxford Concordance to the Bible.*

29. Begg, E. C. M., *The Cult of the Black Virgin*, p. 38.

30. Osman, A., *Moses – Pharaoh of Egypt*, pp. 178-79.

31. Clayton, P. A., *Chronicle of the Pharaohs*, p. 120.

32. Budge, E. A. W., *The Book of the Dead*, p. 201.

33. Smenkhkare is also recorded as Akenkheres. *See* Carpenter, C., *The Guinness Book of Kings, Rulers and Statesmen*, p. 68.

34. Velikovsky, I., *Ages in Chaos*, p. 5.

35. Albany, HRH Prince Michael of, *The Forgotten Monarchy of Scotland*, Element Books, Shaftesbury, 1998, pp. 68-69.

36. Keating, Geoffrey, *The History of Ireland*, (trans. David Comyn and Rev. P. S. Dinneen), 1640; reprinted by Irish Texts Society, London 1902-14, vol. II, pp. 20-21.

37. *Ibid.*, vol. II, p. 17.

38. *Ibid.*, vol. I, p. 233.

39. Seele, *King Aye and the Close of the Amarna Age*, in the *Journal of Near Eastern Studies*, vol. 14, 1955, pp. 168-80.

40. Aldred, C., *Akhenaten – King of Egypt*, p. 222.

41. Smith, Ray Winfield, The *Akhenaten Temple Project*, Aris & Phillips, Warminster, 1976, p. 22.

42. Osman, A., *Moses – Pharaoh of Egypt*, p. 134.

43. Rohl, D., *A Test of Time*, p. 397.

44. Clayton, P. A., *Chronicle of the Pharaohs*, p. 126.

45. *Ibid.*, p. 127.

46. Osman, A., *Moses – Pharaoh of Egypt*, pp. 138-47.

47. Peet, T. E., *Egypt and the Old Testament*, pp. 111-12.

48. Thiering, Barbara, *Jesus the Man*, Transworld, London, 1992, pp. 177 and 196.

49. Peet, T. E., *Egypt and the Old Testament*, p. 28.

50. Clayton, P. A., *Chronicle of the Pharaohs*, pp. 140-41.

51. Osman, A., *Moses – Pharaoh of Egypt*, p. 61.

52. *Ibid.*, p. 43.

53. Clayton, P. A., *Chronicle of the Pharaohs*, p. 142.

54. Osman, A., *Moses – Pharaoh of Egypt*, pp. 48-49; and Velikovsky, I., *Ages in Chaos*, p. 7.

55. Peet, T. E., *Egypt and the Old Testament*, p. 115.

56. *Ibid.*, p. 109; and Osman, A., *Moses – Pharaoh of Egypt*, p. 47.

57. Clayton, P. A., *Chronicle of the Pharaohs*, p. 157.

## 19: MAGIC OF THE MOUNTAIN

1. Porter, J. R., *The Illustrated Guide to the Bible*, 3:61.

2. Osman, A., *Moses – Pharaoh of Egypt*, p. 172.

3. Petrie, Sir W. M. Flinders, *Researches in Sinai*, John Murray, London, 1906, p. 72.

4. *Ibid.*, p. 85.

5. Kitchen, Kenneth Anderson, *Ramesside Inscriptions*, B. H. Blackwell, Oxford, 1975, p. 1; and Osman, A., *Moses – Pharaoh of Egypt*, p. 170.

6. Cerny, Jaroslav (ed.), *The Inscriptions of Sinai*, Egypt Exploration Society, London, 1955, vol. 2, p. 7.

7. *Ibid.*, vol. 2, pp. 45-46.

8. Petrie, Sir W. M. F., *Researches in Sinai*, p. 101.

9. Clayton, P. A., *Chronicle of the Pharaohs*, p. 109.

10. Gardiner, A., *Egyptian Grammar*, Excursion A, p. 72.

11. Carlyon, R., *A Guide to the Gods*, p. 275.

12. Clayton, P. A., *Chronicle of the Pharaohs*, p. 18.

13. Jennings, H., *The Rosicrucians*, p. 107.

14. Carlyon, R., *A Guide to the Gods*, p. 276.

15. Bodnar, Andrea G., Quellette, Michel, Frolkis, Maria, Holt, Shawn E., Chiu, Choy-Pik, Morton, Gregg B., Harley, Calvin B., Shay, Jerry W., Lichtsteiner, Serge, and Wright, Woodring E., *Extension of Life Span by Introduction of Telomerase into Normal Human Cells*, in journal *Science*, vol. 279, 16 January 1998, pp. 349-52.

16. Cerny, J., *The Inscriptions of Sinai*, vol. 2, p. 119.

17. *Ibid.*, vol. 2, p. 205.

18. In the Cairo Museum.

19. *Physical Review A*, vol. 39, no. 5, 1 March 1989.

20. *Nexus*, November 1996, p. 38.

21. The Great Pyramid has been reliably estimated to consist of some 2.3 million blocks. *See* also Hancock, G., *Fingerprints of the Gods*, p. 284.

22. Hodges, Peter, *How the Pyramids were Built*, (ed. Julian Keable), Element Books, Shaftesbury, 1989, p. 123.

23. Jennings, H., *The Rosicrucians*, pp. 4, 108 and 225.

24. Hancock, G., *Fingerprints of the Gods*, p. 298.

25. Edwards, I. E. S., *The Pyramids of Egypt*, Viking, New York, 1986, p. 115.

26. Hancock, G., *Fingerprints of the Gods*, p. 330.

27. Osman, A., *The House of the Messiah*, p. 159.

28. Baikie, J., *The Amarna Age*, p. 241.

29. Osman, A., *The House of the Messiah*, p. 159.

30. Aldred, C., *Akhenaten – King of Egypt*, pp. 203-04.

31. *Ibid.*, p. 286.

32. Baikie, J., *The Amarna Age*, p. 95.

33. Aldred, C., *Akhenaten – King of Egypt*, p. 234.

34. Josephus, F., *The Antiquities of the Jews*, II, 10:2.

35. Alcuin, Flaccus Albinus, Abbot of Canterbury (trans.), *The Book of Jasher*, Longman, London, 1929, section, Testimonies and Notes.

36. Jasher 6:10.

37. Jasher 14:9-33.

38. Jasher 15:1-12.

39. Jasher 15:15-17.

40. Osman, A., *Moses – Pharaoh of Egypt*, p. 184.

41. The Syriac and Ethiopic records identify her as Shípôr.

42. Gardner, L., *Bloodline of the Holy Grail*, p. 86.

43. Clayton, P. A., *Chronicle of the Pharaohs*, p. 123.

44. *Oxford Concordance to the Bible.*

45. Weigall, A., *The Life and Times of Akhenaten*, pp. 138-39.

46. Notably the undated book of Adam which was subsequently translated into Ethiopic in the early Christian era and was later condemned in the Vatican's *Apostolic Constitutions.*

## 20: WISDOM AND THE LAW

1. Osman, A., *Moses – Pharaoh of Egypt*, pp. 165-66.

2. Carlyon, R., *A Guide to the Gods*, p. 266.

3. Osman, A., *Moses – Pharaoh of Egypt*, p. 167.

4. Kramer, S. N., *Sumerian Mythology*, pp. 44 and 59.

5. Aldred, C., *Akhenaten – King of Egypt*, p. 221.

6. Jasher, chaps. 14 to 17.

7. Jasher 19:1.

8. A traditional Jewish view is that the *Pentateuch* was actually written by Moses himself, even though these books are known to have been written centuries later. In the 12th century, the philosopher Moses Maimonides, in formulating the principles of the Jewish faith, upheld the authorship of Moses, but this was questioned in the 17th century by the philosopher Spinoza. Since that time the matter has been a constant area of debate. *See* also Cohn-Sherbok, L. and D., *A Short Reader in Judaism*, pp. 23-35.

9. Now in the Louvre Museum, Paris. *See* also Roux, G., *Ancient Iraq*, p. 169.

10. Hall, M. P., *The Secret Teachings of all Ages*, p. XCVIII.

11. *Ibid.*, p. CLVIb.

12. Ellis, Roger, *Thoth – Architect of the Universe*, Edfu Books, Dorset BH31 6FJ, 1997, p. 32.

13. Founded as *Invisible College* in reign of Charles I (1645), and incorporated under Royal Charter as The Royal Society by Charles II in 1662.

14. Gardner, L., *Bloodline of the Holy Grail*, pp. 322-24.

15. *Boyle's Law* states that at a constant temperature the volume of a (perfect) gas varies inversely in relation to its pressure.

16. Hall, M. P., *The Secret Teachings of all Ages*, p. XXXVII.

17. Bacstrom, Dr Sigismund, *Original Alchemical Manuscripts and Rosicrucian Papers* (18 vols., 18th century). Details of the Rosicrucian *Bacstrom Certificate* and of Bacstrom's dealings with the Comte de Chazal are detailed in Waite, Arthur Edward, *The Brotherhood of the Rosy Cross*, William Rider, London, 1924, pp. 549-60.

18. Breasted, J. H., *The Dawn of Consciousness*, p. 371.

19. *Ibid.*, pp. 377-78.

# CHRONOLOGY

| c.BC | |
|---|---|
| 3,500,000 | Lucy and the first family in Ethiopia |
| 3,000,000 | Early form of *homo erectus* |
| 2,000,000 | *Homo habilis* and Pleistocene Ice Age |
| 800,000 | *Homo erectus* and Old Stone Age |
| 100,000 | Northern Mesopotamian hominoids |
| 70,000 | Neanderthal period. Eljo race prevailed |
| 40,000 | *Homo erectus* still extant in Java |
| 35,000 | The sons of the Gods and daughters of the Eljo |
| | Cro-Magnon period. Naphidem race emerged |
| 30,000 | Neanderthal race extinct |
| | Eljo decimated and Naphidem prevailed |
| 29,500 | Nephilim kingdoms established in Sumer |
| 11,000 | New Stone Age and close of Pleistocene Ice Age |
| 10,000 | Domestic Age in Fertile Crescent |
| 6500 | Bronze Age in Fertile Crescent |
| 5500 | Municipal society in Sumer |
| 4500 | Kurgans migrate and advance wheel culture |
| 4004 | Christian date for Adam and Eve |
| 4000 | Great Flood of southern Mesopotamia |
| 3900 | Age of Civilization and the great cities of Sumer |
| | Introduction of Earthling kingship |
| | Age of the *hu-mannan* (mighty man) |
| | Era of Adâma and Nîn-khâwa (Adam and Eve) |
| | Commencement of Star Fire ritual. |
| 3760 | Jewish date for Adam and Eve |
| 3400 | Cuneiform writing |
| 3200 | Era of Tubal-cain the Vulcan |
| 3050 | First pharaonic dynasty of Egypt |
| 2650 | King Gilgamesh of Uruk |
| 2370 | Sargon the Great of Akkad |
| 2000 | Sumerian King List compiled |
| | Babylon founded. First Tower of Babel |

| | |
|---|---|
| 1960 | Sacking of Ur and migration of the Abram family |
| | Star Fire substituted by Highward Fire-stone |
| 1785 | Dragon Court of Queen Sobeknefru of Egypt |
| 1760 | Jacob-Israel takes Israelites into Egypt |
| 1624 | Eruption of Mount Santorini |
| 1500 | Babylonian Genesis (*Enûma elish*) compiled |
| 1450 | Great White Brotherhood of Pharaoh Tuthmosis III |
| 1400 | Introduction of Aramaic language in Mesopotamia |
| 1334 | Moses and the Israelite Exodus from Egypt |
| | Egyptian laws implemented for Israelites in Canaan |
| 1100 | Hebrews still worshipping the Goddess |
| 1008 | Anointing of King David of Judah |
| 853 | Battle of Karkar (the first precise historical date) |
| 664 | Sacking of Thebes by Ashur-banipal of Assyria |
| | Hebrews still worship the Goddess along with Jehovah |
| 606 | Nebuchadnezzar of Babylon invades Jerusalem |
| 586 | Israelite Captivity begins in Babylon |
| | First books of the Old Testament written |
| 536 | First wave of Israelite captives released from Babylonia |
| 356 | Macedonian Empire of Alexander the Great |
| 100 | Books of the Old Testament concluded |

# GRAND ASSEMBLY OF THE ANUNNAKI

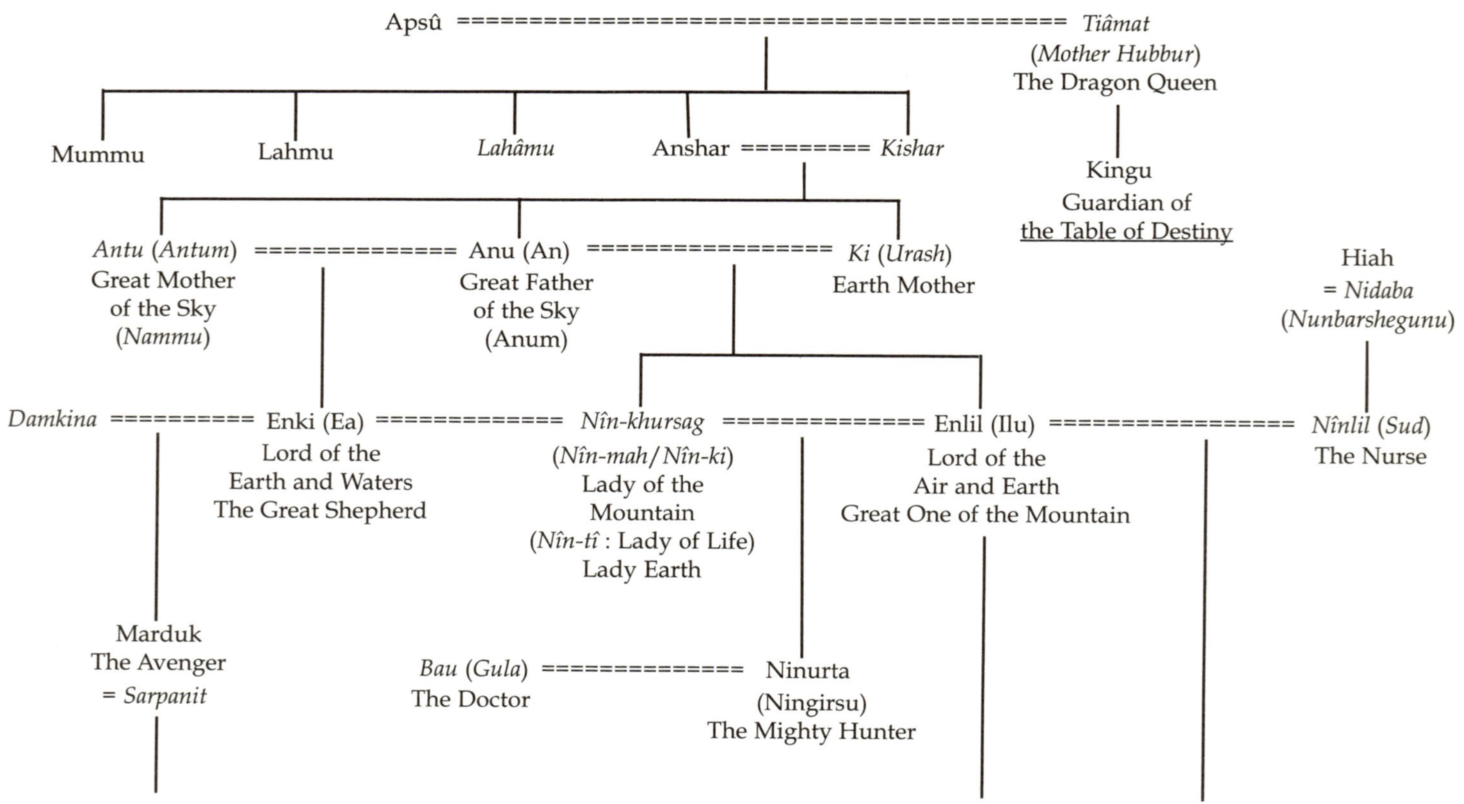

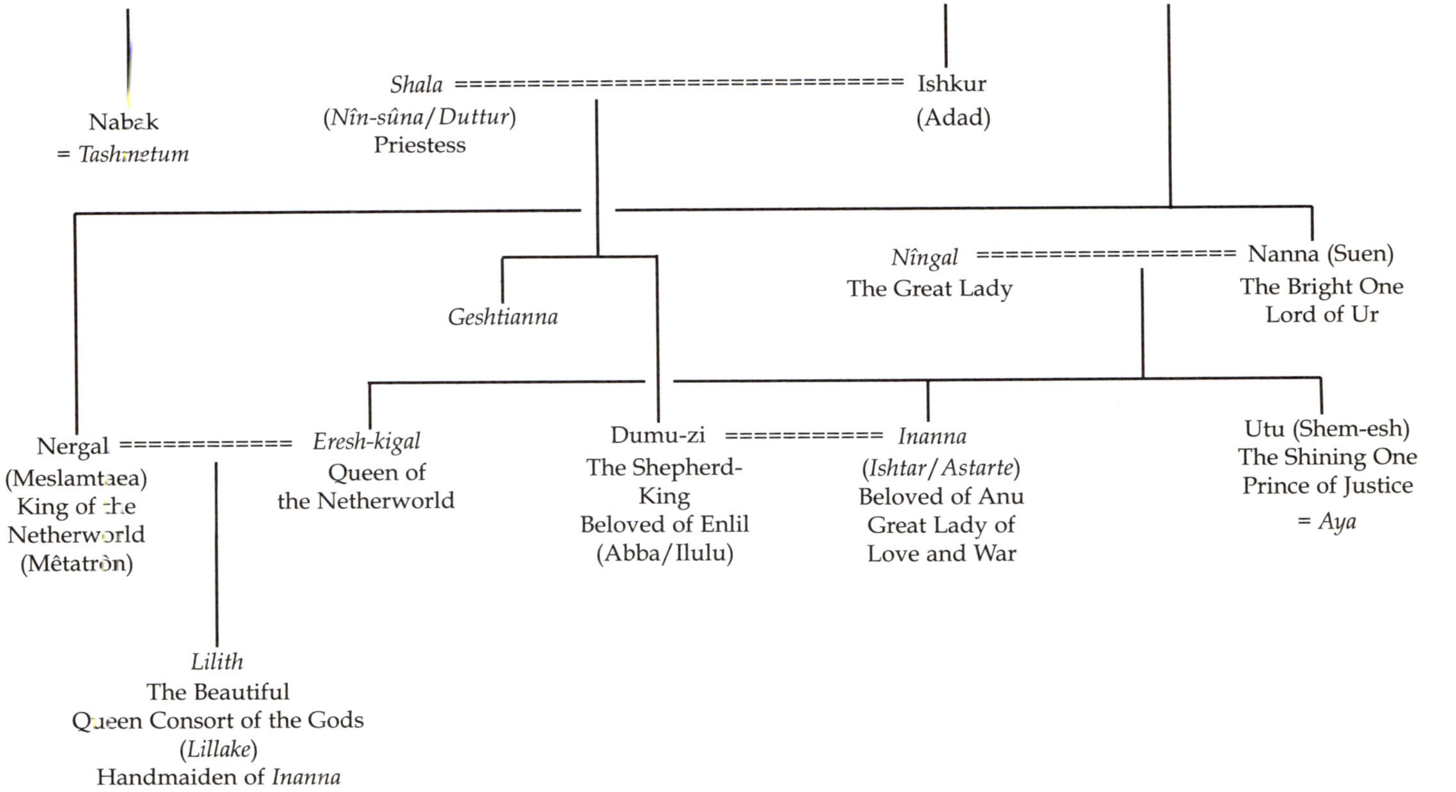

Nabak
= *Tashmetum*
*Shala* ================================ Ishkur
(*Nîn-sûna/Duttur*)
Priestess
(Adad)
*Nîngal* ================== Nanna (Suen)
The Great Lady
The Bright One
Lord of Ur
*Geshtianna*
Nergal ============ *Eresh-kigal*
(Meslamtaea)
King of the
Netherworld
(Mêtatròn)
Queen of
the Netherworld
Dumu-zi =========== *Inanna*
The Shepherd-
King
Beloved of Enlil
(Abba/Ilulu)
(*Ishtar/Astarte*)
Beloved of Anu
Great Lady of
Love and War
Utu (Shem-esh)
The Shining One
Prince of Justice
= *Aya*
*Lilith*
The Beautiful
Queen Consort of the Gods
(*Lillake*)
Handmaiden of *Inanna*

# CHIEFS OF THE TENS OF THE FALLEN ANGELS

From the Book of Enoch

Semîazâz

Arâkîba

Râmâel

Kôkabîel

Tâmîel

Ramîel

Dânel

Ezeqâel

Barâqîjal

Asûel

Armârôs

Batârel

Anânel

Zaqîel

Samsâpâel

Satârel

Tûrel

Jûmjâel

Sarîel

# ANTEDILUVIAN KINGS OF SUMER

From the Sumerian King List

## The Nephilim Kingdoms

*When the kingship was lowered from heaven, the kingship was in Eridu*

In Eridu Al-lulim became king

Then Alagar reigned

*Kingship to Bad-tibira was carried*

In Bad-tibira En-men-lu-anna reigned

Then En-men-gal-anna reigned

And divine Dumu-zi reigned

*Kingship to Larak was carried*

In Larak En-sipa-zi-anna reigned

*Kingship to Sippar was carried*

In Sippar En-men-dur-anna reigned

*Kingship to Shuruppak was carried*

In Shuruppak Ubar-tutu reigned

*The Flood swept thereover*

Ubar-tutu's son was Zi-u-sudra (Uta-napishtim), whose reign was interrupted by the Flood. He was the prototype for the biblical Noah.

## POST-DILUVIAN KINGS OF SUMER

From the Sumerian King List

*After the Flood had swept thereover, when the kingship was lowered from heaven, the kingship was in Kish*

*First attempt at Earthly kingship*

In Kish Ga-[ ]-ur became king

*Earthly kingship fails, and is terminated (destroyed)*
*Kingship reverts back to the Nephilim*

The heavenly Nidaba (queen) then reigned in Kish

Pala-kinatim reigned in Kish

Nangish-lishma reigned in Kish

Bahina reigned in Kish

Bu-an-[ ]-um reigned in Kish

Kalibum reigned in Kish

Qalumu reigned in Kish

Zuqaqip reigned in Kish

*Second introduction of Earthly kingship*

Atabba [Adapa—the Adâma] reigned in Kish
The First Priest-King (Sanga-Lugal)

*Earthly kingship a success*
*Sovereign regalia introduced: tiara, sceptre and shepherd's staff*

In translations of the King List the point is made that some of the early kings may have been simultaneous rather than consecutive

# KINGS OF MESOPOTAMIA (1)

Contemporary with the Bible period from Noah to Peleg
(Excluding 1st dynasty of Kish – *see* Chart: Descents from Lamech and Noah)

| | | | |
|---|---|---|---|
| | 1st Dynasty of URUK | | |
| | Mes-ki-agga-sher (*c*.3000 BC) | | |
| | En-merkar (*c*.2950 BC) | | |
| | Lugal-banda (*c*.2925 BC) | | |
| | Dumu-zi II (*c*.2910 BC) | | |
| | (The Great Shepherd) | | |
| | Gilgamesh (*c*.2860 BC) | | |
| | | 1st Dynasty of UR | 1st Dynasty of LAGASH |
| | | Mes-anne-padda | |
| 2nd Dynasty of KISH | Ur-nungal (*c*.2800 BC) | | |
| | | | Gurshar |
| Shu - [ ] | | A-anne-padda | |
| | Utu-kalamma (*c*.2750 BC) | | |
| Dadasig | Labba- [ ] -ir (*c*.2710 BC) | | Gunidu |
| Magalgalla | E-nun-dara-anna (*c*.2665 BC) | | |
| | | | Ur-Nanshi |
| | | Mes-kiag-nunna | |
| Kalbum | Mes-he (*c*.2610 BC) | | |
| She-è | Melam-anna (*c*.2550 BC) | | A-kurgal |
| Ga-Shub-nunna | Lugal-ki-tun (*c*.2500 BC) | | E-anna-tum I |
| Enbi-Eshtar | | | |
| | | | En-temena |

| | | | |
|---|---|---|---|
| Lugal-mu | | Elulu | |
| En-shakush-anna | | Balulu | |
| | 2nd Dynasty of URUK | | |
| 3rd Dynasty of KISH | | | E-anna-tum II |
| | Lugal-kinishe-dudu (*c.*2450 BC) | | |
| *Ku-baba* | | | |
| (the Barmaid) | | | |
| 4th Dynasty of KISH | | 2nd Dynasty of UR | |
| | | | Lugal-anda |
| Pzur-Sin | | Lugal-kisal-zi | |
| | 3rd Dynasty of URUK | | |
| Ur-Zababa | Lugal-zâgge-si (*c.*2400 BC) | | En-entar-zi |
| Simu-dâr | | Ka-ku | Uru-ka-gina |
| Usi-watâr | | | |

# KINGS OF MESOPOTAMIA (2)

Contemporary with the Bible period from Peleg to Abraham

| | | |
|---|---|---|
| 4th Dynasty of KISH | Dynasty of AKKAD | |
| Sharru-kîn (2371-2316 BC) | | |
| (Sargon I - The Great) | | |
| Eshtar-muti | Rimush (2315-2307 BC) | |
| Ishne-Shamash | | |
| Manishtusu (2306-2292 BC) | | |
| Nannia | | |
| Narâm-Sin (2291-2255 BC) | | |
| Shar-kali-shari (2254-2230 BC) | | |
| Utu-khegal (2120-2114 BC) | | |
| | Restored Dynasty of UR | 2nd Dynasty of LAGASH |
| | Ur-nammu (2113-2096 BC) | |
| | | Ur-baba |
| | Shulgi (2095-2048 BC) | |
| | | Gudea |
| | Amar-sin (2047-2039 BC) | |
| | Shu-sin (2038-2030 BC) | Ur-ningirsu |
| | | Ibbi-sin (2029-2006 BC) |
| | | Ugme |

| Dynasty of ISIN | 1st Dynasty of ASSYRIA | 1st Dynasty of LARSA |
|---|---|---|
| | Zariqum (*c*.2030 BC) | |
| | Pzur-Ashur I (*c*.2010 BC) | Nablânum (2025-2005 BC) |
| Ishbi-Irra (2017-1985 BC) | | |
| | Shalim-Ahum (*c*.1980 BC) | Emisum (2004-1977 BC) |
| Shu-ilishu (1984-1975 BC) | | |
| Iddin-Dagan (1974-1954 BC) | | Samu-um (1976-1942 BC) |
| | Ilushuma (*c*.1950 BC) | |
| Ishme-Dagan (1953-1935 BC) | | |
| | | Zaba-a (1941-1933 BC) |
| Lipit-Ishtar (1934-1924 BC) | | |

# KINGS OF MESOPOTAMIA (3)

Contemporary with the Bible period from Abraham to Miriam

| | | | |
|---|---|---|---|
| Dynasty of ISIN | | | 1st Dynasty of LARSA |
| Ur-ninurta (1923-1896 BC) | | | Gungunum (1932-1906 BC) |
| Bur-Sin (1895-1874 BC) | Amorite Dynasty of BABYLON | 1st Dynasty of ASSYRIA | |
| | [Descent from Hâm] | Erishum I | Abi-sarê (1905-1895 BC) |
| | Shamu-abum (1894-1881 BC) | Sumu-El 1894-1866 BC) | |
| Lipit-Enlil (1873-1869 BC) | Samu-lâwl (1880-1845 BC) | Sargon I | Nûr-Adad (1865-1850 BC) |
| Ira-imitti (1869-1861 BC) | | | |
| Sin-idinam (1849-1843 BC) | | | |
| Enlil Bâni (1860-1837 BC) | | | |
| | Samu-la-ilîm (1844-1835 BC) | Ilâ-kabakabû | Sin-iqîsham |
| Zambia (1836-1834 BC) | | | |
| | Saboum (1834-1831 BC) | | Silli-Adad |
| Iter-pisha (1833-1831 BC) | | 2nd Dynasty of ASSYRIA | |
| | | | Kud-ur-mabuk (1834 BC) |
| Ur-dukuga (1830-1828 BC) | | Shamashi-Adad I | |
| | Apil-sin (1830-1813 BC) | | Warad-Sin (1834-1823 BC) |
| Sin-magir (1827-1813 BC) | | Ishme-Dagan I | |
| | Sin-muballit (1812-1793 BC) | | Rim-Sin (1822-1763 BC) |
| Damiq-ilishu (1816-1794 BC) | | | |
| | | Assur-dugal | |
| | Hammurabi (1792-1750 BC) (The Lawgiver) | | |

| | | | |
|---|---|---|---|
| | | | <u>Kassite Dynasty of LARSA</u> |
| | | <u>3rd Dynasty of ASSYRIA</u> | |
| | Samsu-iluna (1749-1712 BC) | | Gandash (1746-1731 BC) |
| | | Adasi | |
| <u>Dynasty of the SEA LAND</u> | | | Agum I |
| | | Bêl-bani | |
| Iluma-ilu | | | |
| | | Libaiju | |
| | Abi-eshuh (1711-1684 BC) | | Kashtiliash I |
| Damiq-ilishu | | | |
| | | Sharma-Adad I | |
| | Ammi-ditana (1683-1647) | En-tar-sin | Abirattash |
| Gulkishar | | Baza-iju | |
| | | | Ushshi |
| | Ammi-Saducca (1646-1626 BC) | Lulla-iju | |
| | | | Kashtiliash II |
| Peshgal-daramash | | Shuninua | |
| | Samsu-ditana (1625-1595 BC) | Sharma-Adad II | |
| | | | Tashigurmash |
| Aidarkalama | | Erishum III | |
| | | | Harbashipak |
| | <u>Kassite Dynasty of BABYLONIA</u> | Shamashi-Adad II | |
| | | | Tipakzi |
| | | Ishme-dagan II | |
| | Agum (II) (1602-1585 BC) | | Agum II (1602-1585 BC) |

| | |
|---|---|
| | Shamashi-Adad III |
| Burnaburiash I (*c*.1585 BC) | |
| | Ashur-nirâri I |
| Kashtiliash III (*c*.1550 BC) | |
| | Pzur-Ashur III |
| Ulamburiash (*c*.1515 BC) | |
| | Enlil-nasir I |
| Agum III (*c*.1475 BC) | |
| | Nurili (Thri) |
| Kadash-Mankharbe I (*c*.1450 BC) | |
| | Ashu-râbi I |
| Kara-Indash (*c*.1425 BC) | |
| | Ashur-nadin-ahhe I |
| | Enlil-nasir II |
| Kurigalzu I (*c*.1390 BC) | |
| | Ashur-nirâri II |
| Kadash-manenlil I (*c*.1380 BC) | |
| | Ashur-bêl-nisheshu |
| Burnaburiash II (*c*.1375 BC) | Ashur-nadin-ahhe II |
| | Eriba-Adad I |
| Karakhardash II (*c*.1350 BC) | Ashur-uballit I (1365-1330 BC) |

# KINGS OF MESOPOTAMIA (4)

Contemporary with the Bible period from Miriam to King David

Kassite Dynasty of BABYLONIA

Kurigalzu II (1345-1324 BC)
Nazi-Maruttash
Kadashman-Turgu
Kadashman-Enlil II (1279-1265 BC)
Kudurenlil
Shagaraktishuriah

Kashtiliash IV
Tukultininurta I
Enlil-nâdin-shumi
Kadash-Mankharbe II
Adad-shum-iddin
Adad-shum-usur
Melishikhu
Marduk-apal-iddina I
Zababashu-middin
Enlil-nadin-ahhe

Marduk-kabit-ahêshu (1170-1152 BC)
Itti-Marduk-balatu (1151-1143 BC)
Ninurt-anad-inshum (1142-1125 BC)
Nebuchadrezzar I (1124-1103 BC)
Enlil-nadin-apli
Marduk-nadin-ahhê (1099-1081 BC)
Marduk-shapik-zêrmâti

Adad-apal-iddina (1067-1046 BC)

3rd Dynasty of ASSYRIA

Enlil-inirâri (*c.*1330 BC)
Arik-dên-ilu (*c.*1325 BC)
Adad-nirâri I (*c.*1300 BC)
Shalmaneser I (1274-1245 BC)

Tukulti-Ninurta I (1244-1208 BC)

Ashur-nadin-apli (*c.*1207 BC)

Ashur-nirâri III (*c.*1200 BC)

Enlil-kuduruser (*c.*1196 BC)

Ninurta-apal-Ekur I (1192-1180 BC)

Ashur-dân I (1179-1134 BC)

Mutak-kilnusku (1133-1131 BC)
Ashur-rêsh-ishi (1131-1116 BC)
Tiglathpileser I (1115-1077 BC)
Ashur-bêl-kala (1074-1057 BC)

Eriba-Adad II (1056-1054 BC)

Shamashi-Adad IV (1053-1050 BC)
Ashurnasirpal I (1049-1031 BC)

# ANCESTRY OF ADAM AND EVE

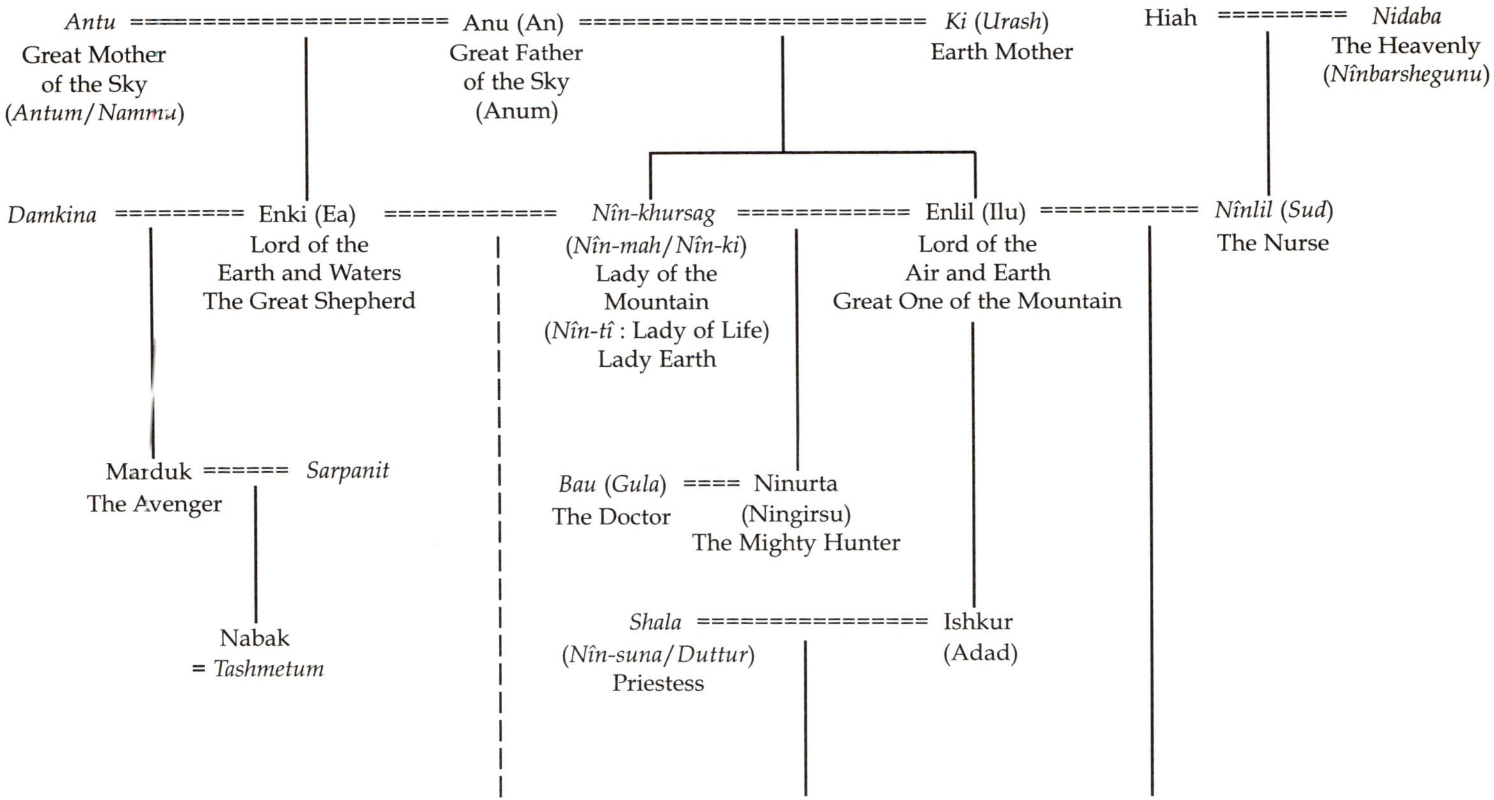

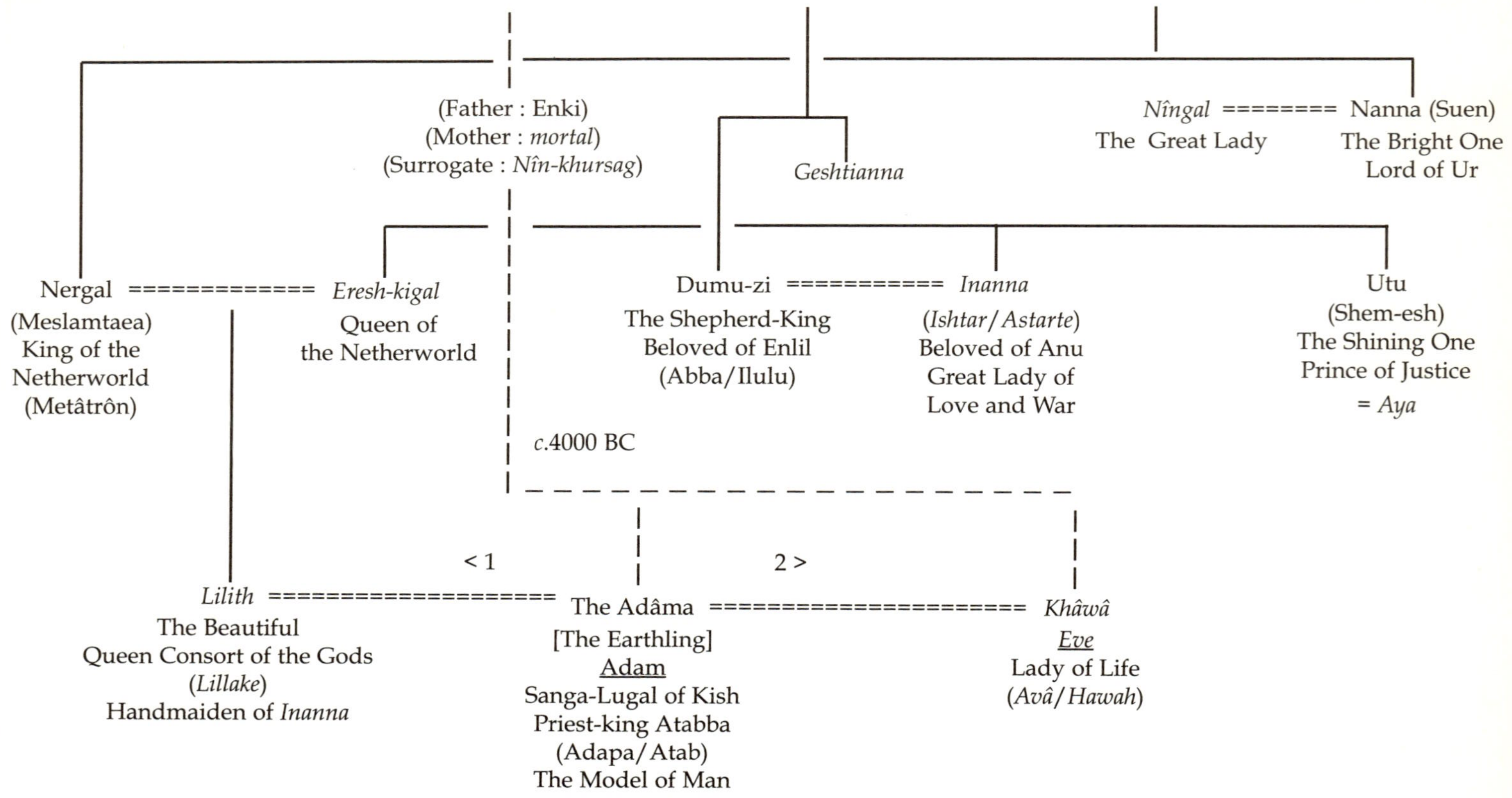

(Father : Enki)
(Mother : mortal)
(Surrogate : Nîn-khursag)
Geshtianna
Nîngal ======== Nanna (Suen)
The Great Lady
The Bright One
Lord of Ur
Nergal ============= Eresh-kigal
(Meslamtaea)
King of the
Netherworld
(Metâtrôn)
Queen of
the Netherworld
Dumu-zi =========== Inanna
The Shepherd-King
Beloved of Enlil
(Abba/Ilulu)
(Ishtar/Astarte)
Beloved of Anu
Great Lady of
Love and War
Utu
(Shem-esh)
The Shining One
Prince of Justice
= Aya
c.4000 BC
< 1
2 >
Lilith ==================== The Adâma ====================== Khâwâ
The Beautiful
Queen Consort of the Gods
(Lillake)
Handmaiden of Inanna
[The Earthling]
Adam
Sanga-Lugal of Kish
Priest-king Atabba
(Adapa/Atab)
The Model of Man
Eve
Lady of Life
(Avâ/Hawah)

# DESCENTS TO CAIN AND SETH

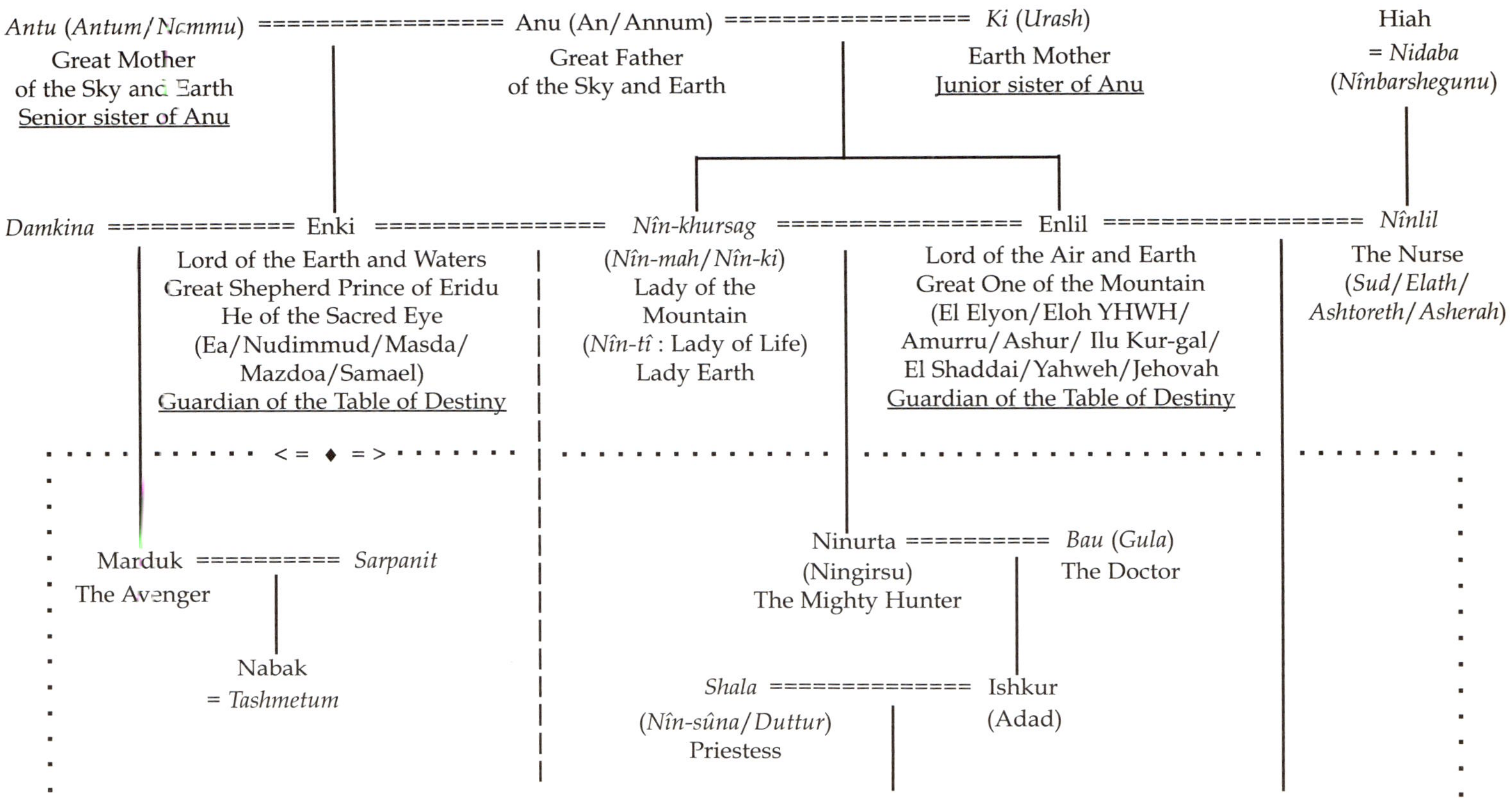

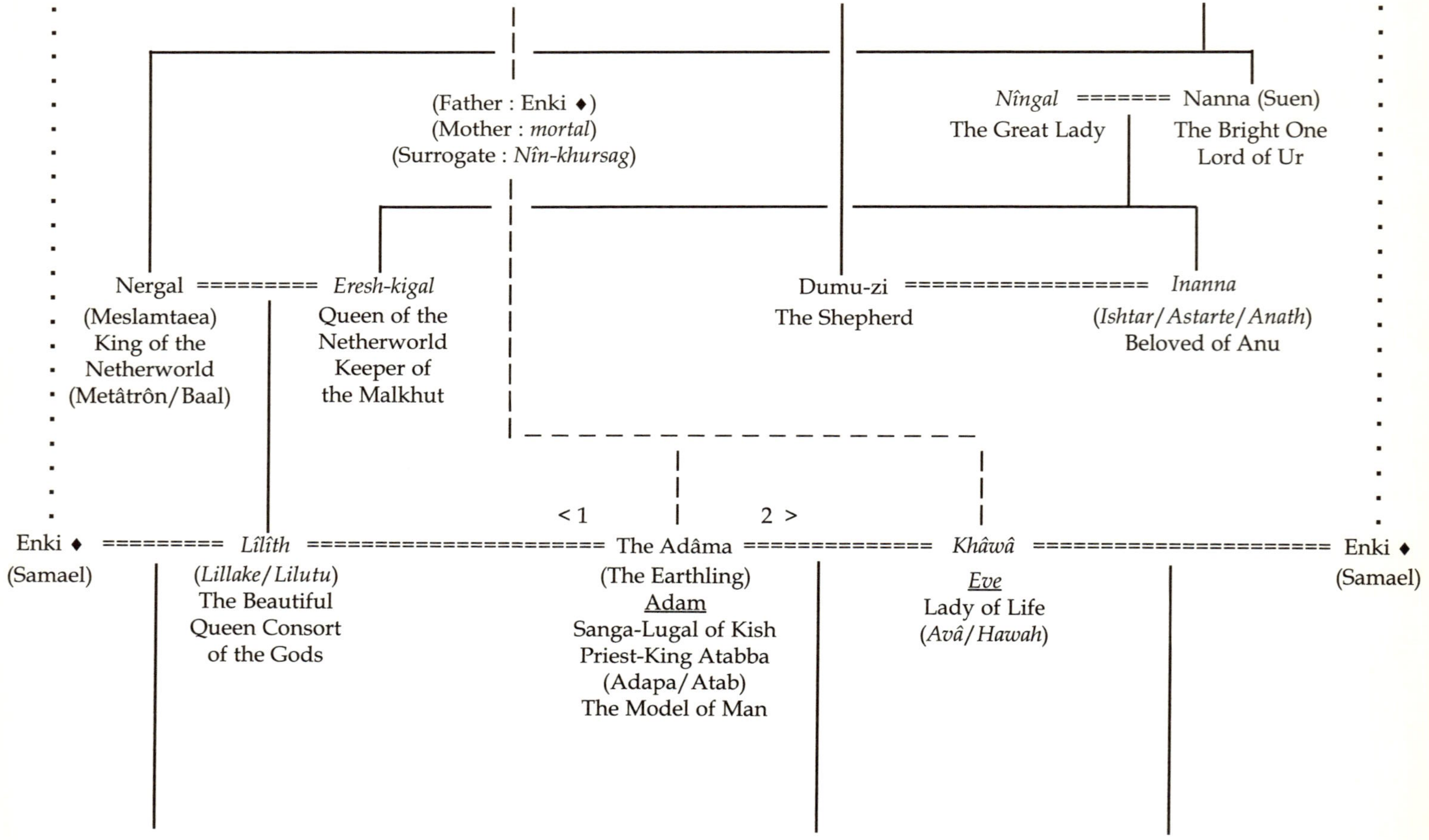
(Father : Enki ♦)
(Mother : mortal)
(Surrogate : Nîn-khursag)
Nîngal ======= Nanna (Suen)
The Great Lady
The Bright One
Lord of Ur
Nergal ========= Eresh-kigal
(Meslamtaea)
King of the
Netherworld
(Metâtrôn/Baal)
Queen of the
Netherworld
Keeper of
the Malkhut
Dumu-zi ================== Inanna
The Shepherd
(Ishtar/Astarte/Anath)
Beloved of Anu
< 1
2 >
Enki ♦ ========= Lîlîth ====================== The Adâma ============== Khâwâ ====================== Enki ♦
(Samael)
(Lillake/Lilutu)
The Beautiful
Queen Consort
of the Gods
(The Earthling)
Adam
Sanga-Lugal of Kish
Priest-King Atabba
(Adapa/Atab)
The Model of Man
Eve
Lady of Life
(Avâ/Hawah)
(Samael)

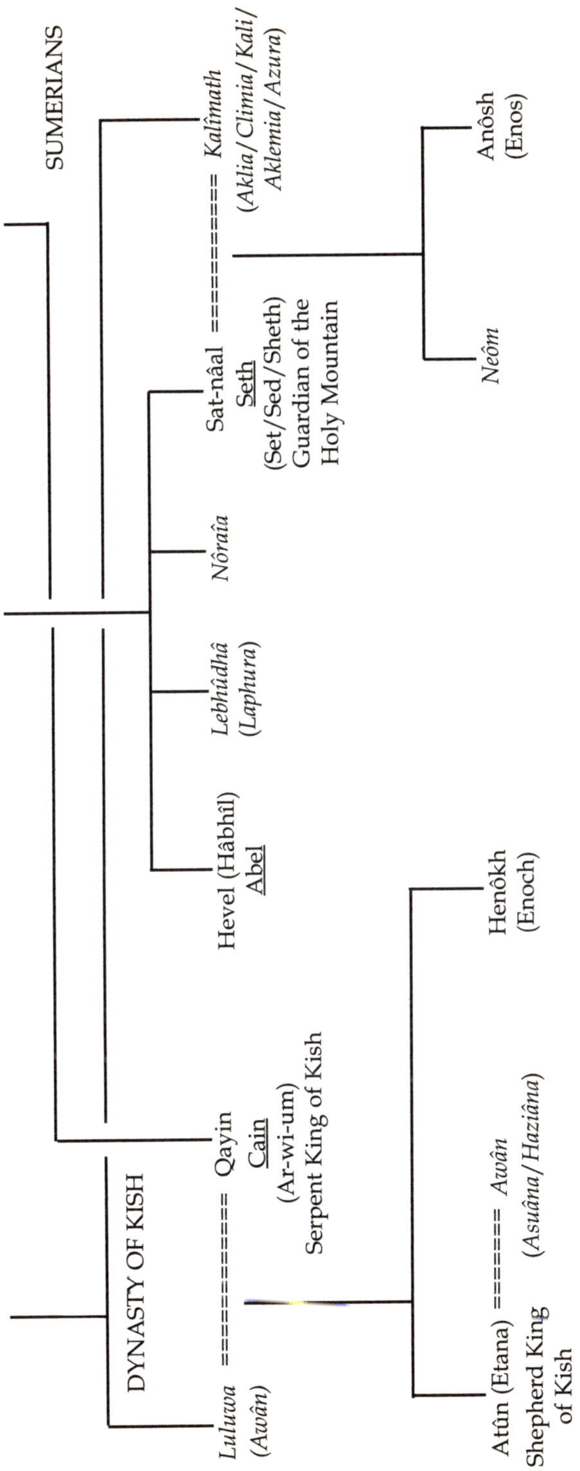
SUMERIANS
DYNASTY OF KISH
Luluwa
(Awân)
Qayin
Cain
(Ar-wi-um)
Serpent King of Kish
Hevel (Hâbhîl)
Abel
Lebhûdhâ
(Laphura)
Nôraîa
Sat-nâal
Seth
(Set/Sed/Sheth)
Guardian of the
Holy Mountain
Kalîmath
(Aklia/Climia/Kali/
Aklemia/Azura)
Atûn (Etana)
Shepherd King
of Kish
Awân
(Asuâna/Haziâna)
Henôkh
(Enoch)
Neôm
Anôsh
(Enos)

# ANCESTRAL LINES OF TUBAL-CAIN AND NOAH

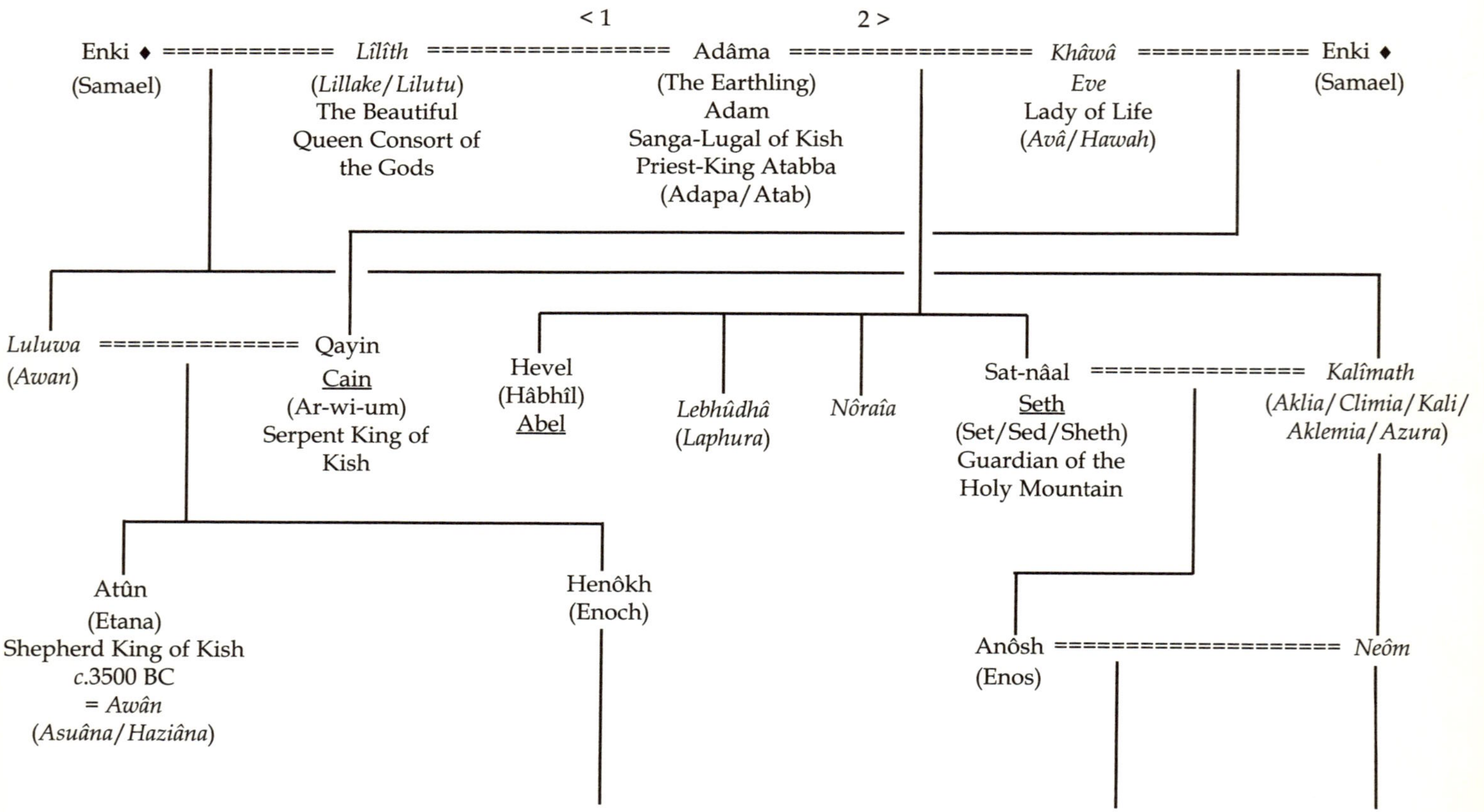

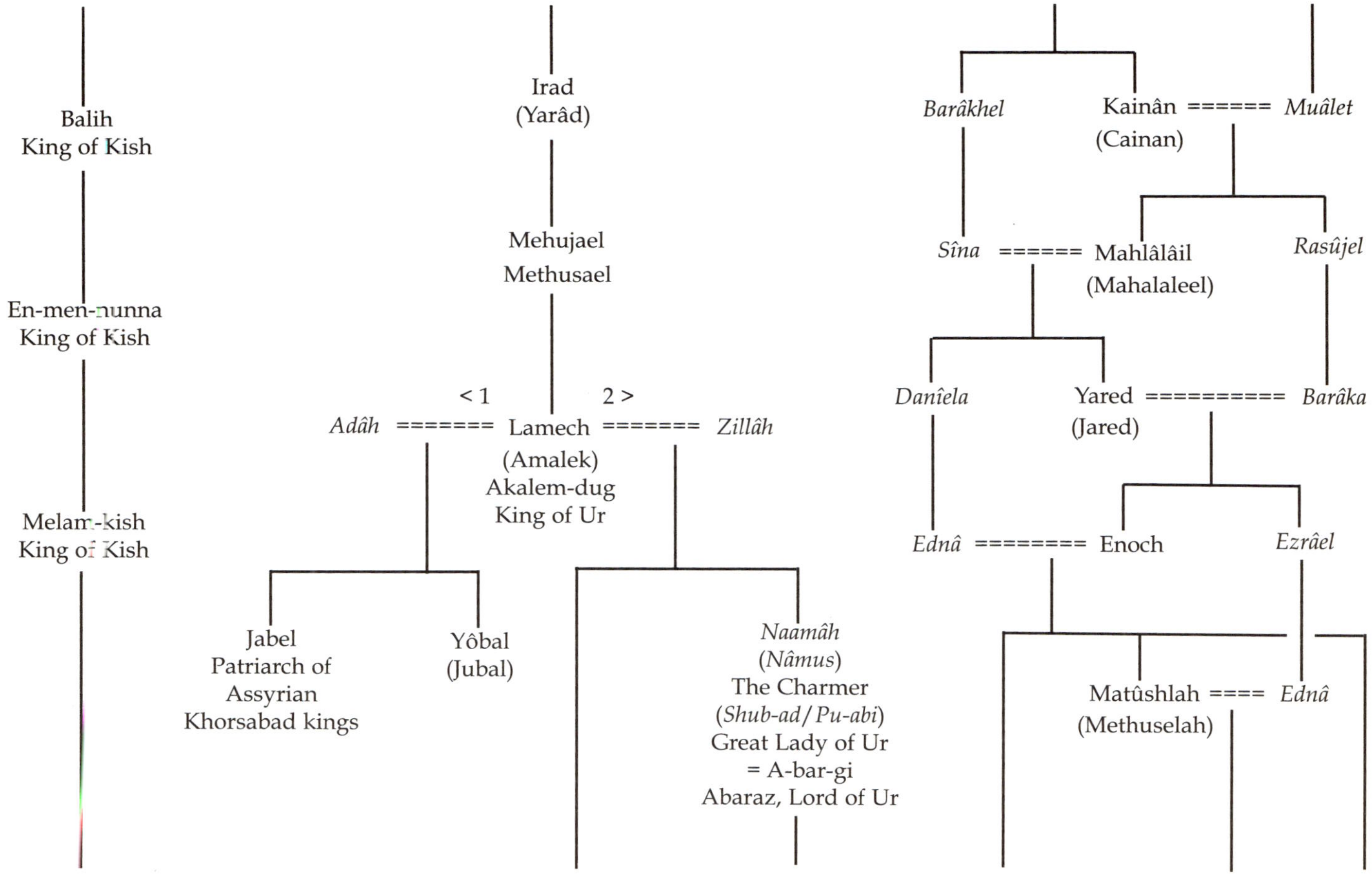
Balih
King of Kish
En-men-nunna
King of Kish
Melam-kish
King of Kish
Irad
(Yarâd)
Mehujael
Methusael
< 1
2 >
*Adâh* ======= Lamech ======= *Zillâh*
(Amalek)
Akalem-dug
King of Ur
Jabel
Patriarch of
Assyrian
Khorsabad kings
Yôbal
(Jubal)
*Naamâh*
(*Nâmus*)
The Charmer
(*Shub-ad*/*Pu-abi*)
Great Lady of Ur
= A-bar-gi
Abaraz, Lord of Ur
*Barâkhel*
Kainân ====== *Muâlet*
(Cainan)
*Sîna* ====== Mahlâlâil
(Mahalaleel)
*Rasûjel*
*Danîela*
Yared ========== *Barâka*
(Jared)
*Ednâ* ======== Enoch
*Ezrâel*
Matûshlah ==== *Ednâ*
(Methuselah)

Bar-sal-nunna
King of Kish

<u>Tubal-cain</u> ======= *Nîn-banda*
(Tôbalkin the Vulcan)
Mes-kalam-dug
King of Ur
Hero of the Good Land
*c*.3200 BC

*Bârakel*

Enoch
= *Rakel*

*Bilânos* ========= Lamech

<u>Noah</u> ========= *Emzârah*
(Nûr /Nôe)
The Righteous One

# DESCENTS FROM LAMECH AND NOAH

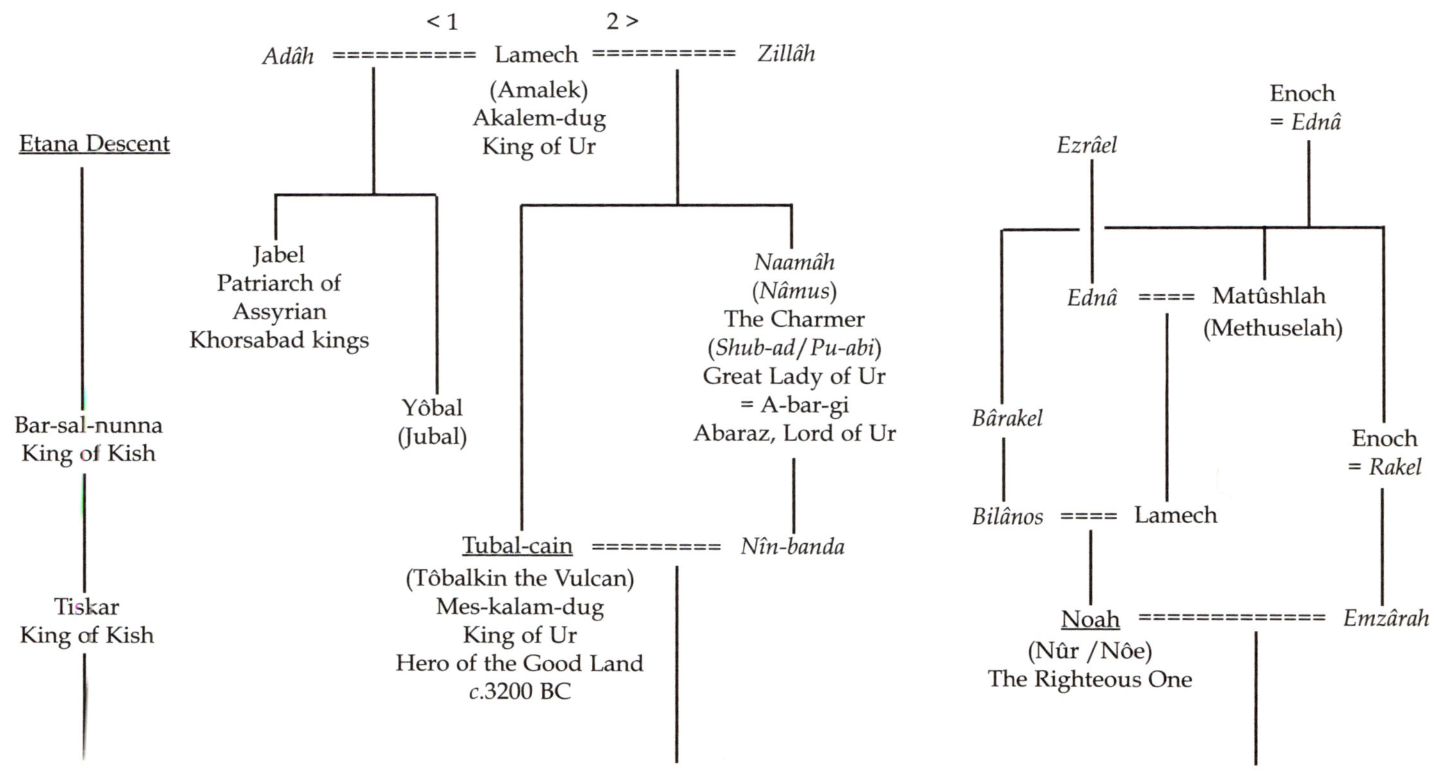

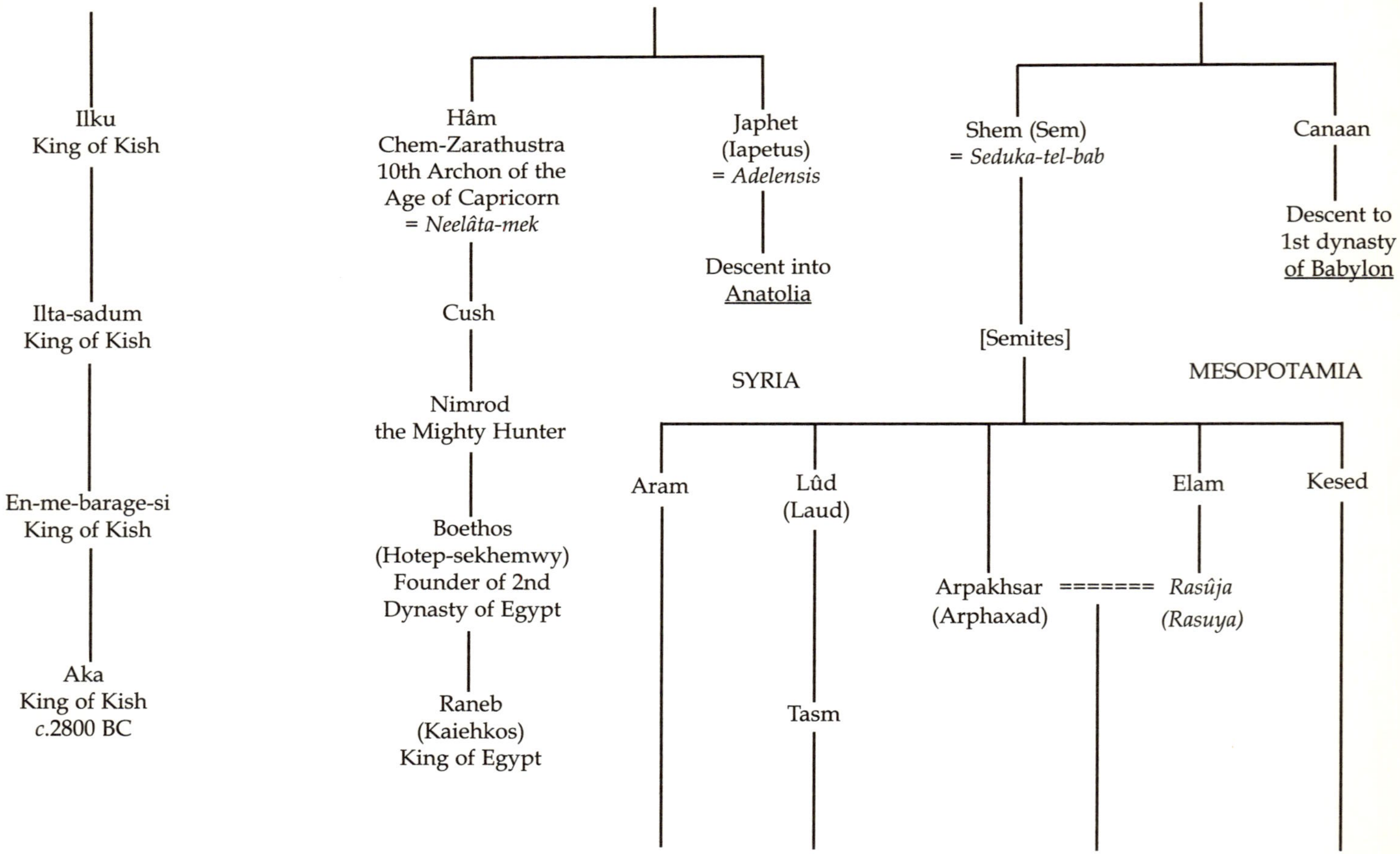
Ilku
King of Kish
Ilta-sadum
King of Kish
En-me-barage-si
King of Kish
Aka
King of Kish
*c.*2800 BC
Hâm
Chem-Zarathustra
10th Archon of the
Age of Capricorn
= *Neelâta-mek*
Cush
Nimrod
the Mighty Hunter
Boethos
(Hotep-sekhemwy)
Founder of 2nd
Dynasty of Egypt
Raneb
(Kaiehkos)
King of Egypt
Japhet
(Iapetus)
= *Adelensis*
Descent into
Anatolia
Shem (Sem)
= *Seduka-tel-bab*
[Semites]
Canaan
Descent to
1st dynasty
of Babylon
SYRIA
MESOPOTAMIA
Aram
Lûd
(Laud)
Tasm
Arpakhsar
(Arphaxad)
=======
*Rasûja*
*(Rasuya)*
Elam
Kesed

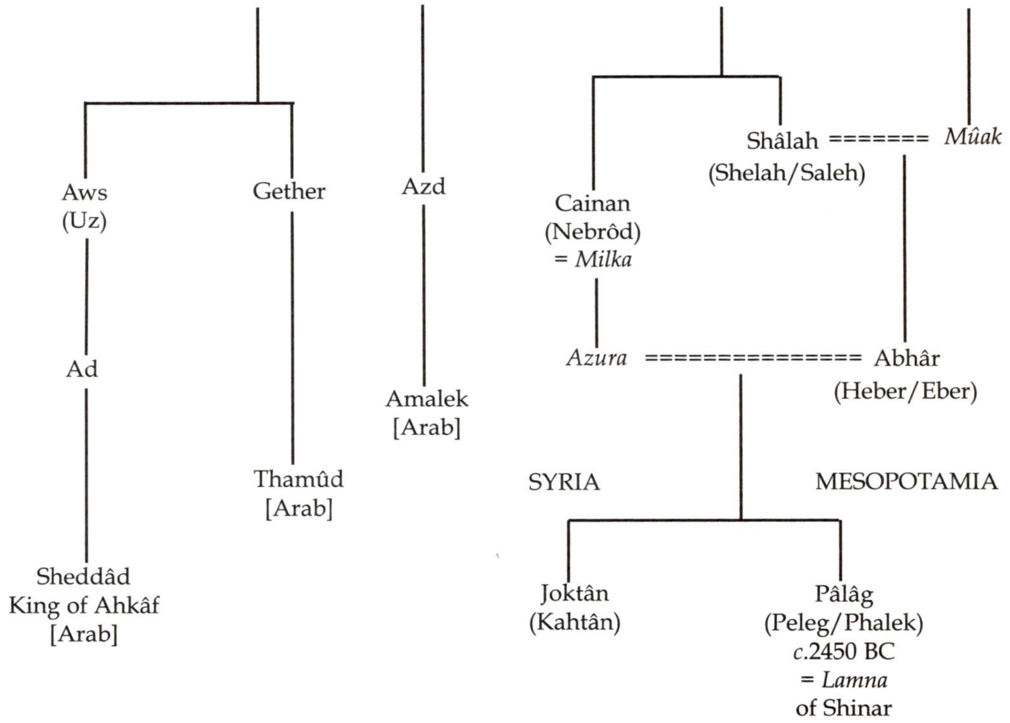
Aws
(Uz)
Ad
Sheddâd
King of Ahkâf
[Arab]
Gether
Thamûd
[Arab]
Azd
Amalek
[Arab]
Cainan
(Nebrôd)
= *Milka*
*Azura*
Shâlah ======= *Mûak*
(Shelah/Saleh)
============== Abhâr
(Heber/Eber)
SYRIA
MESOPOTAMIA
Joktân
(Kahtân)
Pâlâg
(Peleg/Phalek)
*c*.2450 BC
= *Lamna*
of Shinar

# FOREBEARS OF ABRAHAM

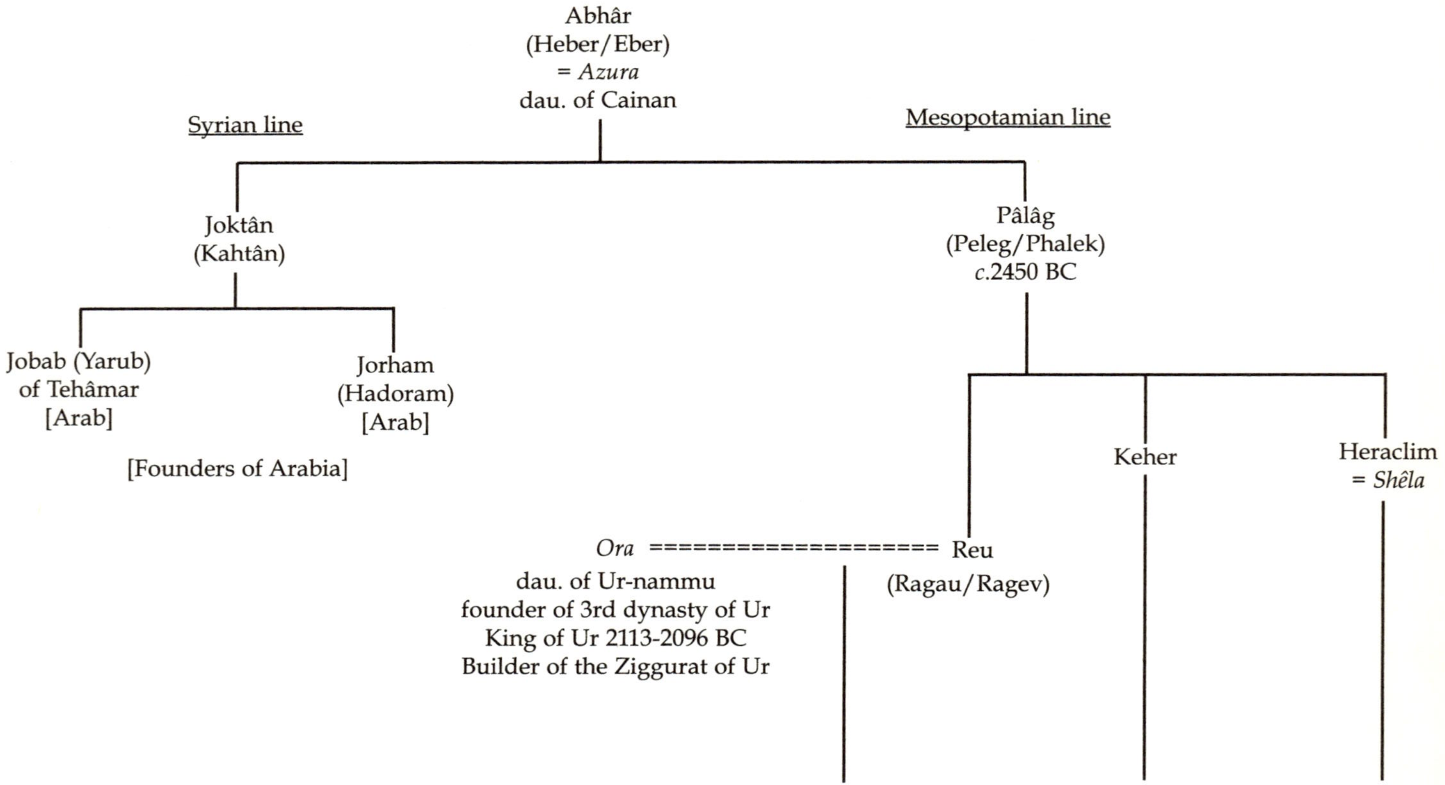

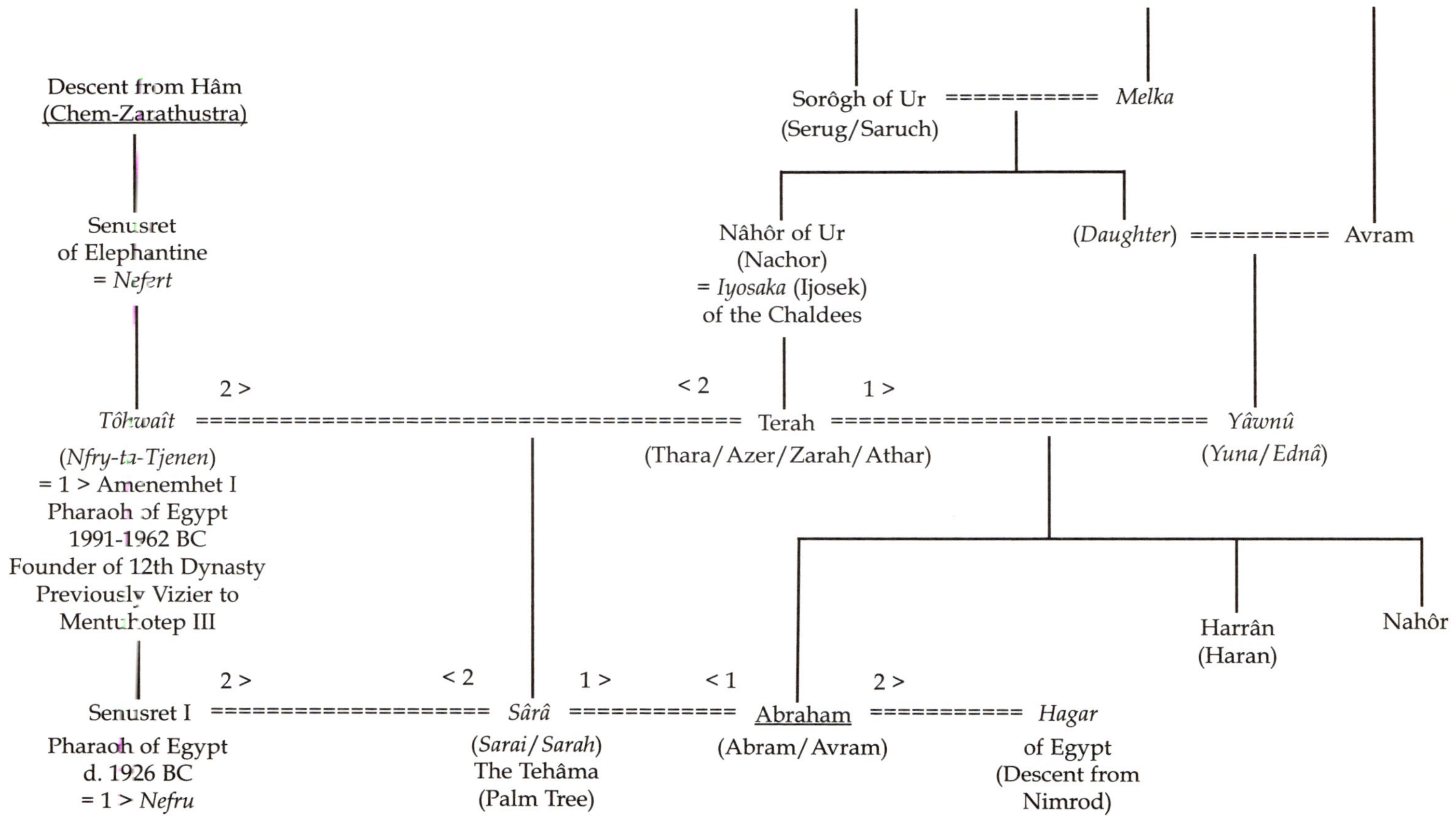
Descent from Hâm
(Chem-Zarathustra)
Senusret
of Elephantine
= *Nefert*
*Tôhwaît*
(*Nfry-ta-Tjenen*)
= 1 > Amenemhet I
Pharaoh of Egypt
1991-1962 BC
Founder of 12th Dynasty
Previously Vizier to
Mentuhotep III
Senusret I
Pharaoh of Egypt
d. 1926 BC
= 1 > *Nefru*
Sorôgh of Ur
(Serug/Saruch)
*Melka*
Nâhôr of Ur
(Nachor)
= *Iyosaka* (Ijosek)
of the Chaldees
(*Daughter*)
Avram
2 >
< 2
Terah
(Thara/Azer/Zarah/Athar)
1 >
*Yâwnû*
(*Yuna/Ednâ*)
*Sârâ*
(*Sarai/Sarah*)
The Tehâma
(Palm Tree)
< 2
1 >
< 1
Abraham
(Abram/Avram)
2 >
*Hagar*
of Egypt
(Descent from
Nimrod)
Harrân
(Haran)
Nahôr

## BIBLICAL AGES OF THE EARLY PATRIARCHS

| | Age (per Genesis) when first son born | Years lived after birth of first son |
|---|---|---|
| Adam | 130 | 800 |
| Seth | 105 | 807 |
| Enos | 90 | 815 |
| Cainan | 70 | 840 |
| Mahalaleel | 65 | 830 |
| Jared | 162 | 800 |
| Enoch | 65 | 300 |
| Methuselah | 187 | 782 |
| Lamech | 182 | 595 |
| Noah | 500 | 450 |
| Shem | 100 | 500 |
| Arphaxad | 35 | 403 |
| Salah | 30 | 403 |
| Eber | 34 | 430 |
| Peleg | 30 | 209 |
| Reu | 32 | 207 |
| Serug | 30 | 200 |
| Nahor | 29 | 119 |
| Terah | 70 | 135 |
| Abraham | | |

# PHARAOHS OF EGYPT (1)

Contemporary with the Bible period from Noah to Peleg

1st Dynasty

Hor-Aha Men (3050-2988 BC)
Djer (Atoti) (2988-2931 BC)
Djet (Uadji/Kenkenes)
Den (Udimu/Semti)
Narmer
Anedjib (Merpeba/Miebis)
Semerkhet (Nekht/Sememphses)
Qa'a (Hedjet/Ka-sen/Bieneches)

2nd Dynasty

Hotep-sekhemwy (Hotepsekheumi/Boethos) (2890-2852 BC)
Raneb (Re-neb/Kaiehkos) (2852-2813 BC)
Nynetjer (Neneter/Neteri-mu/Binothris) (2813-2766 BC)
Seth-Peribsen (Sekhemib/Otlas) (2766-2749 BC)
Khasekhemwy (Khasekham/Necherophes) (2749-2686 BC)

3rd Dynasty—The Old Kingdom

Sanakhte (Nebka/Tyreis) (2686-2668 BC)
Djoser (Netjeriket/Zozer) (2668-2649 BC)
Sekhemkhet (2649-2643 BC)
Khaba (2643-2637 BC)
Huni (2637-2613 BC)

4th Dynasty

Sneferu (Snofru/Snoris) (2613-2589 BC)
Kufu (Cheops) (2589-2566 BC)
Djedefre (Redjedef) (2566-2558 BC)
Khafre (Chepren) (2558-2532 BC)
Menkaure (Mycerinus) (2532-2504 BC)
Shepseskaf (2504-2500 BC)
Sebek-ka-re (Thamphtis) (2500-2498 BC)

5th Dynasty

Userkaf (Ousercheres) (2498-2491 BC)
Sahure (Sephres) (2491-2477 BC)
Neferirkare (Nephercheres/Kakau) (2477-2467 BC)
Shepseskare (Sisires) (2467-2460 BC)
Neferefre (Khaneferre) (2460-2453 BC)
Niuserre (Ini/Rathoures) (2453-2422 BC)
Menkauhor (Kaiu/Mencheres) (2422-2414 BC)
Djedkare (Tancheres/Isesi) (2414-2375 BC)
Unas (Wenis/Onnos) (2375-2345 BC)

# PHARAOHS OF EGYPT (2)

Contemporary with the Bible period from Peleg to Abraham

6th Dynasty

Teti (Otheos) (2345-2333 BC)

Pepi I (Meryre) (Phios) (2332-2283 BC)

Merenre I (2283-2278 BC)

Pepi II (2278-2184 BC)

Merenre II (Mehtimsaf) (2184-2181 BC)

7th & 8th Dynasties—First Intermediate Period

Wadjkare (2181- BC)

Qakare (Iby) (-2161 BC)

9th & 10th Dynasties

Meryibre (Khety) (Akhtoy)

Merykare (Merika-re)

Keneferre

Nebkaure (Akhtoy) (-2040 BC)

11th Dynasty

Intef I (Sehertawy) (2134-2117 BC)

Intef II (Wahankh) (2117-2069 BC)

Intef III (Nakjtnebtepnfer) (2069-2060 BC)

Mentuhotep I (Nebhetepre) (2060-2010 BC)

Mentuhotep II (Sankhkare) (2010-1998 BC)

Mentuhotep III (Nebtawyre) (1997-1991 BC)

# PHARAOHS OF EGYPT (3)

Contemporary with the Bible period from Abraham to Miriam

## 12th Dynasty – The Middle Kingdom

Amenemhet I (Sehetepibre) (Ammenemes) (1991-1962 BC)
Senusret I (Kheperkara) (Sestoris) (1971-1926 BC)
Amenemhet II (1929-1895 BC)
Senusret II (1897-1878 BC)
Senusret III (1878-1841 BC)
Amenemhet III (Nymaatre) (1841-1797 BC)
Amenemhet IV (Maakherure) (1797-1786 BC)
*Queen Sobeknefru* (*Skemiophris*) (1785-1782 BC)

## 13th Dynasty – Second Intermediate Period

Wegaf (Khutawyre) (1782-1778 BC)
Sobekhotep I (*c.*1775 BC)
Ameny Intef IV (Sankhibre) (*c.*1770 BC)
Hor (Auyibre) (*c.*1760 BC)
Sobekhotep II (Sekhemre-khutawy) (*c.*1750 BC)
Khendjer (Userkare) (*c.*1747 BC)
Sobekhotep III (Sekhemre Sewadjtawy) (c.1745 BC)
Neferhotep I (Khasekhemre) (1741-1730 BC)
Sobekhotep IV (Khaneferre) (1730-1720 BC)
Ay (Merneferre) (*c.*1720 BC)
Neferhotep II (Sekhemre Sankhtawy) (*c.*1710 BC)

## 14th Dynasty

Nehesy (Aasehre) (*c.*1700 BC)

## 15th & 16th Dynasties

The Hyksos Delta Kings (consecutive with 17th dynasty)
Descent from Wâlid, Prince of the Hikau-khoswet
*- See separate chart -*

## 17th Dynasty

Sobekemsaf II (Sekhemre Shedtawy) (1700- BC)
Intef VII (Nubkheperre) (*c.*1663 BC)
Tao I (Sanakhtenre) (Seqenenre I) (*c.*1633 BC)
Tao II (Seqenenre II Taa-ken) (1574-1573 BC)
Kamose (Wadjkheperre) (1573-1570 BC)

18th Dynasty – The New Kingdom

Ahmose I (Nebpehtyre) (1570-1550 BC)
Amenhotep I (Djeserkare) (1550-1528 BC)
Tuthmosis I (Akheperkare) (1528-1510 BC)
Tuthmosis II (Akhoperenre) (1510-1490 BC)
*Queen Hatshepsut* (1484-1469 BC)
Tuthmosis III (Menkheperre) (1490-1436 BC)
Amenhotep II (Akheperure) (1436-1413 BC)
Tuthmosis IV (Menkheperure) (1413-1405 BC)
Amenhotep III (Nubmaatre) (1405-1367 BC)
Amenhotep IV (Akhenaten) (1367-1361 BC)
Smenkhkare (Akenkhares) (1361 BC)
Tutankhaten (Tutankhamun) (Nebkheperure) (1361-1352 BC)
Aye (Amunpthis) (1352-1348 BC)
Horemheb (Meryamun) (1348-1335 BC)

## PHARAOHS OF EGYPT (4)

Contemporary with the Bible period from Miriam to King David

<u>19th Dynasty – Ramesside Period</u>

Ramesses I (1335-1333 BC)

Seti I (1333-1304 BC)

Ramesses II – The Great (1304-1237 BC)

[Interregnum]

Merneptah (1236-1202 BC)
Amenmeses (1202-1199 BC)
Seti II (1199-1193 BC)
Siptah (1193-1187 BC)
*Queen Twosret* (*Tausert*) (1187-1185 BC)

<u>20th Dynasty</u>

Setnakhte (1185-1182 BC)

Ramesses III (1182-1151 BC)

Ramesses IV (1151-1145 BC)

Ramesses V (1145-1141 BC)

Ramesses VI (1141-1133 BC)

Ramesses VII (1133-1129 BC)

Ramesses VIII (1129-1126 BC)

Ramesses IX (1126-1108 BC)

Ramesses X (1108-1098 BC)

Ramesses XI (1098-1070 BC)

## HYKSOS DELTA KINGS OF EGYPT

Contemporary with the 17th dynasty of Thebes
(Including Princes of the Levant, and related to the Sea Land dynasty of Babylon)

15th and 16th Dynasties

Wâlid
Prince of the Hikau-khoswet

[Amorites of the Sea Land: Aa-Mu]

Sheshi (Saltis/Ma-yeb-re) (*c*.1663 BC)
Ant-her (Anathar)
Neshi
Beon (Sem-qen)
Apakhnas
Khyan (Khian/Staan /Se-user-en-re)
Yaqeb-her (Yakubher/Mer-user-re)
Apepi I (Apophis/Au-ser-re/Aqun-en-re)
[contemporary with 17th-dynasty Seqenere-Tao I]
Sethos (Nofer-ka-ra)
Inanis (Nub-ka-ra)
Kertos (Kheper-ra)
Kara
Aa-neb-ra
Uazed (Unzed)
Sekt
Sam-ka-ra
Noferui-uah-ra (Neferui-uah-ra)
Maa-ab-ra
Shesha (Assis)
Aa-que (Aaq-er-mu)
Kha-user-ra
Se-khan-ra
Yaqeb-al (Yaqeb-el-mu)
Aa-mu (Aa)
Aa-hotep-ra
Oar
Ykha (Ykha-mu)
Ya (Ya-mu)
Maa-ra
Er-du-ra (Er-du-mu)
Anathar (Anaker)
Yakobaam
Apepi II (Apophis)
Deposed by 18th-dynasty Ahmose I (*c*.1555 BC)

Although the above are shown consecutively, some Hyksos ruled simultaneously. The 15th and 16th dynasties ran in parallel with each other and with the reigns of other Levantine Hyksos kingdoms.

# EGYPT AND THE TRIBES OF ISRAEL

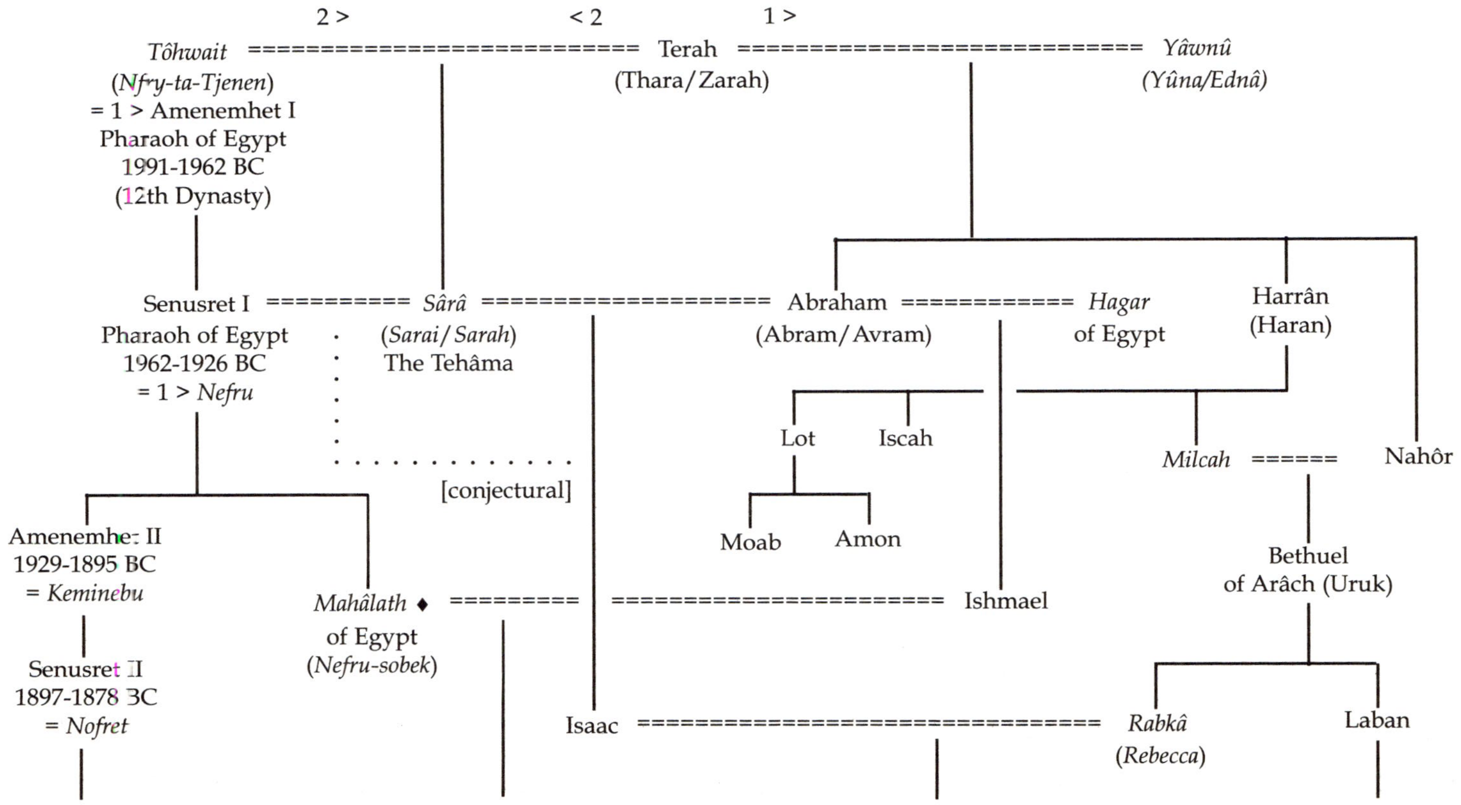

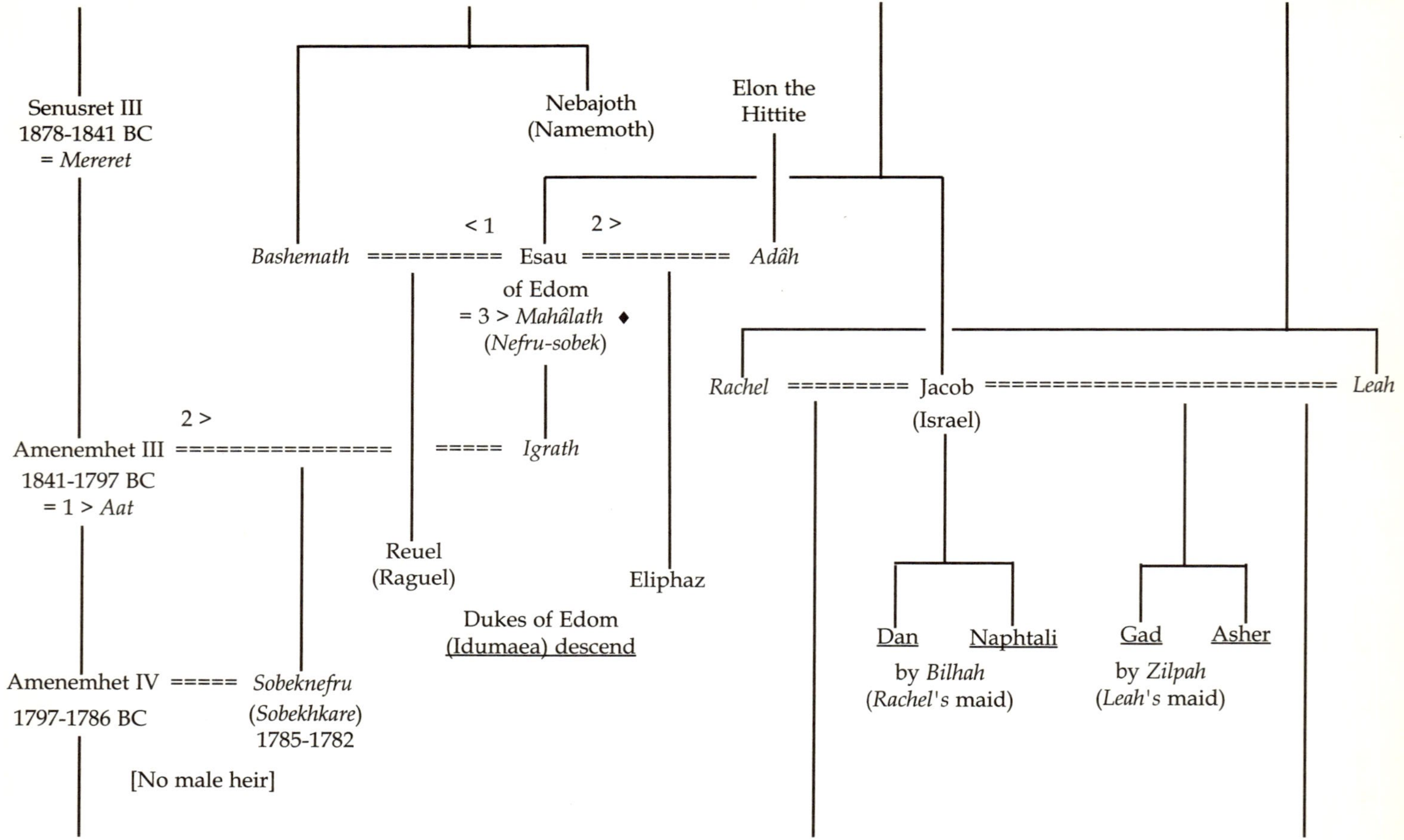
Senusret III
1878-1841 BC
= *Mereret*
Nebajoth
(Namemoth)
Elon the
Hittite
*Bashemath* ========== Esau =========== *Adâh*
< 1
2 >
of Edom
= 3 > *Mahâlath* ◆
(*Nefru-sobek*)
*Rachel* ========= Jacob ========================== *Leah*
(Israel)
Amenemhet III ================ ===== *Igrath*
2 >
1841-1797 BC
= 1 > *Aat*
Reuel
(Raguel)
Eliphaz
Dukes of Edom
(Idumaea) descend
Dan
Naphtali
by *Bilhah*
(*Rachel*'s maid)
Gad
Asher
by *Zilpah*
(*Leah*'s maid)
Amenemhet IV ===== *Sobeknefru*
1797-1786 BC
(*Sobekhkare*)
1785-1782
[No male heir]

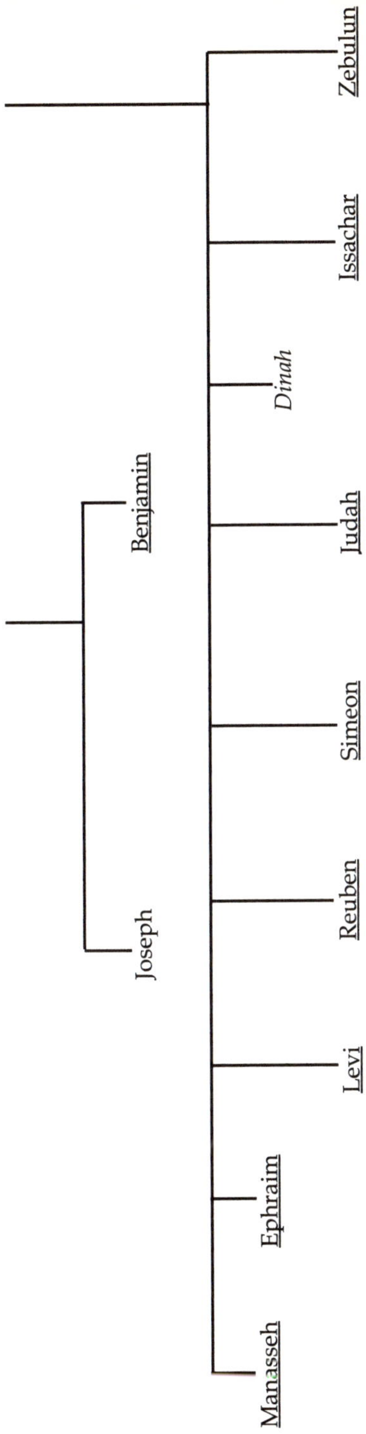
Joseph
Benjamin
Manasseh
Ephraim
Levi
Reuben
Simeon
Judah
*Dinah*
Issachar
Zebulun

# THE EGYPTIAN CONNECTION

Joseph, Moses, Miriam and Aaron

EGYPT
<u>18th Dynasty</u>

Tuthmosis IV
(Menkheperure)
*c.*1413-1405 BC
= *Mutemwiya*

Descent from *Igrath*
<u>dau. of Esau and *Mahâlath*</u>

Padi-pa-ra
(Poti-pherah)
Priest of Ra
= *Zelekha*

Descent from Hâm
(Chem-Zarathustra)
<u>via the Hyksos Delta Kings</u>

Descent from Levi

*Tuya* =================== Yuya the Vizier

(The Asenath)
Priestess
of Neith

Father of the Lord
(Yusuf-Yuya)
<u>Joseph</u>

< 1 2 >

*Sitamun* ======== Amenhotep III ========== *Tiye*

(Nubmaatre)
*c.*1405-1367 BC
= 3 > *Gilukhipa*
Princess of Mitanni

Aye ===================== *Tey*

Father of the God
(Amûnpthis: the Am-râm)
Vizier, Priest and Pharaoh
(*c.*1352-1348 BC
= 2 > *Akhesenpa-aten*
widow of Tutankhamun

Senior Queen
(*Yokâbâr / Jochebed*)
Feeding-mother to
Akhenaton (Moses)
and *Nefertiti*

Anen
Chancellor
(Divine Father)
Priest of Ra

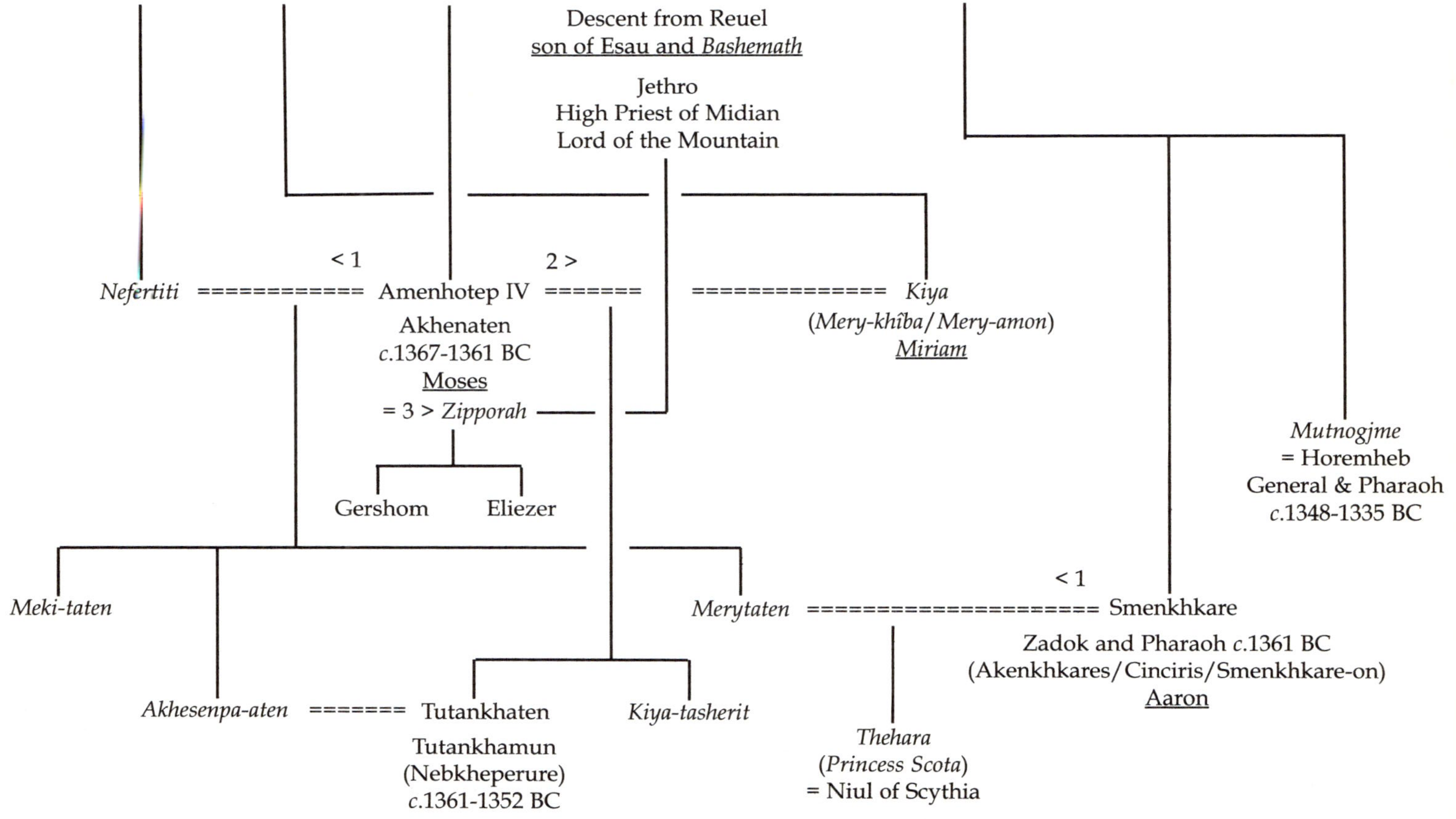
Descent from Reuel
son of Esau and *Bashemath*
Jethro
High Priest of Midian
Lord of the Mountain
*Nefertiti* ============ < 1 Amenhotep IV 2 > ======= ============== *Kiya*
Akhenaten
*c*.1367-1361 BC
Moses
= 3 > *Zipporah*
(*Mery-khîba*/*Mery-amon*)
*Miriam*
Gershom
Eliezer
*Mutnogjme*
= Horemheb
General & Pharaoh
*c*.1348-1335 BC
*Meki-taten*
*Merytaten* ===================== < 1 Smenkhkare
Zadok and Pharaoh *c*.1361 BC
(Akenkhkares/Cinciris/Smenkhkare-on)
Aaron
*Akhesenpa-aten* ======= Tutankhaten
Tutankhamun
(Nebkheperure)
*c*.1361-1352 BC
*Kiya-tasherit*
*Thehara*
(*Princess Scota*)
= Niul of Scythia

## OUT OF EGYPT

From Miriam to King David

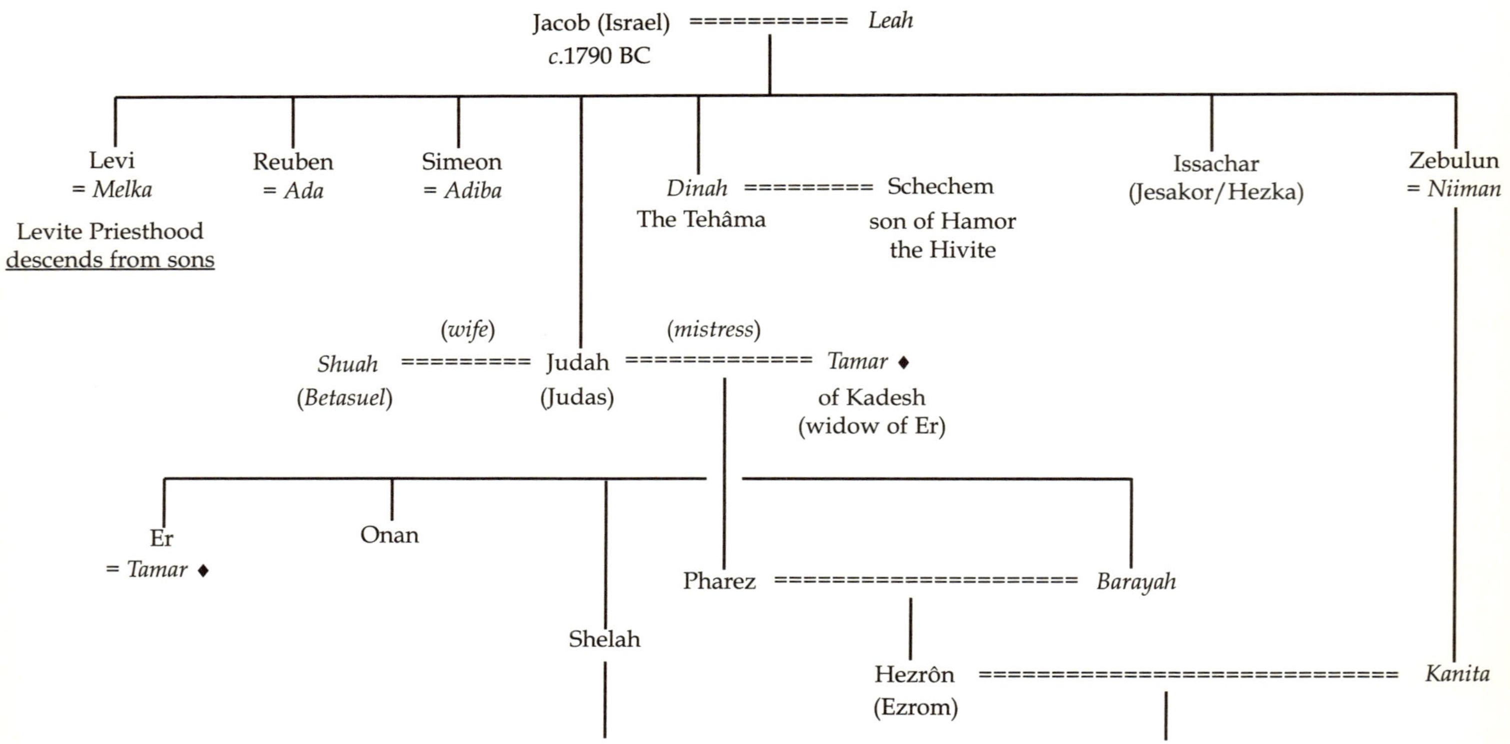

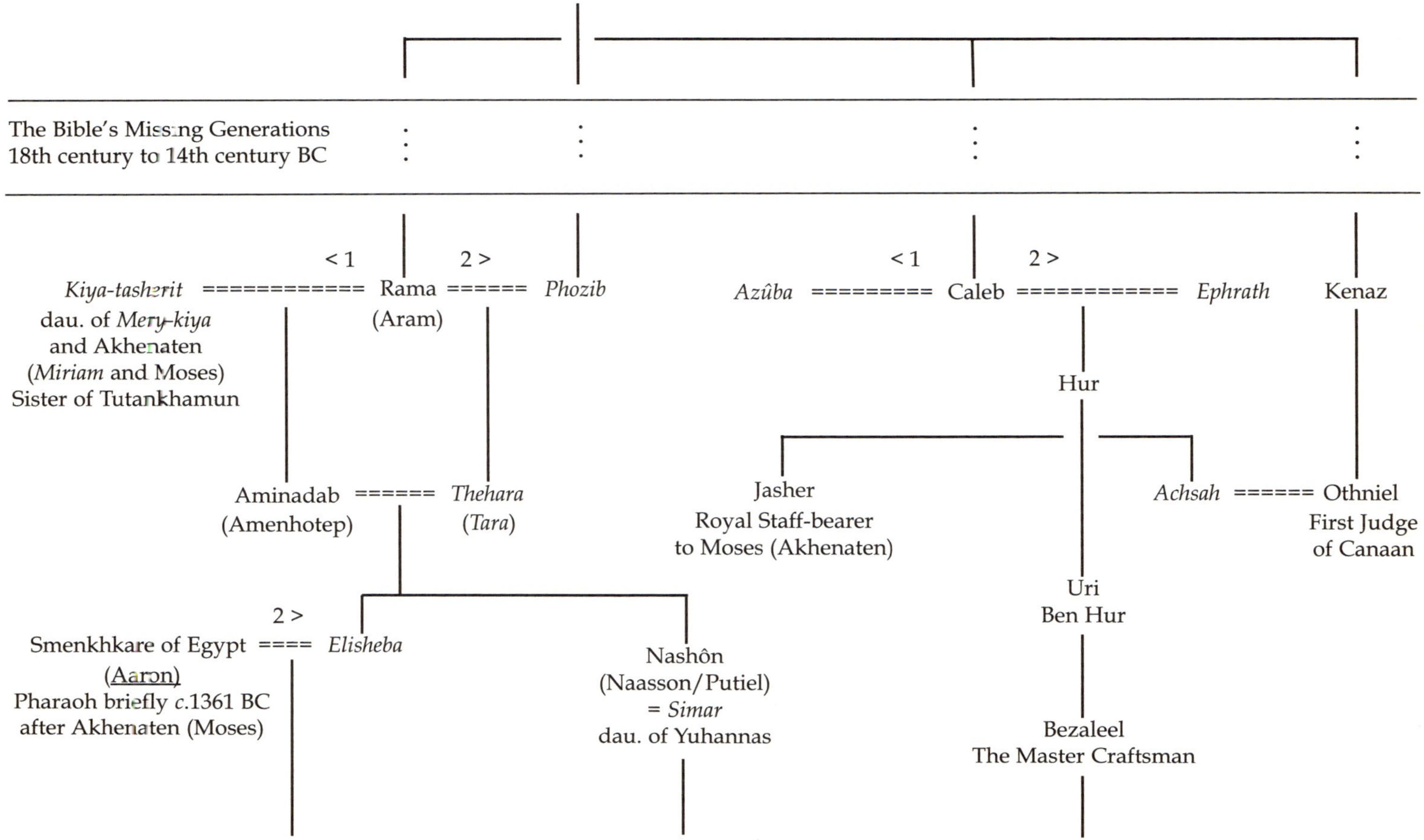
The Bible's Missing Generations
18th century to 14th century BC
< 1
2 >
Kiya-tasherit
dau. of Mery-kiya
and Akhenaten
(Miriam and Moses)
Sister of Tutankhamun
Rama
(Aram)
Phozib
< 1
2 >
Azûba
Caleb
Ephrath
Kenaz
Hur
Aminadab
(Amenhotep)
Thehara
(Tara)
Jasher
Royal Staff-bearer
to Moses (Akhenaten)
Achsah
Othniel
First Judge
of Canaan
Uri
Ben Hur
2 >
Smenkhkare of Egypt
(Aaron)
Pharaoh briefly c.1361 BC
after Akhenaten (Moses)
Elisheba
Nashôn
(Naasson/Putiel)
= Simar
dau. of Yuhannas
Bezaleel
The Master Craftsman

Elieazar =========== (*Daughter*)    Salma ============== *Rachab*

[Aaronite Priests descend]    (Salmon)    (*Rahab / Saphila*)

---

Further four missing Bible generations    :

---

Elimelech
= *Naomi* (*Mara*)

Chilon
= *Orpah*

Mahlon ========= *Ruth* ======================= Boaz
*d.s.p.*    the Moabite    (Booz)

Descent from Lot
< 1    2 >

Obed
= *Abalit*
dau. of Sonas

Jesse
= *Habliar*
dau. of Abrias

David
King of Judah *c.*1008 BC—King of Israel *c.*1001 BC

Canaan was ruled by regional judges until introduction of kingship—first under elected King Saul, and then by *Miriam's* royal line from Egypt under King David of Judah and Israel.

## BABYLONIAN CREATION EPIC AND GENESIS

Their Common Elements

| Enûma elish | Genesis |
| --- | --- |
| Divine spirit is coexistent and coeternal with cosmic matter | Divine spirit creates cosmic matter and exists independently of it |
| Primeval chaos, with darkness enveloping the salt waters | A desolate waste, with darkness covering the deep |
| Light emanates from the gods and the firmament is created above the Earth | Light is created by God and the firmament is created above the Earth |
| Dry land is created on Earth | Dry land is created on Earth |
| The luminaries (sun, moon and stars) are created | The luminaries (sun, moon and stars) are created |
| Man is created | Man is created |
| The gods celebrate | God rests |

# AMENEMOPE AND THE BOOK OF PROVERBS

Examples of Egyptian wisdom literature used in the Bible

| From the Wisdom of Amenemope | From the Proverbs of Solomon |
| --- | --- |
| Incline thine ears to hear my sayings,<br>And apply thine heart to their comprehension.<br>For it is a profitable thing to put them in thy heart.<br>(*Amenemope 1:6*) | Bow down thine ear, and hear the words of the wise,<br>And apply thine heart unto my knowledge.<br>For it is a pleasant thing if thou keep them within thee.<br>(*Proverbs 22:17-18*) |
| Remove not the landmark on the boundary of the fields ....<br>And trespass not on the boundary of the widow.<br>(*Amenemope 7:12-15*) | Remove not the old landmark,<br>And enter not into the fields of the fatherless.<br>(*Proverbs 23:10*) |
| They have made themselves wings like geese,<br>And they have flown to heaven.<br>(*Amenemope 10:5*) | Riches certainly make themselves wings.<br>They fly away as an eagle towards heaven.<br>(*Proverbs 23:4-5*) |
| Better is poverty in the hand of God,<br>Than the riches in the storehouse.<br><br>Better are loaves when the heart is joyous.<br>(*Amenemope 9:5-8*) | Better is little with fear of the Lord,<br>Than great treasure and trouble therewith.<br>Better is a dinner of herbs where love is.<br>(*Proverbs 15:16-17*) |
| Fraternise not with the hot-tempered man.<br>And press not on him for conversation.<br>(*Amenemope 11:13-14*) | Make no friendship with an angry man.<br>And with a furious man thou shalt not go.<br>(*Proverbs 22:24*) |

# BIBLIOGRAPHY


Albany, HRH Prince Michael of, *The Forgotten Monarchy of Scotland,* Element Books, Shaftesbury, 1998.

Albright, William Foxwell, *The Archaeology of Palestine and the Bible,* Fleming H. Revel, New York, 1932.

*Archaeology and the Religion of Israel,* John Hopkins, Baltimore, Md., 1942.

*Yahweh and the Gods of Canaan,* Athlone Press, University of London, London, 1968.

Alcuin, Flaccus Albinus, Abbot of Canterbury (trans.), *The Book of Jasher* (8th-century translation from Hebrew), Longman, London, 1929.

Aldred, Cyril, *Akhenaten, King of Egypt,* Thames & Hudson, London, 1988.

*Egypt to the End of the Old Kingdom,* Thames & Hudson, London, 1992.

Alexander, David and Pat (eds.), *Handbook to the Bible,* Lion Publishing, Oxford, 1983.

Allegro, John M., *The Dead Sea Scrolls,* Penguin, Harmondsworth, 1964.

Alter, Robert (trans.), *Genesis,* W. W. Norton, New York, 1996.

Anati, E, *Palestine Before the Hebrews,* Jonathan Cape, London, 1963.

Armstrong, Karen, *In the Beginning,* Harper Collins, London, 1997.

Ashley, Leonard R. N., *The Complete Book of Devils and Demons,* Robson Books, London, 1997

Aymar, B., *A Treasury of Snake Lore,* Greenberg, New York, 1956.

Bade, William F., *The Old Testament in the Light of Today,* Houghton Mifflin, Boston, Mass., 1915.

Baigent, Michael, with Leigh, Richard and Lincoln, Henry, *The Messianic Legacy,* Jonathan Cape, London, 1986.

Baigent, Michael, and Leigh, Richard, *The Dead Sea Scrolls Deception,* Jonathan Cape, London, 1991.

Baikie, James, *The Amarna Age,* A. & C. Black, London, 1926.

Baines, John, and Málek, Jaromír, *Atlas of Ancient Egypt*, Equinox, Oxford, 1980.

Barbault, Armand, *Gold of a Thousand Mornings*, (trans. Robin Campbell), Neville Spearman, London, 1975.

Barton, George A., *A Sketch of Semitic Origins*, Macmillan, London, 1902.

*The Royal Inscriptions of Sumer and Akkad*, Yale University, New Haven, Conn. 1929.

Beauval, Robert, and Hancock, Graham, *Keeper of Genesis*, William Heinemann, London, 1996.

Becker, Robert O., and Selden, Gary, *The Body Electric*, William Morrow, New York, 1985.

Begg, Ean C. M., *The Cult of the Black Virgin*, Arkana, London, 1985.

Behe, Michael, *Darwin's Black Box*, Free Press, Simon & Schuster, New York, 1996.

Bertholet, Alfred, *A History of Hebrew Civilization*, (trans. A. K. Dallas), G. G. Harrap, London, 1926.

Black, Jeremy, and Green, Anthony, *Gods, Demons and Symbols of Ancient Mesopotamia*, British Museum Press, London, 1992.

Bramley, William, *The Gods of Eden*, Avon Books, New York, 1993.

Breasted, J H., *A History of Egypt*, Hodder & Stoughton, London, 1924.

*The Dawn of Consciousness*, Charles Scribner's Sons, New York, 1934.

Browne, Lewis (ed.), *The Wisdom of Israel*, Michael Joseph, London, 1948.

Budge, Sir Ernest A. Wallis (trans.), *The Book of the Bee*, (translation from Syriac text), Clarendon Press, Oxford, 1886.

*The Book of the Kings of Egypt*, Kegan Paul, London, 1908.

*A Guide to Babylonian and Assyrian Antiquities*, British Museum, London, 1922.

*The Book of the Cave of Treasures*, The Religious Tract Society, London, 1927.

*From Fetish to God in Ancient Egypt*, Oxford University Press, Oxford, 1934.

*The Book of the Dead*, University Books, New York, 1960.

*The Gods of the Egyptians*, Dover Publications, New York, 1969.

Burney, C. F., *Notes on the Hebrew Texts of the Books of Kings*, Clarendon Press, Oxford, 1903.

Burrows, Millar, *What Mean These Stones?*, American School of Oriental Research, New Haven, Conn., 1941.

Butler, E. M., *The Myth of the Magus*, Cambridge University Press, Cambridge, 1948.

Carlyon, Richard, *A Guide to the Gods*, Heinemann/Quixote, London, 1981.

Carpenter, Clive, *The Guinness Book of Kings, Rulers and Statesmen*, Guinness Superlatives, Enfield, 1978.

Cassuto, Umberto, *The Goddess Anath*, (trans. Israel Abrahams), Magnes Press, Hebrew University, Jerusalem, 1971.

Cerny, Jaroslav (ed.), *The Inscriptions of Sinai*, Egypt Exploration Society, London, 1955.

Charles, R. H. (trans.), *The Book of Enoch*, (revised from Dillmann's edition of the Ethiopic text, 1893), Oxford University Press, Oxford, 1906 and 1912.

Charroux, Robert, *Legacy of the Gods*, Sphere, London, 1979.

Chase, Mary Ellen, *Life and Language in the Old Testament*, Collins, London, 1956,

Chiera, Edward, *They Wrote on Clay*, University of Chicago, Chicago, 1938.

Childe, Gordon, *New Light on the Most Ancient Near East*, Routledge & Kegan Paul, London, 1934.

Church, Rev. Leslie F. (ed.), *Matthew Henry's Commentary on the Whole Bible*, Marshall Pickering/Harper Collins, London, 1960.

Churchward, Albert, *The Signs and Symbols of Primordial Man*, Allen & Unwin, London, 1910.

Clayton, Peter A., *Chronicle of the Pharaohs*, Thames & Hudson, London, 1994.

Cohn-Sherbok, Lavinia and Dan, *A Short Reader in Judaism*, Oneworld, Oxford, 1997.

Collins, Andrew, *From the Ashes of Angels*, Michael Joseph, London, 1996.

Collon, D., *First Impressions – Cylinder Seals in the Ancient Near East*, British Museum, London, 1987.

Cook, Stanley A., *The Religion of Ancient Palestine in the Light of Archaeology,* (from the 1925 Schweich Lectures of the British Academy), Oxford University Press, Oxford, 1930.

Cornhill, C. H., *History of the People of Israel,* (trans. W. H. Carruth), Open Court, Chicago, 1898.

Corteggiani, Jean Pierre, *The Egypt of the Pharaohs at the Cairo Museum,* Scala, London, 1987.

Cottrell, Leonard, *The Land of Shinar,* Souvenir Press, London, 1965.

Coulborn, Rushton, *The Origin of Civilized Societies,* Princeton University Press, New Jersey, 1959.

Cremo, Michael A., and Thompson Richard L., *The Hidden History of the Human Race,* Gorvardan Hill, Badger, Calif., 1994.

Cunliffe, Barry (ed.), *The Oxford Illustrated Prehistory of Europe,* Oxford University Press, Oxford,1994.

Curtis, John (ed.), *Early Mesopotamia and Iran – Contact and Conflict 3500-1600 BC,* British Museum, London, 1993.

Danby, Herbert (trans.), *The Mishnah,* Oxford University Press, Oxford, 1933.

Daniel, Glyn, and Paintin, Elaine, (eds.), *The Illustrated Encyclopedia of Archaeology,* Macmillan, London, 1978.

Däniken, Erich von, *Chariots of the Gods,* Souvenir Press, London, 1969.

*The Return of the Gods,* Element Books, Shaftesbury, 1997.

Darwin, Charles, *On the Origin of the Species,* (1872) — New York University Press, New York, (6th edn.), 1988.

David, Rosalie and Anthony, *A Biographical Dictionary of Ancient Egypt,* Seaby, London, 1992.

Dawkins, Richard, *River Out of Eden,* Basic Books, New York, 1995.

Dupont-Sommer, André, *The Jewish Sect of Qumrân and the Essenes,* Valentine Mitchell, London, 1954.

*The Essene Writings from Qumrân,* (trans. Geza Vermes), Basil Blackwell, Oxford, 1961.

Durán, Fray Diego, *Book of the Gods and Rites, and the Ancient Calendar*, (trans. and ed. F. Horcasitas and D. Heyden), University of Oklahoma Press, Oklahoma City, 1971.

Easton, M. G., *The Illustrated Bible Dictionary*, Bracken Books, London, 1989.

Edwards, I. E. S., *The Pyramids of Egypt*, Viking, New York, 1986.

Eisenman, Robert, *Maccabees, Zadokites, Christians and Qumrân*, E. J. Brill, Leiden, 1983.

*The Dead Sea Scrolls and the First Christians*, Element Books, Shaftesbury, 1996.

Ellis, Roger, *Thoth – Architect of the Universe*, Edfu Books, Dorset BH31 6FJ, 1997.

Engnell, Ivan, *Studies in Divine Kingship in the Ancient Near East*, Basil Blackwell, Oxford, 1967.

Epstein, Perle, *Kabalah – The Way of the Jewish Mystic*, Shambhala Pubs., Boston, Mass., 1988.

Eusebius, *The History of the Church from Christ to Constantine*, Penguin, Harmondsworth, 1989.

Farbridge, Maurice H., *Studies in Biblical and Semitic Symbolism*, E. P. Dutton, London, 1923.

Faulkner, R. O., *The Ancient Egyptian Pyramid Texts*, Oxford University Press, Oxford, 1969.

Ferdowsi, *The Epic of the Kings* (*Shah-Nama*), (trans. Reuben Levy and Amin Banani), Arkana/Penguin, Harmondsworth, 1990.

Filby, Frederick, *The Flood Reconsidered*, Pickering & Inglis, London, 1970.

Frankfort, Henri, *Cylinder Seals*, Macmillan, London, 1939.

*Kingship and the Gods*, University of Chicago Press, Chicago, 1948.

*The Birth of Civilization in the Near East*, Williams & Norgate, London, 1954.

*The Art and Architecture of the Ancient Orient*, Penguin, Harmondsworth, 1954.

with Frankfort, H. A., Wilson, J. A., and Jacobsen, T., *Before Philosophy*, Penguin, Harmondsworth, 1951.

Frazer, J. G., *Folklore in the Old Testament – Studies in Comparative Religion*,

Macmillan, London, 1923.

Frazer, Sir James, *The Golden Bough*, Macmillan, London, 1907.

Freer, Neil, *Breaking the Godspell*, New Falcon, Phoenix, Ariz., 1987.

*God Games*, The Book Tree, Escondido, CA, 1998.

Freud, Sigmund, *Moses and Monotheism*, Hogarth Press, London, 1939.

Gadd, C. J., *The Fall of Nineveh*, British Academy & Oxford University Press, Oxford, 1932.

*The Stones of Assyria*, Chatto & Windus, London, 1936.

Gardiner, Alan, *Egyptian Grammar*, Griffith Institute, Ashmolean Museum, Oxford, 1957.

Gardner, Laurence, *Bloodline of the Holy Grail*, Element Books, Shaftesbury, 1996.

*Realm of the Ring Lords*, MediaQuest, Ottery St. Mary,2000.

Geden, Alfred D., *Studies in the Religions of the East*, Charles H. Kelly, London, 1913.

Gelb, I. J., *A Study of Writing*, University of Chicago, Chicago, 1952.

Gilbert, Adrian G., *Magi – The Quest for a Secret Tradition*, Bloomsbury, London, 1996.

Gimbutas, Marija, *The Gods and Goddesses of Old Europe*, Thames & Hudson, London, 1974.

*The Civilization of the Goddess*, Harper Bros, New York, 1991.

Goff, Beatrice, *Symbols of Prehistoric Mesopotamia*, Yale University Press, New Haven, Conn., 1963.

Gordon, Cyrus H., *The Loves and Wars of Baal and Anat*, Princeton University Press, New Jersey, 1943.

Grant, Kenneth, *The Magical Revival*, Skoob Books, London, 1991.

Graves, Robert, *The White Goddess*, Faber & Faber, London, 1961.

*Mammon and the Black Goddess*, Cassell, London, 1965.

with Patai, Raphael, *Hebrew Myths – The Book of Genesis*, Cassell, London, 1964.

Gray, John, *The Canaanites*, Thames & Hudson, London, 1964.

Grimal, Nicholas, *A History of Ancient Egypt*, Basil Blackwell, Oxford, 1992.

Guirand, Felix, *Greek Mythology*, (trans. Delano Ames), Paul Hamlyn, London, 1965.

Halevi, Z'ev ben Shimon, *Adam and the Kabbalistic Tree*, Gateway Books, London, 1974.

Hall, Manly P., *The Secret Teachings of all Ages*, The Philosophical Research Society, Los Angeles, 1989.

Hancock, Graham, *Fingerprints of the Gods*, William Heinemann, London, 1995.

Harris, Z. S., *A Grammar of the Phoenician Language*, American Oriental Society, New Haven, Conn., 1936.

Hawkes, Jaquetta, and Woolley, Sir C. Leonard, *Prehistory and the Beginnings of Civilization*, Harper & Row, New York, 1962.

Hawking, Stephen, *A Brief History of Time*, Bantam Press, London, 1992.

Heidel, Alexander, *The Babylonian Genesis*, University of Chicago Press, Chicago, 1942.

*The Gilgamesh Epic and Old Testament Parallels*, University of Chicago Press, Chicago, 1949.

Herzog, Chaim, and Gichon, Mordechai, *Battles of the Bible*, Greenhill Books, Lionel Leventhal, London, 1997.

Hinz, Walther, *The Lost World of Elam*, Sidgwick & Jackson, London, 1972.

Hocart, A. M., *Kingship*, Oxford University Press, Oxford, 1927.

Hodges, Peter, *How the Pyramids were Built*, (ed. Julian Keable), Element Books, Shaftesbury, 1989.

Hoffman, Michael A., *Egypt Before the Pharaohs*, Routledge & Kegan Paul, London, 1980.

*Holy Bible, The* (King James Authorized Version), Oxford University Press, Oxford.

*Holy Scriptures of the Old Testament, The* (Hebrew and English), The British & Foreign Bible Society, London, 1925.

Hooke, S. H., *The Origins of Early Semitic Ritual*, (from the 1935 Schweich Lectures of the British Academy), Oxford University Press, Oxford, 1938.

*The Siege Perilous*, SCM Press, London, 1956.

Hope, Murry, *The Sirius Connection*, Element Books, Shaftesbury, 1996.

Hudson, David, *Alchemy* (video), Ramtha's School of Enlightenment, PO Box 1210 Yelm, WA, 1995.

*Hutchinson's New 20th Century Encyclopedia*, Hutchinson Publishing, London, 1970 edn.

Ingram, Michael J., *From Atlantis to Doomsday*, Cambridge Desktop Bureau, Cambridge, 1997.

Ions, Veronica, *Egyptian Mythology*, Newnes Books, London, 1986.

Jack, J. W., *The Ras Shamra Tablets – Their Bearing on the Old Testament*, T. & T. Clark, Edinburgh, 1935.

Jackson, F. J. Foakes, *The Biblical History of the Hebrews*, Heffer, London, 1909.

Jacobsen, Thorkild, *The Sumerian King List* (Assyrialogical Studies No.11), University of Chicago Press, Chicago, 1939.

*The Treasures of Darkness – A History of Mesopotamian Religion*, Yale University Press, New Haven, Conn., 1976.

James, E. O., *The Nature and Function of Priesthood*, Thames & Hudson, London 1955.

*Prehistoric Religion*, Thames & Hudson, London, 1958.

*The Cult of the Mother Goddess*, Thames & Hudson, London, 1959.

Jennings, Hargrave, *The Rosicrucians – Their Rites and Mysteries*, Routledge, London, 1887.

Jeramias, Alfred, *The Old Testament in the Light of the Ancient East*, (trans. C. L. Beaumont), Williams & Norgate, London, 1911.

Jones, A. M. H., *The Decline of the Ancient World*, Longman, London, 1966.

Jones, Bernard E., *Freemasons' Book of the Royal Arch*, George G. Harrap, London, 1969.

Jones, Steve, *In the Blood – God, Genes and Destiny*, Harper Collins, London, 1996.

Josephus, Flavius, *The Works of Flavius Josephus: The Antiquities of the Jews, The Wars of the Jews* and *Against Apion*, (trans. William Whiston), Milner & Sowerby, London, 1870.

Kalicz, Nándor, *Clay Gods*, Corvina Kiadó, Budapest, 1970.

Kaufmann, Yehezkel, *The Religion of Israel*, University of Chicago Press, Chicago, 1969.

Keating, Geoffrey, *The History of Ireland*, (trans. David Comyn and Rev. P. S. Dinneen), 1640; reprinted Irish Texts Society, London, 1902-14.

Keil, K. F., *Manual of Biblical Archaeology*, (trans. Peter Christie), T. & T. Clark, Edinburgh, 1888.

Keller, Werner, *The Bible as History*, (trans. William Neil), Hodder & Stoughton, London, 1956.

King, Francis, *The Secret Rituals of the OTO*, C. W. Daniel, London, 1973.

King, L. W., *The Letters and Inscriptions of Hammurabi*, Luzak & Co., London, 1898.

*A History of Babylonia and Assyria*, Chatto & Windus, London, 1910.

*A History of Sumer and Akkad*, Chatto & Windus, London, 1910.

Kingsland, William, *The Gnosis or Ancient Wisdom in the Christian Scriptures*, Allen & Unwin, London, 1937.

Kitchen, Kenneth Anderson, *Ramesside Inscriptions*, B. H. Blackwell, Oxford, 1975.

Knappert, Jan, *The Encyclopedia of Middle Eastern Religion and Mythology*, Element Books, Shaftesbury, 1993.

Knight, Christopher, and Lomas, Robert, *The Hiram Key*, Century, London, 1996.

*Koran, The* (*Al-Qur'an of Mohammed*), (introduction and discourse by Frederick Sale), Chandos/Frederick Warne, London (undated).

Kozloff, Arielle P., and Bryan, Betsy M., *Egypt's Dazzling Sun – Amenhotep III and his World*, Cleveland Museum of Art, Cleveland, 1992.

Kramer, Samuel Noah, *History Begins at Sumer*, Thames & Hudson, London, 1958.

*Sumerian Mythology*, Harper Bros., New York, 1961.

*Mythologies of the Ancient World*, Anchor Books, Garden City, New York, 1961.

*The Sumerians*, University of Chicago, Chicago, 1963.

*The Sacred Marriage Rite*, Indiana University Press, Bloomington, 1969.

Lambert, W. G., *Babylonian Wisdom Literature*, Clarendon Press, Oxford, 1960.

*Enûma Elis*, Clarendon Press, Oxford, 1966.

Lamy, Lucy, *Egyptian Mysteries*, Thames & Hudson, London, 1986.

Langdon, Stephen H., *Tammuz and Ishtar*, Clarendon Press, Oxford, 1914.

Lapidus, *In Pursuit of Gold – Alchemy in Theory and Practice*, (ed. George Skinner), Neville Spearman, London, 1976.

Leakey, L. S. B., *Adam's Ancestors*, Methuen, London, 1953.

Leick, Gwendolen, *A Dictionary of Ancient Near Eastern Mythology*, Routledge, London, 1991.

Lemesurier, Peter, *The Great Pyramid Decoded*, Element Books, Shaftesbury, 1977.

Levi, Eliphas, *Transcendental Magic*, Rider, London, 1923.

Levy, Rachel G., *Religious Conceptions of the Stone Age and Their Influence upon European Thought*, Harper Bros, New York, 1963.

Lewis, H. Spencer, *The Mystical Life of Jesus*, Ancient and Mystical Order Rosae Crucis, San Jose, Calif., 1982.

Lloyd, Seton, *Foundations in the Dust*, Penguin, Harmondsworth, 1955.

Loomis, Roger Sherman, *The Grail – From Celtic Myth to Christian Symbolism*, University of Wales Press, Cardiff, 1963.

Malan, Rev S. C. (trans.), *The Book of Adam and Eve*, (translated from Ethiopic text), Williams & Norgate, London, 1882.

Martin, Malachi, *The Decline and Fall of the Roman Church*, Secker & Warburg, London, 1982.

Mellersh, H. E. L., *The Ancient World – Chronology 10,000 BC to AD 799*, Helicon, Oxford, 1976.

Mertz, Henrietta, *Gods From the Far East*, Ballantyne, New York, 1975.

Miles, Jack, *God – A Biography*, Vintage, New York, USA, 1995.

Milik, J. T., *Ten Years of Discovery in the Wilderness of Judaea*, (trans. J. Strugnell), SCM Press, London, 1959.

Mills, Watson E. (ed.), *Lutterworth Dictionary of the Bible*, Lutterworth Press, Cambridge, 1994.

Milton, John, *Paradise Lost*, Jacob Tonson, London, 1730.

Mivart, St George, *On the Genesis of the Species*, Macmillan, London, 1871.

Montgomery, James A., and Harris, Zellig S., *The Ras Shamra Mythological Texts*, American Philosophical Society, Philadelphia, 1935.

Moorey, P. R. S., *The Ancient Near East*, Ashmolean Museum, Oxford, 1987.

Morfill, W R (trans.), *Book of the Secrets of Enoch*, (ed. R. H. Charles), Clarendon Press, Oxford, 1896.

Morgan, Marlo, *Mutant Message Down Under*, Thorsons/Harper Collins, London, 1994.

Mundkur, Balaji, *The Cult of the Serpent*, State University of New York Press, Albany, NY, 1983.

Murray, Margaret Alice, *The Witch-Cult in Western Europe*, Clarendon Press, Oxford, 1921 (facsimile reprint 1971).

*The God of the Witches*, Sampson Low, London, 1931; reprinted Oxford University Press, Oxford, 1970.

Neumann, Erich, *The Great Mother*, (Princeton University Bollingen Series), Routledge, London, 1963.

Norvill, Roy, *Giants — The Vanished Race of Mighty Men*, Aquarian Press, Wellingborough, 1979.

*The Language of the Gods*, Ashgrove Press, Bath, 1987.

Oakeley, Sir Atholl, *Blue Blood on the Mat*, Anchor Press, Tiptree (undated).

Oates, Joan, *Babylon*, Thames & Hudson, London, 1986.

O'Brien, Christian and Barbara Joy, *Genius of the Few*, Dianthus, Cirncester, 1999.

*The Shining Ones*, Dianthus, Cirncester, 1999.

Olson, Carl (ed.), *The Book of the Goddess: Past and Present*, Crossroad Publishing, New York, 1989.

Oppenheim, A. Leo, *Ancient Mesopotamia – Portrait of a Dead Civilization*, University of Chicago, Chicago, 1964.

Osman, Ahmed, *Stranger in the Valley of Kings*, Souvenir Press, London, 1987.

*Moses – Pharaoh of Egypt*, Grafton/Collins, London, 1990.

*The House of the Messiah*, Harper Collins, London, 1992.

Osterley, W. O. E., *Hebrew Religion – Its Origin and Development*, Macmillan, New York, 1937.

Pagels, Elaine, *The Origin of Satan*, Random House, New York, 1995.

Patai, Raphael, *The Hebrew Goddess*, Wayne State University Press, Detroit, 1967.

*The Jewish Mind*, Charles Scribner's Sons, New York, 1977.

Peet, T. Eric, *Egypt and the Old Testament*, Liverpool University Press, Liverpool, 1922.

Petrie, Sir W. M. Flinders, *Researches in Sinai*, John Murray, London, 1906.

Piggot, Stuart, *The Earliest Wheeled Transport*, Cornell University Press, Ithaca, NY, 1983.

Platt, Rutherford H. (ed.), *The Forgotten Books of Eden*, New American Library, New York, 1974.

Pope, Marvin H. (trans.), *Song of Songs*, Anchor/Doubleday, Garden City, New York, 1977.

Porter, J. R., *The Illustrated Guide to the Bible*, Duncan Baird, London, 1995.

Postgate, Nicholas, *The First Empires*, Elseiver, Phaidon, Oxford, 1977.

Pritchard, James B. (ed.), *Ancient Near Eastern Texts Relating to the Old Testament*, Princeton University Press, New Jersey, 1955.

Ransome, Hilda M., *The Sacred Bee*, Bee Books, Bridgwater, 1937.

Reade, Julian, *Assyrian Sculpture*, British Museum, London, 1983.

*Mesopotamia*, British Museum, London, 1991.

Redford, Donald B., *Akhenaten, the Heretic King*, Princeton University Press, New Jersey, 1984.

Reed, William L., *The Asherah in the Old Testament*, Texas Christian University Press, Fort Worth, Texas, 1949.

Reiter, Dr Russel J., and Robinson, Jo, *Melatonin*, Bantam Doubleday, New York, 1996.

Roaf, Michael, *Cultural Atlas of Mesopotamia and the Ancient Near East*, Equinox, Oxford, 1990.

Robinson, James M. (ed.), *The Nag Hammadi Library*, Coptic Gnostic Library: Institute for Antiquity and Christianity, E. J. Brill, Leiden, 1977.

Rohl, David, *A Test of Time – The Bible from Myth to History*, Century, London, 1995.

Rola, Stanislas Klossowski de, *Alchemy*, Thames & Hudson, London, 1977.

Roney-Dougal, Serena, *Where Science and Magic Meet*, Element Books, Shaftesbury, 1993.

Roux, Georges, *Ancient Iraq*, George Allen & Unwin, London, 1964.

Sadoul, Jacques, *Alchemists and Gold*, (trans. Olga Sieveking), Neville Spearman, London, 1972.

Saggs, H. W. F., *The Greatness that was Babylon*, Sidgwick & Jackson, London, 1988.

Schaeffer, Claude F. A., *The Cuneiform Texts of Ras Shamra-Ugarit*, (from the 1936 Schweich lectures of the British Academy), Oxford University Press, Oxford, 1939.

Schodde, Rev. George H. (trans.), *The Book of Jubilees*, Capital University, Columbus, Ohio (E. J. Goodrich edn.), 1888; reprinted Artisan, Calif., 1992.

Scholem, Gershom G., *Major Trends in Jewish Mysticism*, Thames & Hudson, London, 1955.

*On the Kabbalah and its Symbolism*, Schocken Books, New York, 1965.

Schonfield, Hugh, *The Essene Odyssey*, Element Books, Shaftesbury, 1984.

*The Passover Plot*, Element Books, Shaftesbury, 1985.

Sellers, Jane B., *The Death of Gods in Ancient Egypt*, Penguin, Harmondsworth, 1992.

Seters, John van, *The Hyksos*, Yale University Press, New Haven, Conn., 1966.

Seton-Watson, M. V., *Egyptian Legends and Stories*, Rubicon Press, London, 1990.

Shapiro, Debbie, *The Body Mind Workbook*, Element Books, Shaftesbury, 1990.

Sitchin, Zecharia, *The 12th Planet*, Avon Books, New York, 1978.

*The Stairway to Heaven*, Bear & Co., Santa Fe, New Mexico, 1992.

*When Time Began*, Avon Books, New York, 1993.

Slatyer, William, *Genethliacon*, George Millar, London, 1630.

Smith, George, *The Chaldean Account of Genesis*, Sampson Low & Marston, London, 1876.

Smith, Ray Winfield, and Redford, Donald B., *The Akhenaten Temple Project*, Aris & Phillips, Warminster, 1976.

Smith, Sidney, *Early History of Assyria*, Chatto & Windus, London, 1928.

*Alalakh and Chronology*, Luzak & Co, London, 1940.

Smith, W. Robertson, *The Religion of the Semites*, A. & C. Black, London, 1894.

Sollberger, Edmund, *The Babylonian Legend of the Flood*, British Museum, London, 1984.

Sparks, H. F. D. (ed.), *Apocryphal Old Testament*, Clarendon Press, Oxford, 1984.

Speiser, E. A., *Mesopotamian Origins*, University of Pennsylvania Press, Philadelphia, 1930.

*Biblical and Other Studies*, Harvard University Press, Cambridge, Mass., 1963.

*The Anchor Bible*, (translation from Hebrew text), Doubleday, Garden City, New York, 1964.

Stone, Merlin, *The Paradise Papers*, Virago/Quartet Books, London, 1976.

Stoyanov, Yuri, *The Hidden Tradition in Europe*, Arkana/Penguin, Harmondsworth, 1995.

Strommenger, E., *The Art of Ancient Mesopotamia*, Thames & Hudson, London, 1964.

Suarès, Carlo, *The Cipher of Genesis*, Samuel Weiser, Maine, 1992.

Teisser, Beatrice, *Ancient Near Eastern Cylinder Seals from the Marcopoli Collection*, University of California Press, Berkeley, 1984.

Thiele, Edwin R., *The Mysterious Numbers of the Hebrew Kings*, Kregel, Grand Rapids, Mich., 1983.

Thiering, Barbara, *Jesus the Man*, Transworld, London, 1992.

Thomas, D. Winton (ed.), *Documents From Old Testament Times*, Harper Collins, New York, 1961.

*Times Atlas of Archaeology, The* (*Past Worlds*), Times Books, London, 1988.

*Times Atlas of the Bible, The*, Times Books, London, 1987.

Thompson, R. Campbell, *Semitic Magic*, Luzac & Co., London, 1908.

Vaux, Roland de, *The Early History of Israel to the Period of the Judges*, Darton, Longman & Todd, London, 1978.

Velikovsky, Immanuel, *Worlds in Collision*, (1950), Victor Gollancz, London, 1973.

*Ages in Chaos*, Sidgwick & Jackson, London, 1952.

Vermes, Geza, *The Dead Sea Scrolls in English*, Pelican, Harmondsworth, 1995.

Waite, Arthur E., *The Brotherhood of the Rosy Cross*, William Rider, London, 1924.

*The New Encyclopedia of Freemasonry*, Weathervane, New York, 1970.

Walker, C. B. F., *Cuneiform*, British Museum, London, 1987.

Ward, J. S. M., *Freemasonry and the Ancient Gods*, Simpkin, Marshall, Hamilton & Kent, London, 1926.

Ward, William Hayes, *The Seal Cylinders of Western Asia*, Carnegie Institution, Washington, 1910.

Watterson, Barbara, *Gods of Ancient Egypt*, Sutton, Stroud, 1996.

Weigall, Arthur, *The Life and Times of Akhenaten*, Thornton Butterworth, London, 1910.

Weinberg, Steven Lee (ed.), *Ramtha*, Sovereignty Inc., Eastbound, WA, 1986.

Wellhausen, J., *Prolegomena to the History of Israel,* Scholars Press, Atlanta, Georgia, 1994.

Wells, H. G., *The Outline of History,* Cassell, London, 1920.

Wheeler, Sir Mortimer, *Archaeology From the Earth,* Penguin, Harmondsworth, 1956.

Wigram, W. A., *The Cradle of Mankind,* A. & C. Black, London, 1914.

Williams, Derek, *The Bible Chronicle,* Eagle/Inter Publishing, Guildford, 1997.

Wilson, Colin, *From Atlantis to the Sphinx,* Virgin Books, London, 1996.

with Grant, John, *The Directory of Possibilities,* Webb & Bower, Exeter, 1981.

Wood, David, *Genisis—The First Book of Revelations,* Baton Press, Tunbridge Wells, 1985.

*Geneset – Target Earth,* Bellevue Books, Sunbury on Thames, 1994.

Wood, Michael, *Legacy—A Search for the Origins of Civilization,* BBC Network Books, London, 1992.

Woolley, Sir C. Leonard, *Dead Towns and Living Men,* Oxford University Press, Oxford, 1920.

*Ur of the Chaldees,* Ernest Benn, London, 1929.

*The Development of Sumerian Art,* Faber & Faber, London, 1935.

*A Forgotten Kingdom,* Max Parish, London, 1959.

*The Sumerians,* W. W. Norton, London, 1965.

Yates, Frances A., *The Rosicrucian Enlightenment,* Routledge & Kegan Paul, London, 1972.

Yatri, *Unknown Man,* Sidgwick & Jackson, London, 1988.

# INDEX